A·N·N·U·A·L E·D·I·T·I·O·N·S

Sema Kalaian

Research Methods 01/02

First Edition

EDITORS

Mary Renck Jalongo
Indiana University of Pennsylvania

Currently, Dr. Mary Renck Jalongo is a professor of education at Indiana University of Pennsylvania where she teaches undergraduate and graduate courses in education as well as doctoral-level courses in qualitative research methods and writing for professional publication. She earned her Ph.D. in curriculum and instruction with a minor in measurement and statistics at the University of Toledo. Dr. Jalongo is the author, coauthor, and/or editor of 13 books in the educational field. These publications include scholarly books and successful textbooks. She also has extensive experience writing for a wide array of professional journals and serves as editor-in-chief of *Early Childhood Education Journal* (Kluwer Academic Publishing/Human Sciences Press). Dr. Jalongo has received three national awards for excellence in writing from EdPress and the American Association for Higher Education.

Gail J. Gerlach
Indiana University of Pennsylvania

Dr. Gail Gerlach earned her doctorate at Temple University, and she has extensive experience in teaching research methods. Dr. Gerlach is coauthor of the research methods textbook *Educational Research: A Practical Approach* (Delmar, 1996), which provides relevant, practical, and clear exercises for applying the various concepts and techniques for effective educational research. Additionally, she has coauthored a successful college-level reading and study skills text, *The College Learner: Reading, Studying, and Attaining Academic Success 2nd edition* (Prentice Hall, 1999). Dr. Gerlach serves as chairperson of the Internal Review Board for all research projects produced by students and faculty in a large academic department as well as the coordinator of student teaching.

Wenfan Yan
Indiana University of Pennsylvania

Dr. Wenfan Yan is a professor of education at Indiana University of Pennsylvania. He earned his Ph.D. in educational psychology at the State University of New York at Buffalo. His research and publications focus on large-scale data analysis; cognitive, social, and motivational processes in learning; and applications of educational technology. Dr. Yan is the current president of the American Educational Research Association's Special Interest Group for the Advanced Study of the National Data Base. His published research has appeared in various journals in the fields of cognitive psychology and education, including *Intelligence, Contemporary Educational Psychology, Learning Disabilities Research and Practice*, and *Journal of Cross-Cultural Psychology*. Additionally, Dr. Yan has contributed four chapters on various topics to *The Technology and Teacher Education Annual*.

McGraw-Hill/Dushkin
530 Old Whitfield Street, Guilford, Connecticut 06437

Visit us on the Internet
http://www.dushkin.com

Credits

1. Research: Nature, Purposes, and Basic Concepts
Unit photo—Courtesy of Digital Stock.
2. The Researcher/Practitioner: Standards and Ethics of Practice
Unit photo—United Nations photo by Marta Pinter.
3. Research Beginnings: Theoretical Bases and Question Formulation
Unit photo—Courtesy of McGraw-Hill/Dushkin.
4. Research Means: Collecting and Interpreting Data
Unit photo—© 2000 by PhotoDisc, Inc.
5. Research Ways: Categories of and Approaches to Research
Unit photo—Courtesy of McGraw-Hill/Dushkin.
6. Research Ends: Reporting Research
Unit photo—Courtesy of AT&T Photo Center.
7. Research Aims: Improving Professional Practice
Unit photo—Courtesy of McGraw-Hill/Dushkin.

Copyright

Cataloging in Publication Data
Main entry under title: Annual Editions: Research Methods. 2001/2002.
   1. Research—Methods. I. Jalongo, Mary Renck, *comp.* II. Gerlach, Gail J. *comp.*
III. Yan, Wenfan, *comp.* IV. Title: Research methods.
ISBN 0–07–240437–X   001′.2   80–643193

First Edition

Cover image © 2001 PhotoDisc, Inc.

Printed in the United States of America   1234567890BAHBAH54321   Printed on Recycled Paper

Editors/Advisory Board

Staff

In publishing ANNUAL EDITIONS we recognize the enormous role played by the magazines, newspapers, and journals of the public press in providing current, first-rate educational information in a broad spectrum of interest areas. Many of these articles are appropriate for students, researchers, and professionals seeking accurate, current material to help bridge the gap between principles and theories and the real world. These articles, however, become more useful for study when those of lasting value are carefully collected, organized, indexed, and reproduced in a low-cost format, which provides easy and permanent access when the material is needed. That is the role played by ANNUAL EDITIONS.

New to ANNUAL EDITIONS is the inclusion of related World Wide Web sites. These sites have been selected by our editorial staff to represent some of the best resources found on the World Wide Web today. Through our carefully developed topic guide, we have linked these Web resources to the articles covered in this ANNUAL EDITIONS reader. We think that you will find this volume useful, and we hope that you will take a moment to visit us on the Web at *http://www.dushkin.com* to tell us what you think.

Unlike many other subject areas that students explore during their college careers, research methods often represents almost entirely new terrain. As a result of a lack of familiarity with research, many students approach courses in methodology with a large measure of trepidation. In addition to being editors for *Annual Editions: Research Methods 01/02*, we are experienced instructors of research methods courses, which are required of all students.

Research, at its best, begins with an intriguing question that the researcher yearns to pursue. Because that question has professional, social, and personal significance, it is important to chronicle discoveries in ways that are more credible and persuasive than unsubstantiated opinion, fleeting anecdotal impressions, or disorganized bits of data. Simply stated, research questions matter; therefore it matters how we go about seeking answers. That is where methodology comes in. Research methods are strategies for tackling the tough issues that confront our respective fields and rational routines for pursuing answers.

We proposed *Annual Editions: Research Methods* as a book for the McGraw-Hill/Dushkin series because it was the book of readings we wished we had when teaching research methods courses. At first, we considered lengthy articles that reported on the work of one person or one team of researchers. We immediately thought of examples of studies that we admired because they were original, thorough, and exemplary in a variety of ways. On further consideration, however, we realized that our readers would need something quite different—concise, practical articles that could provide insight into the wide range of strategies that researchers can use. As it turned out, it was far more challenging to find short, helpful articles about research than it was to locate lengthy examples of particular studies. Looking beyond particular examples offered yet another advantage. Now, with our disciplinary blinders taken off, we could envision a book of readings that was adaptable for professionals in a wide range of professions, particularly in the social sciences. Instead of underscoring the lines of demarcation among our fields, we were able to scour through the publications of many fields and find readings that had broader applicability. In doing this, we produced a book so varied in content and level of difficulty that it could simultaneously meet the demands of different audiences ranging from sophisticated undergraduates to graduate students.

As you explore the sections of this, the first edition of *Annual Editions: Research Methods,* you will encounter seven admittedly overlapping and interrelated sections. The seven sections are (1) Research: Nature, Purposes and Basic Concepts, (2) The Researcher/Practitioner: Standards and Ethics of Practice, (3) Research Beginnings: Theoretical Bases and Question Formulation, (4) Research Means: Collecting and Interpreting Data, (5) Research Ways: Categories of and Approaches to Research, (6) Research Ends: Reporting Research, and (7) Research Aims: Improving Professional Practice. Within each category we have clustered together articles that offer useful information and practical applications, as well as raise critical issues about research methods.

As first-time *Annual Editions* series editors, we needed a large measure of guidance from McGraw-Hill/Dushkin's exceptionally competent and supportive editorial and production staff. We thank them for shepherding this project through the stages from conceptualization to publication and for coordinating all of the efforts required for a project of this magnitude. It is a marvel that they work on so many books in this ever-expanding series yet never fail to give the impression that our book is highly valued and eagerly anticipated.

A selective listing of helpful Web sites is included in this volume to further expand your understanding of research methods. These sites are cross-referenced by number to a *topic guide* for locating articles on specific subjects. A *table of contents* with abstracts that summarize each essay, with key concepts in bold italics and a comprehensive *index*, are additional helpful features designed to aid students, researchers, and professionals.

We trust that you will find the readings in this compendium both challenging and rewarding reading material. Please take the time to complete and mail the postage-paid article rating form on the last page to voice your opinions about the selections. We value your input and will use it as we look toward to the next edition of *Annual Editions: Research Methods.*

Mary Renck Jalongo

Mary Renck Jalongo
Editor

Gail J. Gerlach

Gail J. Gerlach
Editor

Wenfan Yan

Wenfan Yan
Editor

Contents

UNIT 1

Research: Nature, Purposes, and Basic Concepts

Five selections in this section look at the practical dynamics of research.

The concepts in bold italics are developed in the article. For further expansion please refer to the Topic Guide and the Index.

UNIT 2

The Researcher/ Practitioner: Standards and Ethics of Practice

The need for ethical research is examined in this unit's four articles.

The concepts in bold italics are developed in the article. For further expansion please refer to the Topic Guide and the Index.

UNIT 3

Research Beginnings: Theoretical Bases and Question Formulation

Four unit selections discuss some of the necessary steps needed in designing research parameters.

The concepts in bold italics are developed in the article. For further expansion please refer to the Topic Guide and the Index.

vii

UNIT 4

Research Means: Collecting and Interpreting Data

Methods for qualitatively interpreting data that has been gathered through various collection processes are considered in this section.

The concepts in bold italics are developed in the article. For further expansion please refer to the Topic Guide and the Index.

UNIT 5

Research Ways: Categories of and Approaches to Research

Five articles consider how sample size, surveys, and qualitative methodology impact effective research.

UNIT 6

Research
Ends:
Reporting
Research

In this unit, four selections
discuss how to best present
accurate and effective research.

The concepts in bold italics are developed in the article. For further expansion please refer to the Topic Guide and the Index.

UNIT 7

Research Aims: Improving Professional Practice

Four articles look at some of the
challenges facing effective and
balanced reporting of research.

The concepts in bold italics are developed in the article. For further expansion please refer to the Topic Guide and the Index.

This topic guide suggests how the selections and World Wide Web sites found in the next section of this book relate to topics of traditional concern to research methods students and professionals. It is useful for locating interrelated articles and Web sites for reading and research. The guide is arranged alphabetically according to topic.

The relevant Web sites, which are numbered and annotated on pages 4 and 5, are easily identified by the Web icon (◉) under the topic articles. By linking the articles and the Web sites by topic, this ANNUAL EDITIONS reader becomes a powerful learning and research tool.

TOPIC AREA	TREATED IN	TOPIC AREA	TREATED IN
Action Research	12. Issues in Teaching Participatory Action Research 13. Practical Issues for Teachers Conducting Classroom Research 24. Action Research: Empowering Teachers to Work with At-Risk Students ◉ **1, 2, 4, 10, 11, 20, 22, 29**	**Focus Groups**	15. Future of Focus Groups ◉ **1**
Applied Research	31. Rethinking Sociology: Applied and Basic Research ◉ **1, 2, 33**	**Human Subjects**	6. Human Subjects and Informed Consent: The Legacy of the Tuskegee Syphilis Study 25. Need for Better Ethical Guidelines for Conducting and Reporting Research ◉ **1, 2, 8, 9, 26**
Basic Research	31. Rethinking Sociology: Applied and Basic Research ◉ **1, 2, 31, 33**	**Independent Variables**	4. Quantitative Research Approaches ◉ **1, 2, 5**
Classroom Research	12. Issues in Teaching Participatory Action Research 13. Practical Issues for Teachers Conducting Classroom Research 24. Action Research: Empowering Teachers to Work with At-Risk Students ◉ **3, 4, 19, 20, 22**	**Informed Consent**	6. Human Subjects and Informed Consent: The Legacy of the Tuskegee Syphilis Study 25. Need for Better Ethical Guidelines for Conducting and Reporting Research ◉ **1, 2, 8, 9, 26**
Critical Evaluation	29. Social Consequences of Bad Research ◉ **1, 2, 30, 33**	**Interviewing**	15. Future of Focus Groups 18. Daily Data Collection: A Comparison of Three Methods ◉ **1, 2, 15, 16, 17, 18**
Data Collection	14. Videotaped Behavioral Observations: Enhancing Validity and Reliability 16. Self-Assessment at Work: Outcomes of Adult Learners' Reflections on Practice 17. Using Electronic Mail to Conduct Research 18. Daily Data Collection: A Comparison of Three Methods 22. Primer in Survey Research ◉ **13, 14, 15, 16, 17, 18, 21, 25, 31, 32, 33**	**Objective Evaluation**	11. Best Kept Secret in Counseling: Single Case (N=1) Experimental Design ◉ **1, 2, 14, 28**
		Observation	14. Videotaped Behavioral Observations: Enhancing Validity and Reliability 24. Action Research: Empowering Teachers to Work with At-Risk Students ◉ **1, 2, 14, 21, 23**
Dissertations	10. Research Students' Early Experiences of the Dissertation Literature Review 26. Education Should Consider Alternative Formats for the Dissertation ◉ **24**	**Paradigms of Thought**	1. Back from Chaos
		Probability Theory	27. Chance and Nonsense: A Conversation about Interpreting Tests of Statistical Significance, Parts I and II ◉ **27**
Ethical Guidelines	8. Ethics, Institutional Review Boards, and the Changing Face of Educational Research 25. Need for Better Ethical Guidelines for Conducting and Reporting Research ◉ **1, 2, 7, 8, 9, 26, 30, 31**	**Qualitative Research**	3. Evolution of Qualitative Research Methodology: Looking beyond Defense to Possibilities 8. Ethics, Institutional Review Boards, and the Changing Face of Educational Research 19. Quantitative Attitudes Questionnaire: Instrument Development and Validation 21. On Writing Qualitative Research 23. New Frontier in Qualitative Research Methodology 30. Future Directions in Qualitative Research 32. Salvaging Quantitative Research with Qualitative Data ◉ **1, 2, 6, 23, 32**
Ethical Issues in Research	6. Human Subjects and Informed Consent: The Legacy of the Tuskegee Syphilis Study 8. Ethics, Institutional Review Boards, and the Changing Face of Educational Research 25. Need for Better Ethical Guidelines for Conducting and Reporting Research 29. Social Consequences of Bad Research ◉ **1, 2, 7, 8, 9, 26, 30, 31**	**Quantitative Research**	4. Quantitative Research Approaches 8. Ethics, Institutional Review Boards, and the Changing Face of Educational Research

● AE: Research Methods

The following World Wide Web sites have been carefully researched and selected to support the articles found in this reader. If you are interested in learning more about specific topics found in this book, these Web sites are a good place to start. The sites are cross-referenced by number and appear in the topic guide on the previous two pages. Also, you can link to these Web sites through our DUSHKIN ONLINE support site at *http://www.dushkin.com/online/*.

The following sites were available at the time of publication. Visit our Web site—we update DUSHKIN ONLINE regularly to reflect any changes.

General Sources

1. Bill Trochim's Center for Social Research Methods
http://trochim.cornell.edu
This site is rich in research materials, including a Knowledge Base online textbook, Web links, a statistical advisor, and papers by Bill Trochim and others.

2. Research Methods in the Social Sciences on the Internet
http://www.library.miami.edu/netguides/psymeth.html
These Web pages link to just about everything you might want to know about research methodology, including a statistics glossary and a glossary of research terms.

Research: Nature, Purposes, and Basic Concepts

3. CSU Institute for Education Reform
http://www.csus.edu/ier/reading.html
This report of building a powerful reading program from research to practice demonstrates many concepts about research.

4. Education & Research Using Internet
http://www.brint.com/Research.htm
This annotated list of Web resources covers issues in research and publication, survey research, qualitative, interpretive, intensive, and action research.

5. Outline of Quantitative Research Design
http://www.coe.uh.edu/coe_kiosk/elcs/doctoral/source/outline_quan.html
Some of the common quantitative research designs can be found at this site. From this site, there are also references to more exhaustive treatments of the designs.

6. Qualitative Research Page
http://www.oit.pdx.edu/~kerlinb/qualresearch/
This site will connect you to the qualitative research Web Ring. Explore it for the theory and role of qualitative research, a bibliography, research ethics, software, and theses.

The Researcher/Practitioner: Standards and Ethics of Practice

7. American Sociological Association's Ethical Standards
http://www.asanet.org/members/ecostand2.html
This list of standards includes subjects such as informed consent, use of deception in research, unanticipated research opportunities, and reporting (including plagiarism).

8. Guidelines for the Conduct of Research Involving Human Subjects at the National Institutes of Health
http://helix.nih.gov:8001/ohsr/guidelines.phtml
These guidelines include historical, ethical, and legal foundations for the policies set forth, as well as the responsibilities

of investigators, collaborative research activities, and the function of the Office of Human Subjects Research.

9. Institutional Review Boards
http://www.madnation.org/bioethics/irb.htm
Published on the Web by MadNation, an organization for people working together for social justice and human rights in mental health, *Institutional Review Boards: A System in Jeopardy* is the testimony of Gary B. Ellis, director of the Office for Protection from Research Risks of the NIH, about the problems of IRBs.

Research Beginnings: Theoretical Bases and Question Formulation

10. Action Research International
http://www.scu.edu.au/schools/sawd/ari/ari-wadsworth.html
In this 20-page paper published on the Web, Yoland Wadsworth asks, "What Is Participatory Action Research?" Her answers cover all bases.

11. Internet Resources for Participatory Action Research
http://www.goshen.edu/soan/soan96p.htm
Web links at this site include Action Learning International, PARnet, Cornell University's site, and many other groups and working papers on the subject.

12. Practitioner Research: The Purposes of Reviewing the Literature within an Enquiry
http://www.scre.ac.uk/spotlight/spotlight67.html
The author, Rae Stark of University of Strathclyde, advises the researcher to use reading the literature through all phases in the research process, not just for the "literature review" that begins the finished research paper. She also tells how not to use the literature.

13. Single-Case Statistical Analysis: Introduction
http://www.unlv.edu/Colleges/Education/EP/scsantro.htm
This site offers an overview of single-case research: the need for it, measurement, and statistical tools.

Research Means: Collecting and Interpreting Data

14. Journal of Undergraduate Research Paper
http://www.clas.ufl.edu/CLAS/jur/0001/stanfordpaper.html
This research study by Meredith Stanford uses videotaping as a technique for observing interaction between autistic children and their families. It demonstrates the type of research that can be aided by the use of videotaping.

15. Oregon Survey Research Laboratory
http://darkwing.uoregon.edu/~osrl/relatdlnks.html
Links to many survey research laboratories are available at this Web page.

16. Social Research Update 19: Focus Groups
http://www.soc.surrey.ac.uk/sru/SRU19.html
This article by Anita Gibbs of the Centre for Criminological Research at Oxford University discusses the use of focus

groups, interviewing techniques and their benefits, problems that arise, and the importance of the moderator.

17. Using E-mail to Survey Internet Users in the United States
http://www.ascusc.org/jcmc/vol4/issue3/sheehan.html
Kim Bartel Sheehan and Mariea Grubbs Hoy offer this report on the methodology that can be used and their assessment of the technology of online sampling.

18. Using the Internet for Quantitative Survey Research
http://www.swiftinteractive.com/white-p1.htm
Here is a discussion by James Watt on using the Internet for quantitative survey research. It includes appropriate populations to use, types of Internet samples, and methods of conducting the surveys.

Research Ways: Categories of and Approaches to Research

19. Education Resources
http://www.mcrel.org/resources/links/action.asp
This series of 14 links to action research and the teacher as researcher covers approaches to curriculum development, action research and social movement, and many other references about the teacher as researcher.

20. Research to Practice Gap in Special Education
http://www.lsi.ukans.edu/jg/bridgap.htm
Here is a list of links to projects such as the Juniper Gardens Children's Project and Project Bridge, considered ideas that work in bridging the gap between research and practice.

21. Survey Research versus Participation Observation
http://www.pitt.edu/~malhotra/cmupstn.doc
Here is an illustrated book on the Web that offers simple ways of looking at the two different approaches to studying people in their natural surroundings.

22. Teacher Research: Action Research Resources
http://ucerc.edu/teacherresearch/teacherresearch.html
Click on Article Text under the title, "Collaborative Action Research Model for Teacher Preparation Program," for a 35-page paper that concerns a model for teacher preparation programs that will enable teachers in the classroom to practice education research.

23. Use of Vignettes in Qualitative Research
http://www.soc.surrey.ac.uk/sru/SRU25.html
This article by Christine Barter and Emma Renold covers the three main purposes in social research for which vignettes may be used, and guidelines for how to use vignettes effectively.

Research Ends: Reporting Research

24. Degree Programs: Dissertation
http://www.me.gatech.edu/me/publicat/handbook/sne/dh.html
This description of the general guidelines for Ph.D. dissertation research is typical of what is required.

25. ERIC Citations for the Concept of Statistical Significance Testing
http://ericae.net/faqs/statsig/ericbib_statsig.htm
From this ERIC page access this group of documents that covers many aspects of statistical significance testing.

26. Guidelines for Ethical Practices
http://www.pitt.edu/~provost/ethresearch.html
These guidelines, which come from the University of Pittsburgh, include the special obligations of the researcher in human subject research, and are representative of guidelines offered by other research entities.

27. Probability Theory: The Logic of Science
http://bayes.wustl.edu/etj/prob.html
This book by E. T. Jaynes is available in a pdf version and can be reached from this Web page.

Research Aims: Improving Professional Practice

28. Andrew Bennett
http://www.georgetown.edu/bennett/
Many articles on case study methods, written by Andrew Bennett of the Department of Government at Georgetown University, are available at this site.

29. Beginner's Guide to Action Research
http://www.scu.edu.au/schools/sawd/arr/guide.html
This extensive resource file on action research suggests that as a methodology, action research is cyclic, participative, and qualitative, and is intended to have both action outcomes and research outcomes

30. Bias in Social Research
http://www.socresonline.org.uk/2/1/2.html
Here is a 19-page discussion of bias in social research, prepared in depth by M. Hammersley and R. Gomm.

31. Pitfalls of Data Analysis
http://www.execpc.com/~helberg/pitfalls/
Subtitled "How to Avoid Lies and Damned Lies," this article discusses in detail the problems with statistics, sources of bias, errors in methodology, and interpretation.

32. Qualitative Research and the Generalizability Question
http://www.nova.edu/ssss/QR/QR4-3/myers.html
This article on the Web discusses the importance of small qualitative studies. Even though they are not generalizable in the traditional sense, they have redeeming qualities.

33. Using Random Assignment in Social Science Settings
http://www.aaas.org/spp/dspp/sfrl/per/per12.htm
This article by Lynette Feder describes the use of random assignment in a research project that was done to prove whether or not individuals guilty of domestic violence should be mandated into counseling. It is an excellent example of how research can have a serious social impact.

We highly recommend that you review our Web site for expanded information and our other product lines. We are continually updating and adding links to our Web site in order to offer you the most usable and useful information that will support and expand the value of your Annual Editions. You can reach us at:
http://www.dushkin.com/annualeditions/.

www.dushkin.com/online/

Unit Selections

1. **Back from Chaos,** Edward O. Wilson
2. **The Connection between Research and Practice,** Mary M. Kennedy
3. **Evolution of Qualitative Research Methodology: Looking beyond Defense to Possibilities,** LeAnn G. Putney, Judith L. Green, Carol N. Dixon, and Gregory J. Kelly
4. **Quantitative Research Approaches,** George A. Morgan, Jeffrey A. Gliner, and Robert J. Harmon
5. **What Is (and Isn't) Research?** Debra Viadero

Key Points to Consider

❖ Discuss the views of thinkers who have influenced various paradigms for human knowledge. Which paradigm suits your personal views?

❖ Which are the possible explanations for the existing gap between research and practice? In what ways can this gap be bridged?

❖ What phases has qualitative research gone through in its development?

❖ Is a thesis or dissertation the only acceptable form of scholarship or should other creative works be considered as ways of fulfilling the requirements for the degree?

 **Links** **www.dushkin.com/online/**

3. **CSU Institute for Education Reform**
   http://www.csus.edu/ier/reading.html
4. **Education & Research Using Internet**
   http://www.brint.com/Research.htm
5. **Outline of Quantitative Research Design**
   http://www.coe.uh.edu/coe_kiosk/elcs/doctoral/source/outline_quan.html
6. **Qualitative Research Page**
   http://www.oit.pdx.edu/~kerlinb/qualresearch/

These sites are annotated on pages 4 and 5.

What counts as research? If you pose that question to most junior high school students in the United States who are being asked to write their first "research paper," they would probably say that it has to do with paraphrasing from encyclopedias and online sources. If you ask a group of college freshmen about research, they are apt to mention such things as frequenting a college or university library (both the bricks-and-mortar type and the virtual library), making notes, and mastering the referencing style demanded by the discipline. By the time that most college students are completing an undergraduate degree or pursuing a graduate degree, they realize that something further is required when conducting research. They have come to think of research, not merely as reprocessing information gleaned from reading, but as creating and contributing to a field in some original way. Reviewing the work of others, important as that may be, is regarded as a beginning rather than an end in itself.

In this introductory section, we provide an expanded definition of research that includes information about the nature of research activity, the overarching purposes of research, and the basic concepts that are foundational to research. The section begins with a leading scientist's historical perspective on major schools of thought about the creation of knowledge, "Back from Chaos" by Edward O. Wilson. Next is an article by Mary Kennedy, "The Connection between Research and Practice," which discusses the perceived gap between research and practice and proposes four possible explanations for this lack of connection. The third article, by LeAnn Putney, Judith Green, Carol Dixon, and Gregory Kelly, delves a bit deeper into the qualitative research traditions and takes the form of a conversation among four qualitative researchers with different backgrounds and perspectives. By way of contrast, George Morgan, Jeffrey Gliner, and Robert Harmon offer a guide to the major categories of quantitative research methods, a helpful "guide to the galaxy."

Unit 1 concludes with a concise statement about useful distinctions between research and other forms of scholarly activity by Debra Viadero, "What Is (and Isn't) Research?"

Back From
CHAOS

by Edward O. Wilson

Enlightenment thinkers knew a lot about everything, today's specialists know a lot about a little, and postmodernists doubt that we can know anything at all. One of the century's most important scientists argues, against fashion, that we can know what we need to know, and that we will discover underlying all forms of knowledge a fundamental unity

I N contrast to widespread opinion, I believe that the Enlightenment thinkers of the seventeenth and eighteenth centuries got it mostly right. The assumptions they made about a lawful material world, the intrinsic unity of knowledge, and the potential for indefinite human progress are the ones we still take most readily to heart, suffer without, and find maximally rewarding as we learn more and more about the circumstances of our lives. The greatest enterprise of the mind always has been and always will be the attempt to link the sciences and the humanities. The ongoing fragmentation of knowledge and the resulting chaos in philosophy are not reflections of the real world but artifacts of scholarship.

The key to unification is consilience. I prefer this word to "coherence," because its rarity has preserved its precision, whereas "coherence" has several possible meanings. William Whewell, in his 1840 synthesis *The Philosophy of the Inductive Sciences*, was the first to speak of consilience—literally a "jumping together" of knowledge as a result of the linking of facts and fact-based theory across disciplines to create a common groundwork of explanation. He wrote, "The Consilience of Inductions takes place when an Induction, obtained from one class of facts, coincides with an Induction, obtained from another different class. This Consilience is a test of the truth of the Theory in which it occurs."

Consilience can be established or refuted only by methods developed in the natural sciences—in an effort, I hasten to add, not led by scientists, or frozen in mathematical abstraction, but consistent with the habits of thought that have worked so well in exploring the material universe.

The belief in the possibility of consilience beyond science and across the great branches of learning is a metaphysical world view, and a minority one at that, shared by only a few scientists and philosophers. Consilience cannot be proved with logic from first principles or grounded in any definitive set of empirical tests, at least not any yet conceived. Its best support is no more than an extrapolation from the consistent past success of the natural sciences. Its surest test will be its effectiveness in the social sciences and the humanities. The strongest appeal of consilience is in the prospect of intellectual adventure and, if even only modest success is achieved, a better understanding of the human condition.

To illustrate the claim just made, think of two intersecting perpendicular lines, and picture the quadrants thus created. Label one quadrant "environmental policy," one "ethics," one "biology," and one "social science."

environmental policy	social science
ethics	biology

We already think of these four domains as closely connected, so rational inquiry in one informs reasoning in the other three. Yet each undeniably stands apart in the contemporary academic mind. Each has its own practitioners, language, modes of analysis, and standards of validation. The result is confusion—and confusion was correctly identified by Francis Bacon, four centuries ago, as the direst of errors, which "occurs wherever argument or inference passes from one world of experience to another."

Next imagine a series of concentric circles around the point of intersection.

environmental policy ⊕ social science
ethics ⊕ biology

As we cross the circles inward toward the point at which the quadrants meet, we find ourselves in an increasingly unstable and disorienting region. The ring closest to the intersection, where most real-world problems exist, is the one in which fundamental analysis is most needed. Yet virtually no maps exist; few concepts and words serve to guide us. Only in imagination can we travel clockwise from the recognition of environmental problems and the need for soundly based policy to the selection of solutions based on moral reasoning to the biological foundations of that reasoning to a grasp of social institutions as the products of biology, environment, and history—and thence back to environmental policy.

Consider this example. Governments everywhere are at a loss regarding the best policy for regulating the dwindling forest reserves of the world. Few ethical guidelines have been established from which agreement might be reached, and those are based on an insufficient knowledge of ecology. Even if adequate scientific knowledge were available, we would have little basis for the long-term valuation of forests. The economics of sustainable yield is still a primitive art, and the psychological benefits of natural ecosystems are almost wholly unexplored.

The time has come to achieve the tour of such domains in reality. This is not an idle exercise for the delectation of intellectuals. The ease with which the educated public, not just intellectuals and political leaders, can think around these and similar circuits, starting at any point and moving in any direction, will determine how wisely public policy is chosen.

To ask if consilience can be gained in the domains of the innermost circles, such that sound judgment will flow easily from one discipline to another, is equivalent to asking whether, in the gathering of disciplines, specialists can ever reach agreement on a common body of abstract principles and evidential proof. I think they can. Trust in consilience is the foundation of the natural sciences. For the material world, at least, the momentum is overwhelmingly toward conceptual unity. Disciplinary boundaries within the natural sciences are disappearing, in favor of shifting hybrid disciplines in which consilience is implicit. They reach across many levels of complexity, from chemical physics and physical chemistry to molecular genetics, chemical ecology, and ecological genetics. None of the new specialties is considered more

than a focus of research. Each is an industry of fresh ideas and advancing technology.

TERROR AND THE ENLIGHTENMENT

THE dream of intellectual unity was a product of the Enlightenment, an Icarian flight of the mind that spanned the seventeenth and eighteenth centuries. A vision of secular knowledge in the service of human rights and human progress, it was the West's greatest contribution to civilization. It launched the modern era for the whole world; we are all its legatees. Then—astonishingly—it failed.

Given the prospect of renewed convergence of the disciplines, it is of surpassing importance to understand both the essential nature of the Enlightenment and the weaknesses that brought it down. Both can be said to have been embodied in the life of the Marquis de Condorcet. No single event better marks the end of the Enlightenment than his death, on March 29, 1794. The circumstances were exquisitely ironic. Condorcet has been called the prophet of the Laws of Progress. By virtue of his towering intellect and visionary political leadership, he seemed destined to emerge from the French

THE ENLIGHTENMENT GOT IT MOSTLY RIGHT. THE FRAGMENTATION OF KNOWLEDGE AND THE CHAOS IN PHILOSOPHY ARE NOT REFLECTIONS OF THE REAL WORLD BUT ARTIFACTS OF SCHOLARSHIP.

Revolution as the Jefferson of France. But in late 1793 and early 1794, as he was composing the ultimate Enlightenment blueprint, *Sketch for a Historical Picture of the Progress of the Human Mind*, he was instead a fugitive from the law, liable to a sentence of death by representatives of the cause he had so faithfully served. His crime was political: He was perceived to be a Girondist, a member of a faction found too moderate—too reasonable—by the radical Jacobins. Worse, he had criticized the constitution drawn up by the Jacobin-dominated National Convention. He died on the floor of a cell in the jail at Bourg-la-Reine, after being imprisoned by villagers who had captured him on the run. They would certainly have turned him over to the Paris authorities for trial. The cause of death is unknown. Suicide was ruled out at the time, but poison, which he carried with him, is nevertheless a possibility; so is trauma or heart attack. At least he was spared the guillotine.

The French Revolution drew its intellectual strength from men and women like Condorcet. It was readied by the growth of educational opportunity and then fired by the idea of the universal rights of man. Yet as the Enlightenment seemed about to achieve political fruition in Europe, something went terribly wrong. What seemed at first to be minor inconsistencies widened into catastrophic failures. Thirty years earlier Jean-Jacques Rousseau, in *The Social Contract,* had introduced the idea that was later to inspire the rallying slogan of the Revolution: "Liberty, Equality, Fraternity." But he had also invented the fateful abstraction of the "general will" to achieve these goals. The general will, he wrote, is the rule of justice agreed upon by assemblies of free people whose interest is only to serve the welfare of the society and of each person in it. When achieved, it forms a sovereign contract that is "always constant, unalterable, and pure." "Each of us puts his person and all his power in common under the supreme direction of the general will, and, in our corporate capacity, we receive each member as an indivisible part of the whole." Those who do not conform to the general will, Rousseau continued, are deviants subject to necessary force by the assembly. A truly egalitarian democracy cannot be achieved in any other way.

Robespierre, who led the Reign of Terror that overtook the Revolution in 1793, grasped this logic all too well. He and his fellow Jacobins understood Rousseau's necessary force to include summary condemnations and executions of all those who opposed the new order. Some 300,000 nobles, priests, political dissidents, and other troublemakers were imprisoned, and 17,000 died within the year. In Robespierre's universe the goals of the Jacobins were noble and pure. They were, as he serenely wrote in February of 1794 (shortly before he himself was guillotined), "the peaceful enjoyment of liberty and equality, the rule of that eternal justice whose laws have been engraved ... upon the hearts of men, even upon the heart of the slave who knows them not and of the tyrant who denies them."

Thus took form the easy cohabitation of egalitarian ideology and savage coercion that was to plague the next two centuries. The decline of the Enlightenment was hastened not just by tyrants who used it for justification but by rising and often valid intellectual opposition. Its dream of a world made orderly and fulfilling by free intellect had seemed at first indestructible, the instinctive goal of all men. The movement gave rise to the modern intellectual tradition of the West and much of its culture. Its creators, among the greatest scholars since Plato and Aristotle, showed what the human mind can accomplish. Isaiah Berlin, one of their most perceptive historians, praised them justly as follows: "The intellectual power, honesty, lucidity, courage, and disinterested love of the truth of the most gifted thinkers of the eighteenth century remain to this day without parallel. Their age is one of the best and most hopeful episodes in the life of mankind." But they reached too far, and their best efforts were not enough to create the sustained endeavor their vision foretold.

THE PERIL OF PERFECTIBILITY

THIS, then, was the problem. Although reason supposedly was the defining trait of the human species, and needed only a little more cultivation to flower universally, it fell short. Humanity was not paying attention. Humanity thought otherwise. The causes of the Enlightenment's decline, which persist today, illuminate the labyrinthine wellsprings of human motivation. It is worth asking, particularly in this winter of our cultural discontent, whether the original spirit of the Enlightenment—confidence, optimism, eyes to the horizon—can be regained. And to ask in honest opposition, *Should* it be regained, or did it possess in its first conception, as some have suggested, a dark-angelic flaw? Might its idealism have contributed to the Terror, which foreshadowed the horrendous dream of the totalitarian state? If knowledge can be consolidated, so might the "perfect" society be designed—one culture, one science—whether fascist, communist, or theocratic.

The Enlightenment itself, however, was never a unified movement. It was less a determined, swift river than a lacework of deltaic streams working their way along twisted channels. By the time of the French Revolution it was very old. It emerged from the Scientific Revolution during the early seventeenth century and attained its greatest influence in the European academy during the eighteenth. Its originators often clashed over fundamental issues. Most engaged from time to time in absurd digressions and speculations, such as looking for hidden codes in the Bible and for the anatomical seat of the soul. The overlap of their opinions was nevertheless extensive and clear and well reasoned enough to bear this simple characterization: They shared a passion to demystify the world and free the mind from the impersonal forces that imprison it.

They were driven by the thrill of discovery. They agreed on the power of science to reveal an orderly, understandable universe and thereby lay an enduring base for free rational discourse. They thought that the perfection of the celestial bodies discovered by astronomy and physics could serve as a model for human society. They believed in the unity of all knowledge, individual human rights, natural law, and indefinite human progress. They tried to avoid metaphysics even as the flaws in and incompleteness of their explanations forced them to practice it. They resisted organized religion. They despised revelation and dogma. They endorsed, or at least tolerated, the state as a contrivance required for civil order. They believed that education and right reason would enormously benefit humanity. A few, like Condorcet, thought that human beings were perfectible and capable of shaping and administering a political utopia.

FRANCIS BACON AND GOD'S MACHINE

SCIENCE was the engine of the Enlightenment. The more scientifically disposed Enlightenment authors agreed that the cosmos is an orderly material construct governed by exact laws. It can be broken down into entities that can be measured and arranged in hierarchies, such as societies, which are made up of persons, whose brains consist of nerves, which in turn are composed of atoms. In principle, at least, the atoms can be reassembled into nerves, the nerves into brains, and the persons into societies, with the whole understood as a system of mechanisms and forces. If one insists on a divine intervention, the Enlightenment philosophers maintained, one should think of the world as God's machine. The conceptual constraints that cloud our vision of the physical world can be eased for the betterment of humanity in every sphere. Thus Condorcet, in an era still unburdened by the ballast of complicating fact, called for the illumination of the moral and political sciences by the "torch of analysis."

The grand architect of this dream was not Condorcet, or any of the other *philosophes* who expressed it so well, but Francis Bacon. Among the Enlightenment founders, he is the one who most endures in spirit, informing us across four centuries that we must understand nature, both around us and within ourselves, in order to set humanity on the course of self-improvement. We must do it knowing that our destiny is in our own hands and that denial of the dream will lead back to barbarism. In his scholarship Bacon questioned the solidity of classical "delicate" learning—those medieval forms based on ancient texts and logical expatiation. He spurned reliance on ordinary scholastic philosophy, calling for a study of nature and the human condition on their own terms and without artifice. He observed that because "the mind, hastily and without choice, imbibes and treasures up the first notices of things, from whence all the rest proceed, errors must forever prevail, and remain uncorrected." Thus knowledge is not well constructed but "resembles a magnificent structure that has no foundation."

By reflecting on all possible methods of investigation available to his imagination, Bacon concluded that the best among them for accurate thought was induction—the gathering of large numbers of facts and the detection of patterns. In order to obtain maximum objectivity, we must entertain only a minimum of preconceptions. Bacon proclaimed a pyramid of disciplines, with natural history forming the base, physics above and subsuming it, and metaphysics at the peak, explaining everything below—though perhaps in powers and forms beyond the grasp of man.

He was neither a gifted scientist ("I can not thridd needles so well") nor trained in mathematics, but he was a brilliant thinker, who founded the philosophy of science. A Renaissance man, he took, in his famous phrase, all knowledge to be his province. Then he stepped forward into the Enlightenment as the first taxonomist and master purveyor of the scientific method.

Bacon defined science broadly to include a foreshadowing of the social sciences and parts of the humanities. The repeated testing of knowledge by experiment, he insisted, is the cutting edge of learning. But to him "experiment" meant more than controlled manipulations in the manner of modern science. It was all the ways in which humanity brings change into the world through information, agriculture, and industry. He believed the great branches of learning to be open-ended and constantly evolving, but he nonetheless wrote eloquently on his belief in the underlying unity of knowledge. He rejected the sharp divisions among the disciplines that had prevailed since Aristotle.

Bacon elaborated on but did not invent the method of induction as a counterpoint to classical and medieval deduction. Still, he deserves the title Father of Induction, on which much of his fame rested in later centuries. The procedure he favored was much more than merely making factual generalizations—such as, to use a modern example, "Ninety percent of plant species have flowers that are yellow, red, or white, and are visited by insects." Rather, he said, *start* with such an unbiased description of phenomena. Collect their common traits into an intermediate level of generality. Then proceed to higher levels of generality—such as, "Flowers have evolved colors and anatomy designed to attract certain kinds of insects, and these are the creatures that exclusively pollinate them." Bacon's reasoning was an improvement over the traditional methods of description and classification prevailing during the Renaissance, but it anticipated little of the methods of concept formation, competing hypotheses, and theory that form the core of modern science.

In psychology, and particularly in the nature of creativity, Bacon cast his vision furthest ahead. Although he did not use the word (it was not coined until 1653), he understood the critical importance of psychology in scientific research and all other forms of scholarship. He had a deep intuition for the mental processes of discovery. He understood the means by which those processes are best systematized and most persuasively transmitted. "The human understanding," he wrote, "is no dry light, but receives an infusion from the will and affections; whence proceed sciences which may be called 'sciences as one would.'" He did not mean by this to distort perception of the real world by interposing a prism of emotion. Reality ought still to be embraced directly and reported without flinching. But it is also best delivered the same way it was discovered, retaining a comparable vividness and play of the emotions.

I do not wish, by ranking Francis Bacon so high, to portray him as a thoroughly modern man. He was far from that. His friend William Harvey, a physician and a real scientist who made a fundamental discovery, the circulation of the blood, noted drily that Bacon wrote philosophy like a Lord Chancellor. His phrases make splendid marble inscriptions and commencement flourishes. The unity of knowledge he conceived is remote from the present-day concept of consilience, far from the deliberate, systematic linkage of cause and effect across the disciplines. His stress lay instead on the common means of inductive inquiry that might optimally serve all the branches of learning. He searched for the techniques that best convey the knowledge gained, and to that end he argued for the full employment of the humanities, including art and fiction, as the best means for developing and expressing science. Science, as he broadly defined it, should be poetry, and poetry science. That, at least, has a pleasingly modern ring.

Bacon's philosophy raised the sights of a small but influential public. It helped to prime the Scientific Revolution, which was to blossom spectacularly in the decades ahead. To this day his vision remains at the heart of the scientific-technological ethic. He was a magnificent figure, standing alone by necessity of circumstance, who achieved that affecting combination of humility and innocent arrogance present only in the greatest scholars.

DESCARTES AND THE THREE COORDINATES

ALL histories that live in our hearts are peopled by archetypes in mythic narratives. This, I believe, is part of Francis Bacon's appeal and the reason that his fame endures. In the tableau of the Enlightenment, Bacon is the herald of adventure. A new world is waiting, he announced; let us begin the long and difficult march into its unmapped terrain. René Descartes, the founder of algebraic geometry and modern philosophy, and France's pre-eminent scholar of all time, is the mentor in the narrative. Like Bacon before him, he summoned scholars to the scientific enterprise; among them came the young Isaac Newton. Descartes showed how to do science with the aid of precise deduction, cutting to the quick of each phenomenon and skeletonizing it. The world is three-dimensional, he explained, so let our perception of it be framed in three coordinates. Today they are called Cartesian coordinates. With them the length, breadth, and height of any object can be exactly specified and subjected to mathematical operations to explore the object's essential qualities. Descartes accomplished this step in elementary form by reformulating algebraic notation so that it could be used to solve complex problems of geometry and, further, to explore realms of mathematics beyond the visual realm of three-dimensional space.

Descartes's overarching vision was of knowledge as a system of interconnected truths that can ultimately be abstracted into mathematics. It all came to him, he said, through a series of dreams in November of 1619, when somehow, in a flurry of symbols (thunderclaps, books, an evil spirit, a delicious melon), he perceived that the universe is both rational and united throughout by cause and effect. He believed that this conception could be applied everywhere from physics to medicine—hence biology—and even to moral reasoning. In this respect he laid the groundwork for the belief in the unity of learning that was to influence Enlightenment thought profoundly in the eighteenth century.

Descartes insisted that systematic doubt was the first principle of learning. By his light, all knowledge was to be laid out and tested on the iron frame of logic. He allowed himself only one undeniable premise, captured in the celebrated phrase *"Cogito ergo sum"*—"I think, therefore I am." The system of Cartesian doubt, which still thrives in modern science, is one in which all assumptions that can be are systematically eliminated, so as to leave only one set of axioms on which rational thought can be based and experiments can be rigorously designed.

Descartes nonetheless made a fundamental concession to metaphysics. A lifelong Catholic, he believed in God as a perfect being, manifested by the power of the idea of such a being in his own mind. That given, he went on to argue for the complete separation of mind and matter. The stratagem freed him to put spirit aside and concentrate on matter as pure mechanism. In works published over the years 1637–1649 Descartes introduced

FRANCIS BACON WAS A MAGNIFICENT FIGURE, WHO ACHIEVED THAT AFFECTING COMBINATION OF HUMILITY AND INNOCENT ARROGANCE PRESENT ONLY IN THE GREATEST SCHOLARS.

reductionism, the study of the world as an assemblage of physical parts that can be broken down and analyzed separately. Reductionism and analytic mathematical modeling were destined to become the most powerful intellectual instruments of modern science. (The year 1642 was a signal one in the history of ideas: with Descartes's *Meditationes de Prima Philosophia* just published and his *Principia Philosophiae* soon to follow, Galileo died and Newton was born.)

As Enlightenment history unfolded, Isaac Newton came to rank with Galileo as the most influential of the heroes who answered Bacon's call. A restless seeker of horizons, stunningly resourceful, he invented calculus before Gottfried Leibniz, whose notation was nevertheless clearer and is the one used today. In company with analytic geometry, calculus proved to be one of the two crucial mathematical techniques in physics and, later, chemistry, biology, and economics.

In 1684 Newton formulated the mass and distance laws of gravity, and in 1687 the three laws of motion. With these mathematical formulations he achieved the first great breakthrough in modern science. He showed that the planetary orbits postulated by Copernicus and proved elliptical by Kepler could be predicted from the first principles of mechanics. His laws were exact and equally applicable to all inanimate matter, from the solar system down to grains of sand—and, of course, to the falling apple that had triggered his thinking on the subject twenty years previously (apparently a true story). The universe, he said, is not just orderly but also intelligible. At least part of God's grand design could be written with a few lines on a piece of paper.

The laws of gravity and motion were a powerful beginning. And they started Enlightenment scholars thinking, Why not a Newtonian solution to the affairs of men? The idea grew into one of the mainstays of the Enlightenment agenda. As late as 1835 Adolphe Quételet was proposing "social physics" as the basis of the discipline soon to be named sociology. Auguste Comte, his contemporary, believed a true social science to be inevitable. "Men," he said, echoing Condorcet, "are not allowed to think freely about chemistry and biology, so why should they be allowed to think freely about political philosophy?" People, after all, are just extremely complicated machines. Why shouldn't their behavior and social institutions conform to certain still-undefined natural laws?

Given its unbroken string of successes during the next three centuries, reductionism may seem today the obvious best way to have constructed knowledge of the physical world, but it was not so easy to grasp at the dawn of science. Western science took the lead in the world largely because it cultivated reductionism and physical law to expand the understanding of space and time beyond that attainable by the unaided senses. The advance, however, carried humanity's self-image ever further from its perception of the remainder of the universe, and as a consequence the full reality of the universe seemed to grow progressively more alien. The ruling talismans of twentieth-century science, relativity and quantum mechanics, have become the ultimate in strangeness to the human mind. They were conceived by Albert Einstein, Max Planck, and other pioneers of theoretical physics during a search for quantifiable truths that would be known to extraterrestrials as well as to our species, and hence certifiably independent of the human mind. The physicists succeeded magnificently, but in so doing they revealed the limitations of intuition unaided by mathematics; an understanding of nature, they discovered, comes very hard. Theoretical physics and

molecular biology are acquired tastes. The cost of scientific advance is the humbling recognition that reality was not constructed to be easily grasped by the human mind. This is the cardinal tenet of scientific understanding: Our species and its ways of thinking are a product of evolution, not the purpose of evolution.

THE CASE FOR DEISM

WE now pass to the final archetype of the epic tableau, the keepers of the innermost room. The more radical Enlightenment writers, alert to the implications of scientific materialism, moved to reassess God himself. They imagined a Creator obedient to his own natural laws—the belief known as deism. They disputed the theism of Judeo-Christianity, whose divinity is both omnipotent and personally interested in human beings, and they rejected the nonmaterial worlds of heaven and hell. At the same time, few dared go the whole route and embrace atheism, which seemed to imply cosmic meaninglessness and risked outraging the pious. So by and large they took a middle position. God the Creator exists, they conceded, but He is allowed only the entities and processes manifest in his own handiwork.

Deistic belief, by persisting in attenuated form to this day, has given scientists a license to search for God. More precisely, it has prompted a small number to make a partial sketch of Him (Her? It? Them?), derived from their professional meditations.

Few scientists and philosophers, however, let alone religious thinkers, take scientific theology very seriously. A more coherent and interesting approach, possibly within the reach of theoretical physics, is to try to answer the following question: Is a universe of discrete material particles possible only with one specific set of natural laws and parameter values? In other words, does the human imagination, which can conceive of other laws and values, thereby exceed possible existence? Any act of Creation may be only a subset of the universes we can imagine. On this point Einstein is said to have remarked to his assistant Ernst Straus, in a moment of neo-deistic reflection, "What really interests me is whether God had any choice in the creation of the world." That line of reasoning can be extended rather mystically to formulate the "anthropic principle," which asserts that the laws of nature, in *our* universe at least, had to be set a certain precise way so as to allow the creation of beings able to ask about the laws of nature. Did Someone decide to do it that way?

The dispute between Enlightenment deism and theology can be summarized as follows. The traditional theism of Christianity is rooted in both reason and revelation, the two conceivable sources of knowledge. According to this view, reason and revelation cannot be in conflict, because in areas of opposition, revelation is given the higher role—as the Inquisition reminded Galileo in Rome when he was offered a choice between orthodoxy and pain. In contrast, deism grants reason the edge, and insists that theists justify revelation with the use of reason.

Traditional theologians of the eighteenth century, faced with the Enlightenment challenge, refused to yield an inch of ground. Christian faith, they argued, cannot submit itself to the debasing test of rationality. Deep truths exist that are beyond the grasp of the unaided human mind, and God will reveal them to our understanding when and by whatever means He chooses.

Given the centrality of religion in everyday life, the stand of the theists against reason seemed . . . well, reasonable. Eighteenth-century believers saw no difficulty in conducting their lives by both ratiocination and revelation. The theologians won the argument simply because they saw no compelling reason to adopt a new metaphysics. For the first time, the Enlightenment visibly stumbled.

The fatal flaw in deism is thus not rational at all but emotional. Pure reason is unappealing because it is bloodless. Ceremonies stripped of sacred mystery lose their emotional force, because celebrants need to defer to a higher power in order to consummate their instinct for tribal loyalty. In times of danger and tragedy especially, unreasoning ceremony is everything. Rationalism provides no substitute for surrender to an infallible and benevolent being, or for the leap of faith called transcendence. Most people, one imagines, would very much like science to prove the existence of God but not to take the measure of his capacity.

Deism and science also failed to systematize ethics. The Enlightenment promise of an objective basis for moral reasoning could not be kept. If an immutable secular field of ethical premises exists, the human intellect during the Enlightenment seemed too weak and shifting to locate it. So theologians and philosophers stuck to their original positions, either by deferring to religious authority or by articulating subjectively perceived natural rights. No logical alternative seemed open to them. The millennium-old rules sacralized by religion seemed to work, more or less. One can defer reflection on the celestial spheres indefinitely, but daily matters of life and death require moral decisiveness.

HOW SELF-KNOWLEDGE LEADS TO TOTALITARIANISM

ANOTHER, more purely rationalist objection to the Enlightenment program remains. Grant for argument's sake that the most extravagant claims of the Enlightenment's supporters proved true and scientists could look into the future to see what course of action was best for humanity. Wouldn't that trap us in a cage of logic and revealed fate? The thrust of the Enlightenment, like the Greek humanism that prefigured it, was Promethean: the knowledge it generated

THERE HAVE ALWAYS BEEN TWO KINDS OF ORIGINAL THINKERS— THOSE WHO UPON VIEWING DISORDER TRY TO CREATE ORDER, AND THOSE WHO UPON ENCOUNTERING ORDER TRY TO CREATE DISORDER.

was to liberate mankind by lifting it above the savage world. But the opposite might occur: if scientific inquiry diminishes the conception of divinity while prescribing immutable natural laws, then humanity can lose what freedom it already possesses. Perhaps only one social order is "perfect" and scientists will find it—or, worse, falsely claim to have found it. Religious authority, the Hadrian's Wall of civilization, will be breached, and the barbarians of totalitarian ideology will pour in. Such is the dark side of Enlightenment secular thought, unveiled in the French Revolution and expressed more recently by theories of "scientific" socialism and racialist fascism.

Still another concern is that a science-driven society risks upsetting the natural order of the world set in place by God, or by billions of years of evolution. Science given too much authority risks conversion into a self-destroying impiety. The godless creations of science and technology are in fact powerful and arresting images of modern culture. Frankenstein's monster and Hollywood's Terminator (an all-metal, microchip-guided Frankenstein's monster) wreak destruction on their creators, including the naive geniuses in lab coats who arrogantly forecast a new age ruled by science. Storms rage, hostile mutants spread, life dies. Nations menace one another with world-destroying technology. Even Winston Churchill, whose country was saved by radar, worried after the atom-bombing of Japan that the Stone Age might return "on the gleaming wings of Science."

THE RISE OF ROMANTICISM

FOR those who thus feared science as Faustian rather than Promethean, the Enlightenment program posed a grave threat to spiritual freedom— even to life itself. What is the answer to such a threat? Revolt! Return to natural man, reassert the primacy of individual imagination and confidence in immortality. Find an escape to a higher realm through art; promote a Romantic revolution. In 1807 William Wordsworth, in words typical of the movement then spreading over Europe, evoked the aura of a primal and serene existence beyond reason's grasp.

Our Souls have sight of that immortal sea
Which brought us hither,
Can in a moment travel thither,
And see the Children sport upon the shore,
And hear the mighty waters rolling evermore.

With Wordworth's "breathings for incommunicable powers" the eyes close, the mind soars, the inverse square distance law of gravity falls away. The spirit enters another reality, beyond the reach of weight and measure. If the constraining universe of matter and energy cannot be denied, at least it can be ignored with splendid contempt. Beyond question, Wordsworth and his fellow English Romantic poets of the first half of the nineteenth century conjured works of great beauty. They spoke truths in another tongue, and guided the arts still further from the sciences.

Romanticism also flowered in philosophy, where it placed a premium on rebellion, spontaneity, intense emotion, and heroic vision. Searching for aspirations available only to the heart, its practitioners dreamed of mankind as part of boundless nature. Rousseau, although often listed as an Enlightenment *philosophe*, was actually the founder and most extreme visionary of the Romantic philosophical movement. To him, learning and social order were the enemies of humanity. In works from 1750 (*Discourse on the Sciences and the Arts*) to 1762 (*Emile*) he extolled the "sleep of reason." His utopia is a minimalist state in which people abandon books and other accouterments of intellect in order to cultivate good health and enjoyment of the senses. Humanity, Rousseau claimed, was originally a race of noble savages in a peaceful state of nature, and was later corrupted by civilization—and by scholarship. Religion, marriage, law, and government are deceptions created by the powerful for their own selfish ends. The price paid by the common man for this high-level chicanery is vice and unhappiness.

Where Rousseau invented a stunningly inaccurate form of anthropology, the German Romantics, led by Goethe, Hegel, Herder, and Schelling, set out to reinsert metaphysics into science and philosophy. The product, *Naturphilosophie*, was a hybrid of sentiment, mysticism, and quasi-scientific hypothesis. Johann Wolfgang von Goethe, pre-eminent among its expositors, wanted most of all to be a great scientist. He placed that ambition above literature, to which he became an immortal contributor. His respect for science as an idea, an approach to tangible reality, was unreserved, and he understood its basic tenets. Analysis and synthesis, he liked to say, should alternate as naturally as breathing in and breathing out. At the same time, he was critical of the mathematical abstractions of Newtonian science, thinking physics far too ambitious in its goal of explaining the universe.

Goethe can easily be forgiven. After all, he had a noble purpose—nothing less than the coupling of the soul of the humanities to the engine of science. He would have

grieved had he foreseen history's verdict: great poet, poor scientist. He failed in his synthesis through lack of what is today called the scientist's instinct—not to mention the necessary technical skills. Calculus baffled him, and some said he could not tell a lark from a sparrow. But he loved nature in a profoundly spiritual way. One must cultivate a close, deep feeling for Nature, he proclaimed. "She loves illusion. She shrouds man in mist, and she spurs him toward the light. Those who will not partake of her illusions she punishes as a tyrant would punish. Those who accept her illusions she presses to her heart. To love her is the only way to approach her." In the philosophers' empyrean, I imagine, Bacon has long since lectured Goethe on the idols of the mind. Newton will have lost patience immediately.

Friedrich Schelling, the leading philosopher of the German Romantics, attempted to immobilize the scientific Prometheus not with poetry but with reason. He proposed a cosmic unity of all things, beyond the understanding of man. Facts by themselves can never be more than partial truths. Those we perceive are only fragments of the universal flux. Nature, Schelling concluded, is alive—a creative spirit that unites knower and known, progressing through greater and greater understanding and feeling toward an eventual state of complete self-realization.

In America, German philosophical Romanticism was mirrored in New England Transcendentalism, whose most celebrated adherents were Ralph Waldo Emerson and Henry David Thoreau. The Transcendentalists were radical individualists who rejected the overwhelmingly commercial nature of American society that came to prevail during the Jacksonian era. They envisioned a spiritual universe built entirely within their personal ethos. They were nevertheless more congenial to science than their European counterparts—witness the many accurate natural-history observations in *Faith in a Seed* and other writings by Thoreau.

THE AGE OF NARROW SPECIALIZATION DAWNS

NATURAL scientists, chastened by such robust objections to the Enlightenment agenda, mostly abandoned the examination of human mental life, yielding to philosophers and poets another century of free play. In fact, the concession proved to be a healthy decision for the profession of science, because it steered researchers away from the pitfalls of metaphysics. Throughout the nineteenth century knowledge in the physical and biological sciences grew at an exponential rate. At the same time, newly risen like upstart duchies and earldoms, the social sciences—sociology, anthropology, economics, and political theory—vied for territory in the space created between the hard sciences and the humanities. The great branches of learning emerged in their present form—natural sciences, social sciences, and the humanities—out of the unified Enlightenment vision.

The Enlightenment, defiantly secular in orientation while indebted and attentive to theology, had brought the Western mind to the threshold of a new freedom. It waved aside everything, every form of religious and civil authority, every imaginable fear, to give precedence to the ethic of free inquiry. It pictured a universe in which humanity plays the role of perpetual adventurer. For two centuries God seemed to speak in a new voice to humankind.

By the early 1800s, however, the splendid image was fading. Reason fractured, intellectuals lost faith in the leadership of science, and the prospects for a unity of knowledge sharply declined. The spirit of the Enlightenment lived on in political idealism and the hopes of individual thinkers. In the ensuing decades new schools sprang up like shoots from the base of a shattered tree: the utilitarian ethics of Bentham and Mill, the historical materialism of Marx and Engels, the pragmatism of Charles Peirce, William James, and John Dewey. But the core agenda seemed irretrievably abandoned. The grand conception that had riveted thinkers during the previous two centuries lost most of its credibility.

Science traveled on its own way. It continued to double every fifteen years in practitioners, discoveries, and technical journals, as it had since the early 1700s, finally starting to level off only around 1970. Its continuously escalating success began to give credence again to the idea of an ordered, explainable universe. This essential Enlightenment premise gained ground in the disciplines of mathematics, physics, and biology, where it had first been conceived by Bacon and Descartes. Yet the enormous success of reductionism, its key method, worked perversely against any recovery of the Enlightenment program as a whole. Precisely because scientific information was increasing at a geometric pace, most researchers thought little about unification, and even less about philosophy. They thought, What works, works. They were still slower to address the taboo-laden physical basis for the workings of the mind, a concept hailed in the late 1700s as the gateway from biology to the social sciences.

There was another, humbler reason for the lack of interest in the big picture: scientists simply didn't have the requisite intellectual energy. The vast majority of scientists have never been more than journeymen prospectors. That is truer than ever today. They are professionally focused; their education does not open them to the wide contours of the world. They acquire the training they need to travel to the frontier and make discoveries of their own—and make them as fast as possible, because life at the edge is expensive and chancy. The most productive scientists, installed in million-dollar laboratories, have no time to think about the big picture, and see little profit in it. The rosette of the U.S. National Academy of Sciences, which the 2,100 elected members wear on their lapels as a mark of achievement, contains a center of sci-entific gold surrounded by the purple of natural philosophy. The eyes of most leading scientists, alas, are fixed on the gold.

We should not be surprised, therefore, to find physicists who do not know what a gene is, and biologists who guess that string theory has something to do with violins. Grants and honors are given in science for discoveries, not for scholarship and wisdom. And so it has ever been. Francis Bacon, using the political skills that lofted him to the Lord Chancellorship, personally importuned the English monarchs for funds to carry forth his great scheme of unifying knowledge. He never got a penny. At the height of his fame Descartes was ceremoniously awarded a stipend by the French court. But the account remained unfunded, helping to drive him to the more generous Swedish court, in the "land of bears between rock and ice," where he soon died of pneumonia.

The same professional atomization afflicts the social sciences and the humanities. The faculties of higher education around the world are a congeries of experts. To be an original scholar is to be a highly specialized world authority in a polyglot Calcutta of similarly focused world authorities. In 1797, when Jefferson took the president's chair at the American Philosophical Society, all American scientists of professional caliber and their colleagues in the humanities could be seated comfortably in the lecture room of Philosophical Hall. Most could discourse reasonably well on the entire world of learning, which was still small enough to be seen whole. Their successors today, including 450,000 holders of the doctorate in science and engineering alone, would overcrowd Philadelphia. Professional scholars in general have little choice but to dice up research expertise and research agendas among themselves. To be a successful scholar means spending a career on membrane biophysics, the Romantic poets, early American history, or some other such constricted area of formal study.

Fragmentation of expertise was furthered in the twentieth century by modernism in the arts, including architecture. The work of the masters—Braque, Picasso, Stravinsky, Eliot, Joyce, Martha Graham, Gropius, Frank Lloyd Wright, and their peers—was so novel and discursive as to thwart generic classification, except perhaps for this: The modernists tried to achieve the new and provocative at any cost. They identified the constraining bonds of tradition and self-consciously broke them. Many rejected realism of expression in order to explore the unconscious. Freud, as much a literary stylist as a scientist, inspired them and can justifiably be included in their ranks. Psychoanalysis was a force that shifted the attention of modernist intellectuals and artists from the social and political to the private and psychological. Subjecting every topic within their domain to the "ruthless centrifuge of change," in the American historian Carl Schorske's phrase, they meant proudly to assert the independence of twentieth-century high culture from the past. They were not nihilists; rather, they sought to create

THE WORLD WILL SOMEHOW BECOME CLEARER, AND WE WILL GRASP THE TRUE STRANGENESS OF THE UNIVERSE. THE STRANGENESS WILL ALL PROVE TO BE CONNECTED, AND TO MAKE SENSE.

a new level of order and meaning. They were complete experimentalists who wished to participate in a century of radical technological and political change and to fashion part of it entirely on their own terms.

Thus the free flight bequeathed by the Enlightenment, which disengaged the humanities during the Romantic era, had by the middle of the twentieth century all but erased hope for the unification of knowledge with the aid of science. The two cultures described by C. P. Snow in his 1959 Rede Lecture, the literary and the scientific, were no longer on speaking terms.

THE RIDDLE OF POSTMODERNISM

ALL movements tend toward extremes, which is approximately where we are today. The exuberant self-realization that ran from Romanticism to modernism has given rise now to philosophical postmodernism (often called post-structuralism, especially in its more political and sociological expressions). Postmodernism is the ultimate antithesis of the Enlightenment. The difference between the two can be expressed roughly as follows: Enlightenment thinkers believed we can know everything, and radical postmodernists believe we can know nothing.

The philosophical postmodernists, a rebel crew milling beneath the black flag of anarchy, challenge the very foundations of science and traditional philosophy. Reality, the radicals among them propose, is a state constructed by the mind. In the exaggerated version of this constructivism one can discern no "real" reality, no objective truths external to mental activity, only prevailing versions disseminated by ruling social groups. Nor can ethics be firmly grounded, given that each society creates its own codes for the benefit of equivalent oppressive forces.

If these premises are correct, it follows that one culture is as good as any other in the expression of truth and morality, each in its own special way. Political multiculturalism is justified; each ethnic group and sexual preference in the community has equal validity and deserves communal support and mandated representation in educational agendas—that is, again, if the premises are correct. And they must be correct, say their promoters, because to suggest otherwise is bigotry, which is a car-

dinal sin. Cardinal, that is, if we agree to waive in this one instance the postmodernist prohibition against universal truth, and all agree to agree for the common good. Thus Rousseau redivivus.

Postmodernism is expressed more explicitly still in deconstruction, a technique of literary criticism. Its underlying premise is that each author's meaning is unique to himself; neither his true intention nor anything else connected to objective reality can reliably be determined. His text is therefore open to fresh analysis and commentary from the equally solipsistic world in the head of the reviewer. But the reviewer, too, is subject to deconstruction, as is the reviewer of the reviewer, and so on in infinite regress. That is what Jacques Derrida, the creator of deconstruction, meant when he stated the formula "*Il n'y a pas de hors-texte*" ("There is nothing outside the text"). At least, that is what I think he meant, after reading him, his defenders, and his critics with some care. If the radical postmodernist premise is correct, we can never be sure what he meant. Conversely, if that *is* what he meant, perhaps we are not obliged to consider his arguments further. This puzzle, which I am inclined to set aside as the "Derrida paradox," is similar to the Cretan paradox (a Cretan says "All Cretans are liars"). It awaits solution, but one should not feel any great sense of urgency in the matter.

Scientists, held responsible for what they say, have not found postmodernism useful. The postmodernist posture toward science, in turn, is one of subversion. It contains what appears to be a provisional acceptance of gravity, the periodic table, astrophysics, and similar stanchions of the external world, but in general the scientific culture is viewed as just another way of knowing, and, moreover, a mental posture contrived mostly by European and American white males.

One is tempted to place postmodernism in history's curiosity cabinet, alongside theosophy and transcendental idealism, but it has seeped by now into the mainstream of the social sciences and the humanities. It is viewed there as a technique of metatheory (theory about theories), by which scholars analyze not so much the subject matter of a scientific discipline as the cultural and psychological factors that explain why particular scientists think the way they do. The analyst places emphasis on "root metaphors," those ruling images in the thinker's mind whereby he designs theories and experiments. Here, for example, is the psychologist Kenneth Gergen explaining how modern psychology is dominated by the metaphor of human beings as machines:

> Regardless of the character of the person's behavior, the mechanist theorist is virtually obliged to segment him from the environment, to view the environment in terms of stimulus or input elements, to view the person as reactive to and dependent on these input elements, to view the domain of the mental as structured (constituted of interacting elements), to segment behavior into units that can be coordinated to the stimulus inputs, and so on.

Put briefly, and to face the issue squarely, psychology is at risk of becoming a natural science. As a possible remedy for those who wish to keep it otherwise, and many scholars do, Gergen cites other, perhaps less pernicious root metaphors of mental life that might be considered, such as dramaturgy, the marketplace, and rule-following. Psychology, if not allowed to be contaminated with too much biology, can accommodate endless numbers of theoreticians in the future.

As diversity of metaphors has been added to ethnic diversity and gender dualism and then politicized, schools and ideologies have multiplied explosively. Usually leftist in orientation, the more familiar modes of general postmodernist thought include Afrocentrism, constructivist social anthropology, "critical" (that is, socialist) science, deep ecology, ecofeminism, Lacanian psychoanalysis, Latourian sociology of science, and neo-Marxism—to which must be added all the bewildering varieties of deconstructionism and New Age holism swirling round about and through them.

Their adherents fret upon the field of play, sometimes brilliantly, usually not, jargon-prone and elusive. Each in his own way seems to be drifting toward that *mysterium tremendum* abandoned in the seventeenth century by the Enlightenment—and not without the expression of considerable personal anguish. Of the late Michel Foucault, the great interpreter of political power in the history of ideas, poised "at the summit of Western intellectual life," the literary critic George Scialabba has perceptively written,

> Foucault was grappling with the deepest, most intractable dilemmas of modern identity. . . . For those who believe that neither God nor natural law nor transcendent Reason exists, and who recognize the varied and subtle ways in which material interest—power—has corrupted, even constituted, every previous morality, how is one to live, to what values can one hold fast?

How and to what indeed? To solve these disturbing problems, let us begin by simply walking away from Foucault, and existentialist despair. Consider this rule of thumb: to the extent that philosophical positions both confuse us and close doors to further inquiry, they are likely to be wrong.

To Foucault I would say, if I could (and I do not mean to sound patronizing), it's not so bad. Once we get over the shock of discovering that the universe was not made with us in mind, all the meaning the brain can master, and all the emotions it can bear, and all the shared adventure we might wish to enjoy, can be found by deciphering the hereditary orderliness that has borne our species through geological time and stamped it with the residues of deep history. Reason will be advanced to new levels, and emotions played in potentially infinite patterns. The true will be sorted from the false, and we will understand one another very well, the more quickly because we are the same species and possess biologically similar brains.

To those concerned about the growing dissolution and irrelevance of the intelligentsia, which is indeed alarming, I suggest that there have always been two kinds of original thinkers—those who upon viewing disorder try to create order, and those who upon encountering order try to protest it by creating disorder. The tension between the two is what drives learning forward. It lifts us upward on a zigzagging trajectory of progress. And in the Darwinian contest of ideas order always wins, because—simply—that is the way the real world works.

As today's celebrants of unrestrained Romanticism, the postmodernists enrich culture. They say to the rest of us, Maybe, just maybe, you are wrong. Their ideas are like sparks from fireworks explosions that travel away in all directions, devoid of following energy, soon to wink out in the dimensionless dark. Yet a few will endure long enough to cast light in unexpected places. That is one reason to think well of postmodernism, even as it menaces rational thought. Another is the relief it affords those who have chosen not to encumber themselves with a scientific education. Another is the small industry it has created within philosophy and literary studies. Still another, the one that counts most, is the unyielding critique of traditional scholarship it provides. We will always need postmodernists or their rebellious equivalents. For what better way to strengthen organized knowledge than continually to defend it from hostile forces? John Stuart Mill correctly observed that teacher and learner alike fall asleep at their posts when there is no enemy in the field. And if somehow, against all the evidence, against all reason, the linchpin falls out and everything is reduced to epistemological confusion, we will find the courage to admit that the postmodernists were right, and in the best spirit of the Enlightenment we will start over again. Because, as the great mathematician David Hilbert once said, capturing so well that part of the human spirit expressed through the Enlightenment, *"Wir müssen wissen. Wir werden wissen."* ("We must know, we will know.")

THE PROMISE OF CONSILIENCE

IF contemporary scholars work to encourage the consilience of knowledge, I believe, the enterprises of culture will eventually devolve into science—by which I mean the natural sciences—and the humanities, particularly the creative arts. These domains will continue to be the two great branches of learning in the twenty-first century. Social science will split within each of its disciplines, a process already rancorously begun, with one part folding into or becoming continuous with biology, and the other fusing with the humanities. Its disciplines will continue to exist but in radically altered form. In the process the humanities, embracing philosophy, history, moral reasoning, comparative religion, and interpretation of the arts, will draw closer to the sciences and partly fuse with them.

The confidence of natural scientists, I grant, often seems overweening. Science offers the boldest metaphysics of the age: the faith that if we dream, press to discover, explain, and dream again, thereby plunging repeatedly into new terrain, the world will somehow become clearer and we will grasp the true strangeness of the universe. And the strangeness will all prove to be connected and make sense.

In his 1941 classic *Man on His Nature,* the British neurobiologist Charles Sherrington spoke of the brain as an "enchanted loom," perpetually weaving a picture of the external world, tearing down and reweaving, inventing other worlds, creating a miniature universe. The communal mind of literate societies—world culture—is an immensely larger loom. Through science it has gained the power to map external reality far beyond the reach of a single mind, and in the arts it finds the means to construct narratives, images, and rhythms immeasurably more diverse than the products of any solitary genius. The loom is the same for both enterprises, for science and for the arts, and there is a general explanation of its origin and nature and thence of the human condition.

In education the search for consilience is the way to renew the crumbling structure of the liberal arts. During the past thirty years the ideal of the unity of learning, bequeathed to us by the Renaissance and the Enlightenment, has been largely abandoned. With rare exceptions American colleges and universities have dissolved their curricula into a slurry of minor disciplines and specialized courses. While the average number of undergraduate courses per institution has doubled, the percentage of mandatory courses in general education has dropped by more than half. Science was sequestered at the same time; as I write, only a third of colleges and universities require students to take at least one course in the natural sciences. The trend cannot be reversed by force-feeding students with some of this and some of that across the branches of learning; true reform will aim at the consilience of science with the social sciences and the humanities in scholarship and teaching. Every college student should be able to answer this question: What is the re-

lation between science and the humanities, and how is it important for human welfare?

Every public intellectual or political leader should be able to answer that question as well. Already half the legislation coming before Congress has important scientific and technological components. Most of the issues that vex humanity daily—ethnic conflict, arms escalation, overpopulation, abortion, environmental destruction, and endemic poverty, to cite several of the most persistent—can be solved only by integrating knowledge from the natural sciences with that from the social sciences and the humanities. Only fluency across the boundaries will provide a clear view of the world as it really is, not as it appears through the lens of ideology and religious dogma, or as a myopic response solely to immediate need. Yet the vast majority of our political leaders are trained primarily or exclusively in the social sciences and the humanities, and have little or no knowledge of the natural sciences. The same is true of public intellectuals, columnists, media interrogators, and think-tank gurus. The best of their analyses are careful and responsible, and sometimes correct, but the substantive base of their wisdom is fragmented and lopsided.

A balanced perspective cannot be acquired by studying disciplines in pieces; the consilience among them must be pursued. Such unification will be difficult to achieve. But I think it is inevitable. Intellectually it rings true, and it gratifies impulses that arise from the admirable side of human nature. To the extent that the gaps between the great branches of learning can be narrowed, diversity and depth of knowledge will increase. They will do so because of, not despite, the underlying cohesion achieved. The enterprise is important for yet another reason: It gives purpose to intellect. It promises that order, not chaos, lies beyond the horizon. Inevitably, I think, we will accept the adventure, go there, and find what we need to know.

Edward O. Wilson is the Research Professor and Honorary Curator in Entomology at Harvard University. Two of his books have been awarded the Pulitzer Prize in the general nonfiction category: *On Human Nature* (1978) and *The Ants* (1990). Wilson's article in this issue is taken from his book *Consilience: The Unity of Knowledge,* which was published by Knopf in April 1998.

The Connection Between Research and Practice

MARY M. KENNEDY

This article reviews four hypotheses that have been put forward to account for a perceived lack of connection between research and practice: (a) research needs to be more authoritative, (b) research needs to be more relevant, (c) research needs to be more accessible, and (d) the education system itself is inherently too stable or too unstable and therefore unable to respond coherently to research findings. A brief history of thought within each of these hypothesis is offered, and the place of education researchers in the larger education context is discussed.

In the past few decades, members of AERA seem to have become increasingly skeptical about the potential for research to improve practice. My "baseline" for this observation is roughly the late 1960s and early 1970s, when both researchers and research funding agencies were relatively optimistic about the role of research in improving education: National labs and research centers were legislated in 1963, federal funding for educational research rose some 2000% during the 1960s (Bloom, 1966), and a new National Institute of Education was formed in 1972. In 1978, Patrick Suppes published a book celebrating the impact of educational research (Suppes, 1978). Throughout this period, members of AERA seemed convinced that research would soon produce universal truths about teaching and learning that teachers would, could, and should implement. In fact, along with federal funding for research came federal funding for dissemination as well to ensure that teachers learned about the latest findings from research.

Now, if I can borrow an old saw from G. K. Chesterton, the historian, it is tempting to say that the main thing we have learned from educational research is that we have not learned much from educational research. Witness the article Carl Kaestle published in 1993 titled "The Awful Reputation of Educational Research."

But this trend toward pessimism extends well back from my baseline of the 1960s and 1970s. There was another period of intense optimism at the beginning of the century, documented by Geraldine Clifford (1973) in the *Second Handbook of Research on Teaching*. That wave of optimism was also accompanied by a stream of disappointments—Clifford quoting Thorndike as expecting his research to reach practice in some 30–50 years, William Bagley in 1934 expressing disappointment at how little influence research had had, W. W. Charters worrying in 1948 about the lack of influence research had had on practice, Stephen Corey in 1954, and Julian Stanley in 1957. Viewed from that vantage point, Carl Kaestle's 1993 article is simply extending a century-long tradition.

One difference between the more recent and the earlier phases of optimism and pessimism is that this time we have studied the problem more systematically. During its heyday in the 1970s, the National Institution of Education created an entire division devoted to dissemination efforts, and that division sponsored a great deal of research on research use. Researchers studied the dissemination and use of research as a topic in its own right and also studied the implementation of innovations derived from research.

From these efforts, we now have a virtual catalogue of reasons for this perceived lack of usefulness of educational research. The reasons hypothesized for the apparent failure of research to influence teaching can be grouped into four general hypotheses: (a) The research itself is not sufficiently *persuasive or authoritative;* the quality of educational studies has not been high enough to provide compelling, unambiguous, or authoritative results to practitioners. (b) The research has not been *rele-*

MARY M. KENNEDY *is a professor at Michigan State University, 116F Erickson Hall, East Lansing, MI 48824. Her specialties are teacher learning, research use, and education policy.*

From *Educational Researcher,* Vol. 26, No. 7, October 1997, pp. 4-12. © 1997 by the American Educational Research Association. Reprinted by permission of the publisher.

vant to practice. It has not been sufficiently practical, it has not addressed teachers' questions, nor has it adequately acknowledged their constraints. (c) Ideas from research have not been *accessible to teachers.* Findings have not been expressed in ways that are comprehensible to teachers. (d) The education system itself is intractable and unable to change, or it is conversely inherently unstable, overly susceptible to fads, and consequently unable to engage in systematic change. Either of these characteristics—excessive instability and excessive stability—render it incapable of responding reliably to educational research.

The Persuasiveness and Authority of Research

Much of the discussion about the merits of research from the 1940s through the 1960s was focused on research design. The goal was to isolate variables and define their relationships with other variables. Causal relationships were especially important, and researchers designed studies in the hope that they could control for all possible rival interpretations. The need for control was one of the main reasons researchers wanted to conduct their research in the laboratory. Design considerations were so central to the thinking of educational researchers that a chapter on research design that appeared in the first *Handbook of Research on Teaching* was reprinted as an independent monograph and became required reading for graduate students for at least a decade. This was, of course, Campbell and Stanley's (1963/1969) "Experimental and Quasi-Experimental Designs in Research on Teaching." Campbell and Stanley brought to our attention the notion of rival hypotheses and listed several of them that we needed to control for. Their admonitions made comparison groups important and made random assignment to groups one of the central criteria for sound research design. Early on in their article, they define their premise as follows:

> This chapter is committed to the experiment: as the only means for settling disputes regarding educational practice, as the only way of verifying educational improvements, and as the only way of establishing a cumulative tradition in which improvements can be introduced without the danger of a faddish discard of old wisdom in favor of inferior novelties. (Campbell & Stanley, 1963, pp. 2)

It wasn't just designs that preoccupied researchers. We argued about the use of covariates, the reliability of change scores, the appropriate unit of analysis in nested school designs, ways of teasing out interaction effects, and every other conceivable methodological issue you could imagine.

The problem with this line of thinking was that it discouraged research on complex approaches to teaching, for such studies could not be mounted with sufficient control over external influences on learning. In fact, it limited researchers' abilities even to think about such teaching. Consider, for instance, an educational reform called discovery learning that was popular in the 1960s. Like the current reform movement, that one aimed to foster more self-reliant learners and a greater command over the fundamental ideas in the various academic disciplines. In a critique of the research evidence supporting discovery learning, Lee Cronbach (1966) said we needed more persuasive evidence of its effectiveness. Yet even as he described what would count as good research, he conceded that "If all my recommendations were followed, research would become impossibly elaborate" (Cronbach, 1966, p. 77).

In fact, researchers who studied educational phenomena in the field rarely did manage to control for all the extraneous variables. Each major study of that period became mired in methodological debates over whether the inferences its authors made were justified. From Rosenthal and Jacobson's *Pygmalion in the Classroom* (1968) to Coleman's *Equality of Educational Opportunity* (Coleman, 1966) to *Findings From the Follow Through Planned Variation Study* (Kennedy, 1978), methodologists quibbled over confounding variables, measurement problems, methodological biases, and competing interpretations of the data. While such arguments are a necessary part of the process of developing knowledge, they also have side effects that may only become apparent later. In this case, these debates had several side effects. First, they became so esoteric that only the most sophisticated methodologists could follow the debates. Less-qualified researchers and practitioners couldn't possibly track the nuances of reasons for why findings should or should not be believed. Second, although the debaters believed that more carefully designed studies would settle these issues once and for all, the main thing their audiences learned from the debates was that the issues were hopelessly complicated and might never be resolved. Finally, the debates diverted attention from other educational issues. I recall sitting on a proposal review panel for the National Institute of Education in which the strongest proposal *from a design point of view* was an offer to conduct further analyses of Coleman's EEO data. But a practitioner on our review panel strongly objected to funding that project, saying she was tired of seeing all the research money being spent on increasingly esoteric arguments over one study when there were so many other pressing problems facing the schools that were not being addressed.

Most of the arguments about design began to exhaust themselves by the late 1970s without ever producing the ideal, definitive research designs that had been hoped for. Even Lee Cronbach threw in the towel in 1975, when he conceded not only that it was impossible to design studies that could take into account all the relevant variables, but that even if we succeeded at that, the findings from social research would not accumulate over time but instead would "decay" because the social contexts were constantly changing (Cronbach, 1975). We will never, he concluded, be able to generate stable findings that can provide the basis for theories about social phenomena, including the phenomenon of teaching and learning.

But we still argue about design, still worry about how to know if our designs are yielding reliable knowledge. Contemporary discussions about design have taken a different turn, however, as Ann Brown's (1992) article on "Design Experiments" illustrates. Brown grants that we cannot eliminate all possible rival hypotheses and argues that our goal should be to accommodate these other variables rather than control them. She argues that, if research is to produce important knowledge, it has to occur within the natural constraints of real classrooms and must accommodate as best it can the multiple confounding influences that are there.

The Relevance of Research

The second line of thinking about research and practice focuses on the kinds of problems teachers actually have and the kinds of problems researchers are trying to solve. Concerns about relevance frequently motivate the U.S. Department of Education's Office of Educational Research and Improvement to require research grantees to involve teachers in the design of their work, on the assumption that such involvement will force researchers to attend more to teachers' questions and concerns. They have also led to recommendations for collaborative research (Bennett & Desforges, 1985; Huberman, 1989).

Concerns about relevance developed partly in response to the heavy emphasis on authority that permeated the 1960s. Shulman, for instance, argued strongly in 1970 that research needed to move out of the laboratory and into the classroom because the precision gained in the laboratory was purchased at the expense of classroom relevance. At that time, laboratory studies of learning focused mainly on individual learning, whereas teachers worked with groups of learners. Laboratory studies focused mainly on learning nonsense syllables, while teachers were concerned about teaching subject matter. In the intervening decades, educational research has indeed moved to the field. Yet it is still not uncommon for teachers to dismiss research because the classrooms involved in the research differ from their own classrooms—different socioeconomic groups, for instance, or different cultural settings.

Though we may not have solved the relevance dilemma, we have certainly progressed toward understanding it. In fact, in an article published in the *Second Handbook of Research on Teaching,* Dan Lortie (1973) mentioned what he called an "odd gap" in the literature on teaching: There was no research on teachers' beliefs and teachers' conceptions of their work. Lortie found it odd that this gap existed, but I think it is safe to say that the gap has been filled in the intervening 25 years.

Moreover, the research that has been done in the past two decades has actually been quite fruitful for researchers, if not for teachers, in that it has given us vivid descriptions of classroom life, shown us how teachers manage that life, and shown us how teachers think about their practice. Very few naturalistic studies of schools and teaching were done in the first half of the century, but the last two decades have been filled with such studies.

One of the earliest of these studies was Jackson's (1968) *Life in Classrooms.* Jackson claimed that classroom life was characterized by crowds, praise, and power. The fact that students are always grouped with 20 or 30 others means that they must wait in line, wait to be called on, wait for help, and tolerate interruptions and disruptions in their work. That's the crowd part. Teachers control most actions and events and decide what the group will do and how much deviation from the plan will be tolerated. That's the power part. Teachers also give and withhold praise and do so publicly so that students always know which students are favored or not favored by the teacher. That is both praise and power.

Another early and important study was Dan Lortie's (1975) *Schoolteacher,* which didn't involve observing classrooms, but instead focused on teachers and what they thought about their work. One of many important concepts that Lortie introduced was that of *uncertainty.* The presence of 20 to 30 children in a single classroom means there are 20 to 30 possibilities for an interruption in one's plans. Even apart from these routine disturbances, though, students may get into fights with one another, get sick, or simply ask a question that is difficult to answer. All of these actions, from major to minor, are disruptions to the scenarios that teachers have planned and make it difficult for teachers to predict with any certainty how a lesson will proceed, how long it will take, whether students will find it engaging, or whether they will "get it."

Nor can teachers often say with certainty at the close of a lesson whether it went well or whether students "got it." A teacher may think that students were engaged, attentive, and learning on one day, only to discover the next day that they don't recall much at all from the day before. These experiences accumulate to give teachers the feeling that learning is a mysterious process, one that they don't understand and certainly don't control (Huberman, 1983).

A third important insight into teaching and teachers comes from several studies of student adaptations to school life. Students, for the most part, would rather be elsewhere and tend, therefore, to be either disengaged or overtly defiant of teachers' efforts, so that teachers often find themselves negotiating and bargaining with students who, for their part, strive to simplify their tasks, postpone the deadlines for assignments, minimize their workload, and maximize the grades they are given (Sedlak, Wheeler, Pullin, & Cusick, 1986).

This portrait of classroom life puts teachers in quite a different world from that of the researchers I described earlier. When these two communities are characterized in this way, it is hard to imagine research being helpful to teachers. It is too pristine, too fussy, too concerned with justification.

On the other hand, both researchers and teachers aim to increase certainty. That should give them something in common. Perhaps the problem, then, has more to do with how each group tries to cope with uncertainty. For researchers, it is a matter of improving study designs, checking and verifying, and replicating. Certainty comes about through intellectual processes. For teachers, certainty is often achieved by *creating predictability* within the classroom. Many teachers respond to classroom life by defining clear and unambiguous classroom routines. That way, students know what to expect from the teacher and the teacher knows what to expect from the students. Keeping students busy also is a way of avoiding confrontation and reducing the possibilities for disruption. Both teachers and students prefer routine, familiar tasks to more novel and open-ended tasks. Routines increase predictability and decrease anxiety for both teachers and students.

But Doyle (1986) showed us that an unfortunate result of routines was that everyone's attention gets diverted from the substantive meaning of academic work to procedures, routines, schedules, and products. The need to manage the group focuses teachers' attention on getting tasks done rather than on the quality of the work that is done (Carter & Doyle, 1987), and the need to assign grades focuses teachers' attention on product standards and completion deadlines rather than on the intellectual content or merits of the work. As teachers and students focus on these tasks, meaning gets lost (Doyle, 1986). Academic content is transformed from issues to lists (McNeil, 1988). Rules and routines give teachers a way to respond to student bargaining, a set of criteria for grading student work, a way to increase predictability, and a way of ascertaining whether the class as a whole has "progressed."

These insights into classroom life help us understand teachers' situations much better than we ever did in the past and give us some suspicions for why research might not be perceived as particularly relevant to teachers. Whatever knowledge research may provide, it can rarely guide teachers toward concrete strategies or routines that can accommodate all of the constraints they are trying to manage. There is quite a bit of research, for instance, that has contributed to the current reform movement advocating conceptual or constructivist approaches to teaching, and much of it suggests that the approaches to teaching advocated by reformers might actually benefit students more than traditional teaching strategies do. But how can such research persuade teachers to do things differently when the strategies they currently use solve so many problems and satisfy so many constraints?

In fact, research on teacher thinking also led to a new version of the relevance hypothesis. In the 1960s, the relevance hypothesis usually meant that researchers were not addressing the questions that teachers had about their practice or the research was not done in classroom contexts that represented most teachers' classrooms. The contemporary version of the relevance hypothesis is that research findings need to be in *an epistemological form* that better matches the realities of classroom life. In 1983, for instance, Bolster said

> I believe the fundamental requirement of any inquiry which hopes to be consonant with the teachers' perspective on teaching is that it must view human behavior as reflexive. . . . Significant knowledge of any social situation, therefore, consists of an awareness of the emerging meanings that participants are developing and the specific ways that these meanings are functioning to shape their endeavors and thus the characteristics of the situation itself. (Bolster, 1983, pp. 303)

Since then, numerous researchers have advocated case studies, ethnographies, and, more recently, narratives (Carter, 1993; Connelly & Clandinin, 1990) as forms of research that might better approximate classroom reality and, therefore, be more relevant to teachers. So the current version of the relevance hypothesis has extended the concept of focusing on teachers' questions to incorporate the idea of actually *viewing the classroom as teachers view it.*

The Accessibility of Research

The third hypothesis accounting for the apparent lack of connection between research and practice focuses on teachers' lack of access to research findings. This has always been Congress's favorite hypothesis, and it has led to sponsorship of regional labs, ERIC clearinghouses, a National Diffusion Network, and many other endeavors whose essential purpose is to somehow carry research findings from the ivory tower into the classroom.

At the same time that these efforts were being expanded, though, researchers were studying their influence on teachers. Their work has led to new understandings about what makes research accessible to teachers and how teachers use research that is accessible. In the 1960s, when people talked about an "impact" from research, they meant that teachers were applying specific techniques that had been found by researchers to be effective. But studies of research use showed that research was more likely to be used *conceptually* than *instrumentally.* That is, practitioners did not take from research tools that could be directly applied in their classrooms, but instead took ideas: concepts that could, especially when combined with other ideas and with their own experiences, help them understand their situations or help them invent specific responses to local situations (Kennedy, 1983). Even when teachers were trying to implement specific classroom innovations, we discovered that they did not *adopt* innovations, but instead *adapted* them (Berman & McLaughlin, 1975, 1978).

A second finding from this line of work was that teachers' own prior beliefs and values were important influences on their practice (Kagan, 1992), not just in the direct sense of dictating what was important to accomplish, but also in the indirect sense of influencing how receptive teachers were to ideas they might encounter from research or from colleagues (Hollingsworth, 1989). The presence of such prior beliefs and values creates a dilemma for researchers—and for reformers, more generally—for it suggests that changing practice cannot occur simply by *informing* teachers. If teachers are sympathetic with a reform agenda, they will be receptive to its research findings, but if they are not at least sympathetic, they will probably not be persuaded by the research no matter how authoritative or relevant it is.

The centrality of beliefs and values has also become apparent outside of teaching, in other contexts where researchers have examined the stability and malleability of beliefs. Certain types of beliefs are found to be much more resistant to change, and they tend to be the beliefs teachers rely on (Pajares, 1992; Rokeach, 1968). Beliefs that are most resistant to change are

- *Those that are formed during childhood.* Most teachers' beliefs are formed while they themselves are students in school observing their teachers and envisioning the kind of teachers they themselves would be.
- *Those that are closely associated with our identities.* Teachers' beliefs about teaching are important to their definitions of themselves as teachers.
- *Those that are part of interlocking networks of beliefs.* Teachers' beliefs about how students learn are associated with their beliefs about the appropriate role for teachers to play in classrooms, the nature of school subjects, and so on.

This third line of reasoning suggests that the problem of accessibility is not merely one of placing research knowledge within *physical* reach of teachers; but rather one of placing research knowledge within the *conceptual* reach of teachers, for if research encouraged teachers to reconsider their prior assumptions, it might ultimately pave the way for change. It also suggests that persuasiveness may require more than simply strong research design and that relevance may require more than a similar context or a relevant question. Instead—or, perhaps, in addition—the potential for research to contribute to practice depends on its ability to influence teachers' *thinking*.

The Stability (and Instability) of the Education System

Each of the hypotheses I described above—the persuasiveness and authority of educational research, the rele-

vance of educational research, and the accessibility of educational research—represent an attempt to explain why research has not had more influence on practice and, concomitantly, to offer suggestions for changes in the character of research that would increase its value to teachers. In so doing, all of these arguments assume that research could influence practice if we improved our methods, our questions, our dissemination, or some other feature of our work. The fourth hypothesis for the apparent lack of connection between research and practice suggests that the problem lies not in research but in the education system itself. Many features of education mitigate against the potential for research, some because they stabilize the system and some because they destabilize it.

One important contributing factor here in the United States is our decentralized governance. Education governance in the United States is more decentralized than governance in almost any other country in the world. We have no centralized curriculum, no centralized examination system, no centralized textbooks, no centralized standards for teachers, and no centralized curriculum for teacher education. Some of these matters are determined by states; many are determined locally. Even when states define policies in these areas, they tend to define them loosely. And even when defined locally, our local school systems are not very tightly coupled (Weick, 1976), and teachers have a fair degree of autonomy in their daily practice.

Another contributing factor is that the population we serve is remarkably heterogeneous, perhaps more so than any other country in the world. Not only are we racially and ethnically diverse, but families have come here from numerous other countries and have brought their own customs and values with them. Such diversity increases the difficulty of creating a coherent curriculum that can adequately accommodate our many interests. As early as 1938, Willard Waller observed that our cultural heterogeneity constituted a conservative influence on the curriculum, for the points where agreement could be reached among various groups tended to be mundane points.

There are also arguments that our system is inherently unstable. Meyer (1983), for instance, argued that decentralized decisionmaking and community control of schools make our system especially susceptible to fads as local teachers, parents, and other education constituents search for new ways to improve their education. These fads come and go so rapidly that it is rarely possible to generate a real knowledge base about any of them. Consequently, innovations are justified by exaggerated claims, theoretical virtues, and anecdotes. Proposals for change are justified as moral imperatives rather than as proven ideas, and persuasion occurs through publicity rather than through reasoned argument. His observation is not new: Woodring (1964) evaluated the reforms that were popular in the early sixties—the use of teaching machines, for instance, and the use of team teaching—in search of some underlying psychological principles and concluded that they mainly derived from social and political pressures rather than from clearly stated psychological principles. Similarly, Callahan (1962) concluded after examining the history of education administration that American schools are extremely vulnerable to public pressures and that this vulnerability is built into our pattern of local support and local control. Larry Cuban's (1990) take on the problem is that the combination of decentralized decision-making and multiple constituencies requires schools to simultaneously hold multiple and conflicting goals, many of which are not very well defined. At the same time, the loose coupling of local school districts protects teachers from the various waves of reform and counterreform that circle their classrooms.

The lack of coherent direction is particularly apparent in our textbooks. Both the Second International Mathematics Study (McKnight et al., 1989) and the Third International Mathematics and Sciences Study (Schmidt et al., 1996) found American textbooks to be more fragmented and superficial than texts in most other countries. They were longer, covered more topics, and devoted more space to review and repetition, so that individual topics were repeated often but were treated with little depth. Similar conclusions have been drawn from examinations of mathematics curricula at other grade levels (e.g., Porter, 1989) and from examinations of texts in other subjects (Brophy, 1990; Gagnon, 1987). Tyson-Bernstein and Woodward (1986) concluded from their review that textbook publishers, in an effort to please everyone, try to include as many topics as possible rather than taking the time to develop a few central ideas.

Even the contemporary reform is not coherent. Some of us think the reform is aimed at clearing up confusions by aligning texts, tests, teacher preparation, and standards so that the system as a whole is unified. Some of us think the reform is aimed at changing the character of teaching and learning toward more constructive approaches, authentic learning tasks, or "bigger" ideas so that students are more intellectually engaged and academic content is more rigorous and more conceptual. Still others think the reform is aimed at decentralizing the system even more by introducing charter schools and/or vouchers and giving parents more power, through market systems, over their children's education. Like past reforms, none of these ideas has a sufficient knowledge base to justify massive expenditures, and, like past reforms, these ideas will probably fade away before such a knowledge base is developed.

So we have a system that can be characterized by a lack of agreed-on goals, a lack of shared guiding principles, no central authority to settle disputes, decentralized decisionmaking, a continual stream of new fads and fancies, limited evidence to support or refute any particular idea, textbooks that manage the conflicts by including all possible ideas and giving no serious attention to any of them, and reforms that are running at cross-purposes to each other.

Ironically, at the same time we decentralize our educational decisions more than most other countries, and permit numerous fads and conflicting ideas to constantly compete, we also give our teachers less time than most other countries do to formulate their curricula and to develop their daily lessons. According to OECD's Centre for Educational Research and Innovation (1995), teachers in the United States spend more hours per year directly teaching students than teachers in other nations do. The extensive amount of time they spend in class leaves them painfully little time to think about any aspect of their teaching (Fullan, 1994). It should not be surprising, then, to learn that many teachers do not see any underlying order to classroom events (Huberman, 1983), for they haven't the time to examine their experiences to find underlying order.

These two views of the education system—as large, cumbersome, and unchanging on one hand and as disorganized and driven by fads on the other—are not incompatible. Most of our fads and fancies are more observable in rhetoric than they are in practice, as Cuban's (1984) history has shown us, and those that do influence practice tend to alter its more superficial features rather than altering the fundamental character of teaching and learning (Applebee, 1991; Cohen, 1990; Peterson, 1990). Teachers may adopt new devices such as math manipulatives, for instance, and not adopt the conceptual underpinnings that justify these devices.

Not only are these two portraits of our system compatible; they are related. The multiplicity and ambiguity of goals that press against local educators, combined with their lack of time to actually think through any new ideas that present themselves, severely limit the capacity of all actors in the system to think hard about their practices and to pursue a steady course in any one new direction. These pressures encourage a kind of defensive rigidity in which practitioners protect themselves from substantial changes by making slight adjustments at the margins, by claiming they have already made the changes that reformers propose, or by claiming that research justifies their existing practices.

But the problem of multiple, conflicting, and ill-defined goals is not unique to the United States and does not derive solely from our unique system of governance. Indeed, most other countries have far more centralized systems than we have, but do not have any more evidence of research use. Many of them are susceptible to fads—often emigrating from the United States—and all are susceptible to multiple and conflicting goals for their education systems and to shifting policy climates and public sentiments as perceptions of national strengths and weaknesses change over time.

All are also susceptible to certain universal sources of stability. One such source, first noticed by Dan Lortie (1975), is that teachers learn their practice through an extended apprenticeship of observation. Unlike practitioners in virtually all other professions, teachers observe practitioners for 13 years before they even begin their formal preparation for their work. Many of their deepest beliefs about teaching and learning derive from this apprenticeship of observation.

Lortie's observation was reinforced by Cuban's (1984) history of teaching, a study aimed at trying to understand why some features of the system change while others don't. Though there have been numerous changes in our education system over time—including the expansion of the system to include all children, the gradual raising of education requirements for teachers, the introduction of graded classrooms, and so forth—none of these changes touches the most basic feature of the system—the character of interactions between teachers and students within classrooms. Cuban concluded that teaching practices have remained relatively unchanged in part because of structural constraints on practice and in part because of the stability of teachers' beliefs about what should occur in their classrooms.

Cohen (1988), too, suggests that it may be wrongheaded to expect substantial change in teaching practices. He suggests that the stability of teaching practices derives from the nature of teaching itself. Teaching is analogous to psychotherapy or social work in that its aim is to improve other human beings—a task for which clear strategies remain elusive and in which practitioners depend on clients' motivation and ability for their success. Cohen argues that the uncertainty of the work interacts with the practitioners' dependency on clients. For instance, if teachers attempt more difficult goals, they automatically decrease the certainty that they will succeed and increase their dependence on their students' abilities and motivations. They become more vulnerable. Lortie (1975) also found that the uncertainties of teaching encourage more conservative practices, and March (1991) also argued that the exploration of new ideas introduces more risk of failure than does the exploitation of existing ideas. When trying new ideas, returns are less certain and more remote in time. When exploiting existing ideas, on the other hand, returns seem more certain, quick, and predictable.

Add to the long apprenticeship of observation and the ambiguity of teaching itself a multiplicity of educational goals—and, in fact, an increasing proliferation of goals as more and different cultural groups press for acknowledgement of their own values—and the enterprise becomes too complex to manage unless some limitations are self-imposed. These self-imposed limitations contribute to the stability of the enterprise and foster a reluctance to seriously entertain the many laudable ideas that reformers and researchers so frequently ask for.

Educational Research As a Part of the Education System

Now here's the rub: These inherent characteristics of education also limit the possibilities for researchers to produce a stable or coherent body of knowledge that could be useful to practitioners. The constant conflict over goals and directions for education spills over into research agendas. Educational research, or funding for education research, has been characterized as fragmented, unstable, and subject to repeated shifts in foci (Chall, 1967; Dershimer, 1976; Dershimer & Iannaccone, 1973) in part because of disputes over what the terrain consists of and who is in charge (Lagemann, 1996). The central federal agency for educational research, the U.S. Department of Education's Office of Educational Research and Improvement, has been found on more than one occasion to be lacking both focus and continuity (Atkinson & Jackson, 1992; Bick & Jackson, 1994), and federal funding for educational research has been constantly threatened since the federal-funding heyday of the 1960s. Disputes among researchers, combined with political and public disputes about education itself, make it difficult for the sponsors of educational research to forge and sustain focused research agendas.

Particularly telling is the overwhelming attention we give to arguments about how we should conduct our work. We sometimes seem to argue more about how to acquire new knowledge than about what knowledge we have already managed to acquire, in part because we disagree about what counts as new knowledge. We argue about research methodology, and we argue about the role we should play in our interactions with education practitioners. In the fifties and sixties, we argued about basic versus applied research; today we argue about quantitative and qualitative research. We envision roles for ourselves that range from the committed action researcher originally advocated by Kurt Lewin (Lewin, 1946, 1948) to the dispassionate social experimenter advocated by Donald Campbell (1969, 1973). Some of us even argue that research has had too great an influence and is responsible for some the problems that now ail schools (Coleman, 1975; Richardson-Koehler, 1987). These arguments about methods and roles are not unrelated to more broad arguments about the goals of education, for different approaches to research often entail different assumptions about the nature of educational practice and about how research can or should contribute to it.

It might be tempting to think that we would make more progress if we concentrated on conceptual contributions to practice rather than on discrete innovations, perhaps giving people new ways to think about old problems or perhaps focusing on ideas that are large enough to encompass many aspects of practice (Anderson & Burns, 1990; Fenstermacher, 1982; Shavelson, 1988). Historically, though, we have tended to shift our central concepts almost as often as we shift our attention to specific practices. We have embraced behaviorism, task analysis, cognitive development, and, most recently, social constructivism, each in the hope of finding a single guiding metaphor that captures the essence of teaching and learning. But as theoretical ideas gain popularity, they also lose their precise meaning and consequently lose their explanatory power (Cronbach & Suppes, 1969). Before educational ideas have time to be systematically developed and refined, their critics become so numerous that the ideas are replaced by other ideas.

Viewing research as a part of a larger system that contains multiple, competing, and often ill-defined goals, the connection between research and practice is not one in which research influences practice, as many researchers might hope, nor one in which practice influences research, as many might hope, but rather one in which both research and practice are influenced by, and are perhaps even victims of, the same shifting social and political context.

Discussion

Each of the hypotheses described in this article rests on assumptions about what the relationship *should be* between research and practice. Much of the work invested in developing persuasive research designs, for instance, was premised on the notion that research should provide generalizable statements because such generalizations would yield what Kliebard (1993) calls "rules of action." Early versions of the relevance hypothesis and the accessibility hypothesis also assumed this role, and researchers thought that if only research addressed teachers' questions and if only teachers knew about the findings, they would indeed use some of the generalizations that had been found.

But later versions of these two hypotheses were based on different assumptions. As the relevance hypothesis extended from studying teachers' questions to viewing the classroom in the way teachers view it and as the accessibility hypothesis moved from physical accessibility to conceptual accessibility, these two hypotheses seemed to rest on an assumption that research should provide new and better understanding of the dynamics of teaching and learning, new perspectives rather than new rules of action (Shavelson, 1988). This view of the contribution of research leaves teachers with considerable professional judgment as to how they might draw on these insights to make their moment-to-moment decisions. Lampert (1985), for instance, argued that we need to view teachers not as technical production managers, but instead as dilemma managers who routinely balance among competing goals as they design their courses of action. I suspect most researchers now acknowledge this view of teachers and aim to provide guidance and insights more than rules of action.

The accessibility hypothesis, however, introduces a new dilemma for us, for research that is conceptually accessible to teachers may be research that does *not* challenge assumptions or introduce new possibilities. Chinn and Brewer (1993) showed the many ways in which all of us—from scientists to children—can reject research findings that are incongruous with our prior beliefs. If that is the case, then, conceptually accessible research could be research that further reinforces the stability of the education enterprise rather than research that challenges assumptions or offers new insights. To the extent that research that introduces new ideas is inherently less conceptually accessible to teachers, then we researchers also become dilemma managers.

The fourth hypothesis, which identifies the ambiguity and conflict inherent in the education enterprise as the culprit for the apparently modest role of research, follows naturally from the third, for as researchers have adopted the goals of providing new insights and of challenging old ideas, they have discovered the intransigence of prior beliefs, the frequent popularity of untested fads, and the frequent lack of receptivity to tested ideas. All of these phenomena lead us to realize that the ideas that are conceptually accessible to policymakers or teachers are not necessarily the ideas that have been most carefully developed or argued.

This fourth hypothesis, then, suggests that researchers have no particular authoritative advantage in the public arena. It views our role as on par with that of reformers and other education advocates. We become simply another group of players in the continuing debate about education. We use different methods and often adopt a posture of neutrality, but our influence in the ongoing debate sometimes seems to depend more on our advocacy than on our evidence.

But the fourth hypothesis also suggests that researchers are susceptible to the same varying waves of fads and reforms as teachers are. If this is so, then our own shifting paradigms and research agendas reflect social moods and public sentiments as much as new developments in theory or new empirical findings.

Conclusion

The disillusionment many of us feel, and that many of our audiences feel, probably stems from false expectations. Our audiences continue to believe that research should provide reliable and relevant rules for action, rules that can be put to immediate use (Shavelson, 1988). Many of us still seek such results. But many others are beginning to search for other contributions.

Is this progress? Despite our numerous changes in paradigms, research interests, and assumptions about how we contribute to practice and despite our debates over method, we have learned a tremendous amount about our enterprise in the past several decades. We now have a much deeper understanding both about what we are capable of doing and about how we can contribute to practice. We also are more aware that we cannot avoid the political processes, though as Donmoyer (1995) pointed out, we are still uncertain of our political position.

This improved understanding of the system in which we work and the system we aim to assist leads to new and different research questions and new and different research designs. And to the extent that our work reflects more adequately the ambivalent and ambiguous character of education, it may become more persuasive and more relevant, and perhaps as it does, it may also become more conceptually accessible.

Note

An earlier version of this article was presented at the annual meeting of the American Educational Research Association, New York, April 1996.

References

Anderson, L. W., & Burns, R. B. (1990). The role of conceptual frameworks in understanding and using classroom research. *South Pacific Journal of Education, 18*(1), 5–18.

Applebee, A. N. (1991). Informal reasoning and writing instruction. In J. F. Voss, D. N. Perkins, & J. W. Segal (Eds.), *Informal reasoning and education* (pp. 225–246). Hillsdale, NJ: Erlbaum.

Atkinson, R. C., & Jackson, G. B. (Eds.). (1992). *Research and educational reform: Roles for the Office of Educational Research and Improvement.* Washington, DC: National Academy of Sciences Press.

Bennett, N., & Desforges, C. (1985). Ensuring practical outcomes from educational research. In M. Shipman (Ed.), *Educational research: Principles, policies, and practices* (pp. 81–96). Philadelphia: Falmer Press.

Berman, P., & McLaughlin, M. W. (1975). *Federal programs supporting educational change: Vol. 5. Executive summary.* Santa Monica, CA: The Rand Corporation.

Berman, P., & McLaughlin, M. W. (1978). *Federal programs supporting change: Implementing and sustaining innovations.* Santa Monica, CA: The Rand Corporation.

Bick, K., & Jackson, G. B. (1994). Research and educational reform: A study of the federal role in the United States' educational research and development. In T. Tomlinson & A. C. Tuijnman (Eds.), *Educational research and reform: An international perspective* (pp. 69–79). Washington, DC: OERI and OECD.

Bloom, B. (1966). Twenty-five years of educational research. *American Educational Research Journal, 3*(3), 211–221.

Bolster, A. S. (1983). Toward a more effective model of research on teaching. *Harvard Educational Review, 53*(3), 294–308.

Brophy, J. (1990). *The de facto national curriculum in elementary social studies: Critique of a representative sample.* East Lansing, MI: Michigan State University Center for the Learning and Teaching of Elementary Subjects.

Brown, A. (1992). Design experiments: Theoretical and methodological challenges in creating complex interventions in classroom settings. *The Journal of the Learning Sciences, 2*(2), 141–178.

Callahan, R. E. (1962). *Education and the cult of efficiency.* Chicago: The University of Chicago Press.

Campbell, D. T. (1969). Reforms as experiments. *American Psychologist, 24*(4), 409–429.

Campbell, D. T. (1973). The social scientist as methodological servant of the experimenting society. *Policy Studies Journal, 2*, 72–75.

Campbell, D. T., & Stanley, J. C. (1969). *Experimental and quasi-experimental designs for research.* Chicago: Rand McNally. (Originally published 1963)

Carter, K. (1993). The place of story in the study of teaching and teacher education. *Educational Researcher, 22*(1), 5–12, 18.

Carter, K., & Doyle, W. (1987). Teachers' knowledge structures and comprehension processes. In J. Calderhead (Ed.), *Exploring teacher thinking* (pp. 147–160). London: Cassell.

Centre for Educational Research and Innovation. (1995). *Education at a glance: OECD indicators.* Paris: Organization for Economic Cooperation and Development.

Chall, J. S. (1967). *Learning to read: The great debate.* New York: McGraw Hill.

Chinn, C. A., & Brewer, W. K. (1993). The role of anomalous data in knowledge acquisition: A theoretical framework and implications for science instruction. *Review of Educational Research, 63*(1), 1–49.

Clifford, G. J. (1973). History of the impact of education research. In R. M. S. Travers (Eds.), *Second handbook of research on teaching* (pp. 1–46). New York: Macmillan.

Cohen, D. K. (1988). Plus ça change. In P. Jackson (Ed.), *Contributions to educational change; Perspectives on research in practice issues. National Society for the Study of Education series on contemporary issues* (pp. 27–84). Berkeley, CA: McCutchan.

Cohen, D. K. (1990). A revolution in one classroom: The case of Mrs. Oublier. *Educational Evaluation and Policy Analysis, 12*(3), 311–329.

Coleman, J. (1966). *Equality of educational opportunity.* Washington, DC: U.S. Department of Health, Education and Welfare.

Coleman, J. A. (1975). Comment. In A. M. Rivlin & P. M. Timpane (Eds.), *Planned variation in education* (pp. 173–175). Washington, DC: The Brookings Institute.

Connelly, F. M., & Clandinin, D. J. (1990). Stories of experience and narrative inquiry. *Educational Researcher, 19*(5), 2–14.

Cronbach, L. J. (1966). The logic of experiments on discovery. In L. S. Shulman (Ed.), *Learning by discovery: A critical appraisal* (pp. 76–92). Chicago: Rand McNally.

Cronbach, L. J. (1975). Beyond the two disciplines of scientific psychology. *American Psychologist, 30*(2), 116–127.

Cronbach, L. J., & Suppes, P. (Eds.). (1969). *Research for tomorrow's schools: Disciplined inquiry for education.* New York: National Academy of Education and Macmillan.

Cuban, L. (1984). *How teachers taught: Constancy and change in American classrooms, 1890–1980.* White Plains, NY: Longman.

Cuban, L. (1990). Reforming again, again, and again. *Educational Researcher, 19*(1), 3–13.

Dershimer, R. A. (1976). *The federal government and educational R&D.* Lexington, MA: Lexington Books.

Dershimer, R. A., & Iannaccone, L. (1973). Social and political influences on educational research. In R. M. W. Travers (Ed.), *Second handbook of research on teaching* (pp. 113–121). Chicago: Rand McNally.

Donmoyer, R. (1995). Empirical research as solution and problem: Two narratives on knowledge use. *International Journal of Educational Research, 23*(2), 151–168.

Doyle, W. (1986). Content representation in teachers' definitions of academic work. *Journal of Curriculum Studies, 18*(4), 365–379.

Fenstermacher, G. D. (1982). On learning to teach effectively from research on teaching effectiveness. *Journal of Classroom Interaction, 17*(2), 7–12.

Fullan, M. G. (1994). Teachers as critical consumers of research. In T. Tomlinson (Ed.), *Educational research and reform: An international perspective.* Washington, DC: U.S. Department of Education.

Gagnon, P. (1987). Democracy's untold story. *American Educator, 11*(2), 19–25.

Hollingsworth, S. (1989). Prior beliefs and cognitive change in learning to teach. *American Educational Research Journal, 26*(2), 160–189.

Huberman, M. (1983). Recipes for a busy kitchen. *Knowledge, Creation, Diffusion, Utilization, 4*(4), 478–510.

Huberman, M. (1989). Predicting conceptual effects in research utilization: Looking with both eyes. *Knowledge in Society: The International Journal of Knowledge Transfer, 2*(3), 6–24.

Jackson, P. (1968). *Life in classrooms.* New York: Holt Rhinehart and Winston.

Kaestle, C. F. (1993). The awful reputation of educational research. *Educational Researchers, 22*(1), 23–31.

Kagan, D. M. (1992). Implications of research on teacher belief. *Educational Psychologist, 27*(1), 65–90.

Kennedy, M. M. (1978). Findings from the Follow Through Planned Variation Study. *Educational Researchers, 7*(6), 3–11.

Kennedy, M. M. (1983). Working knowledge. *Knowledge: Creation, Diffusion, Utilization, 5*, 193–211.

Kliebard, H. M. (1993). What is a knowledge base, and who would use it if we had one? *Review of Educational Research, 63*(3), 295–303.

Lagemann, E. C. (1996). *Contested terrain: A history of education research in the United States, 1890–1990.* Chicago: The Spencer Foundation.

Lampert, M. (1985). How do teachers manage to teach? Perspectives on the problems of practice. *Harvard Educational Review, 55,* 178–194.

Lewin, K. (1946). Action research and the minority problem. *Journal of Social Issues, 2*(4), 34–46.

Lewin, K. (1948). *Resolving social conflicts.* New York: Harper.

Lortie, D. C. (1973). Observations on teaching as work. In R. W. M. Travers (Ed.), *Second handbook of research on teaching* (pp. 474–497). Chicago: Rand McNally.

Lortie, D. C. (1975). *Schoolteacher.* Chicago: The University of Chicago Press.

March, J. G. (1991, April). *Exploration and exploitation in education.* Paper presented at the annual meeting of the American Educational Research Association, Chicago.

McKnight, C. C., Crosswhite, F. J., Dossey, J. A., Kifer, E., Swafford, J. O., Travers, K. J., & Cooney, T. J. (1989). *The underachieving curriculum: Assessing U.S. school mathematics from an international perspective.* Champaign, IL: Stipes.

McNeil, L. M. (1988). *Contradictions of control: School structure and school knowledge.* New York: Routledge.

Meyer, J. W. (1983). Innovation and knowledge use in American public education. In J. W. Meyer & W. R. Scott (Eds.), *Organizational environments: Ritual and rationality* (pp. 233–260). Beverly Hills, CA: Sage.

Pajares, M. F. (1992). Teachers' beliefs and educational research: Cleaning up a messy construct. *Review of Educational Research, 62*(3), 307–332.

Peterson, P. (1990). Doing more in the same amount of time: Cathy Swift. *Educational Evaluation and Policy Analysis, 12*(3), 261–280.

Porter, A. C. (1989). A curriculum out of balance: The case of elementary school mathematics. *Educational Researcher, 18*(5), 9–15.

Richardson-Koehler, V. (1987). What happens to research on the way to practice? *Theory Into Practice, 26*(1), 38–43.

Rokeach, M. (1968). *Beliefs, attitudes and values: A theory of organization change.* San Francisco: Jossey Bass.

Rosenthal, R., & Jacobson, L. (1968). *Pygmalion in the classroom.* New York: Holt, Rhinehart and Winston.

Schmidt, W., & others. (1996). *Characterizing pedagogical flow: An investigation of mathematics and science teaching in six countries.* Dordrecht, the Netherlands: Klewer Publishing.

Sedlak, M. W., Wheeler, C. W., Pullin, D. C., & Cusick, P. A. (1986) *Selling students short: Classroom bargains and academic reform in the American high school.* New York: Teachers College Press.

Shavelson, R. J. (1988). Contributions of educational research to policy and practice: Constructing, challenging, changing cognition. *Educational Researcher, 17*(7), 4–11, 22.

Shulman, L. S. (1970). Reconstruction of educational research. *Review of Educational Research, 40*(3), 371–396.

Suppes, P. (Ed.). (1978). *Impact of research on education: Some case studies.* Englewood Cliffs, NJ: Prentice Hall.

Tyson-Bernstein, H., & Woodward, A. (1986). The great textbook machine and prospects for reform. *Social Education, 50,* 41–45.

Waller, W. (1938). Contributions to education of scientific knowledge about the organization of society and social pathology. In G. M. Whipple (Ed.), *The scientific movement in education. Thirty-seventh yearbook of the National Society for the Study of Education, Part II* (pp. 445–460). Bloomington, IL: Public School Publishing Company.

Weick, K. E. (1976). Educational organizations as loosely coupled systems. *Administrative Sciences Quarterly, 21,* 1–19.

Woodring, P. (1964). Reform movements from the point of view of psychological theory. In E. R. Hilgard (Ed.), *Theories of learning and instruction. Sixty-third yearbook of the National Society for the Study of Education* (pp. 286–305). Chicago: NSSE.

Manuscript received October 16, 1996
Revision received May 16, 1997
Accepted May 28, 1997

LeAnn G. Putney
University of Nevada, Las Vegas, USA

Judith L. Green
Carol N. Dixon
Gregory J. Kelly
University of California, Santa Barbara, USA

Evolution of qualitative research methodology: Looking beyond defense to possibilities

For this particular rendition of the *RRQ* Conversations column, the Editors asked us to provide a dialogue about the evolution of qualitative research methodology. When we initiated the dialogue, we considered putting together a historical overview, then moving on to what we envisioned qualitative educational research becoming in the future. As we continued, we found that the political realm surrounding our dialogue was changing the direction, scope, and content of our discussion, leading to a reflexive revisioning not unlike the realities of the research we undertake.

We still intend to examine where qualitative research may be headed in light of where it has been, but with the understanding that we are facing some critical political decisions that may very well change how qualitative research is viewed by the public. We will also caution the reader that our view of qualitative research is one situated historically and theoretically. Therefore, we will not presume to speak for all of qualitative research but will speak from our disciplinary and theoretical positions about methodological issues facing qualitative researchers in education.

Constructing a Conversation

In this Conversation, we bring together four educational researchers with different expertise and backgrounds who have developed a common framework for approaching qualitative research. The first member of this Conversation is LeAnn Putney from the University of Nevada, Las Vegas, USA, a research educator concerned with teaching-learning processes, who brings a sociocultural and sociohistorical perspective to her research and this dialogue. The other three members are Judith Green, Carol Dixon, and Greg Kelly from the University of California, Santa Barbara, USA. Judith and Carol are literacy educators and cofounders of the Santa Barbara Classroom Discourse Group and bring an ethnographic and sociolinguistic perspective to this Conversation. Greg, a science educator, brings a philosophy of science (epistemological) perspective to the dialogue. All have engaged in qualitative research, individually and collectively. The collaborative effort of this Conversation is just one example of the networking and extension of a research community that leads to joint publications as well as new ways of thinking about interests that we have in common.

The common framework we have developed is one that is concerned with understanding *what* our epistemological stance permits us to examine as well as *how* it informs and limits our point of view. This concern has also led us to explore how all research programs shape the questions that can be asked, the methods that are used, the theoretical frameworks that guide the research and explanatory phases of such projects (what we call orienting and explanatory theories), and the knowledge that can be constructed using these approaches. In this Conversation we share with you some of the issues that we have struggled with as we have sought ways of engaging in qualitative research, teaching qualitative research approaches, and publishing the findings from our individual and collective work.

This particular Conversation began as a result of a keynote talk, "From Roots to Renaissance: The Path Traveled by Qualitative Researchers," that Judith, Carol, and Greg prepared for the 1998 Conference on Qualitative Research in Education in Athens, Georgia. In their keynote, they highlighted a historical look at qualitative research, in terms of methodology and theoretical perspective, as well as future expectations for qualitative researchers. LeAnn initiated a continuation of this dialogue by outlining a possible direction for our collective voice.

Our original intent was to send this outline back and forth over e-mail, each adding to it and sending it around for the others to review and edit. However, we found that the distance between us and the round-robin approach was too disjointed and did not allow the synergy of ideas that could be achieved through face-to-face, in-the-moment dialogue.

We decided to convene in Santa Barbara by gathering together some notes, a laptop computer, a tape recorder, some good cookies, and freshly brewed coffee to get this Conversation rolling. Soon we were moving together in person where the e-mail dialogue just could not take us. The document began to take shape as we moved back and forth from the philosophy of science to the historical underpinnings that we wanted to make visible.

This meeting gave us the framework for what was to occur next and served as a springboard for subsequent sessions that could now take place using phone and e-mail to continue the Conversation. We continued sending the edited pieces back and forth to all involved. In this way, the dialogue became a blending of voices, with the different perspectives still an integral part of a collective voice as represented in the range of citations provided.

Through this and previous dialogues we have stretched our understandings of what it means to do research, what theoretical perspectives contribute to and guide our work, and how the research perspectives we select shape what we can do, say, and know—or in other words, what philosopher Kenneth Strike (1974, p. 103) called "the expressive potential" of our research. Strike introduced this argument more than 2 decades ago in an important yet often overlooked article, "On the Expressive Potential of Behaviorist Language." His abstract captured his perspective, treating peripheralism and associationism as the two central doctrines. He argues that these doctrines

> place semantic and syntactical constraints on acceptable language for the discussion of human beings, and assess the consequences of these doctrines for the description of educational goals and methods. It is shown that peripheralism and associationism are philosophical doctrines inherited from British Empiricism, and that they are more appropriately treated as part of the philosophy of psychology, rather than as testable empirical claims. It is argued that the constraints that this philosophy places on a language render it incapable of expressing some meaningful educational goals, rule out some meaningful empirical hypotheses, and undermine some important ethical distinctions. (p. 103)

We build on the construct of expressive potential of research programs to explore the history of qualitative research in education in order to consider where we have been, where we are currently, and to suggest where the future might take us. We intend to show that qualitative researchers (a) have achieved a degree of success in the past 2 to 3 decades; (b) are, like other educational researchers, facing a crisis of confidence at the public and policy levels; and (c) have a solid foundation to address this crisis and thus expand and enhance the expressive potential of the language(s) to guide research programs from various qualitative traditions.

The historical journey

One way to understand the history of qualitative research, and how a multivocal community of practice has developed, is through the work of a philosopher of science, Helen Longino (1993). She argued that

> Scientific knowledge . . . is an outcome of the critical dialogue in which individuals and groups holding different points of view engage with each other. It is constructed not by individuals but by an interactive dialogic community. A community's practice of inquiry is productive of knowledge to the extent that it facilitates transformative criticism. (p. 112)

To guide this critical dialogue in the development of disciplinary knowledge (including methodological perspectives within a discipline), Longino proposed four criteria as necessary to achieve the "transformative dimension of critical discourse" (p. 112). The community of practice must be characterized by:

1. Publicly recognized forums for the critique of evidence, of methods, and of assumptions and reasoning.
2. A tolerance of dissent, and a change of beliefs and theories over time in response to the critical discourse taking place within it.
3. Publicly recognized standards by reference to which theories, hypotheses, and observational practices are evaluated and by appeal to which criticism is made relevant to the goals of the inquiring community.
4. Equality of intellectual authority, by developing consensus, not as the result of the exercise of political or economic power or of the exclusion of dissenting perspectives; it must be the result of critical dialogue in which all relevant perspectives are represented.

We view the current perspectives constituting qualitative research as an outcome of the critical dialogues that have occurred over the past 3 decades, both within the community of practice associated with qualitative research traditions and with scholars from other research traditions. The productive and transformative nature of the critical dialogues will become evident as we examine the direction of qualitative research in education.

The struggle for recognition: Phase 1

The earliest phase of the development of qualitative traditions within education can be characterized as a struggle for recognition for the value of qualitative research. This phase saw two sets of concerns. The first was raised by educational researchers grounded in core disciplines (e.g., anthropology, sociology, and social psychology) that served as the foundation for ethnographic directions in qualitative research in education. The second was initiated by those drawing distinctions between qualitative methods and dominant paradigms of that time.

In the earliest part of this phase, educational researchers often took up the labels of qualitative traditions without understanding the historical grounding as noted by Rist. For example, in an article in the *Educational Researcher*, Rist (1980) argued that those who had previously engaged in observational research often took up the term *ethnography* as the label for their work without taking up the theoretical frameworks associated with ethnography or understanding the purpose of ethnography (i.e., the study of culture).

This issue was raised across the next 2 decades by others grounded in anthropology and other social science traditions (e.g., Green & Wallat, 1981; Heath, 1982; Jacob, 1987, 1988; Wolcott, 1992). The critical discourse in this period was one of critique that served to make visible the challenges facing educational researchers who were adopting and adapting methodologies that had originated in other disciplines and fields of study.

The second concern was addressed through the purposeful use of dichotomies as a tool to initiate a critical discourse about the distinctions between qualitative methods and other paradigms. Dichotomies posed included qualitative-quantitative, naturalist-positivist, and interpretive-positivistic-critical approaches (see, e.g., Guba, 1990; Lancy, 1993; LeCompte & Preissle, 1993; Lincoln & Guba, 1985). We present two examples drawn from work in the United States (Lincoln & Guba, 1985) and in Great Britain (Halfpenny, 1979, also cited in Burgess, 1984) to illustrate the contrastive and contentious nature of these dichotomies. The first is the naturalist-positivist dichotomy found in the initial work of Lincoln and Guba (1985) as presented in Figure 1.

Figure 1 The naturalist-positivist dichotomy

Axioms about	Positivist paradigm	Naturalist paradigm
The nature of reality	Reality is single, tangible, and fragmentable	Realities are multiple, constructed, and holistic
The relationship of knower to the known	Knower and known are independent, a dualism	Knower and known are interactive, inseparable
The possibility of generalization	Time- and context-free generalizations (nomothetic statements) are possible	Only time- and context-bound working hypotheses (idiographic statements) are possible
The possibility of casual linkages	There are real causes, temporally precedent to or simultaneous with their effects	All entities are in a state of mutual simultaneous shaping, so that it is impossible to distinguish causes from effects
The role of values	Inquiry is value free	Inquiry is value bound

The second example comes from the work of Halfpenny (1979, also cited in Burgess, 1984) and is represented in the comparison of sociological terms of Figure 2.

By drawing attention to these epistemological differences, early qualitative researchers sought to open space for new languages, approaches, and perspectives, thus challenging the dominant paradigms. Through these challenges, researchers identified a range of questions and issues that could, and could not be addressed by previous paradigms; voices that could, and could not be heard; and educational processes and practices that could, and could not be described, interpreted, and articulated. In this way, they made visible the expressive potential of the different research methods and traditions and how the selective nature of those traditions limited the basis for knowledge construction within the educational research community (Strike, 1974; 1989).

One inadvertent consequence of this early phase and its dichotomies was a focus on methodology, with less attention to theory-method relationships. Birdwhistell (1977) captured the problematic nature of this separation:

> I have come to the conclusion that the past twenty-five years have seen a separation of theory from methods of research procedure. This tendency becomes manifest in the choice and analysis of import of problem, in the location of observational site, in the preliminary isolation of data, in the development of relevant, consistent and explicit techniques of observation, in the recording and storage of data, in the orientation of rules of evidence, and, finally, in the methods of data and evidence assessment and presentation that permit and assist in ordering reexamination, and research. (pp. 104–105)

This recognition of the separation of theory-method relationships and the need to examine the expressive potential of each research tradition with its methodology marked the onset of the second phase of the critical dialogues. The transformation of the critical dialogues can be seen in the publication of research handbooks and books and journal issues on comparative methods across disciplines within education.

Critical dialogues on theory-method relationships: Phase 2

We begin the discussion of the directions in this phase by examining the role of handbooks. These handbooks are of two types. One explores issues of educational research by focusing on general issues of curriculum (Jackson, 1992) or teaching (Gage, 1963; Travers, 1973; Wittrock, 1986). The other type examines methodological issues of teaching and learning in particular disciplines—e.g., reading (Pearson, Kamil, Barr, & Mosenthal, 1991), language arts (Flood, Heath, & Lapp, 1997; Flood, Jensen, Lapp, & Squire, 1991),

and science (Gabel, 1994). These handbooks generally include sections on methodology and paradigms for research as well as syntheses of research (e.g., mathematics, science, arts, and reading), thus providing a basis for potentially exploring theory-method relationships.

For example, in the *Handbook of Research on Teaching* (3rd ed., Wittrock, 1986), there was a series of methodological and comparative chapters: Linn (1986) on "Quantitative Methods in Research on Teaching," Erickson (1986) on "Qualitative Methods in Research on Teaching," and Evertson and Green (1986) on "Observation as Inquiry and Method." These chapters show how methodological decisions are framed by particular theoretical orientations that, in turn, have

---

Figure 2 The quantitative-qualitative dichotomy of Halfpenny (1979)

Quantitative	Qualitative
hard	soft
dry	wet
fixed	flexible/fluid
abstract	grounded
explanatory	descriptive/exploratory
scientific	pre-scientific
objective	subjective
deductive	inductive
hypothesis testing	speculative/illustrative
value free	political
rigorous	non-rigorous
nomothetic	idiographic
atomistic	holistic
positivist	interpretivist
imposes sociological theory	exposes actors' meanings
empiricist/behaviorist	phenomenological
universalistic	relativistic
survey	case study
bad	good
good	bad

---

particular implications for how the phenomena can be observed, recorded, described, interpreted, and explained.

Similarly, the newest handbook for literacy educators (Flood, Heath, & Lapp, 1997) includes a broad range of theories and approaches. As a comparative reading of the handbooks makes visible, the choice to engage in research from one perspective precludes asking particular questions, masks particular dimensions of the complex world of educational processes and practices, and constitutes a situated look at the phenomena of interest, regardless of whether qualitative or quantitative methods are used.

In contrast, other handbooks focused on research methods, both within and outside the field of education—for example, *The Handbook of Qualitative Research in Education* (LeCompte, Millroy, & Preissle, 1992), and *The Handbook of Qualitative Research* (Denzin & Lincoln, 1994). These handbooks sought to introduce new paradigms and to make visible a range of perspectives and theory-method relationships.

One way that we view these handbooks is that they provide a potential public forum for seeing differences among perspectives and approaches. While this forum makes available the diversity of perspectives, it does not necessarily lead to the critical discourse called for by Longino (1993). One notable exception is the chapter by Erickson (1986) in which he explicitly constructs a comparative argument to show why a new language and its associated approach are needed.

Among the changes suggested by Erickson and others (e.g., Bogdan & Biklen, 1992; Eisner, 1991; Hammersley & Atkinson, 1995; LeCompte & Preissle, 1993; Lincoln & Guba, 1985) was a focus on the emic, or insider, point of view. This call intersects with concerns in teacher education for exploring reflective practice and theory in use (Clandinin & Connelly, 1988; Schon, 1984). The effect of these calls and volumes was to open to question who counts as researcher and what counts as research when researchers count (or not).

Erickson's (1986) argument pointed to how changes in intellectual lineage, theoretical commitments, and conceptualization of phenomena led to what Rorty (1989) called new vocabularies or language games. Rorty captured the value of new languages, as well as the problematic nature of trying to talk across languages, when he argued for a philosophy that "does not work piece by piece, analyzing concept after concept, or testing thesis after thesis" (p. 9). Rather, he argues that it works holistically and pragmatically by asking the reader to try thinking in a new and different way, or more specifically, to "try to ignore the apparently futile traditional questions by substituting the following new and possibly interesting questions.' It does not pretend to have better candidates for doing the same old thing, which we did when we spoke in the old way. Rather it suggests that we might want to stop doing those things and do something else. But it does not argue for this suggestion on the basis of antecedent criteria common to the old and the new language games. For just insofar as the new language really is new, there will be no such criteria" (p. 9).

Rorty's argument suggested that considerations of new and possibly interesting questions, in lieu of futile traditional questions, leads researchers to consider the pragmatic value of various vocabularies and the ways these describe and explain phenomena. Erickson's critique of positivist research approaches and his argument for a new perspective, one grounded in interpretive traditions, illustrate why the new cannot be written in the language of the old. If we now bring these arguments together with the concept of expressive potential, we establish a basis for engaging in the critical discourse called for by Longino (1993). Such a discourse will need to examine what each approach offers, what questions each addresses, and what purpose(s) each seeks to achieve.

Critiques of what counts as qualitative research: Phase 3

We have come to understand that at this phase of the historical journey, a critical discourse related to qualitative methodology has emerged, raising questions of what counts as qualitative research and who counts as qualitative researchers. In this section, we present two sources from this emerging critical discourse that led us to pose these questions. Two articles, each presenting a particular point of view on how to define qualitative research and who counts as qualitative researchers form the center of this discussion—Jacob (1987; 1988) and Wolcott (1992).

Jacob, in articles published in the *Review of Educational Research* (1987) and the *Educational Researcher* (1988), defined *qualitative* in terms of the core traditions that gave rise to different approaches and theoretical perspectives: human ethnology, ecological psychology, holistic ethnography, cognitive anthropology, ethnography of communication, and symbolic interactionism. These articles, when they were published, gave rise to a range of critical discourses and point-counterpoint discussions across national boundaries (Atkinson, Delamont, & Hammersley, 1988; Buchmann & Floden, 1989; Jacob, 1989; Lincoln, 1989). These dialogues challenged her taxonomy, arguing that it was not inclusive of the full range of qualitative perspectives, particularly ones used by researchers in the U.K. While we find her articles helpful, in that they frame one way of viewing a complex and diffuse field, we view any characterization or taxonomy as excluding particular perspectives and as being located in a particular historical period.

Wolcott (1992) in *The Handbook of Qualitative Research in Education* attempted to avoid such characterization of perspectives by exploring the interrelatedness among qualitative approaches by examining strategies across disciplines and perspectives. Through the analogy of a many-branched tree, Wolcott provided a visual means to conceptualize the common roots among the many diverse qualitative strategies.

In his representation, Wolcott (1992) proposed four different sets of qualitative strategies (i.e., archival, interview, nonparticipant observation, and participant observation), each forming a branch of a tree that he called qualitative inquiry. In this way, Wolcott was able to move the critical dialogue beyond categorical divisions to an exploration of commonalities and differences among a broad range of qualitative approaches.

These critiques, as well as comparative reviews (e.g., Miles & Huberman, 1994; Tesch, 1990), made visible the complexity contained in the label qualitative research. This complexity does not appear to be well understood outside the communities constituting qualitative research, thus contributing in part to the current crisis of confidence facing those engaged in this enterprise.

However, for those within the community of qualitative researchers, these critiques have been highly productive in the spirit of Longino's arguments (1993). They are productive in that they provide a way for such researchers to locate themselves and others in a complex nexus of interconnected, yet diffuse, set of communities engaged in educational research. They are also productive in that they make visible the expressive potential of different approaches and strategies, the languages entailed by the various traditions, and the ranges of questions that can and cannot be posed and addressed by each.

Toward an alternative critical discourse: Phase 4

During the period of critique described above, a second body of work exploring multiple perspectives on common data, or on comparing different perspectives to a common problem, also developed. This body of work provided a way of seeing what the differences in perspective or approach make to our understanding of educational phenomena. We identified a range of books and journal articles in which authors explicitly explored the expressive potential of different perspectives, both within qualitative traditions and across multiple theoretical perspectives.

We were able to identify a range of illustrative volumes and articles dedicated to examining differing points of view or theoretical orientations. These volumes examined different perspectives and theoretical traditions grounding literacy research (Beach, Green, Kamil, & Shanahan, 1992), framing discourse analysis of common classroom data sets (e.g., Green & Harker, 1988; Koschmann, in press; van Dijk, 1985), exploring different traditions for the study of narrative (e.g., Casey, 1995; Cortazzi, 1993; Godmundsdottir, 1997; Hatch & Wisniewski, 1995; Kryatzis & Green, 1997), examining ways different theoretical traditions shape the analysis of conceptual change in science teaching contexts (e.g., Guzzetti & Hynd, 1998), exploring current and emerging theoretical frameworks for research on classroom learning (Marshall, 1992; 1996), and comparing theories of child development (Thomas, 1979).

These volumes provide illustrations of how the expressive potential of differing traditions can be explored, and the value of comparative work in making this visible. In this section, we present two approaches to comparative work on methodology to illustrate

how a comparative approach brings clarity to this complex issue by making visible the expressive potential of each. These articles show how comparative approaches provide ways of understanding how choices among perspectives lead to particular claims and thus to particular knowledge construction.

The articles in Green and Harker (1988) described approaches to discourse analysis used to analyze common data sets. Each section of the book forms a set of planned contrasts. In the first section, three different discourse traditions were contrasted with the use of a single data set: sociolinguistic (Green, Weade, & Graham, 1988), semantic/propositional analysis (Harker, 1988), and literary/story grammar analysis (Golden, 1988). In the second section, differing sociolinguistic approaches to questioning were explored from a single data set (Morine-Dershimer, 1988a, 1988b; Ramirez, 1988; Shuy, 1988; Tenenberg, 1988).

In the final section, individual authors or teams of authors used multiple perspectives to examine the same event (Bloome & Theodorou, 1988; Marshall & Weinstein, 1988; Rentel, 1988; Wallat & Piazza, 1988). This volume showed how expressive potential is influenced by the particular theoretical framework selected, even within a tradition (e.g., sociolinguistics), as well as across traditions (e.g., sociolinguistic, literary, and semantic analyses). These chapters show how different disciplines shape particular questions, approaches, literature, and claims that, in turn, limit what knowledge about educational processes and practices (e.g., story reading, questioning, writing, spelling, and discussing content across disciplines) can be constructed through each discipline and related approaches.

In his monograph on *Narrative Analysis,* Cortazzi (1993) reviewed different theoretical and methodological perspectives on narrative, exploring what each potentially contributes to the study of teacher narratives. He examined narrative as it has been used in the study of teaching as well as models of narrative across disciplines outside of education: anthropology, literary theory, psychology, sociology, and sociolinguistics. He concluded the monograph with a description of how he analyzed the narratives of primary teachers in a school lunch room. Each chapter on models and approaches described the questions that can be addressed, the problems of interest, the theoretical literature, and the constructs used and provided examples of the different types of analyses and the models of narrative underlying or constituted by each. He also drew implications and applications of each tradition or approach for the use of the methods and theories within education, thus making visible the expressive potential of these traditions an their related approaches.

These volumes are illustrative of two growing areas of qualitative research, not all-inclusive. The citations provided at the beginning of this section point to others who contribute to our understanding of the expressive potential of differences within qualitative traditions, or in Wolcott's sense, strategies. Further, we see these volumes as providing a model that goes beyond mere critique of categories.

Building on the arguments about the nature of a research language by Rorty (1989) and Strike (1974), this model can move us to and frame the ongoing critical discourse for which Longino (1993) called. By examining what each tradition makes visible and what it contributes to our understanding of educational phenomena, we lay a foundation for assessing its appropriateness for the question of concern and its contribution to knowledge construction; that is to say, for addressing the criteria for qualitative research and other forms of educational research as proposed by Howe & Eisenhart (1990). One of the key dimensions of the criteria they proposed was that an article must be assessed within the tradition used by the authors. The review-within-disciplines approach they proposed had been adopted by journals in recent years across disciplines (e.g., counseling and clinical psychology and literacy) as well as in selection of reviewers for national programs (e.g., American Educational Research Association, National Research Council, and International Reading Association).

On what qualitative research contributes: Some key points

While these debates have been ongoing, qualitative research has made contributions to knowledge about educational processes, particularly in the area of literacy. A description of the full range of the contributions of qualitative research is beyond the scope of this Conversation. However, to illustrate the kinds of contributions that qualitative research has made to our understanding of literacy, we present several findings that have influenced our own work on the relationships of discourse, knowledge construction, and literate practices within and across disciplines.

Qualitative research approaches have enabled us to explore and understand systematically and theoretically the local and situated nature of classroom life and how that life is consequential for particular members or groups. Specifically, qualitative approaches have provided ways of transcribing and analyzing the discursive construction of everyday events, of examining the consequential nature of learning within and across events, and of exploring the historical nature of life within a social group or local setting.

Qualitative research has also provided insights into the emic, or insider, knowledge needed by members of a group to participate in socially and academically appropriate ways. For example, outsiders coming into the classroom or a social situation cannot understand, as members do, what is required; what counts as knowledge; and who has access to what, when, where, and under what conditions. This work has also provided information about why and how miscommunication among actors occurs, particularly when such actors are members of different groups (e.g., administrators-teachers, ethnic groups, genders).

Qualitative approaches and the theories guiding them have also made us aware of different voices and the need to consider whose voice will be represented, how, in what ways, and for what purposes. These approaches suggest the need to consider and make visible the voices of particular individuals, participants, groups, and communities that have traditionally not been heard.

Finally, given the need to examine what people know, understand, and produce within and across local settings, at particular points in time, or through particular modes of communication, qualitative research has demonstrated the need to develop grounded understandings of phenomena constructed in and through the everyday actions and activity of people within particular settings (e.g., students' constructs, what counts as knowing, how teacher actions support or constrain the opportunities students have for learning, and what counts as knowing and doing science). For us, then, qualitative research has provided ways for understanding the local and situated nature of everyday life; how this life is consequential for those who are members, as well as those seeking membership; and for exploring how equity of access to academic knowledge and societal resources are locally constructed in and through the actions of people in local settings.

Future directions: A closing and an opening

In this dialogue, we described different phases in the development of qualitative research and briefly considered how qualitative research contributes to our understanding of educational phenomena and processes. We presented this evolution as sets of critical dialogues that have made visible the complex and substantive contributions of the various traditions and perspectives of qualitative researchers. As we argued, the roots for new directions in this dialogue are in place, and a critical discourse as framed by Longino (1993) is crucial for future development. In this concluding section, we suggest why such discourses are needed and who needs to participate in them.

One of the groups that needs to engage in such dialogues is the educational research community. As our discussion of the history of qualitative research suggests, just how this discourse will be undertaken, who is part of this community, and what perspectives count are not so evident. As new traditions are created or those from other disciplines are adapted, we need to explore their expressive potentials and determine how they contribute to the questions we have within education.

For example, as we seek understandings of the potential of recent directions in poststructuralism, postmodernism, deconstruction, feminist theories, and other research perspectives, we will need to understand how they contribute to the study of educational phenomena as well as how they can be applied to educational issues and questions. As part of these dialogues, we will also need to examine how, and in what ways, the different traditions and perspectives might be combined or inform each other. These issues are critical ones within the educational research community if we are to assess the contribution of these different perspectives and research approaches.

However, as we argued at the onset of this Conversation, there are other participants who need to be part of the new directions. Past dialogues, while valuable in building the substantive foundation that currently exists, have not included those outside of education, leading to the current crisis of confidence facing educational research in general, not merely for qualitative researchers. As Stroufe (1997, p. 26) argued in an article on the reputation of educational research, there currently exists a "dissing [disrespecting] of educational researchers" by policy makers and governmental agencies.

We believe that while some of the dissing is due to political issues, another factor contributing to the dismissal of educational research comes from the lack of inclusion of those outside educational research in the current and past dialogues. In the past, the dialogues have occured within the educational research community, ignoring other communities that are interested in the value and outcomes of educational research (e.g., policy makers, teachers, administrators, parents, students, legislators).

Many of these dialogues appear to those outside the educational research community as unnecessary or as creating a Tower of Babel. By not including such publics in our dialogues, we have missed an important opportunity to help them develop understandings of the contributions of the new perspectives, to explore how these differences among perspectives influence what can be known, and, perhaps most important, to acquire the knowledge and language associated with the different perspectives. In other words, we have not helped them to understand the expressive potential of these new and emerging perspectives, and what they contribute that is important to consider.

The current dialogues in various public arenas show that these publics do not understand the value of multiple perspectives; often, according to Stroufe, this leads them to dismiss such research as anecdotal.

The response to the lack of inclusion of some members of these publics has been clear. Some policy makers and government agency representatives have promoted a particular view of what counts as scientific research in education.

For example, in a recent U.S. congressional session, a particular view of educational research found its way into proposed legislation in the Reading Excellence Bill (HR 2614). In that bill, research that would count for funding educational programs was defined as "replicable and reliable scientific research." This public inscription ignores much of the scholarship on replicability and reliability in science that raises questions about the uses of replication and the extent to which replication exists separate from specific studies under consideration within particular communities of practice in each of the sciences (e.g., Barnes & Edge, 1982; Collins, 1985; Jasanoff, Markle, Petersen, & Pinch, 1995; Kelly, Carlsen, & Cunningham, 1993; Tuana, 1989).

This definition ignores the work that shows that individual students do not live large-scale, replicable lives. They live local and situated ones. Large-scale research studies mask differences that shape student lives. Further, these actions suggest that the different publics that researchers seek to address are drawing on perspectives and languages that are comfortable to them. Their actions suggest that they may be unaware of or explicitly ignoring the limitations of such work for local communities.

This state of affairs suggests that while progress has been made in the acceptance and development of qualitative research, the current context for educational research, and qualitative research in particular, is once again a contested terrain. The contested terrain suggests another reason for continuing the critical dialogues so that we might transform them from ones of contention to ones in which evidence of the value of each approach or perspective might be examined.

This form of critical discourse has the potential of moving beyond arguments about mere methodological difference to arguments that explore the contribution of different perspectives to the complex and dynamic issues facing educators and learners in our culturally and socially diverse world. Such dialogues have the potential for helping those participating in the discourse to explore how these perspectives shape particular views of children, teachers, parents, settings, schools, social institutions, culture, class, ethnicity, race, gender, economic conditions, and educational goals and outcomes. Without this information, we will not be able to assess the adequacy and appropriateness of different frameworks for addressing particular educational issues.

Answers to these questions must be considered across all approaches and by all stakeholders, not just by qualitative researchers, if we are to get beyond the divide that currently separates educational researchers from their publics and understand how and which of these perspectives contribute to the goal of equity of access to education. In the area of literacy, such conversations will allow us to explore what counts as literacy and who counts as literate, when literacy counts (c.f. Heap, 1980; Soares, 1992).

REFERENCES

ATKINSON, P., DELAMONT, S., & HAMMERSLEY, M. (1988). Qualitative research traditions: A British response to Jacob. *Review of Educational Research, 58,* 231–250.

BARNES, B., & EDGE, D. (Eds.). (1982). *Science in context: Readings in the sociology of science.* Cambridge, MA: MIT Press.

BEACH, R., GREEN, J., KAMIL, M., & SHANAHAN, T. (1992). *Multiple perspectives on research in literacy.* Urbana, IL. National Conference for Research in English.

BIRDWHISTELL, R. (1977). Some discussion of ethnography, theory, and method. In J. Brockman (Ed.), *About Bateson: Essays on Gregory Bateson* (pp. 103–144). New York: E. P. Dutton.

BLOOME, D., & THEODOROU, E. (1988). Analyzing teacher-student and student-student discourse. In J. Green & J. Harker (Eds.), *Multiple perspective analyses of classroom discourse* (pp. 217–248). Norwood, NJ: Ablex.

BOGDEN, R.C., & BIKLEN, S. K. (1992). *Qualitative research for education: An introduction to theory and methods* (2nd ed.). Boston: Allyn & Bacon.

BUCHMANN, M., & FLODEN, R.E. (1989). Research traditions, diversity, and progress. *Review of Educational Research, 58,* 241–248.

BURGESS, R.G. (1984). *The research process in educational setting: Ten case studies.* London: Falmer Press.

CASEY, K. (1995). The new narrative research in education. In M. Apple (Ed.), *Review of research in education: Volume 21* (pp. 211–253). Washington, DC: American Educational Research Association.

CLANDININ, D.J., & CONNELLY, F. M. (1988). Studying teachers' knowledge of classrooms: Collaborative research. *Journal of Educational Thought, 22*(2A), 269–282.

COLLINS, H.M. (1985). *Changing order: Replication and induction in scientific practice.* London: Sage.

CORTAZZI, M. (1993). *Narrative analysis.* London: Falmer Press.

DENZIN, N.K., & LINCOLN, Y.L. (1994). *The handbook of qualitative research.* Thousand Oaks, CA: Sage.

EISNER, E.W. (1991). *The enlightened eye: Qualitative inquiry and the enhancement of educational practice.* New York: Macmillan.

ERICKSON, F. (1986). Qualitative methods in research on teaching. In M. Wittrock (Ed.), *Handbook of research on teaching* (3rd ed., pp. 119–161). New York: Macmillan.

EVERTSON, C., & GREEN, J. (1986). Observation as inquiry and method. In M. Wittrock (Ed.), *Handbook of research on teaching* (3rd ed., pp. 162–213). New York: Macmillan.

FLOOD, J., HEATH, S.B., & LAPP, D. (Eds.). (1997), *Handbook for literacy educators: Research in the communicative and visual arts.* New York: Macmillan.

FLOOD, J., JENSEN, J., LAPP, D., & SQUIRE, J. (Eds.) (1991). *Handbook of research on teaching the English language arts.* New York: Macmillan.

GABEL, D. (1994). *Handbook of research on science teaching and learning.* New York: Macmillan.

GAGE, N.L. (Ed.) (1963). *The handbook of research in teaching.* Chicago: Rand McNally.

GODMUNDSDOTTIR, S. (Ed.). (1997). *International Journal of Teaching and Teacher Education, 13*(1).

GOLDEN, J. (1988). The construction of a literary text in a story reading lesson. In J. Green & J. Harker (Eds.), *Multiple perspective analysis of classroom discourse* (pp. 71–106). Norwood, NJ: Ablex.

GREEN, J., & HARKER, J. (Eds.). (1988). *Multiple perspective analyses of classroom discourse.* Norwood, NJ: Ablex.

GREEN, J. L. & WALLAT, C. (1981). Mapping instructional conversations: A sociolinguistic ethnography. In J. Green & C. Wallat (Eds.), *Ethnography and languages in educational settings* (pp. 161–195). Norwood, NJ: Ablex.

GREEN, J.L, WEADE, R., & GRAHAM, K. (1988). Lesson construction and student participation: A sociolinguistic analysis. In J. Green & J. Harker (Eds.), *Multiple perspective analyses of classroom discourse* (pp. 11–48). Norwood, NJ: Ablex.

GUBA, E. (1990). *The paradigm dialog: Options for social science inquiry.* Beverly Hills, CA: Sage.

GUZZETTI, B., & HYND, C. (Eds.). (1998). *Perspectives on conceptual change: Multiple ways to understand knowing and learning in a complex world.* Mahwah, NJ: Erlbaum.

HALFPENNY, P. (1979). The analysis of qualitative data. *Sociological Review, 4,* 799–825.

HAMMERSLEY, M., & ATKINSON, P. (1995). *Ethnography: Principles in practice* (2nd ed.). New York: Routledge.

HARKER, J.O. (1988). Contrasting the content of two story-reading lessons: A propositional analysis. In J. Green & J. Harker (Eds.), *Multiple perspective analyses of classroom discourse* (pp. 49–78). Norwood, NJ: Ablex.

HATCH, J.A., & WISNIEWSKI, R. (1995). *Life history and narrative.* London: The Falmer Press.

HEAP, J. (1980). What counts as reading? Limits to certainty in assessment. *Curriculum Inquiry, 10*(3), 265–292.

HEATH, S. B. (1982). Ethnography in education; Defining the essentials. In P. Gillmore & A.A. Glatthorn (Eds.), *Children in and out of school: Ethnography and education* (pp. 33–55). Washington, DC: Center for Applied Linguistics.

HOWE, K., & EISENHART, M. (1990). Standards for qualitative (and quantitative) research: A prolegomenon. *Educational Researcher, 19*(4), 2–9.

JACKSON, P.W. (1992). *Handbook of research on curriculum.* New York: Macmillan.

JACOB, E. (1987). Qualitative research traditions: A review. *Review of Educational Research, 57,* 1–50.

JACOB, E. (1988). Clarifying qualitative research: A focus on traditions. *Educational Researcher, 17*(1), 16–24.

JACOB, E. (1989). Qualitative research: A defense of traditions. *Review of Educational Research, 59,* 229–235.

JASANOFF, G.E., MARKLE, J.C., PETERSEN, J., & PINCH, T. (Eds.). (1995). *Handbook of science and technology studies.* Thousand Oaks, CA: Sage.

KELLY, G.J., CARLSEN, W.S., & CUNNINGHAM, C.M. (1993). Science education in sociocultural context; Perspectives from the sociology of science. *Science Education, 77,* 207–220.

KOSCHMANN, T. (Ed.). (in press). *Discourse processes.*

KYRATZIS, A., & GREEN, J.L. (1997). Jointly constructed narratives in classrooms: Co-construction of friendship and community through language. *International Journal of Teaching and Teacher Education, 13*(1), 17–37.

LANCY, D.F. (1993). *Qualitative research in education: An introduction to the major traditions.* White Plains, NY: Longman.

LECOMPTE, M.D., MILLROY, W.L., & PREISSLE, J. (Eds.). (1992). *The Handbook of qualitative research in education.* San Diego, CA: Academic Press.

LECOMPTE, M.D., & PREISSLE, J. (1993). *Ethnography and qualitative design in educational research* (2nd ed.). San Diego, CA: Academic Press.

LINCOLN, Y. (1989). Qualitative research: A response to Atkinson, Delamont, and Hammersley. *Review of Educational Research, 59,* 237–239.

LINCOLN, Y. & GUBA, E. (1985). *Naturalistic inquiry.* Newbury Park, CA; Sage.

LINN, R.L. (1986). Qualitative methods in research on teaching. In M. Wittrock (Ed.), *Handbook of research on teaching* (3rd ed., pp. 92–118). New York: Macmillan.

LONGINO, H.E. (1993). Subjects, power, and knowledge: Description and prescription in feminist philosophies of science. In L. Alcoff & E. Potter (Eds.), *Feminist epistemologies* ([pp. 101–120). New York: Routledge.

MARSHALL, H. (Ed.). (1992) *Redefining student learning: Roots of educational change.* Norwood, NJ: Ablex.

MARSHALL, H. (Ed.). (1996). *Educational Psychologist, 31*(3/4).

MARSHALL, H.H., & WEINSTEIN, R.S., (1988). Beyond quantitative analysis: Recontextualization of classroom factors contributing to the communication of teacher expectations. In J. Green &

J. Harker (Eds.), *Multiple perspective analyses of classroom discourse* (pp. 249–280). Norwood, NJ: Ablex.

MILES, M.B., & HUBERMAN, A.M. (1994). *Qualitative data analysis: A sourcebook of new methods* (2nd ed.). Thousand Oaks, CA: Sage.

MORINE-DERSHIMER, G. (1988a). Comparing systems: How do we know? In J. Green & J. Harker (Eds.), *Multiple perspective analyses of classroom discourse* (pp. 195–214). Norwood, NJ: Ablex.

MORINE-DERSHIMER, G., (1988b). Three approaches to sociolinguistic analysis: Introduction. In J. Green & J. Harker (Eds.), *Multiple perspective analyses of classroom discourse* (pp. 107–112). Norwood, NJ: Ablex.

PEARSON, P.D., KAMIL, M., BARR, R., & MOSENTHAL, P. (Eds.). (1991). *Handbook of research on reading.* New York: Longman.

RAMIREZ, A. (1988). Analyzing speech acts. In J. Green & J. Harker (Eds.), *Multiple perspective analyses of classroom discourse* (pp. 135–164). Norwood, NJ: Ablex.

RENTEL, V. (1988). Cohesive harmony in children's written narratives: A secondary analysis. In J. Green & J. Harker (Eds.), *Multiple perspective analyses of classroom discourse* (pp. 281–308). Norwood, NJ: Ablex.

RIST, R.C. (1980). Blitzkrieg ethnography: On the transformation of a method into a movement. *Educational Researcher, 9*(2), 8–10.

RORTY, R. (1989). *Contingency, irony, and solidarity.* New York: Cambridge University Press.

SCHON, D.A. (1984). *The reflective practitioner: How professionals think in action.* New York: Basic Books.

SHUY, R. (1988(). Identifying dimensions of classroom language. In J. Green & J. Harker (Ed.), *Multiple perspective analyses of classroom discourse* (pp. 113–134). Norwood, NJ: Ablex.

SOARES, M.B. (1992). Literacy assessment and its implications for statistical measurement. *Current surveys and research in statistics* (Publication No. SCR-E-62). Paris: UNESCO.

STRIKE, K.A. (1974). On the expressive potential of behaviorist language. *American Educational Research Journal, 11*, 103–120.

STRIKE, K.A. (1989). *Liberal justice and the Marxist critique of education.* New York: Routledge.

STROUFE, G.E. (1997). Improving the "awful reputation" of educational research. *Educational Researcher, 26*(7), 26–29.

TENENBERG, M. (1988). Diagramming question cycle sequences. In J. Green & J. Harker (Ed.), *Multiple perspective analyses of classroom discourse* (pp. 165–194). Norwood, NJ: Ablex.

TESCH, R. (1990). *Qualitative research: Analysis types and software tools.* New York: Falmer Press.

THOMAS, R.M. (1979). *Comparing theories of child development.* Belmont, CA: Wadsworth.

TRAVERS, R. (1973). *The handbook for research on teaching* (2nd ed.). New York: Macmillan.

TUANA, N. (1989). *Feminism and science.* Bloomington, IN: Indiana University Press.

VAN DIJK, T. (Ed.). (1985). *Handbook of discourse analysis: Vol. 1. Disciplines of discourse.* New York: Academic Press.

WALLAT, C., & PIAZZA, C. (1988). The classroom and beyond: Issues in the analysis of multiple studies of communicative competence. In J. Green & J. Harker (Eds.), *Multiple perspective analyses of classroom discourse* (pp. 309–343). Norwood, NJ: Ablex.

WITTROCK, M. (Ed.). (1986). *Handbook of research on teaching* (3rd ed.). New York: Macmillan.

WOLCOTT, H.F. (1992). Posturing in qualitative inquiry. In M.D. LeCompte, W.L. Millroy, & J. Preissle (Eds.), *The handbook of qualitative research in education* (pp. 3–52). San Diego, CA: Academic Press.

Received June 1, 1998
Final revision received September 30, 1998
Accepted October 5, 1998

Quantitative Research Approaches

GEORGE A. MORGAN, PH.D., JEFFREY A. GLINER, PH.D., AND ROBERT J. HARMON, M.D.

In this column we describe our conceptual framework for quantitative research approaches (such as randomized experimental, quasi-experimental, and descriptive). The research literature is inconsistent, but we think that it is important to make logical, consistent, and conceptually important distinctions among different approaches to research. We believe that this framework and labeling are helpful because the terminology (a) is more appropriate, (b) is more logically consistent, (c) helps make the leap from approaches and designs to selection of appropriate statistics, (d) provides appropriate guidance about inferring cause and effect, (e) separates approaches and data collection techniques, which are conceptually orthogonal, and (f) deals well with complex studies because the approaches relate to research questions and not necessarily to whole studies.

Remember from the column on variables (Harmon and Morgan, 1999, p. 784) that we distinguish between active and attribute independent variables. An *active* independent variable is a variable such as a treatment, workshop, or other intervention that is manipulated (i.e., either given to or withheld from a group of participants), usually within a specified period of time *during* the study. One level of the independent variable, perhaps a new therapy, is given to one group of participants and another level of the independent variable, perhaps a traditional therapy, is given to another group of participants. A variable that is not given or withheld in the study is called an *attribute* independent variable because it is a measure of a characteristic of the person. Ethnicity and type of disability are considered to be attribute variables because a subject cannot be assigned to an ethnicity or disability group. However, if determined by the institutional review board to be ethical, some state characteristics of participants, such as anxiety, can be manipulated. If some participants are assigned to an anxiety-reduction condition and others to a control condition, anxiety would be considered an active variable in that study. Usually anxiety is measured, not manipulated, and is considered to be an attribute variable.

Figure 1 indicates that the general purpose of all 5 of the approaches, except the descriptive, is to explore relationships (in the broad sense) between or among variables. We point this out to be consistent with the notion that all common parametric statistics are relational and with the typical phrasing of research questions and hypotheses as investigating the relationship between 2 or more variables. Note that these approaches really apply to a research question, not necessarily to an entire study, which may have many research questions and use more than one approach. Figure 1 also indicates the specific purpose, type of research question, and general type of statistic used in each of the 5 approaches.

Research Approaches With an Active (or Manipulated) Independent Variable

Randomized Experimental Approach. This approach provides the best evidence about cause and effect. For a research approach to be called randomized experimental, 2 criteria must be met. First, the independent variable must be active (i.e., be a variable that is given, such as a treatment). Second, the researcher must *randomly assign participants to groups* or conditions. As you can see from Table 1, this latter criterion is what differentiates experiments from quasi-experiments.

Quasi-Experimental Research Approach. Researchers do not agree on the definition of a quasi-experiment. Our definition is implied in Table 1; there must be an active/manipulated independent variable, but the participants are not randomly assigned to the groups. Much applied research involves groups that are already intact, such as clinic participants, where it is not possible to change

Accepted June 30, 1999.

Dr. Morgan is Professor of Education and Human Development, Colorado State University, Fort Collins, and Clinical Professor of Psychiatry, University of Colorado School of Medicine, Denver. Dr. Gliner is Professor of Occupational Therapy and Education, Colorado State University, Fort Collins. Dr Harmon is Professor of Psychiatry and Pediatrics and Head, Division of Child Psychiatry, University of Colorado School of Medicine, Denver.

The authors thank Helena Chmura Kraemer for helpful feedback and Nancy Plummer for manuscript preparation. Parts of the column are adapted, with permission from the publisher and the authors, from Gliner JA and Morgan GA (in press), Research Methods in Applied Settings: An Integrated Approach to Design and Analysis. Mahwah, NJ: Erlbaum. Permission to reprint or adapt any part of this column must be obtained from Erlbaum.

Reprint requests to Dr. Harmon, CPH Room 2K04, UCHSC Box C268-52, 4200 East Ninth Avenue, Denver, CO 80262.

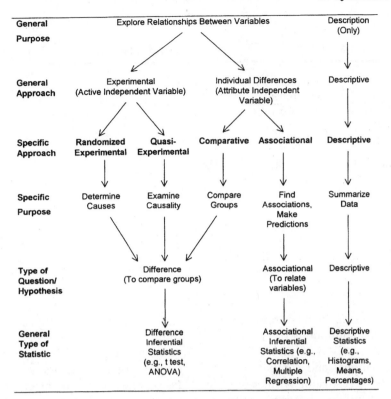

Fig. 1 Schematic diagram showing how the general type of statistic and hypothesis/question used in a study corresponds to the purposes and the approach. ANOVA = analysis of variance.

those assignments and divide the participants *randomly* into experimental and control groups. Such research is considered to be quasi-experimental and the designs are called nonequivalent comparison group designs. We divide the quasi-experimental approach into strong, moderate, and weak designs. In the strong quasi-experimental designs, participants are already in a few similar intact groups, but the treatment (rather than the participants) is randomly assigned to these groups. In a moderate strength quasi-experimental design, the participants again are in intact groups, but the investigator is not able to randomly assign the treatment to certain groups. Instead, the investigator takes advantage of a situation where it is known that one setting (e.g., clinic) will receive the intervention and another (one hopes) similar setting will not receive the intervention. In weak quasi-experimental designs, the participants have assigned themselves to the groups by volunteering to be in the treatment or control group. In the weak quasi-experimental approach, the groups are likely to be very different and, thus, pose a serious threat to internal validity. Quasi-experiments, especially moderate and weak ones, do not provide good evidence about the cause of changes in the dependent variable.

Research Approaches That Have Attribute Independent Variables

Table 1 shows that in most ways the associational and comparative approaches are similar. The distinction be-

tween them, which is implied but not stated in most research textbooks, is in terms of the number of levels of the independent variable. This distinction between comparative and associational approaches is made only for heuristic/educational purposes. In the associational approach, the independent variable is assumed to be continuous rather than have a few levels or categories. *Neither* approach provides evidence for attributing cause and effect.

It is common for survey research to include both comparative and associational as well as descriptive research questions, and therefore use all 3 approaches. It is also common for experimental studies to include attribute independent variables such as gender and, thus, use both experimental and comparative approaches. The approaches are tied to types of independent variables and research questions, not necessarily to whole studies.

Comparative Research Approach. Table 1 shows that, like randomized experiments and quasi-experiments, the comparative approach, sometimes called *ex post facto*, usually has a few levels or categories for the independent variable and makes comparisons between groups. Studies that use the comparative approach compare groups based on a few levels of an attribute independent variable.

The randomized experimental, quasi-experimental, and comparative approaches tend to use the same types of inferential statistics, often a *t* test or analysis of variance. Figure 1 illustrates this point, which we think helps with the difficult task of deciding what statistic to use.

TABLE 1

A Comparison of the Five Basic Quantitative Research Approaches

Criteria	Randomized Experimental	Quasi-Experimental	Comparative	Associational	Descriptive
Random assignment of participants to groups by the investigator	Yes	No	No	No (only one group)	One group
Independent variable is active	Yes	Yes	No (attribute)	No (attribute)	No independent variable
Independent variable is controlled by the investigator[a]	Usually	Sometimes	No	No	No
Independent variable has only a few levels/categories	Usually	Usually	Usually	Sometimes	No independent variable
Association between variables or comparison groups	Yes (comparison)	Yes (comparison	Yes (comparison)	Yes (association)	No

[a] Although this is a desired quality of randomized experimental quasi-experimental designs, it is not sufficient for distinguishing between these two approaches.

Associational Research Approach. In this approach, the independent variable is often continuous or has a number of ordered categories, usually 5 or more. To show the similarity of the associational and comparative approaches, suppose that the investigator is interested in the relationship between IQ and self-concept in children. If IQ, the independent variable, had been divided into high and low groups, the research approach would be comparative. The associational approach would treat the independent variable, IQ, as continuous. In other words, all participants would be in a single group measured on 2 continuous, hopefully normally distributed, variables: IQ and self-concept. Correlation and multiple regression are statistical methods commonly used with the associational approach.

Although for correlation technically there is no independent variable, it is important to think about which variable is presumed to be the independent or predictor variable and which is the dependent/outcome variable for a particular research question. This is important not only when doing regression statistics but because researchers almost always have some direction of "effect" in mind even if their statistics do not prove cause.

In both the comparative and associational approaches, some things (e.g., analysis of covariance or partial correlation) can be done to strengthen internal validity but neither approach is inherently stronger. Students learn that a high correlation does not prove cause and effect, but they also need to know that neither does a highly significant *t* test, if the approach is comparative (or quasi-experimental). We prefer the term "associational" to "correlational" because the approach is more than, and should not be confused with, a specific statistic.

Descriptive Research Approach

Most research books use a broader definition for descriptive research or do not seem to have a dear definition, using "descriptive" almost as a synonym for

exploratory, or sometimes correlational research. We think it is clearer and less confusing to restrict the term "descriptive research" to questions and studies that use only *descriptive statistics*, such as averages, percentages, histograms, and frequency distributions, that are not tested for statistical significance.

This approach is different from the other 4 in that only one variable is considered at a time so that no comparisons or associations are determined. The descriptive approach does not meet any of the criteria such as random assignment of participants to groups. While most research studies include some descriptive questions (at least to describe the sample), few stop there. In fact, it is rare these days for published quantitative research to be purely descriptive, in our sense; researchers almost always study several variables and their relationships. However, political polls and consumer surveys may be interested only in describing how voters as a group react to issues or what products a group of consumers will buy. Exploratory studies of a new topic may describe only what people say or feel about that topic. Furthermore, qualitative/naturalistic research may be primarily descriptive.

Approaches Versus Data Collection Techniques

We think that it is inappropriate to mix data collection methods with approaches. Hendricks et al. (1990) pointed out that this confusion/oversimplification exists in many psychology texts. We agree with them that data collection techniques, such as surveys and observations, are conceptually orthogonal to what we call approaches. Observation and questionnaires can be used, even if they usually are not, with any of the 5 approaches.

REFERENCES

Harmon RJ, Morgan GA (1999), Research problems and variables. *J Am Acad Child Adolescent Psychiatry* 37:784–785
Hendricks B, Marvel MK, Barrington BL (1990), The dimension of psychological research. *Teach Psychol* 17:76–82

What Is (and Isn't) Research?

**As education scholarship comes under the microscope,
the question takes on new importance.**

By Debra Viadero

At a national conference in 1994, two prominent education researchers—Howard Gardner and Elliott W. Eisner—started a lively debate that would go on for two more years. The question was: Should novels count as doctoral dissertations in education?

It's the kind of question that might be dismissed out of hand in medicine, physics, or any of the other "hard sciences." But in education, a field in which alternative forms of research proliferate like gnats in springtime, the debate has serious implications.

At its heart are differing views about what constitutes good education research. And how do you know it when you see it?

"There are so many alternative paradigms in education research that we're not really agreed upon what knowledge counts and what's good research," says Penelope L. Peterson, the dean of the school of education and social policy at Northwestern University in Chicago.

Such questions are taking on a new urgency now, as education research and the federal system that feeds it come under the microscope at the national level. A host of com-missions, advisory groups, former U.S. Department of Education officials, and other interested parties this year have sought to spell out what researchers ought to be studying, how they ought to conduct those studies, how the federal government can best support the whole enterprise, and how to ensure that findings get used in real schools and classrooms.

The implications of this soul-searching are important. How education scholars decide what "counts" could ultimately raise or lower the field's credibility with the teachers and policymakers increasingly hungry for advice. If education researchers can't determine for themselves what good scholarship is, how can anyone else?

Mixing of Traditions

To some degree, all the social sciences, tied up as they are in measuring complex and unpredictable qualities of human behavior, wrestle with the same issues. Even medical researchers—often held up as exemplars by critics of their education counterparts—use different methodologies to point them to conclusions. They might, for example, draw on both lung-tissue samples and epidemiological studies to study the effects of smoking, notes Lorrie A. Shepard, the president of the American Educational Research Association, a Washington-based group representing 23,000 researchers.

But in education, the growth of so many different forms of research may be more pronounced because the field itself is an amalgam of academic traditions. Anthropologists, psychologists, economists, political scientists, sociologists, and historians—to name a few—all engage in eduction research. And the tools they use in their work range from questionnaires to field notes to videotapes.

Education researchers do surveys, longitudinal studies that track students' progress over time, and meta-analyses—a statistical technique that enables researchers to summarize effects found across many studies. They might delve into national databases, or into schools themselves with strictly controlled experiments or quasi-experiments to find out if an educational intervention really makes a difference. They might sit for months in classrooms and produce narrative descriptions of teachers, schools, classrooms, and thinking processes at work.

They might even write novels.

Psychology an Early Model

The Gardner-Eisner debates were no pie-in-the-sky intellectual exercises. By 1994, the first year the two scholars took up the topic, Hofstra University in Hempstead, N.Y., had already accepted a novel as a doctoral dissertation in education, according to one scholar who took part in those debates.

"In a sense, this flowering of methods is a healthy consequence of the fact that we've outgrown some of the methodological strait-jackets we lived in 30 or 40 years ago," said Alan H. Schoenfeld, the AERA's immediate past president and an education professor at the University of California, Berkeley. "But now I think there's probably too much, in the sense that the number of methods we have now will either turn out not to be robust or will be eclipsed by other things."

In earlier decades, education research predominantly modeled itself on psychological studies. Experiments were often conducted in laboratories, rather than real schools, and the results were always neatly quantifiable. Gradually, however, some researchers came to believe that the traditional methodologies weren't giving them the whole story. The study of schooling, they reasoned, needed to take place in schools and other real-life contexts.

What is more, statistical studies examining simply whether or not an intervention worked only scratched the surface. If a new program or classroom technique succeeded, statistics couldn't answer the big question: Why?

Notions of objectivity also came into question. Even though standard empirical or quasi-scientific studies may give the appearance of objectivity, some academics pointed out, the outcomes could easily be biased by the researchers' choices of measures or comparison groups.

Thus was born a move, which became almost a flood during the 1980s, toward more descriptive studies, known as qualitative research. At the same time, interest revived in research done by teachers and in "action research"—where researchers themselves often are active participants in the changes they are studying. Why bother to try to be a dispassionate observer, some proponents of those approaches may have reasoned, when objectivity may be an impossible goal?

Good vs. Bad

Now the pendulum is swinging again.

"There's beginning to be some serious skepticism about the movement in education toward qualitative analysis," Marshall S. Smith, the Education Department's acting deputy secretary, told researchers last month at a meeting in Cambridge, Mass., organized by the American Academy of Arts and Sciences. "People are beginning to realize that case studies are only useful when they're well-grounded in theory."

Part of the problem has been that descriptive studies, some of them involving a single school or classroom, don't carry much weight with policymakers. And while some qualitative studies have drawn accolades for their elegance, their detail, and their ability to shine a spotlight on what really goes on in some classrooms or in the minds of learners, others did little to the field's collective knowledge.

"It's not qualitative versus quantitative," Henry M. Levin, an education professor at Teachers College, Columbia University, told the Cambridge gathering. "It's good research versus bad research, and the qualitative field opens up a lot more possibilities for bad research."

Even when qualitative research is good, some scholars note, there is no mechanism that enables such findings to accumulate so that they become more than anecdotes and isolated stories.

An example of this type of solid, experimental work that policymakers are demanding is a noted Tennessee study on the effects of smaller classes. The study, begun in 1985, is also significant in that it set out to examine a question with direct and far-reaching policy implications.

With more than $12 million in total funding from the state legislature, researchers from the Student/Teacher Achievement Ratio, or STAR, project conducted a classic experiment in which thousands of students from 79 schools across the state were randomly assigned to either small classes of 15 to 18 students or classes of 22 to 25 students.

The researchers found that students from the smaller classes outscored their counterparts in every year of study. Those students held on to their academic edge years after returning to larger classes. (*See Education Week, May 5, 1999.*)

All but ignored when it was first published widely in 1990, the study has since drawn the eye of state legislators and President Clinton. And the findings have become powerful ammunition in the movement to reduce class sizes in the early grades.

Cost a Factor

What made the STAR study so influential, experts say, was its use of a random-assignment research methodology that reduced the risk of bias and made it possible to look across different school populations.

If the Tennessee researchers could pull off that kind of rigorous, scientific experiment on such a large scale, proponents of such experimental methods say, why can't other education researchers?

But conducting reliable random-assignment studies also presents some practical challenges. A big one is cost—a major concern in a field that is widely considered to be underfunded.

"The Tennessee study is a good example of the expense involved in doing [such research] on a scale that's credible," says the AERA's Ms. Shepard, who is a professor of education and research methods at the University of Colorado at Boulder. "It's clear that doing this in education means bigger-scale investments."

Another practical obstacle is that school districts sometimes find it hard to refuse parents' demands to include or exclude their children in experimental groups. Accommodating such wishes can dilute a study's strength.

"The chances for controlling for what we should be controlling for are pretty slim," says Lauren B. Resnick, a co-director of the Learning Research and Development Center at the University of Pittsburgh. "There are problems with that approach, but there are certain questions that can be addressed that way."

And certain questions that can't. One example Mr. Schoenfeld, the former AERA president, cites is studies on "metacognition," or people's awareness of their own learning strategies.

Standards for Research?

The bigger issue for many researchers is defining and maintaining quality in the midst of all the ferment in their profession. And they are divided over whether setting common standards for education research would help.

"If anyone right now were to say, 'These are the standards, and they're carved in stone,' they'd wind up setting the field back rather than mov-ing it forward," Mr. Schoenfeld says. But, he adds, within particular academic disciplines, "there are serious questions to ask about what kinds of claims you can make and on what grounds."

To some extent, research standards already exist. Academic journals act as gatekeepers when they send prospective articles out for peer review. Reviewers also screen the funding proposals that come before the Education Department's office of educational research and improvement.

But one recent federal report questions whether the OERI's peer-review panels are doing an adequate job. The report by the National Educational Research Policy and Priorities Board notes that while most peer reviewers appear to be qualified for the task, a few panels that screened proposals for research competitions held in 1996 and 1997 had few or no members with any expertise in research. (*See Education Week, March 24, 1999.*)

The Education Department is considering creating standing review panels whose members would work together over longer periods of time, learn from one another, and reach consensus on some common evaluation standards.

"There's no getting away, at the end of the day, that quality is to some considerable degree in the eyes of the beholder," says C. Kent McGuire, the department's assistant secretary in charge of the OERI. "But I think these things need to be publicly discussed, and the field needs to worry about quality."

Different Notions of 'Research'

So, is a novel a valuable enough piece of research to qualify as a dissertation? Or is it just a piece of fiction, with little value for those trying to build better schools?

After two years of talking, neither Mr. Gardner nor Mr. Eisner had moved any closer to agreeing on whether a novel could be a dissertation.

Mr. Gardner remained skeptical. "Not only is art not true, it makes no effort toward truth," the Harvard University scholar, best known for his "multiple intelligences" theory, said the last time the two debated the topic, in 1996. "It seems to me the essence of research is effort, however stumbling, to find out as accurately as you can what's happening and then to report it accurately."

For his part, Mr. Eisner, of Stanford University, conceded that while a novel might not be an appropriate vehicle for every sort of research imaginable, it could create deeper, more empathic understandings in its readers and convey some things that facts cannot reveal.

"If you want to know what it feels like to be an associate professor when you're 54, 'Who's Afraid of Virginia Wolf?' is a good way to find that out," he said in that exchange three years ago. "Exploring new forms of inquiry is part of trying to create an intellectual climate in schools of education where those contributions are not excluded because they don't match the existing categories."

Unit 2

Unit Selections

Key Points to Consider

❖ What basic ethical principles should be followed when human beings are the participants in a research project?

❖ Outline the most important errors that can occur in synthesizing research in education and describe specific strategies that can be used to avoid these errors.

❖ Discuss the ethical guidelines that institutional review boards follow in approving/rejecting faculty members' and students' research proposals.

❖ What criteria should researchers keep in mind in selecting credible pieces of evidence to support historical research?

 **Links** **www.dushkin.com/online/**

These sites are annotated on pages 4 and 5.

To paraphrase the well-known physicist Werner Heisenberg, an expert may be thought of as someone who not only knows the worst mistakes that can be committed in a field but also knows how to avoid them.

Unit 2 highlights the worst mistakes in research methods, beginning with the unethical treatment of human subjects as detailed in Carol Heintzelman's account of the scandalous Tuskegee Syphilis Study. Michael Dunkin's article, "Types of Errors in Synthesizing Research in Education," outlines nine common errors in synthesizing research and ways to avoid them.

The third reading selection for this unit examines the essential role of institutional review boards in monitoring research, as described by Kenneth Howe and Katharine Cutts Dougherty. The authors set forth criteria that should govern both quantitative and qualitative research projects. Unit 2 concludes with Carl Kaestle's explanation of standards for quality in historical research, or how historians "know when they know something," which appeared in the Fall 1992 issue of *History of Education Quarterly*. Kaestle describes the criteria for deciding which evidence is credible and why.

The Researcher/Practitioner: Standards and Ethics of Practice

Human Subjects and Informed Consent:

The Legacy of the Tuskegee Syphilis Study

Carol A. Heintzelman

"... it must have been an experiment, like the one conducted on black men in Alabama, who were injected with the virus that causes syphilis, then studied as they sickened and died. The kind of experiment that would not have been hazarded on European or white American subjects."

—Alice Walker, *Possessing the Secret of Joy*

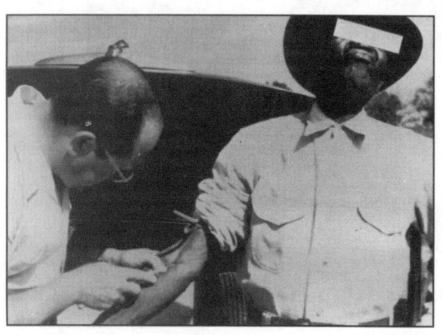

National Archives

A U.S. Public Health Service official takes a blood sample from an unidentified subject of the government's 1932 study of syphilis.

The Tuskegee study of untreated syphilis in African American males is the longest non-therapeutic experiment conducted on human subjects in medical history. Begun in 1932 by the United States Public Health Service (USPHS), the study was purportedly designed to determine the natural course of untreated latent syphilis in some 400 African American men in Tuskegee, Macon County, Alabama. The research subjects, all of whom had syphilis when they were enrolled in the study—contrary to the urban mythology that holds "black men in Alabama ... were injected with the virus that causes syphilis"—were matched against 200 uninfected subjects who served as a control group.

The subjects were recruited with misleading promises of "special free treatment," that were actually spinal taps done without anesthesia to study

From *Scholars: Research, Teaching, and Public Service,* Fall 1996, pp. 23-29. © 1996 by Carol A. Heintzelman. Reprinted by permission.

the neurological effects of syphilis, and were enrolled without their informed consent. The subjects received heavy metals therapy, standard treatment in 1932, but were denied antibiotic therapy when it became clear in the 1940s that penicillin was a safe and effective treatment for the disease. And again, when penicillin became widely available by the early 1950s as the preferred treatment for syphilis, this therapy was withheld. On several occasions, the USPHS actually sought to prevent treatment.

The first published report of the study appeared in 1936, with subsequent papers issued every four to six years until the early 1970s. In 1969, a committee at the federally-operated Center for Disease Control decided the study should continue. Only in 1972, when accounts of the study first appeared in the national press, did the Department of Health, Education and Welfare (DHEW) halt the experiment. At that time, 74 of the test subjects were still alive; at least 28, but perhaps more than 100, had died directly from advanced syphilis. An investigatory panel appointed by DHEW in August 1972 found the study "ethically unjustified" and argued that penicillin should have been provided to the men. As a result, the National Research Act, passed in 1974, mandated that all federally funded proposed research with human subjects be approved by an institutional review board. By 1992, final payments were made under an agreement settling the class action lawsuit brought on behalf of the Tuskegee Study subjects.

Medical Results

What, if any, were the medical results of the study? Doctors Joseph Caldwell, Eleanor Price, Arnold Schroeter, and Gerald Fletcher, of the Center for Disease Control in Atlanta, reported in 1973 that after nearly four decades of study that the rates of aortic regurgitation or insufficiency (blood rushing or surging backward into the aorta from the heart) and cardiovascular morbidity (heart/blood ves-

sel disease) occurred equally in the 127 surviving syphilitic and control subjects.

Earlier in 1968–1970, researchers found that two of the living 76 syphilitics and two of the 51 controls had aortic regurgitation. Following the introduction of penicillin to the remaining survivors, only one of the syphilitics had received no treatment. As a result of the administration of penicillin, the two subjects who suffered from syphilitic aortic valve disease experienced improvement in their condition. Autopsies revealed that the

> *It was common medical knowledge in 1932 that untreated syphilis produced increased disability and premature death.*

syphilitics were more likely to experience major or minor damage to the aortic valve and that the detection rates of local heart muscle scarring was equal in the syphilitic and control groups.

The study provided mostly contributory information, conclusions known and confirmed by earlier studies, mainly in Oslo, Norway at the end of the nineteenth century. It was common medical knowledge in 1932 that untreated syphilis produced increased disability and premature death. The Tuskegee Study confirmed this.

Many questions emerge about ethical issues in research, medicine, law, and especially public health. Should the results of an immorally conducted study continue to serve as the "gold standard" in the clinical understanding of syphilis? How should society balance protecting vulnerable classes of subjects and seeing that minorities are not only adequately represented in clinical trials, but also reap the benefits from them? What lingering meanings does the Tuskegee Syphilis Study have in the African American

community? How do those meanings affect current efforts to conduct biomedical research while providing effective community health care? Underlying all of these are questions about the messages race, or other kinds of difference, carry concerning medicine, healthcare, and research in our culture.

"For Research Purposes"

Of particular concern is the practice of withholding treatment from a control group to assess by comparison whether a given treatment is effective. If the group receiving treatment improves more than the control group over time, then researchers can claim the treatment caused improvement. A control group, comparable to the treatment group in all other ways, allows researchers to claim that improvement in the treatment group was due to the treatment and would not have occurred in its absence.

But the basic question remains, does the benefit gained from the research outweigh the risk of withholding treatment from the control group? And its corollary, is it ethical to offer untested treatments? Also, when treatment is withheld, more subtle ethical issues can arise: To what extent do research activities interfere with the delivery of services to patients?

The USPHS regarded the Tuskegee Study as a classic "study in nature" rather than as an experiment. "The rationale was that the conditions existed 'naturally' and that the men would not have been treated anyway, according to the premise that shaped the study—that African Americans, being promiscuous and lustful, would not seek or continue treatment," according to historian Allan M. Brandt in the December 1978 Hastings Center Report. Since the test of untreated syphilis seemed "natural" because the USPHS presumed the men would never seek or submit to treatment, the Tuskegee Study became a self-fulfilling prophecy.

But the study had one serious flaw in its research: the majority of the patients had been given antibiotic treatment at some point, although it was inadequate. This compromised the study's objective of following the course of truly untreated syphilis.

By 1969, little medical knowledge had resulted from the study. Autopsies had been conducted in poor conditions and tissue samples for germs had not been done. Many of the patients had received inadequate treatment from sources unconnected with the study. It would have appeared to have been sound medical practice to evaluate and treat the men individually at this time. But as late as 1969, the USPHS continued to withhold penicillin treatment to the surviving subjects, even though it recommended the therapy in all cases of syphilis, regardless of the stage.

Patient welfare was consistently overlooked, although there have been multiple attempts to justify why penicillin treatment was withheld. For example, some felt that repair of existing damage would be minimal and others felt that the damage that could result from reactions to the penicillin therapy, including fever, angina, and ruptured blood vessels, would outweigh its benefits. At the time of the Tuskegee Study no data was available on the efficiency of penicillin treatment in late syphilis and short and long-term toxic effects of drugs had not been well documented. In short, when the study was evaluated periodically, researchers judged the benefits of non-treatment outweighed the benefits of treatment.

It was unethical to withhold penicillin from the non-treatment group. Moreover, the subjects were never given a choice about continuing in the study once penicillin had become available; in fact, they were prevented from getting treatment.

The Tuskegee Syphilis Study was further flawed because at the beginning of the study in 1932, the men in the non-treatment group had received antibiotic treatment. Bad science and bad medicine were practiced by switching newly infected men in the control group, subjects who tested positive for syphilis after the study began in 1932, into the participant

group at various points in time as the study unfolded, a practice which affected the outcome for this group. These men should have been replaced by non-syphilitic control subjects. Both practices are examples of poor research involving human subjects and resulted in study bias of the results. No effort was made to protect the men or their families. The researchers kept participants from becoming aware of the disease or of the treatments available. They also failed to aggressively follow-up on diagnosed medical problems unrelated to the syphilis. Placebos were given and many of the men assumed they were receiving adequate medical care. James Jones reports in *Bad Blood: The Tuskegee Syphilis Experiment* that subjects had a naive trust in the medical authorities: "We trusted them because of what we thought they could do for us, for our physical condition," and "We were just going along with the nurse. I thought [the doctors] was doing me good."

From a historical perspective, physicians felt that African American men of rural Alabama would not have even approached the standards for receiving adequate treatment as accepted in 1932 due to their poverty, lack of education, and health conditions. "Attempts at treatment if unsuccessful because of irregularity, might have made the men in the early latent group a reservoir of infection in a promiscuous population," notes R. H. Kampmeier in a November 1974 article in *Southern Medical Journal*. "No evidence exists," he continues, "to indicate that 'adequate' treatment would

Certificate distributed in the late 1950s to each of the surviving subjects of the Tuskegee Syphilis Study.

have protected them against cardiovascular syphilis, nor does evidence exist that 'adequate' treatment in those early days would have extended the shortened life expectancy which attends chronic syphilis." No evidence suggests that penicillin treatment for the men in 1953, two or more decades after infection, would have altered the prognosis. However, the lack of treatment shows the men were not seen as patients, but as research subjects.

Not offering penicillin treatment to the men is the gravest charge against the study. The decision was made based on several factors including the quiescent state of the disease, assumptions about the participants, and fear related to the danger of lethal reactions if the men were to receive penicillin. So treatment was not offered, and even when the experiment ended in 1972, the remaining funds could not be used for treatment, according to USPHS grant guidelines.

Informed Consent

Informed consent refers to telling potential study participants about all aspects of the research that might reasonably influence their decision to participate. People often are asked to sign a consent form which describes the elements of the research. To deceive potential participants is to deny them the ability to determine their own destinies. Although consensus exists about the general principle of informed consent, a major unresolved issue is exactly how far researchers' obligations extend to research subjects. A second issue surrounding informed consent involves pressure a person might feel to agree, or a lack of understanding of precisely what he or she is agreeing to.

Tuskegee Study investigators took advantage of participants who were socio-economically deprived and who had previously experienced low levels of care. Their contacts were doctors and nurses whom they perceived as authoritarian figures. Eunice Rivers, a nurse involved with the study for most of its history served as a bridge between the traditional culture of the participants and the elite culture of the USPHS, representatives of medical science. Edward Berkowitz, social historian, sees the study as an example of comparative provincialism and isolation. Researchers regarded the participants as neither belonging to "their" community nor as people whose lives could or would be affected by what the researchers did. The African American community personified the localism of a racially segregated society, while the white researchers personified a scientific and bureaucratic community that had developed an ethical system separate from other institutions of society

The Tuskegee Syphilis Study Investigatory Panel believed in 1972 that the participants had volunteered; however, the men had not. Unfortunately the USPHS deceived recruits, who were told and believed they were getting free treatment from government doctors for a serious disease. It was

never explained that the survey was designed to detect syphilis. Doctors used the expression "bad blood," which was a colloquialism for everything from anemia to leukemia, and never defined it for the subjects. Subjects were never told they had syphilis, the course of the disease, or the treatment, which consisted of spinal taps, described as "spinal shots." Participation in the study did not remedy their situation. Instead, the consequences were just the opposite. Not only did the USPHS fail to inform subjects of the risks of joining this study it failed to gain their free and voluntary consent.

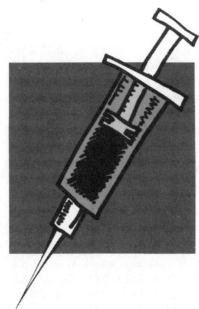

Several questions about informed consent remain unanswered. What were patients told? What did they understand about their "bad blood?" Did they know about treatment entitlements? If they knew, did they care? At this point, it is not known if they had been properly informed whether they would have accepted two years of proposed therapy when the study began in 1932.

Research Issues

The research process of the Tuskegee Syphilis Study contained numerous deficiencies. The USPHS has not produced any written protocol showing the original intent of the study, the objectives of the study or how

those objectives were to be met. The study lacked a long range plan, as well as validity and reliability assurances. In addition, the validity of the database was questionable. The overall experimental design was of questionable value for a long-term study. Moreover, neither the USPHS nor any of the participating investigators ever published any comprehensive report.

The gathering of partially treated subjects was fortuitous. In fact, there were more of these than untreated subjects. Between 1932 and 1936, data from the partially treated group of 275 subjects was incorporated into the investigation of the chronic syphilitics. In 1933, some test subjects were removed and others added. After 1936, this group was no longer reported on. Among the control subjects, who started without syphilis, it was not known how many had contracted the disease; however, those that did develop syphilis did receive treatment. A more serious flaw was the creation of subdivisions within the untreated group, those who came to the study with syphilis: one group of syphilitics received no treatment and the other group of syphilitics did accept treatment (reports indicated some did) but never left the experimental group. The men in the subgroup who did accept treatment had accepted inadequate treatment in the beginning of the study. Since their syphilis was not cured, they continued in the untreated group. By doing this, the researchers compromised the validity of their study. These men should have been removed from the untreated group and placed in the control group where they could continue to receive adequate treatment.

The underlying premise of the data-gathering phase was likewise flawed. Investigators felt that participants were able to give adequate information about how long they had had "bad blood," although they never told them they were infected with syphilis. Since all of the patients were culled from a population of latent syphilitics, the duration of their infection was not known. It was not clear from the

National Archives

Nurse Eunice Rivers "served as a bridge between the traditional culture of the participants and the elite culture of the USPHS."

data collected if the men's health problems were caused by syphilis or other factors. To make this determination, it was necessary to do autopsies, for which the men's families each received $50 dollars to cover burial expenses.

Another flaw in the research process was the lack of supervision by an independent review board, a given in today's human subject experiments. In 1932, when the study began, the concept of an independent review board was unknown.

Also, the continuity of the study was seriously weakened by changes in key personnel over the 40 years, changes significant because of the lack of a clearly defined protocol and standardization procedures. In addition, the subjects of the study consisted of African American males only, although the study purported to examine differences in rates of syphilitic heart disease between African American males and white males.

The Tuskegee Syphilis Study continued even after the USPHS adopted a Code of Research Ethics, a result of the Nuremberg Trials and the ensuing Nuremberg Code regarding medical research in human subjects. The key question of the study was never answered. The project was terminated because, "no scientific knowledge of any consequence would be derived

from its continuance," as medical researcher William Curran has noted. In short, 400 human beings were denied therapy in the interest of a medical experiment that was fundamentally worthless.

Other Issues

Numerous other ethical issues surrounded the study:

■ Alabama had passed a law in 1927 which required the reporting and treatment of several venereal diseases, including syphilis, by medical personnel. The USPHS ignored the state law, choosing to disregard the impact of untreated syphilis on wives of the married men who were subjects.

■ Accurate records were not kept. The number of subjects who died from syphilis was never known. The number of survivors was estimated to be between 76 and 111 and the number dying was estimated between 28 and 101.

■ Beliefs within the medical profession about the nature of African Americans, sexual behavior, and disease clouded the study. As a result, the health of an entire community was jeopardized by leaving a communicable disease untreated.

A related ethical issue deals with professional self-regulation and scientific bureaucracy. Although no comprehensive report was ever published, the

study was reported in medical journals for nearly 40 years without protest from anyone in the medical community. The investigating doctors never questioned the morality of the study. And, the DHEW had no mechanism for periodic reassessment of the ethics and scientific value of studies being conducted.

■ Good science is incompatible with bad ethics; researchers engaged in immoral conduct with subjects cannot generate useful or valid scientific findings. Yet the findings are still widely cited by the contemporary biomedical community. In fact, the moral issues of the study continue to be overlooked.

■ An unresolved dilemma relating to human subject research is the conflict between the dynamics of race and medical research. If difference is ignored and all groups or persons are treated similarly, unintended harm may result from the failure to recognize racially correlated factors. If differences among groups of persons are recognized and attempts are made to respond to past injustices or special burdens, the effort is likely to reinforce existing negative stereotypes that contributed to the emphasis on racial differences in the first place.

Consequences

The Tuskegee Syphilis Study forced the nation to rethink and redefine practices involving human experimentation, especially those involving minority populations. As a consequence of the Tuskegee Syphilis Study, the DHEW established a National Human Investigation Board, and legislation was passed requiring the establishment of Institutional Review Boards.

A class action suit, filed in the 1970s on behalf of the survivors, resulted in no new law and avoided the issue of government responsibility for injury in such an experiment. Each survivor received a settlement of approximately $40,000.

The most enduring legacy of the Tuskegee Syphilis Study is its repercussions in the African American community which have implications in light of the AIDS epidemic. The study laid the foundations for African Americans' continued distrust of public health officials; it reinforced views about the medical establishment and the federal government, as well as disregard for African Americans' lives. To some, the study demonstrated how effectively the government could exterminate African Americans through a conspiratorial partnership of key science institutions—the USPHS, the Macon County Health Department, and the Tuskegee Institute, where the autopsies were performed. Although community outreach efforts have done much to combat the misconceptions, there seems to be evidence that African Americans did not seek treatment

for AIDS in the early 1980s because of distrust of health care providers regarding the diagnosis, prognosis, and treatment of AIDS.

"As a symbol of racism and medical malfeasance, the Tuskegee Study may never move the nation to action, but it can change the way Americans view illness," says history professor James H. Jones. "Hidden within the anger and anguish of those who decry the experiment is a plea for government authorities and medical officials to hear the fears of people whose faith has been damaged, to deal with their concerns directly, and to acknowledge the link between public health and community trust," the specialist in bioethical issues continues. "Government authorities and medical officials must strive to cleanse medicine

of social infection by eliminating any type of racial or moral stereotypes of people or their illnesses."

Carol A. Heintzelman is professor of social work at Millersville University of Pennsylvania. She recently published a review of Social *Work: A Profession of Many Faces (7th edition)* by A. T. Morales and B. W. Sheador in *BPD Update.*

Types of errors in synthesizing research in education

Nine types of errors occurring in three stages of the process of synthesizing research are described and illustrated with examples from a recent synthesis of research on teacher professional growth. Types of errors include the exclusion of relevant literature and erroneously attributing findings to studies.

Michael J. Dunkin

Nine types of errors occurring in three stages of the process of synthesizing research are described and illustrated with examples from a recent synthesis (Kagan, 1992) of research on teacher professional growth. Errors can occur in the initial identification and collection of reports of research, in the analysis of documents, and in the final stage of reaching generalizations about the whole body of research. Types of errors include the exclusion of relevant literature, wrongly reporting details such as sample size, erroneously attributing findings to studies, and stating unwarranted conclusions about the research reviewed. Implications for reviewers and users of reviews are considered.

In the last 20 years a large body of literature on ways of synthesizing research in education has developed (Dunkin, 1994; Walberg, 1986). Approaches to gleaning the accumulated findings of that research have varied from the narrative through vote counting or box scores to meta-analysis. Some of these approaches make more demands on the conceptual and interpretative skills of the synthesizer than others and, therefore, contain more scope for error and bias than others, although all approaches are subject to the fallibility of the synthesizers and those upon whom they necessarily rely. It is important that the validity

of all syntheses be tested, for they are the main ways in which assessments can be made about the accumulation and development of research-based knowledge.

Syntheses of research are influential in regard to subsequent research, policy, and practice. They provide the empirical bases for applications for research grants, for higher-degree dissertations and theses, and for individual and institutional research. They are used by policymakers in designing strategies for development, and they are used to guide practitioners in the enhancement of professional activity. They provide the contents of highly regarded publications in handbooks, encyclopedias, and textbooks and become the best known statements of the state of knowledge on the topics to which they are addressed.

The processes by which syntheses of research are conducted and disseminated are, therefore, crucially important, because they determine the quality of the syntheses and which syntheses are available publicly for the above purposes. If the synthesizers allow systematic biases to affect their selection of studies to review, if they fail to recognize that some authors of the original sources were wrong in announcing their findings, if they allow their own priorities to affect the findings they report to the exclusion of contrary findings, then there is

the potential for a synthesis that is seriously flawed. The likelihood that a poor synthesis would survive the rigorous refereeing process employed by prestigious scholarly journals is undoubtedly very small. Nevertheless, the consequences of such a mistake warrant contemplation, for they could be whole programs of misguided research, policy, and practice.

The purposes of this article are to suggest the stages at which a synthesizer is at risk of making mistakes, to present a typology of errors that can be made, and to illustrate the typology with errors made in a recent synthesis-namely, Kagan's (1992) review of studies on professional development among preservice and beginning teachers.

Stages in the Occurrence of Error

There are three stages at which synthesizers might make errors. The first, the primary stage, is when the synthesizer searches the literature and selects from it the items judged relevant to the topic of the review. Errors made at this stage result in bias that might lead to conclusions that represent the findings of only part of the research and omit the findings of the rest,

From *Review of Educational Research*, Vol. 66, No. 2, Summer 1996, pp. 87-97. © 1996 by the American Educational Research Association. Reprinted by permission of the publisher.

or that give equal status to the findings of good and poor research.

At the secondary stage, the reviewer analyzes the literature selected in order to identify context, methods, and the findings of each study included. This is the stage at which the variety of errors made is greatest. As detailed below, error in identifying facts about contexts and methods leads to the misclassification of studies, and errors in identifying and reporting findings introduce error into the next stage of the synthesis.

This next stage, the tertiary stage, occurs when the synthesizer accumulates the findings identified in the previous stage in order to reach generalizations about the topic under investigation. Errors brought forward from the primary and secondary stages have their fullest impact at this stage, for they can lead to invalid generalizations.

Types of Reviewer Error: Primary Stage Errors

Type 1: Unexplained selectivity. These are errors in which the reviewer excludes research which comes within the declared scope of the review without explaining or justifying the exclusion. The outcome of this error is that the conclusions of the reviewer cannot be held to apply to the whole defined field of concern. It is possible, for example, that the findings of the body of the excluded research contradict those of the included research, and that reliance on the latter alone produces a biased picture of the state of knowledge in the field. Contemporary facilities for conducting literature searches and developing bibliographies are so advanced that these errors can seldom be explained in terms of understandable reviewer ignorance of the existence of the excluded work.

In her critique of Kagan's (1992) review, Grossman (1992) specified 16 studies that came within the declared boundaries of the review but had been ignored. She also drew attention to the fact that a surprisingly high proportion of the papers analyzed had been written by just two authors, which suggests that relevant papers by other authors had been ignored. If Grossman was right, then the review cannot be regarded as adequately representing the state of research knowledge on teacher professional growth, because of the presence of Type 1 errors.

Type 2: Lack of discrimination. Not all research on the same topic is of equal quality. Much of the literature available to a reviewer consists of tentative reports in the form of conference papers presented by authors seeking feedback prior to preparation of final drafts, which may or may not be submitted for publication in refereed scholarly journals. One test, therefore, of the quality of a conference paper is whether

or not it subsequently appears in one version or another, perhaps under a different title, in a refereed journal. In their efforts to be up-to-date, reviewers often do not wait that long, and rely on conference papers themselves. Clearly, this is a risky practice which can result in preliminary findings being accorded the same status as findings contained in journal articles that have survived rigorous refereeing and editing processes. This is not to say that all conference papers are defective or that all journal articles are free of weaknesses. In either case, reviewers should be vigilant that they distinguish between good and poor research, lest they give equal status to both.

Grossman (1992) accused Kagan (1992) of having committed this type of error but did not specify examples of poor research reviewed. This is possibly the most difficult type of error to identify, because criteria for evaluating research are usually controversial, and judges sometimes disagree on the difference between good and poor research. Most of the studies included in Kagan's review had been published in refereed journals, but 11 were cited as conference papers presented at Annual Meetings of the American Educational Research Association. Three of those papers could not be obtained for present purposes. Hollingsworth (personal communication, September 29, 1994) reported that she did not coauthor the paper cited as "Lidstone and Hollingsworth (1990)," and attempts to contact the other cited author were unsuccessful. The paper was not listed in the main, printed program of the meeting at which it was said to be presented, and it seems not to have been published elsewhere. The paper cited as "Wendel (1989)" was also unavailable for this analysis. It did not appear in the main, printed program of the meeting concerned, and repeated attempts to locate the paper were unsuccessful. Finally, the paper by Cochran-Smith (1989) was revised and subsequently published (Cochran-Smith, 1991) under a different title. During the years covered by Kagan's review (1987 through 1991), the present author was the editor of *Teaching and Teacher Education: An International Journal of Research and Studies*. Three of the papers reviewed by Kagan were submitted for publication in that journal and were subsequently rejected.[1]

The unavailability and/or nonpublication of some papers in their original form, the form which was used in Kagan (1992), may well indicate something about their quality and give justification to Grossman's (1992) criticism.

Secondary Stage Errors

As mentioned above, Grossman (1992) criticized Kagan (1992) mainly for making

two types of errors, which have been classified as primary stage errors here. She said little, however, about the types of errors described below that also were found in Kagan's synthesis.

Type 3: Erroneous detailing. These errors consist of incorrect statements of the sampling, methods, designs, procedures, and contexts of the studies reviewed. In some cases, the reports reviewed are about parts of larger projects and contain descriptions of the larger projects as well as the relevant parts. Details of the whole are sometimes thought to apply to the part when, in fact, they do not. In other cases, the reviewer accepts an opening statement of sample size without recognizing that attrition occurred and that the data actually came from a smaller sample. Errors in the reporting of methods, procedures, designs, and contexts can lead to the misclassification of studies so that they do not share the essential characteristics that are supposed to make them comparable with other studies.

In Kagan (1992) the sample sizes of four studies were reported inaccurately. In one case (Calderhead & Robson, 1991) the sample size was said to be 12, when it was 7; in another (McDaniel, 1991) it was said to be 22, when it was 3; in a third study (Borko et al., 1991), it was said to be 38, when it was just 1; and in the fourth (Wildman, Niles, Magliaro, & McLaughlin, 1989) it was said to be 15, with in-depth profiles of 4, when in fact the 15 were the subject of an earlier report (Wildman, Magliaro, Niles, & McLaughlin, 1988), and only the 4 case studies were reported in the publication reviewed. The main problem in these cases was that the papers reviewed were sometimes reports of parts of larger studies. The larger sample sizes were true of the full-scale studies, but the parts of these studies being dealt with in the review had smaller sample sizes. Thus, all four errors were in the direction of larger sample size, so that the reader was led to believe that the accumulated findings of those four studies came from a total of 87 novice teachers, when in fact they came from a total of just 15!

Other Type 3 errors were made in reporting data gathering procedures. For example, concerning the study by Aitken & Mildon (1991), it was claimed in Kagan (1992) that only interviews were used, when in fact there were workshop presentations, written preparations for these workshop presentations, self-evaluations, peer evaluations, written autobiographies, written responses to workshops, and researchers' field notes.

A more serious error concerning these types of details led to the complete misclassification of three studies. The Laboskey (1991) study was classified in Kagan (1992) as being concerned with the "image of self as teacher" (p. 146). Laboskey made no reference to self-image, and nowhere in the paper was anything said about the "central role" that self-image was said by the reviewer to play. In the section headed "Requisites for Growth During Practica and Student Teaching," the review summarized six studies which, it was claimed, "examined how candidates' knowledge of teaching changed during a practicum, student teaching, or the course of an entire preservice program" (p. 140). In fact, one of the studies (Gore & Zeichner, 1991) did not investigate change at all. Then, the study by Chamberlin & Vallance (1991), included in the group supposed to be "comprehensive evaluations of practica or student teaching experiences," was said to involve student teachers in spending half of each day in a 9-hour "block course" in classrooms. In fact, the student teachers in this study spent only half a day per week for 9 weeks in classrooms. The other studies reviewed in that section involved either 1 or 2 semesters or 1 year of full-time student teaching and were, therefore, clearly not comparable to the misclassified study. Needless to say, the findings of that study could not legitimately be claimed to contribute to any accumulation of evidence that might be perceived in the rest of the group.

Type 4: Double counting. This error consists of listing different reports from the same project as providing additional confirmation of the same finding. The risk of this error occurring seems to be present particularly when there is multiple reporting of results of the one project. This can be difficult to detect, especially given that titles and lists of authors are sometimes changed. While it might be expected that these multiple reports would contain acknowledgements of each other's existence, this does not always happen. Reviewers, therefore, have to be especially vigilant not to assume that independent studies have been reported.

Kagan (1992) included one very interesting Type 4 error involving double counting. This involved the case studies reported by Bullough and his colleagues. Bullough, Knowles, and Crow (1989) reported case studies of three beginning teachers named Bonnie, Lyle, and Helena. Then Bullough (1990) wrote about Helena alone, but called her Heidi, without mentioning that they were one and the same. Next, Bullough and Knowles (1990) wrote about Lyle alone, without mentioning the earlier write-up on Lyle. Finally, Bullough and Knowles (1991) wrote about Bonnie alone, except that this time Bonnie was called Barbara; it was revealed in an endnote that Barbara "chose to have her real name used" (p. 139). This endnote was not signaled at any place in the text where the name "Barbara" was used, but, rather, was added to another, quite unrelated note. Only by ac-

cident could a reader discover the information about the change of name. Kagan was apparently unaware of these strange occurrences and so treated these publications as though they were all reporting independent studies.

The effect of this Type 4 error was that Kagan (1992) claimed that six cases had been found, when there were in fact only three. To those who consider such matters as the replicability or frequency of occurrence of findings to be important, this error is significant.

Type 5: Nonrecognition of faulty author conclusions. Authors of original reports of research do not always represent their findings fully in their statements of conclusions. If reviewers uncritically accept such statements, they risk continuing the misrepresentation. The occurrence of this error can be contributed to by the original author, who may be biased to the extent of selectively incorporating only expected or hoped-for findings in statements of conclusions.

One example of a Type 5 error that occurred in Kagan (1992) involved the report by Weinstein (1990). Weinstein studied all 38 student teachers enrolled in one section of an introductory course required for formal admission to a teacher education program in the northeastern United States. On the basis of responses to an initial questionnaire which asked "How well do you think you will do during student teaching?," 15 were selected for interview. Students had also been asked to list the strengths and weaknesses they considered when answering that question. The 15 were then interviewed to explore topics in depth and answer questions about ways in which their thinking had changed during the semester. Of the 15, 12 agreed to be interviewed in the following semester. The questionnaire was administered in the autumn semester on the first and last days of class. Interviews were conducted in the following spring.

After reporting the results of her analyses of the data, Weinstein concluded, "What is most striking about the data reported here is the lack of change that occurred during the semester" (p. 285). In Kagan (1992), Weinstein's conclusion regarding change was repeated as follows: "Despite coursework and field experiences, the candidates' beliefs about teaching and themselves as teachers remained unchanged throughout the semester" (p. 140). In fact, Weinstein's findings were as follows:

(1) There was a significant decrease in optimism (p < .OS), "although students remained extremely optimistic" (p. 282).

(2) "Explanations for the self-ratings given at the end of the semester were similar to those given at the beginning of the semester. Students continued to stress caring (32%) [down from 45%] and enthusi-

asm (40%) [up from 32%]. However, nonteaching experiences with children were rarely mentioned (40% at the beginning of the semester versus 2.6% at the end (p < .0001); instead, 18% of the students (in contrast to an initial 3%) now cited a knowledge of teaching gained from the course or the associated field experience (p = .03)" (p. 283).

(3) "Conceptions of a 'really good teacher' remained largely the same; however, there were some interesting changes. Ability to maintain discipline was now mentioned by 50% of the students (p = .OS) [up from 37%], as was enjoyment or enthusiasm for teaching (p < .01) [up from 23%]. Fewer subjects cited ability to motivate students (p = .09) [from 34% to 18%] and willingness to spend extra time and effort (p = .08) [from 32% to 16%]. There was also an increase in responses dealing with the ability to meet the diverse needs of individual students (from 5% to 19%, p = .07)" (pp. 284–285). Weinstein also found that there was a decrease in mentions of "professional behavior" from 10% to 0% (p < .OS), but this was not mentioned in the text of her report.

None of these findings by Weinstein regarding change was mentioned in Kagan (1992), and so the conclusion was a gross misrepresentation of the facts, probably due to uncritical acceptance of Weinstein's clearly unwarranted conclusion.

Type 6: Unwarranted attributions. This error consists of reviewers claiming that studies yield findings or reach conclusions that they do not. In an extreme form, this error can even consist of attributing findings to studies when the design limitations of the studies do not permit such findings to be reached, or when the studies do not even set out to investigate the subject of the attributed finding.

One glaring Type 6 error was found in Kagan's (1992) treatment of the Hollingsworth (1989) report. In the review, it was said that

> Hollingsworth (1989) identified four factors that appeared to affect the acquisition of classroom knowledge by the novices: (a) their images of themselves as learners; (b) an awareness that they needed to temper initial beliefs and come to terms with classroom management; (c) the presence of a cooperating teacher who was a role model that facilitated growth; (d) placement with a cooperating teacher whose ideas and practices were somewhat different from the student teacher's beliefs. Modeling seasoned teachers was not sufficient to promote conceptual change; cognitive dissonance was needed to force novices to confront and modify their personal beliefs. (p. 145)

This is what Hollingsworth (1989) wrote:

> For those who did [reach a balanced managerial style], there seemed to be at least four explanatory factors that helped them acquire that knowledge: (a) a role image of themselves as learners and critics of teaching, which allowed for error and change; (b) an awareness that they needed to change their initial beliefs to come to terms with classroom organization; (c) the cooperating teacher and/or university supervisor as role models and facilitators of that change; and (d) a notion of having something worth teaching that demanded student cooperation. (p. 174)

Attributing to Hollingsworth (1989) the finding concerning cognitive dissonance was a Type 6 error in Kagan (1992).

Type 7: Suppression of contrary findings. Original reports sometimes contain findings that are actually contradictory of the generalizations which a reviewer claims they support. It is not necessarily the case in these instances that findings consistent with the reviewer's generalization are not contained in the reports; it is just that other, contradictory findings that are reported are ignored. Avoidance of Type 7 errors does not necessarily demand that reviewers acknowledge every single finding of a study, but it does require acknowledgement of every single finding that is contrary to a generalization a reviewer intends to make about the findings of the body of research concerned.

Grossman (1992) hinted that there was a Type 7 error in Kagan (1992) when she argued that in the part of her study (Grossman, 1989) "not directly addressed" by the review there was no evidence that preservice teachers complained that a particular course was "too theoretical" (p. 174).

Perhaps the most severe Type 7 error, however, was referred to above concerning the Gore and Zeichner (1991) study. Gore and Zeichner were concerned with levels of reflective thought exhibited by student teachers. Theirs was a case study concerned with action research and reflective teaching in preservice teacher education. The authors reported an analysis of the written reports of the action research projects conducted by 18 student teachers during the 1988–1989 academic year "to explore the extent to which action research seemed to be contributing to reflective teaching practice as we have defined it; that is, reflection within all three domains of rationality" (p. 129). The three domains were technical, practical, and critical rationality (Van Manen, 1977). Student teachers kept journals; conducted some formal observations of other classes; prepared, taught, and

evaluated a unit of work; and conducted action research.

Gore and Zeichner (1991) discovered three broad groups of action research projects: (a) a small number in which there was "clear concern for moral and political issues as integral to the project" (p. 129), which they categorized as displaying critical rationality; (b) a larger number in which there was "some concern for these issues but [the writer] did not develop the ideas" (p. 129), which they categorized as displaying practical rationality; and (c) projects more than half of which "revealed no explicit concern for moral and political issues at all" (p. 129), which they categorized as displaying technical rationality.

In Kagan (1992) it was said that there was "little evidence of reflection; what little they did find consisted of technical rationality, the lowest level" (p. 142). This was not true. At least 6 of the 18 cases studied (Jo, Bruce, Melinda, Helen, Leslie, and Annette) were classified as displaying either critical or practical rationality, the two levels of reflection ranked above technical rationality. By denying the actual findings obtained and thereby committing a Type 7 error, the reviewer drew unwarranted conclusions about the influence of preservice teacher education upon student teachers' cognitive performance.

Tertiary Stage Errors

The tertiary stage of a synthesis is that at which the reviewer seeks to assemble the evidence of the individual studies according to the main topics or issues investigated, in order to see whether meaningful and justifiable generalizations (syntheses) can be stated about them. The questions asked are, Do they add up?, and, If so, to what? Errors at this stage can lead to the statement of invalid generalizations and to the failure to recognize valid ones. Of course, errors made at the primary and secondary stages seriously threaten the validity of generalizations at the tertiary stage, but it is also possible that errors can emerge at this stage for the first time.

Type 8: Consequential errors. These are generalizations that are flawed as a consequence of errors made at earlier stages. Errors of any of the first seven types during the primary and secondary stages affect the validity of the findings of the body of studies that the reviewer attempts to synthesize at the tertiary stage. Colloquially, this problem has been captured in the well-known phrase "garbage in, garbage out!" Valid generalizations cannot be reached from erroneous conclusions about the individual studies that are part of a review.

The Kagan (1992) synthesis addressed the question "Do preservice candidates change their personal beliefs and images

during the course of a teacher education program?" (p. 156) and constructed the generalization that "the personal beliefs and images that preservice candidates bring to programs of teacher education usually remain inflexible" (p. 154). Later, it was claimed that "all but one study indicated that personal beliefs remained stable" (p. However, it has been demonstrated (Dunkin, 1995) that the reverse was the case and that most of the studies cited did find substantial change. It seems that the review's representation of four of the studies (McDaniel,1991; McLaughlin,1991[2]; Pigge & Marso,1989; Weinstein, 1990) contained Type 7 errors, and that Type 6 errors had been made with another two (Calderhead & Robson, 1991; Gore & Zeichner, 1991), neither of which reported findings about change or lack of it. As a consequence of these errors, a Type 8 error was made in Kagan (1992) in the generalization about change in preservice teachers' beliefs.

Type 9: Failure to marshall all evidence relevant to a generalization. When a reviewer, in the process of formulating conclusions, fails to recognize that a study contains evidence relevant to a generalization, he or she commits this type of error. This is different from a Type 1 error. It is not that an entire study is omitted from the review but that one or more of the study's findings are not included in the assembling of evidence bearing upon the generalization in question.

In Kagan (1992), Type 9 errors were made when the reviewer failed to assemble evidence provided by Bullough et al. (1989), Grossman (1989), and Levin and Ammon (1992) concerning the generalization that university courses are not sufficiently relevant to the needs of student teachers and that such courses fail to provide novices with adequate procedural knowledge of classrooms. In the review, it was claimed that there was extensive support for that proposition (p. 162), but contrary evidence provided in the three studies cited above was ignored. The review failed to report Levin and Ammon's finding that university courses were effective in securing growth in student teachers' pedagogical conceptions. Furthermore, the review did not mention that Grossman had shown what could happen in the absence of teacher education courses and had concluded that "teacher education coursework can help prospective teachers acquire knowledge about what students are likely to find difficult in a particular subject, and a realistic sense of students' interests, abilities, understandings, and misconceptions concerning specific topics" (p. 206). Moreover, the review did not refer to the following conclusion reached by Bullough et al.:

> All three teachers had adequate theoretical knowledge about teaching,

exposure to and practice of appropriate teaching skills; indeed, they completed the same preservice teacher education program together. What they initially lacked were useful understandings of the contexts in which they would work and, particularly for Lyle, consistent, grounded, and accurate understandings of themselves as teachers. (p. 231)

Bullough et al. argued that teacher educators could do more to help prospective teachers answer the question "Who am I?" but that the understanding of school contexts was primarily the responsibility of school districts and principals.

The failure to bring the above findings by Bullough et al. (1989), Grossman (1989), and Levin and Ammon (1992) to bear on this generalization constituted a Type 9 error.[3]

Conclusions

The main concern to arise from this presentation of the types of errors facing reviewers is the trustworthiness of their syntheses. It has been argued that all nine types of error were present in just one synthesis (Kagan, 1992). If that is the case, it seems clear that no reliance should be placed on that synthesis. But does it say anything about other syntheses? Surely, readers of these works cannot go to the trouble of the detailed scrutiny required to check the validity of every synthesis before they decide whether or not to rely on them. Not even referees or editors can be expected to subject syntheses in manuscript form to the painstaking inquiry process required to establish their validity. In this respect, a synthesis of research is probably no different from the individual studies included in the review, all of which, themselves, are subject to error at every stage of their construction.

The only feasible, systematic approach to quality assurance in regard to syntheses of research is to educate educational researchers, all of whom conduct their own syntheses of research whenever they write a dissertation, a grant proposal, or a research report, to look for the types of errors identified here, and in the more general requirements of good scholarship. Moreover, potential users of syntheses should be encouraged to develop a healthy skepticism toward them. The availability of a typology of synthesizer errors should assist in both processes.

The author would like to thank the anonymous referees and the editors for their helpful advice in bringing this paper to the state of publishability. They are not in any way responsible for any errors that might be found in it.

Notes

1. It would be a breach of editorial ethics to disclose the identities of the authors of those papers.
2. In Kagan (1992) it was mistakenly claimed that McLaughlin (1991) had been published in the *Alberta Journal of Educational Research*.
3. A detailed analysis of errors found in Kagan (1992) concerning research on first year and beginning teachers is to be found in Dunkin (in press).

Received March 7, 1995. Revision received January 16, 1996. Accepted March 19, 1996.

References

Aitken, J. L., & Mildon, D. (1991). The dynamics of personal knowledge and teacher education. *Curriculum Inquiry, 21,* 141–162.

Borko, H., Eisenhart, M., Underhill, R. G., Brown, C. A., Jones, D., & Agard, P. C. (1991, April). To teach mathematics for conceptual or procedural knowledge: A dilemma of learning to teach in the "new world order" of mathematics education reform. Paper presented at the Annual Meeting of the American Educational Research Association, Chicago, IL.

Bullough, R. V., Jr. (1990). Supervision, mentoring, and self-discovery: A case study of a first-year teacher. *Journal of Curriculum and Supervision, 5,* 338–360.

Bullough, R. V., Jr., & Knowles, J. G. (1990). Becoming a teacher: Struggles of a second-career beginning teacher. *International Journal for Qualitative Studies in Education, 3,* 101–112.

Bullough, R. V., Jr., & Knowles, J. G. (1991). Teaching and nurturing: Changing conceptions of self as teacher in a case study of becoming a teacher. *International Journal for Qualitative Studies in Education, 4,* 121–140.

Bullough, R. V., Jr., Knowles, J. G., & Crow, N. A. (1989). Teacher self-concept and student culture in the first year of teaching. *Teachers College Record, 91,* 209–233.

Calderhead, J., & Robson, M. (1991). Images of teaching: Student teachers' early conceptions of classroom practice. *Teaching and Teacher Education, 7,* 1–8.

Chamberlin, C., & Vallance, J. (1991). Reflections on a collaborative school-based teacher education project. *Alberta Journal of Educational Research, 37,* 141–156.

Cochran-Smith, M. (1989, March). Of questions, not answers: The discourse of student teachers and their school and university mentors. Paper presented at the Annual Meeting of the American Educational Research Association, San Francisco, CA.

Cochran-Smith, M. (1991). Learning to teach against the grain. *Harvard Educational Review, 61,* 279–310.

Dunkin, M. J. (1994). Teaching, synthesizing research on. In T. Husen and T. N. Postlethwaite (Eds.), The international encyclopedia of education: Research and studies (2nd ed., Vol. 10, pp. 6235–6240). Oxford, England: Pergamon Press.

Dunkin, M. J. (1995). Synthesising research in education: A case study of getting it wrong. *Australian Educational Researcher, 22*(1), 17–33.

Dunkin, M. J. (in press). Synthesising research in education: A case study of getting it wrong, Part 2. *Asia-Pacific Journal of Teacher Education.*

Gore, J. M., & Zeichner, K. M. (1991). Action research and reflective teaching in preservice teacher education: A case study from the United States. *Teaching and Teacher Education, 7,* 119–136.

Grossman, P. L. (1989). Learning to teach without teacher education. *Teachers College Record, 91,* 192–208.

Grossman, P. L. (1992). Why models matter: An alternate view on professional growth in teaching. *Review of Educational Research, 62,* 171–179.

Hollingsworth, S. (1989). Prior beliefs and cognitive change in learning to teach. *American Educational Research Journal, 26,* 160–189.

Kagan, D. M. (1992). Professional growth among preservice and beginning teachers. *Review of Educational Research, 62,* 129–169.

Laboskey, V. K. (1991, April). Case studies of two teachers in a reflective teacher education program: "How do you know?" Paper presented at the Annual Meeting of the American Educational Research Association, Chicago, IL.

Levin, B. B., & Ammon, P. (1992). The development of beginning teachers' pedagogical thinking: A longitudinal analysis of four case studies. *Teacher Education Quarterly, 19*(4), 19–37.

McDaniel, J. E. (1991, April). Close encounters: How do student teachers make sense of the social foundations? Paper presented at the Annual Meeting of the American Educational Research Association, Chicago, IL.

McLaughlin, H. J. (1991). The reflection on the blackboard: Student teacher self-evaluation. *International Journal for Qualitative Studies in Education, 4,* 141–159.

Pigge, F. L., & Marso, R. N. (1989, March). A longitudinal assessment of the affective impact of preservice training on prospective teachers. Paper presented at the Annual Meeting of the American Educational Research Association, San Francisco, CA.

Van Manen, M. (1977). Linking ways of knowing with ways of being practical. *Curriculum Inquiry, 6,* 205–228.

Walberg, H. J. (1986). Syntheses of research on teaching. In M. C. Wittrock (Ed.), Handbook of research on teaching (3rd ed., pp. 214–229). New York: Macmillan.

Weinstein, C. S. (1990). Prospective elementary teachers' beliefs about teaching: Implications for teacher education. *Teaching and Teacher Education, 6,* 279–290.

Wildman, T. M., Magliaro, S. G., Niles, J. A., & McLaughlin, R. A. (1988, April). Sources of teaching problems and the ways beginners solve them: An analysis of the first two years. Paper presented at the Annual Meeting of the American Educational Research Association, New Orleans, LA.

Wildman, T. M., Niles, J. A., Magliaro, S. G., & McLaughlin, R. A. (1989). Teaching and learning to teach: The two roles of beginning teachers. *Elementary School Journal, 88,* 471–93.

MICHAEL J. DUNKIN is Professor, School of Teacher Education, The University of New South Wales–St. George Campus, P.O. Box 88, Oatley, NSW, Australia 2223; m.dunkin@unsw.edu.au. He specializes in research on teaching and teacher education.

Ethics, Institutional Review Boards, and the Changing Face of Educational Research

KENNETH R. HOWE   KATHARINE CUTTS DOUGHERTY

Educational research has enjoyed special exemptions from formal ethical oversight of research on human subjects since the original mandate from the federal government that such oversight must occur. Although interpreting these exemptions has always been a potential source of controversy and conflict for university Institutional Review Boards, the burgeoning use of qualitative methods has further complicated matters. This article discusses the original rationale for special exemptions for educational research and then examines which varieties of qualitative educational research are consistent with it and which varieties are not. The article also examines the formal ethical oversight of student research practica, an issue also complicated by the advent of qualitative methods. Specific policies are offered both for determining which varieties of qualitative research should qualify for the special educational exemptions and for formally overseeing student research practica.

Educational research has historically enjoyed a special status with respect to formal ethical oversight because a significant portion of it is singled out for "exempt" status in the Code of Federal Regulations for the Protection of Human Subjects (45 CFR 46). Determining precisely which educational research projects should qualify as exempt has always been a source of conflict, potential as well as real, between educational researchers and the university Institutional Review Boards (IRBs) responsible for interpreting and applying the federal regulations. (The ambiguity of "exempt," to be discussed later, is an important part of the problem). However, this source of conflict has become more pronounced over approximately the last decade, as the face of educational research has been changed by the ever-increasing use of qualitative methods. Because of the *intimate* and *open-ended* features of qualitative methods (also to be discussed later), their increased prominence within educational research raises new ethical issues with which educational researchers must grapple. These features also provide the impetus for taking a closer look at the general rationale and criteria for affording educational research a special status vis-à-vis IRB review.

In this article we will discuss several ethical issues associated with qualitative research, with a particular emphasis on the role of IRBs. This emphasis squares with what initially motivated our reflection, namely, controversies between education faculty and the IRB at our university about what should be required of educational research to adequately protect human subjects—controversies rooted in uncertainty about how to apply key provisions of the Code of Federal Regulations and about how to fill in the gaps where the regulations are largely silent. Three such controversies will be the focus of our analysis: the interpretation of the special exemptions for educational research, the accommodation of qualitative research methods, and the oversight of student research practica.

Preliminary to our analysis, however, we will make a few remarks about our position regarding IRB oversight of educational research, for it is by no means universally shared among educational researchers and is itself a source of controversy.

Generally speaking, we believe IRB oversight is a good thing (granting that the ways in which IRBs actually function sometimes leave much to be desired). Contrary to our view, many educational researchers challenge IRB oversight on the grounds that it is researchers, not members of IRBs, who possess the specialized knowledge and experience needed to appreciate the ethical nuances associated with different research methods and different research contexts. They charge IRBs with, among other things, obstructing academic freedom, obstructing the free pursuit of knowledge, and being especially hostile toward qualitative research (e.g., Murphy & Johannsen, 1990). Accordingly, these researchers question the legitimacy of IRBs' looking over their shoulders and demanding they fill out the designated forms.

KENNETH HOWE *is associate professor, University of Colorado, School of Education, Campus Box 249, Boulder, CO 80309. He specializes in the philosophy of education, the philosophy of educational research, and applied and professional ethics.*
KATHARINE CUTTS DOUGHERTY *recently received her PhD in education from the University of Colorado. She teaches in the Verona-Sherrill School District in New York.*

From *Educational Researcher*, Vol. 21, No. 9, December 1993, pp. 16-21. © 1993 by the American Educational Research Association. Reprinted by permission of the publisher.

In our estimation, this view is misguided. In the first place, the portrait of researchers assumed is a bit unrealistic. Although moral abominations in social research are rare (but consider Milgram[1]), other pressures—for instance, pressures to "publish or perish"—are real and ubiquitous, and one need not be a bad person to be tempted to cut ethical corners in response to them, especially if cutting corners is the norm. Furthermore, one need not be a bad person to sometimes be oblivious to ethical worries that others are able to detect, particularly others who have a good deal of experience with the pertinent issues. The portrait of researchers assumed also misconstrues the nature of ethics, inasmuch it commits what the ethicist Robert Veatch (1977) labels the "fallacy of generalized expertise." For example, just as physicians qua physicians have no special expertise regarding whether a women should accept a slightly greater risk of death from breast cancer by opting for radiation therapy over a mutilating mastectomy, educational researchers qua educational researchers have no special expertise regarding whether parents should be given the opportunity to refuse to have their children involved in a given educational research project. Indeed, given their aims and interests, physicians and educational researchers are probably in the worst position to make these judgments. It is for this reason that 45 CFR 46 requires IRBs to be staffed by persons who represent a range of perspectives and interests, including at least one member of the community who is not affiliated with the university and at least least one member whose chief interests are nonscientific (e.g., member of the clergy, lawyer, or ethicist).

In the second place, although IRBs are often overly bureaucratic and discharge their duties in a rather perfunctory manner that takes too lightly the ethical complexities involved (Christakis, 1988; Dougherty & Howe, 1990), they are the only formal mechanism in the United States for overseeing social research (McCarthy, 1983). The shortcomings in the practices exemplified by IRBs is insufficient to abandon or radically change this oversight tool. The alternative of no policing or self-policing is likely to have worse consequences, on balance, than the consequences associated with the institution of IRBs, especially if the choice is to err on the side of overzealousness in protecting human subjects rather than generating social scientific knowledge. Furthermore, remedies for these shortcomings are not altogether lacking (e.g., Silva & Sorrells, 1988, suggest ways for IRBs to enhance informed consent by focusing on the process of consent rather than the wording of the consent form). Finally, IRBs can serve an important educational function. In our experience (which we suspect reflects what is generally true), the IRB is the chief, and often only, locus of reflection and debate about the ethics of social research.

Assuming, then, that IRBs both serve a legitimate function and are here to stay, we now return to the three controversies introduced previously.

The Interpretation of Special Exemptions for Educational Research

Paragraph 46.101(b)(1) of 45 CFR 46 singles out the following kinds of educational research as "exempt" from its requirements:[2]

> Research conducted in established or commonly accepted educational settings involving *normal educational practices* [italics added] such as (i) research on regular and special educational instructional strategies, or (ii) research on the effectiveness of or the comparison among instructional techniques, curricula or classroom management methods.

This provision potentially includes a large part of educational research, but is so vaguely worded as to leave much room for competing interpretations among educational researchers and local IRBs. In view of the inherent vagueness of this provision, it will be useful to begin with a brief examination of its history and rationale.[3]

The first policies set up for the protection of human subjects were done with a primary focus on biomedical research, which had already shown itself to be potentially harmful to the subjects involved. At that time, in the early 1960s, research in the social sciences was not believed to be hazardous to those involved because it did not involve any "invasive" procedures. However, as the National Institutes of Health, and then the Department of Health and Human Services, became involved, the initial guidelines were seen as more and more problematic. Thus, in the 1970s a national commission was set up for the protection of human subjects which thoroughly reviewed policies for the social sciences, including education. With the commission using essentially the same model as medical research, the idea of an independent review board and the emphasis on the need for informed consent prevailed in the new policies on social research.

The commission made provisions in its final recommendations to allow some discretion on the part of IRBs to reduce the burden placed upon them. Specifically, a series of thresholds were developed that defined three levels of review: exempt (no IRB review), expedited (review by a representative of the IRB), and full IRB review. The commission also reduced the burden placed upon IRBs by giving prospective research subjects, through the vehicle of informed consent, a significant role in determining the worth and moral acceptability of research projects for which they are recruited. (Partly because of this, the issue of informed consent has become of paramount concern for research in the social sciences.)

The commission believed that educational research, in particular, required less stringent oversight than other varieties of social research, both because the risks were perceived as slight and because district- and school-based procedures to screen and guide research were believed to already exist. Thus, the commission believed that educational research was one area where the IRBs' role could be minimized, especially since it believed that mechanisms of accountability for educational research were already in place at the local level. Accordingly, it crafted 45 CFR 46 so as to provide explicit exemptions for educational research.

The commission, nonetheless, mandated in 45 CFR 46 that some sort of administrative review (e.g., by department or college) would take place in every case of research involving human subjects. As a consequence, the apparent wide latitude afforded educational research was significantly narrowed by many universities as they went about the task of articulating the purview and responsibilities of their IRBs. In particular, IRBs typically do not permit educational researchers (or any other social researchers, for that matter) to decide for themselves whether their research is exempt from the 45 CFR 46 regulations. Instead, in order to comply with the 45 CFR 46 requirement that all research involving human subjects undergo some kind of institutional review (and perhaps because of some prodding from federal agencies[4]), many universities simply extended the scope of their IRBs (Dougherty & Howe, 1990). Under this system, if an educational researcher believes that his or her research is exempt, then he or she submits a proposal to the IRB indicating that the proposed research is of this kind. A delegated member of the IRB then decides whether the research is exempt from certain requirements of the regulations (e.g., informed consent) and may proceed as proposed, or whether it should go before the full IRB committee. In short, in many universities "exempt" has come to mean exempt from certain requirements and full committee review, not exempt from IRB oversight altogether.

This interpretation of "exempt" will be assumed hereafter. An important consequence of it is that IRBs, not educational researchers, are responsible for determining when educational research qualifies as exempt from the normal requirements of 45 CFR 46, and this engenders potential conflicts between educational researchers and IRBs. For taking the responsibility for determining what educational research satisfies the exemptions in 45 CFR 46 out of the hands of educational researchers, and placing it in the hands of IRBs, makes the IRBs the arbiter of key questions such as what constitutes "normal educational practice." This is problematic for educational researchers because IRBs are composed mostly of university faculty who have little knowledge of the workings of public schools.

With this brief historical digression in hand, we may now return to the issue of how to interpret paragraph 46.101(b)(1). Two related questions need be addressed: (a) What kind of educational research should qualify as exempt, and (b) who should make this determination?

The first question may be answered by explicating the rationale employed by the commission. In particular, certain educational research has features that should qualify it for special exemptions, namely, educational research

that is very low risk and aimed at evaluating and improving normal instructional practices. First, such research is often indistinguishable from or closely resembles the kinds of activities in which schools engage informally as part of their normal efforts to evaluate instruction (e.g., trying out new instructional methods and materials and assessing their effectiveness). Second, such research promises rather immediate benefits regarding instructional practice at the sites of research, exclusive of or in addition to the more customary social science aim of contributing to "generalizable knowledge." Both of these features mitigate the ethical concern attending much social research that only the investigators rather than the subjects (participants) and institutions under investigation stand to benefit from the conduct of research.

This leads to the second question of who should make the determination of when educational research satisfies the above description. We are skeptical of the commission's claim that local school authorities can be depended upon to independently oversee educational research conducted by universities, for there is no evidence to support this assumption—indeed, many rest their approval solely on the approval of the university IRB (Dougherty & Howe, 1990). But we are also skeptical of allowing educational researchers to decide for themselves whether their research should be judged exempt. As we observed earlier, educational researchers are not necessarily the best judges of what research should be permitted and under what constraints.

Notwithstanding what our arguments so far might suggest, we share the concern of other educational researchers about whether the typical IRB is composed of individuals who are in a good position to determine when educational research should quality as exempt, that is, qualify as "normal educational practice." In our view, there is an answer to the question of how to make such a determination that stops short of the extreme of permitting educational researchers to decide for themselves, or placing the decision exclusively in the hands of IRBs. Our suggestion is to formally include school people in the review process, particularly regarding the judgment of what is to count as "normal educational practice." (This suggestion strikes us as so straightforward and simple that we were amazed to find that it is novel; Dougherty & Howe, 1990.)

We do not advocate including school people as arbiters regarding educational research. We advocate including them in order to provide an additional, needed perspective in the IRB review process. Given this proviso, including school people in the review process can take at least two forms. First, IRBs might include in their regular membership a person who works in the schools and who has broad knowledge of local norms and practices, and that person could take special responsibility for determining whether a proposal for educational research should be classified as exempt. Second, IRBs might develop a procedure whereby an appropriate representative of the school at which the research is to be conducted assures the IRB that the proposed research constitutes "normal educational practice" and satisfies certain other conditions regarding risks, benefits, confidentiality, and the like.[5]

Either kind of policy has the advantage of requiring the active involvement of school people in determining what educational research should qualify as normal—a determination that they are typically in a better position to make than members of an IRB and about which they are likely to be less biased than educational researchers. In particular, the second policy—requiring the input of school people closely connected to the site(s) of research—also helps ensure that school people will be explicitly involved in evaluating, and will therefore be knowledgeable about, the research proposed for and conducted in their schools.

The Accommodation of Qualitative Research Methods

Our discussion in the preceding section is partially responsive to the changed face of educational research to the extent that our suggested policies could result in exempt status for certain qualitative research techniques (e.g., short interviews of students regarding a lesson). Because we include certain provisos, however—that such techniques not be too personal, not depart in any significant way from what ordinarily goes on in given schools, and not require students to forgo educational benefits as a result of being pulled out for such activities (see note 5)—our suggested policy alternatives serve largely to cull the more traditional educational research methods and aims from the newer, qualitative ones. As a consequence, much qualitative research presently conducted in schools would not qualify as exempt and would be subject to the same IRB requirements as social research generally.

We wittingly and explicitly embrace this outcome. In our view, qualitative research has two features—intimacy and open-endedness—that both significantly muddy the ethical waters and exclude much of it from the scope of the special 45 CFR 46 exemptions for educational research.

Qualitative research is intimate (in comparison with experimental research) because it reduces the distance between researchers and "subjects." Indeed, there is a tendency to abandon reference to "subjects"—*for* whom "treatments" are to be developed—in preference to "participants"—*with* whom "meanings" are to be negotiated. The methods associated with this general emphasis engender certain potential ethical difficulties that do not typically attend experimental methods. Interviewing, for example, requires one-to-one contact as well as removing children from their "normal" educational activities. Video- and audiotaping create records that pose a potential threat to confidentiality.

Qualitative research is open-ended (again, in comparison with experimental methods) because parameters and a mapped research direction—instead of having to be set at the outset—unfold during the course of the investigation. This significantly complicates obtaining participants' "fully informed consent" before the research begins because research directions will constantly be renewed and revised as a result of the researcher's activities and discoveries along the way. In particular, the prior weighing of research risks and benefits, not unproblematic in the case of experimental research, is further complicated by the open-ended nature of qualitative research.

In light of these features of qualitative research, it should be borne in mind that the special exemptions for educational research were formulated prior to the advent of qualitative methods in educational research. These special exemptions were justified on the grounds that educational research is extremely low risk and does not substantially deviate from practices routinely conducted by schools themselves for the purposes of evaluating and improving curricula, testing, and teaching methods. When educational research departs from this model to take a close look at social structure and to establish an intimate relationship with participants, there is not justification for providing it with greater latitude than other social research merely because it has to do with education, is conducted in schools, or is conducted by educational researchers.

Viewed another way, the advent of more intimate and open-ended methods in educational research creates a distinction between educational research as conceived in 45 CFR 46 and what might be termed social research on education. The latter variety includes much of "qualitative" research and is "educational research" by virtue of only its topics and settings, not its aims and methods. In its aims and methods, this kind of educational research is thus indistinguishable from the work of other researchers, particularly fieldwork sociologists and anthropologists, working in other contexts. According, it should receive no especially liberal treatment with respect to the protection of human subjects.

As we have already intimated, the issue of informed consent is especially tangled and contested where qualitative methods are involved. However, we cannot accept the suggestion (e.g., by Lincoln, 1990; Murphy & Johannsen, 1990) that, because the informed consent requirements of 45 CFR 46 were initially designed primarily for biomedical and experimental research, they are inappropriate for qualitative research. Informed consent is central to research ethics per se, not to any particular kind of research method: It is the principle that seeks to ensure that human beings retain their autonomy and judge for themselves what risks are worth taking for the purpose of furthering scientific knowledge. It just so happens that accomplishing these aims is more difficult in the case of qualitative research than in experimental research for two reasons, having to do with the distinguishing features of qualitative research discussed previously. First, because qualitative research typically involves more intimate interpersonal relationships among researchers and subjects (participants), it is more ethically charged and unpredictable from the outset. Second, because qualitative research is open-ended regarding its questions, participants, and modes of analysis, informed consent, even if obtained to a reasonable degree initially, can decay over time as the research process unfolds. (This contrasts with experimental research, in which the description of "treatments," their duration, and what is being looked for can be stated relatively precisely ahead of time.)

We are thus led to the conclusion that instead of abandoning or loosening the requirement of informed consent for qualitative research, we should, if anything, make it more demanding. We are not alone in advancing such a suggestion. One proposal for more demanding consent procedures has been advanced by a pair of qualitative educational researchers (Cornet & Chase, 1989) in response to the issue of open-endedness. In particular, they suggest (and have tried out) periodic reaffirmations of consent as a study unfolds. In a similar vein, Smith (1990), also a qualitative educational researcher, has suggested reconceiving informed consent in the context of qualitative research as ongoing "dialogue." To also take into account the intimacy of qualitative methods, we might take this one step further and add the requirement that someone other than the researcher(s) obtain the consent. This would help mitigate the potential for subjects (participants) to be subtly pressured to continue in studies from fear of possible repercussions for withdrawing or from a sense of personal obligation to the researcher(s).

The Oversight of Student Research Practica

As qualitative methods in educational research have proliferated, so have undergraduate and graduate courses that teach their use. Such courses often take the form of practica, in which students try out and practice the qualitative techniques. Just as the advent of qualitative methods in educational research prompts closer scrutiny of the question of what kinds of educational research should qualify as exempt, their introduction into courses prompts closer scrutiny of the question of whether such student research should fall within the preview of IRBs.

The 45 CFR 46 regulations nowhere explicitly refer to research practica. Instead, they apply to university "research," which they define as "a systematic investigation designed to develop or contribute to generalizable knowledge." Given that most research that is required as part of a course is variously perceived as no more than a "trial run," a "pilot study," "getting one's hands a little dirty" (Dougherty & Howe, 1990), and, in particular, not as an attempt to contribute to generalizable

knowledge, it would seem that it should not fall within the scope of the regulations.

Although the appeal to the criterion of whether an activity "contributes to generalizable knowledge" is certainly germane to its ethical dimensions—for example, it is related to the intent of an activity and to whether information about individuals will become public—it is quite insensitive to the ethical dimensions of the interactions between persons, particularly the intimate ones associated with qualitative methods. Furthermore, given the nature of such interactions, one can reasonably ask whether neophytes, just learning to interact with research subjects (participants), might require more, not less, oversight than experienced researchers.

In this connection, our preceding observations about the potential for increased ethical difficulties associated with qualitative research—particularly its intimacy and open-endedness—apply *a fortiori* to student research in courses. There simply is no defense for the kind of policy common among university IRBs (Dougherty & Howe, 1990) in which the ethical standards and procedures governing studies done by the most inexperienced members of a research community are lax or nonexistent in comparison with those governing studies by its more experienced members. (Compare medical students' interactions with patients.)

On the other hand, it does not necessarily follow that student research in courses should be subject to the very same review procedures as faculty research, in which each and every student activity must be submitted to the IRB. A sensible policy would be not too cumbersome relative to the protections it provides for human subjects. In our view, a workable alternative places responsibility on course instructors to judge when a student activity is exempt and when it should be submitted to the IRB.[6] Such a policy provides some oversight but avoids the absurdity that research which would be reviewed by the full IRB if conducted by a faculty member escapes such review if conducted by a student. On the other hand, it also avoids burdening students and instructors with preparing, and IRBs with reviewing, numerous virtually risk-free exercises (e.g., passive observation of public behavior) whose function is merely to provide students with practice in applying data collection techniques.

In addition to being ethically sound, this kind of policy also has a desirable educational spin-off. To comply with its requirements, instructors and students alike must familiarize themselves with the ethical requirements of research involving human subjects, particularly regarding the different levels of review associated with different kinds of research activities. Such issues typically receive too little attention, and too late. (Students often don't give ethics a thought until—surprise!—they learn they must have their dissertation proposals approved by the IRB.)

Insofar as more sophisticated and ethically complex research requires normal IRB review, this policy will no doubt inhibit instructors from encouraging and students from conducting such research. But this is not a bad thing, for students just learning to conduct research involving human subjects are the least prepared to grapple successfully with ethically complex situations that arise in the course of planning and carrying it out.

Conclusion

The general arguments of this article are not to likely endear us to educational researchers, particularly qualitative researchers who believe their methods and special problems are poorly understood by IRBs. We should make clear that we offer our arguments tentatively and with humility, not with the intent to inflame those who may substantially disagree with us. On the other hand, we wouldn't mind being responsible for providing the spark that might prompt more serious and sustained attention by both university IRBs and the educational research community to the issues we have raised—and to the ethics of educational research more generally.

Notes

The research on which this article is partially based was funded by the University of Colorado at Boulder Graduate School.

1. Stanley Milgram conducted a series of studies on obedience in which he deceived subjects into believing they were participating in the investigation of the relationship between punishment and learning (see, e.g., University of Pennsylvania, 1969). In one experimental situation, subjects communicated with a sham subject whom they could hear but not see. They were instructed to read a series of unrelated words to the sham subject, ask the sham subject to repeat the words, and administer an electric shock, which increased in severity, each time the sham subject responded incorrectly. Placed in front of the subjects was a board for administering the shocks (also a sham). It had a number of switches, ranging from low voltages to very high voltages that were accompanied by a warning that they shouldn't be used.

    As the sham subject responded incorrectly more and more, and the intensity of the (sham) shocks increased, he began to say ouch to protest that he wanted to stop, to claim he had a bad heart, and ultimately to fall silent. As these events unfolded, subjects began to protest that the experiment should stop, but a researcher (part of the sham) would insist that they continue, no matter what the (sham) subject did. A surprising number of subjects continued to administer what they believed to be real shocks until they reached the highest level, even after the sham subject had presumably been rendered unconscious if not dead.

    Milgram's studies are ethically objectionable (and would never be permitted today) for the extreme distress (if not permanent harm) experienced by subjects that resulted from the related actions of deceiving subjects, failing to obtain their informed consent, and refusing to permit them to withdraw from the research.

2. Paragraph 46.101(b)(2) singles out another variety of educational research as exempt: "Research involving use of *educational tests* (italics added). . . . if information taken from these sources is recorded in such a manner that subjects cannot be identified directly or through identifiers linked to the subjects." We have not included this exemption in our discussion because, at least at our university, it has not been an issue. This does not mean, of course, that it does not have the potential to raise serious ethical questions, particularly given the current clamor for more and more testing.

3. Our subsequent discussion of these issues depends heavily on an interview with Charles MacKay, former deputy director of the

Office for the Protection of Research Subjects (OPPR), as reported in Dougherty and Howe, 1990.

4. A review of this article suggested that this is probably the case. We have no reason to doubt this claim. Indeed, our IRB periodically distributes the *Human Research Report*, and the October 1991 issue is devoted to a discussion of the increasing scope of IRBs mandated by new federal regulations.

5. This is the kind of policy that has been adopted at the University of Colorado at Boulder (with the approval of the School of Education Faculty). It reads as follows:

    In order for a project involving educational research to be reviewed under the exempt category, the investigator must supply a letter from the appropriate school district official that certifies the project meets the following conditions:
    The research activities will:
    1. not differ in any significant ways from the normal range of activities of the classroom, school, or district
    2. involve only customary and noncontroversial instructional goals
    3. not deny any students educational benefits they would otherwise receive
    4. promise direct benefits (at least in the form of evaluative information) to the classroom, school, or district
    5. incorporate adequate safeguards to protect the privacy (i.e., anonymity or confidentiality) of all individuals who might be subjects of the research
    OR
    6. involve only existing data on students that is, or is to be rendered, non-identity specific.

6. We are familiar with two variants of this policy. Michigan State University employs a policy as roughly described in the body of this article, in which instructors are solely responsible for making the judgment of when student activities should be subject to IRB review. At the University of Colorado at Bolder, instructors collaborate with liaisons from the IRB in making these decisions.

References

Christakis, N. (1988). Should IRB's monitor research more strictly? *IRB: A Review of Human Subjects Research, 10*(2), 8–9.

Cornett, J., & Chase, S. (1989, March). *The analysis of teacher thinking and the problem of ethics: Reflections of a case study participant and a naturalistic researcher.* Paper presented at the Annual Meeting of the American Educational Research Association, San Francisco.

Dougherty, K., & Howe, K. (1990). *Policy regarding educational research: Report to the subcommittee on educational research of the human research committee* (unpublished manuscript).

Lincoln, Y. (1990). Toward a categorical imperative for qualitative research. In E. Eisner & A. Peshkin (Eds.), *Qualitative inquiry in education: The continuing debate* (pp. 277–295). New York: Teachers College Press.

McCarthy, C. (1983). Experiences with boards and commissions concerned with research ethics in the U.S. In K. Berg & K. Tranoy (eds.), *Research ethics* (pp. 111–123). New York: Liss.

Murphy, M., & Johannsen, A. (1990). Ethical obligations and federal regulations in ethnographic research and anthropological education. *Human Organization, 49*(2), 127–134.

Howe, K., & Eisenhart, M. (1990). Standards for qualitative (and quantitative) research: A prolegomenon. *Educational Researcher, 14*(8), 2–9.

Silva, M., & Sorrell, J. (1988). Enhancing comprehension of information for informed consent: A review of empirical research. *IRB: A Review of Human Subjects Research, 10*(1), 1–5.

Smith, L. (1990). Ethics in qualitative field research: An individual perspective. In E. Eisner & A. Peshkin (Eds.), *Qualitative inquiry in education: The continuing debate* (pp. 258–276). New York: Teachers College Press.

University of Pennsylvania. (1969). Obedience. Philadelphia: Author.

Veatch, R. (1977). Case studies in medical ethics. Harvard University Press: Cambridge, MA.

Received September 28, 1992
Revision received November 13, 1992
Accepted July 13, 1992

Standards of Evidence in Historical Research: How Do We Know When We Know?

Carl F. Kaestle

This article seeks to give a brief response to the question, how do historians know when they know something? The question involves ideas about certitude and truth, and most historians today would make very modest claims about certitude or truth in our statements about the past. Many would echo Charles Beard, who said sixty years ago, "We hold a damn dim candle over a damn dark abyss."[1] Today the historical profession is fragmented, ideologically diverse, and somewhat relativistic, a situation that is applauded by some and bemoaned by others.

It was not always so. Many of Beard's contemporaries embarked on a quest for objective knowledge. Peter Novick's recent book *That Noble Dream* charts the development of a "commitment to the reality of the past, and to truth as correspondence to that reality." To develop expertise, authority, and professional status, these historians of the early twentieth century ignored James, Dewey, Beard, and other troublesome relativists and established a standard of truth according to the "consensus of the competent." Objectivity became an ideal; ideology was eschewed.[2]

That commitment has been shaken in the past twenty years by forces within and outside of the discipline. In the wake of Thomas Kuhn's history, even the truths of the physical and biological sciences are seen as relative and impermanent, and the influential neo-pragmatist Richard Rorty says we must abandon "the neurotic Cartesian quest

Carl F. Kaestle is William F. Vilas Professor of Educational Policy Studies and History at the University of Wisconsin–Madison. An earlier version of this paper was given at a panel discussion, entitled "Standards of Evidence in Education Research," chaired by Professor Andrew Porter of the University of Wisconsin–Madison, held at the annual meeting of the American Educational Research Association in Boston, 19 April 1990.

From *History of Education Quarterly*, Fall 1992, pp. 361-366. © 1992 by *History of Education Quarterly*.

for certainty," and develop instead "standards relative to the changing purposes of disciplinary communities in changing circumstances."[3] The development of new subject matter, and with it new perspectives in women's history, minority history, radical history, and gay history, have further diversified the truths promoted in contemporary history. What's left? Are we all like Rorty's "cooperative freshman," who proclaims that contrary propositions are equally valid?[4] No, there is some sense of better and worse ways of arguing, more-viable and less-viable generalizations about the past. Where do historians turn for standards?

Because history does not have highly developed methodology around which there is consensus, and because historians are continually scavenging other disciplines for methods or theories, we might look to those external sources for guidance on the question, how do we know when we know? For example, some historians discovered computers and statistics twenty years ago, and started talking about R-squares and chi-squares. But do statistical procedures and standards of significance help us know when we know? Well, of course, when arguing about the statistical significance of some numbers, one has to adopt the standards of the discipline from which you have borrowed the method. But these measures of significance have only a peripheral role in answering the question of certitude in historical work, partly because only a small minority of historians use such techniques and partly because such standards of significance tell us little about the importance of the numbers or how to interpret them.

A second potential external source of standards of truth for historians is theories about social structure, social change, and human nature, whether from economics, sociology, political economy, or anthropology. At the crudest level, those few historians who might be doctrinaire disciples of an existing, comprehensive social theory already know the truth, or at least they know the important truths, before they begin. So, their honest answer to the question, how do we know when we know? would be: "We knew as soon as we persuaded ourselves of the truth of the governing body of the theory." Few historians in the United States use social theory in such a dogmatic way, and even in such ideologically regulated academic settings as the former Soviet Union, no truths were totally secure. A Soviet historians' joke said, "The future is certain; only the past is unpredictable."[5] At the other extreme, those who utterly reject social theory and treat history as mere chronicling nonetheless bring to their work implicit assumptions about the way the world works. Using theory more self-consciously and creatively, historians can create a dialog between it and their data, each informing the other. Social theories, then, can help us decide how to seek the

truth and can shape our answers. They do not (unless we use them like recipe books) answer the question, how do we know when we know?

A third potential external source for standards of truth in historical writing is the philosophy of history, a branch of philosophy pursued at every major research university and totally ignored by practicing historians. Bernard Bailyn went to a seminar on philosophy and history convened by Sidney Hook in 1962, and he said, "Let me put it bluntly. I have never once felt it necessary to work out precise answers to questions of objectivity and subjectivity, the nature of fact, etc.—in order to advance my work in history."[6] Working historians have other problems, said Bailyn, such as anomalies in existing data or discrepancies between data and existing explanations, or how to frame good historical problems, spot false questions, think creatively about what data is relevant, choose the right words for generalizations, and use metaphor appropriately in explanation. These problems are generally not in the province of philosophers of history.

Following Bailyn, I will answer the question, how do we know when we know? by looking internally at some historical work, taking examples from the history of literacy. What are the implicit standards that tell us when to accept a historical generalization?

First, we must define the question a little better. If the issue is certainty, we must ask: certainty about what kinds of issues, and certainty for whom? Regarding what kinds of issues we're talking about, it's not hard to get consensus on many low-level matters we call "factual," such as "Horace Mann was born in 1796 in Franklin, Massachusetts." The more certainty we have (collectively) about something historical, the more trivial it is likely to be. On the other hand, the more significant and interpretive the generalization, the less certain we will be about it. (Of this truth, by the way, I'm absolutely certain.)

Regarding the question, certainty for whom? historical truth is plural, relative, and tentative on issues of importance. If we drop the demand for unanimous assent, there are lots of historical truths around: Franklin Roosevelt was a great president; American civilization is superior; and slavery was the main cause of the Civil War (also, of course, those other truths: Franklin Roosevelt was a terrible president; American civilization is vicious; and slavery was not the main cause of the Civil War). The most popular answers to these kinds of questions may vary depending on the mood of the times, the best recent research, and other factors, but there will always be dissenters, because historical truths are social truths.

Now let me turn to some pragmatic work that illustrates some movement toward certitude in the history of literacy. There are two main approaches to the history of literacy. The first, starting around twenty-five years

ago, aimed to determine who was literate, who was illiterate, and to compare their characteristics, with some attention to the ideology of literacy and how it is acquired. This approach had matured by about five years ago. The methodological points had been argued and explored (for example, does signing a document equate with reading ability?); the questions had stabilized (for example, the relevance of religion, industrialization, and gender); and there had been much counterpoint between local and national studies. Thus, big syntheses like those of Harvey Graff and Rab Houston were made possible.[7]

We can use this initial body of work in the history of literacy to see how consensus was worked out on a particular issue, the relationship of literacy rates and industrialization. In a classic article on literacy in England from 1600 to 1900, Lawrence Stone pointed out that the industrial revolution of the late eighteenth and early nineteenth centuries began during a time of stagnant literacy rates. Not only did British industrialization take off during a lull in literacy growth, but the immediate local impact of industrialization upon education and literacy was negative.[8] This view was pressed by Michael Sanderson, who discovered declining school enrollment and literacy rates in industrializing Lancashire. Why? Because early factory work did not require literacy for most workers, and child labor interfered with education.[9] Reanalyzing the same data, Thomas Laqueur suggested that Sanderson's Lancashire decline could be attributed to massive population increases without adequate institutions for education; Laqueur attributed the reversal of the downtrend to schooling efforts arising from industrialization and urbanization.[10] From this debate began to emerge an understanding that although the long-run impact of industrialization on a region was to increase literacy, the short-run effect in factory towns was socially disruptive and inhibited the acquisition of literacy.

Evidence from other settings reinforced this picture. François Furet and Jacques Ozouf explored the relationship between literacy and industrialization in France, where the expansion of literacy ran very much along socially stratified lines and corresponded with the growth of the market economy. In general, towns had higher literacy rates, because they had concentrations of literate occupations and educating agencies. But the nineteenth century brought a decline in urban literacy, for the same reasons as in England. Furet and Ozouf distinguished between the higher-literacy, old, commercial towns and the lower-literacy, new, industrial towns."[11] Maris Vinovskis and I made similar findings for schooling in nineteenth-century Massachusetts.[12] The emerging picture, then, is one in which literacy is correlated with economic growth in a region but is depressed temporarily by industrialization. Rising literacy rates were associated with commerce, the professions, schooling, and gradual population concentration. But literacy rates were inhibited by child labor, rapid population growth, and the stresses of early industrialization. In short, literacy was boosted by the commercial aspects of urbanization, not the industrial aspects.[13]

The work on industrialization and literacy illustrates three ways in which progress toward viable generalizations can be made: first, there was a dialog between local and national studies, a dialog of micro- and macro-analysis; second, generalizations were developed that reconciled previously contradictory generalizations; and third, the results were confirmed by studies from different countries—a form of replication by comparative history.

Thus, the history of rudimentary literacy rates has matured and has produced some generalizations that seem to garner considerable consensus. The other, newer way to look at the history of literacy, is to explore the uses of literacy, to make the actors active, to connect readers and texts in history. This effort is messy, there are very faint borders around the subject, there is little literature on it, and the evidence is murky. But there are many scholars converging on the need for such work and on the basic concept of uniting readers and text in the history of literacy, as there are also in literary criticism, in reading research, and in communication research. In this kind of situation, with a relatively new, problematic line of inquiry, we need many little studies, innovations in methods, and much speculation about the relation of theory and historical research. Frustration can come from a sense of chaos and lack of motion. Bailyn's metaphor for it is a lot of horses pawing at the ground and not going anywhere yet. But it is a necessary stage, in which we set questions, agendas, share tentative hypotheses, and get ready to move.

After we get beyond this stage, we should be able to say, a few years from now, that some historical generalizations about the uses of literacy fit the evidence better than others. How will we know when we know? When things start falling into place according to the kind of internal and implicit standards of historical dialog that I mentioned: consonance of micro- and macro-levels of analysis, synthesis of contradictory claims, and reinforcement across regions or nations. Even then, of course, the answers will be impermanent, but by these standards, some answers are still better than others. Some give us a little better light for looking into the abyss.

Notes

1. Charles Beard, cited in a communication by Robert F. Smith, *American Historical Review* 94 (Oct. 1989): 1247.
2. Peter Novick, *That Noble Dream: The "Objectivity Question" and the American Historical Profession* (Cambridge, 1988), 1, 51.
3. Richard Rorty, cited in Novick, *Noble Dream,* 540–41.
4. Ibid.
5. Cited in Lawrence Levine, "The Unpredictable Past: Reflections on Recent American Historiography," *American Historical Review* 94 (June 1989): 671.
6. Bernard Bailyn, "The Problems of the Working Historian: A Comment," in *Philosophy and History: A Symposium,* ed. Sidney Hook (New York, 1963), 94.
7. Harvey Graff, *The Legacies of Literacy: Continuities and Contradictions in Western Culture and Society* (Bloomington, 1987); R. A. Houston, *Literacy in Early Modern Europe: Culture and Education, 1500–1800* (New York, 1988).
8. Lawrence Stone, "Literacy and Education in England, 1640–1900," *Past and Present 42* (1969): 69–139.
9. Michael Sanderson, "Literacy and Social Mobility in the Industrial Revolution in England," *Past and Present 56* (1972): 75–104.
10. Thomas W. Laqueur, "Literacy and Social Mobility in the Industrial Revolution," *Past and Present 64* (1974): 96–107.
11. François Furet and Jacques Ozouf, *Lire et Écrire: L'alphabetisation des francois de Calvin à Jules Ferry* (Paris, 1977), published in English as *Reading and Writing: Literacy in France from Calvin to Jules Ferry* (Cambridge, 1982).
12. Carl F. Kaestle and Maris A. Vinovskis, *Education and Social Change in Nineteenth-Century Massachusetts* (New York, 1980).
13. See Carl F. Kaestle et al., *Literacy in the United States: Readers and Reading since 1880* (New Haven, Conn., 1991), ch. 2.

Unit 3

Unit Selections

Key Points to Consider

❖ Outline the six stages in students' conceptions of the literature review. Which one best describes your current perspective on the process?

❖ What variables need to be considered before and while conducting a single-case study?

❖ What are the distinguishing characteristics of action research?

❖ Which practical issues concern teachers who are conducting classroom research?

Links

www.dushkin.com/online/

These sites are annotated on pages 4 and 5.

One of the most challenging questions confronting students of research is where to begin. As any research methods textbook will attest, researchers begin by closely examining the work of others, a process referred to as reviewing the literature. As Christine Bruce's research on graduate students suggests, a high-quality review of the relevant literature requires more than skimming a group of articles, taking notes, and writing a report. Students who review the literature gradually enter into the professional dialogue about their domains of interest in a deeper way as they gain experience as scholars. Then, Duane Lundervold and Marilyn Belwood's article reminds readers that, above all, research methods must be matched to research questions. They describe appropriate applications of single-case experimental design in the field of counseling. Often the questions that researchers raise have a practical side and they seek to render a decision based on carefully collected data that has important implications for a particular group in a particular context. That is where participatory action research, the topic of Paule McNicoll's article, comes in as he describes the challenges of teaching action-oriented research in the field of sociology. In the field of education, teachers are encouraged to become researchers in their own practice by becoming more thoughtful observers of learners and instructional practices. This topic is addressed by the fourth and final article, "Practical Issues for Teachers Conducting Classroom Research," co-authored by Marilyn Rousseau and Brian Kai Yung Tam.

Research Beginnings: Theoretical Bases and Question Formulation

RESEARCH STUDENTS' EARLY EXPERIENCES OF THE DISSERTATION LITERATURE REVIEW

ABSTRACT The phenomenon of a dissertation literature review is explored from a 'second-order' perspective. Writdten responses from 41 neophyte research scholars from various disciplines in an Australian university were gathered in response to two questions: 'What do you mean when you use the words "literature review"?' and 'What is the meaning of a literature review for your research?' A phenomenographic analysis identified six conceptions, or ways of experiencing, literature reviews: literature review as a list, literature review as a search, literature review as a survey, literature review as a vehicle for learning, literature review as a research facilitator, and literature review as a report. The conceptions represent differing relations between student researchers and the literature. The range of conceptions suggests that the supervisors of postgraduates and other teachers interested in the literature review process need to accept literature reviews as a problem area for students and develop strategies to help them.

By *CHRISTINE SUSAN BRUCE,* Queensland University of Technology

Introduction

Literature reviews are a long-standing tradition in research and scholarship. Despite the abundance of examples of literature reviews, definitions of the phenomenon are scarce and little research has been done into aspects of the genre itself. Cooper (1988, p. 107) comes closest to providing a definition which covers all styles of literature review:

> First, a literature review uses as its database reports of primary or original scholarship, and does not report new primary scholarship itself. The primary reports used in the literature may be verbal, but in the vast majority of cases reports are written documents. The types of scholarship may be empirical, theoretical, critical/analytic, or methodological in nature. Second, a literature review seeks to describe, summarise, evaluate, clarify and/or integrate the content of primary reports.

Cooper (1988, p. 109) also outlines a taxonomy according to which literature reviews may be defined in terms of their focus, goals, perspectives, coverage, organisation and audience.

At the university in which this research was conducted, as in many others, learning to review the literature receives different emphases in different courses depending upon the importance it is accorded by individual lecturers and course co-ordinators. As may be expected, this is the case in both undergradu-

ate and postgraduate contexts. When students enter a postgraduate research programme, their exposure to the nature, process and purposes of a literature review is, therefore, likely to vary. Nevertheless, most students undertaking higher degree research are confronted with having to complete a literature review as a significant component of their research. Typically, the literature review forms an important chapter in the thesis, where its purpose is to provide the background to and justification for the research undertaken. Where the style of the thesis permits, sections of the literature review may appear in different chapters. In both these cases, examiners of the thesis will normally expect that the thesis will demonstrate a competent accomplishment of a literature review. The importance of the literature review is reinforced by Nightingale (1984, p. 144) who, in recommending alternative styles of presentation of postgraduate research, indicates that the work should be accompanied by a literature review.

Research manuals for postgraduate students provide them with a range of orientations to the literature review. It is variously described as "an interpretation and synthesis of published research" (Merriam, 1988, p. 6), a research project in its own right (Brent, 1986, p. 137), and "a task that continues throughout the duration of the thesis" (Anderson et al., 1970, p. 17). The latter point out that it "shows how the problem under investigation relates to previous research". Leedy (1989, p. 66) stresses the function of literature reviews as being to "look

From *Studies in Higher Education*, Vol. 19, Issue 2, 1994, pp. 217-230. © 1994 by Taylor & Francis Ltd., P.O. Box 25, Abingdon, Oxfordshire, OX14 3UE, England. Reprinted by permission.

again at the literature... in... an area not necessarily identical with, but collateral to, your own area of study". Borg & Gall (1989, p. 114) write:

> the review of the literature involves locating, reading and evaluating reports of research as well as reports of casual observation and opinion that are related to... the planned project. It is aimed at obtaining a detailed knowledge of the topic being studied.

In view of the guidance provided in research handbooks, literature reviews in the context of postgraduate study may be defined in terms of process and product. The process involves the researcher in exploring the literature to establish the status quo, formulate a problem or research enquiry, to defend the value of pursuing the line of enquiry established, and to compare the findings and ideas of others with his or her own. The product involves the synthesis of the work of others in a form which demonstrates the accomplishment of the exploratory process. Ultimately, the intention of writing the review is to "demonstrate a professional grasp of the background theory" (Phillips & Pugh, 1987, p. 53) to the student's research. Extrapolating this definition from research manuals available to students does not, however, provide insights into their interpretations of this phenomenon. The range of available approaches in fact suggests that research students are likely to have varying understandings and experiences of the literature review.

This paper reports a phenomenographic exploration of students' conceptions of a literature review in the context of an information skills subject for higher degree students offered by the university library. As co-ordinator of this subject I adopted the approach that students working on a literature review should engage in exploring, discussing and challenging their own conceptions of this phenomenon. The phenomenographic approach was chosen as its interest is in the qualitatively different ways in which a phenomenon is experienced, rather than in the nature of the phenomenon itself.

Research Method

The phenomenographic approach is used in this study to identify the qualitatively different ways in which research students experience the literature review. Phenomenography as a research approach evolved out of an interest in describing phenomena as seen, experienced or understood by individuals (Marton, 1981, 1986). "The basic idea of phenomenography is that each phenomenon can be experienced or conceptualised in a limited number of qualitatively different ways, and it is the task of phenomenography to map

these understandings" (Marton, 1988, p. 196). The approach, developed by Marton and others at the University of Gothenburg, Sweden, has been adopted by educational researchers elsewhere, particularly in Britain and Australia. In recent years it has led to the espousal of 'phenomenographic pedagogy', which is "concerned with ways of facilitating conceptual change by the learner in context" (Bowden, 1990, p. 1).

Most phenomenographic research has involved investigating conceptions of phenomena in an academic discipline, or academic tasks such as learning and essay writing. Until now investigations have also concentrated on learners in schools and undergraduate courses. Others have explored conceptions in a community setting. This study extends the interest of phenomenographic research into the arena of postgraduate study and supervision. The research techniques adopted in this study, and described below, are guided by strategies recommended by Marton & Saljo (1984) and Saljo (1988).

The Students

The 41 participants were students engaged in higher degree research at an Australian university. All students were participating in a semester-long subject, which I both co-ordinated and taught, designed to assist them with information retrieval and management. They attended classes for the subject in groups of approximately 12. Masters and doctoral candidates enrolled in research and course work degrees formed the core of the overall group, although a few students in the honours year participated also. Some students were at the beginning stages of their research. Others had been working for a little more than 6 months. Subject areas represented included information systems, public health, architecture, genetic engineering, biology, nursing, engineering, geology and education.

Eliciting Students' Conceptions

As the motivation for this research was the improvement of student learning, 'data gathering' was integrated into teaching-learning processes. To introduce the subject I asked students to reflect upon their understanding of a literature review. They did this by responding to two questions: 'What do you mean when you use the words "literature review"?' and 'What is the meaning of a literature review for your research?' Following open-ended writing in response to the above questions, students discussed with each other their interpretations of the literature review. Their written responses then formed the data from which the students' conceptions of a literature review were derived.

The above questions were chosen as a result of a pilot study which indicated the need for direct questions about the nature of a literature review. Indirect questions trialled during the pilot resulted in students asking me 'What is a literature review?' The questions used, therefore, were direct, non-technical and open-ended as is usual in phenomenographic research. This type of question allows respondents to choose the way in which they structure their response. The questions are also intended to be analogous to Saijo's "What do you mean by learning?" (Saljo, 1979, p. 445).

Analysis involved interpretation of students' writing to uncover conceptions of the literature review, thus revealing qualitatively different ways in which they experienced a literature review. The 'way of proceeding' advocated by Marton & Saijo (1984) was adhered to, to ensure that conceptions were allowed to emerge from the data rather than being imposed upon it. The cases, or units for analysis, were sections of writing rather than individual students, meaning that at times more than one conception is evident in the discourse of one individual. The outcome of the analysis is a series of categories of description, each of which represents a conception.

Verifying the Categories of Description

To check the soundness of the categories created to describe the conceptions, a colleague classified students' responses using a procedure similar to that reported by Renstrom et al. (1990, p. 557). Before consultation between the two 'judges' about how students' writing should be classified, agreement was achieved in 34 of the 41 cases. This represents a consensus of 83.5%. Agreement was reached in all but two cases after discussion of the contentious extracts. This represents a post-consultation consensus of 95%. Saljo (1988) indicates that "in most cases, the inter-judge consensus is between 80 and 90%". In the two cases where uncertainty remained in the minds of the coders, this was due to ambiguity in the students' writing.

Saljo (1988, p. 46) suggests other strategies for verifying the categories including:

- comparison with other studies, (which I have taken to mean other writing about the phenomenon);
- the possibility of describing learning, in this case about the literature review, as a change from the one conception to another; and
- the possibility of constructing an 'outcome space' which is a diagrammatic representation of the logical relations between the categories.

The results of this study meet all these criteria.

Six Conceptions of a Literature Review

Students' writing about the literature review, even in the early stages of reviewing the data, suggested qualitatively different ways of understanding the phenomenon. Take, for example, the following extracts:

Literature review–to obtain more knowledge regarding:

- anatomy
- physiology
- pathology
- technique in scanning
- usefulness in type of examination...

With regard to my research the literature review is being done to increase my knowledge of the subject as in what is known of the physiological development of the vessels, disease processes, what conditions affect the vessels' well being, what medical techniques are used in improving the vessels... (Transcript 2)

Transcript 2, above, focuses on the potential of the literature to add to the students' knowledge base. Transcript 3, below, however, goes beyond this to focus on the value of the literature review in guiding and justifying the students' research:

Literature review provides an introduction and justification for the purpose of your study. Introduction to the subject area by researching what materials/resources/articles are relevant to your topic. The literature review also provides an overview of what has been studied... the review of the more recent material can provide valuable guidelines for the purpose of your study, for example using information reviewed, then your study may be an extension in the field... The l.r. is important for providing a basis for justifying your research area, based on conclusions made by previous researchers... (Transcript 3)

A recursive analysis of the data led to the emergence of six qualitatively different ways in which the literature review was experienced. It was variously experienced or understood as a listing of pertinent literature, as a search for information, as a survey of the discipline's knowledge base, as a vehicle for learning, as a research facilitator and as a report. Each of the conceptions is amplified in the following categories of description.

In the categories of description each conception may also be seen to have a referential and a structural aspect. The referential aspect, that is, the meaning of the conception, is denoted by the category name and the statement of the terms in which the literature review is seen or understood. The structural aspect, that is, the way in which the conception is formed, is identified in the statement of what the student researcher is focusing on. It is the particular act of focusing which in fact makes the referential aspect of the conception possible. For example, in the 'literature review as a search' conception it is the focus on the act of looking for literature which leads to the experienced meaning of a literature review as a search. In the 'literature review as research facilitator' conception, however, the focus of attention is the student's research which leads to the experienced meaning of the literature review as a research facilitator. Finally, sample quotes from students' writing illustrate each conception. (The numbers in brackets indicate the transcript from which each quote was taken.)

The Literature Review as a List

In this conception the literature review is seen/understood as a listing/collection of items representing the literature of the subject. The student researcher's focus is on discrete items, journal articles, books, newspapers. The list may include one or more elements of a bibliographic citation, a description of each item (critical or non-critical), relevant keywords and journals.

> Keywords to be used in the search should also be included. Any journals that are particularly useful should be noted. These could be monitored for future developments. (5)

> Items included in the review can be general or specific, theoretic or applications. (12)

> The list of articles includes the authors' names and year of publication as well as a concise summary of the main points of the research article. (22)

> Includes journal articles, books, newspapers, conference reports, statistics. (25)

The Literature Review as a Search

In this conception the literature review is seen/understood as the process of identifying relevant information/literature. The student researcher's focus is on the act of finding or looking for literature which may involve going through a source of some kind (e.g. journal article, indexing data bases) to identify useful information.

> Locating articles about the same topic. (14)

> I... wish to do a broad search in a specific area..., and a narrow search in other areas, where particular issues are important. (17)

> It involves a broad search of the literature in a particular area and/or a related area. (26)

> Finding information on your topic area. (30)

> Provides other important sources of information to pursue in the form of bibliographies. (38)

The Literature Review as a Survey

In this conception the literature review is seen/understood as an investigation of past and present writing or research in one or more areas of interest. The student researcher's focus is on the literature, the knowledge base or discourse of the discipline(s) including research methodologies. This investigation of the literature may be active (critical/analytical) or passive (non-critical/descriptive).

> A survey of disciplines involved in my research topic. (1)

> The information reviewed gives you a total scan of the area. (3)

> A search of the relevant scientific works to establish what has been already done in the research area. (9)

> Need to see what's been written about computational aspects in this field. (12)

> The review of literature can help obtain the current level of knowledge in a particular field. In addition forward thinking and hypotheses are put into print and give the reader the opportunity to consider the opinions and research of others. (17)

The Literature Review as a Vehicle for Learning

In this concept the literature review is seen/understood as having an impact on the researcher. The student researcher's focus is on his or her gain in knowledge or understanding which is derived from reading the literature. There may be an element of using the literature as a sounding board for checking ideas or testing personal perceptions.

> Increase personal interest in subject area. (25)

> Gaining a thorough understanding of the subject. (29)

> Provide background knowledge on the topic when the research is first being undertaken. (33)

> The literature review is being done to increase my knowledge of the subject. (2)

The Literature Review as a Research Facilitator

In this conception the literature review is seen/understood as relating specifically to the research being, or about to be, undertaken. The research student's focus is on his or her research in one or more of its various stages, from identifying a topic, supporting a methodology, providing a context, to changing the direction of the research. The literature review is conceived as supporting, influencing, directing, shaping or changing the student's research.

> The literature review is important for providing a basis for justifying your research, based on conclusions made by previous researchers. (3)

> Search for inspiration. (6)

> The literature review gives direction in a chosen topic and can introduce methods of data measurement and reduction which you can utilise. (8)

> Helps refine research questions. (21)

> Work by other researchers to provide a jumping board for own research, relevant overlapping work, ideas to incorporate into own work. (24)

The Literature Review as a Report

In this conception the literature review is seen/understood as a written discussion of the literature drawing on investigations previously undertaken. The research student's focus is on framing a written discourse about the literature which may be established as a component part of a thesis or other research report.

> Finally it becomes a product which is incorporated into a lot of other text. It must have a place there. It must have something to contribute to the final report of the research I am doing. (16)

> I consider the literature review to be the scholarship section of the thesis, and as such should reflect a competent refraining of literature on a topic. (20)

> For my research all of the above was covered... the topic was subdivided into five subtopics. Three of the subtopics were similarly subdivided. (32)

> Thus a literature review need not be a lengthy dialogue of what has previously been written, yet be an overview pointing out the important facts. (48)

The Outcome Space

Logical relationships between the six categories describing students' early experiences of the literature review may be depicted in an outcome space (see Fig. 1). An outcome space in phenomenographic research is a graphic depiction of the logical relations between the 'outcomes' of the research, that is, the categories of description. It is a pictorial representation of the "space over which the students' thoughts ranged" (Renstrom et al., 1990, p. 558). Saljo (1988, p. 44) conjures the picture of a "map of territory in terms of which we can interpret how people conceive of a reality".

The outcome space of research students' conceptions of a literature review schematises further the differences noted in the categories of description. It shows that the survey incorporates both the list and search conceptions, and that the vehicle for learning and research facilitator conceptions go beyond the notion of a survey. Finally, the report conception, whilst incorporating the other conceptions, represents a synthesis of understandings derived through the earlier conceptions.

The phenomenon of the literature review can also be understood in terms of varying relations between the student researcher and the literature. Therefore, the outcome space also depicts the varying relations between the student researcher and the literature. These 'relations' are described in terms of direct and indirect interaction with the literature. Thus, the list and search conceptions represent 'indirect interaction', meaning that the researcher is working with an item belonging to the class of tertiary sources which represent the primary literature, for example, bibliographic citations or an indexing and abstracting service. The remaining conceptions, on the other hand, represent 'direct interaction', meaning that the researcher is working with source material, rather than, for example, a representative abstract. The logic relating each category in the outcome space is summarised below.

FIG. 1. Outcome space of conceptions as a literature review.

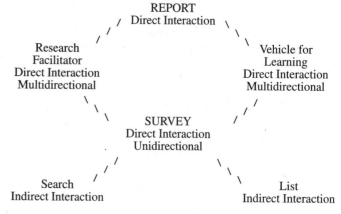

Literature review as a list. In this conception there is no direct interaction between the student researcher and the literature. The primary focus is on the listing rather than on the knowledge contained within the literature represented; therefore the relation between the student and the literature is indirect.

Literature review as a search. In this conception the interaction between the student researcher and the literature is also indirect. The researcher focuses on the literature search process. Source materials act as an intermediary directing the researcher towards or providing an awareness of existing literature.

Literature review as a survey. In this conception the interaction between the student researcher and the literature shifts from indirect to direct in that the student's focus is on the literature, with his/her interest centred on the knowledge base of the discipline. The interaction is, however, unidirectional in that the student's attention is towards and remains with the literature. In the following conceptions, which are described as 'multidirectional', the student's attention moves beyond the literature.

Literature review as a vehicle for learning. In this conception the interaction between the student researcher and the literature is also direct. However, the student's focus is beyond the literature and on his or her personal development. Here the interaction is multidirectional in that the literature is also actively influencing the researcher. There is, however, no influence on the research project.

Literature review as a research facilitator. In this conception the interaction between the researcher and the literature is also direct. It differs from 'vehicle for learning' in that a different dimension is added to the impact of the literature. The impact of the literature moves beyond influencing the researcher to have an impact on the research project. Thus both this and the 'vehicle for learning conception' are more advanced than the survey conception whilst continuing to incorporate it.

Literature review as a report. In this conception the interaction between researcher and the literature remains direct. The interaction is, however, terminal, in that it finally ceases to shape the research or expand the personal horizons of the researcher. The report is not only a synthesis of literature relevant to the research, it is a final representation of interaction with the literature.

Discussion of Results

Students' views of a dissertation literature review upon entering a course of higher degree research cannot be taken for granted. In particular, it cannot be assumed that there are common understandings of this aspect of research amongst students. This sug-

gests that supervisors must be alert to possible variations in students' thinking about literature reviews and explore these with them. It may be useful to share the conceptions identified here, to introduce students to a range of ways of interpreting their literature review and to help them move towards experiences and understandings appropriate to their own research context.

The six conceptions identified in this study may be described as being progressively more encompassing. Each of the conceptions subsume those on lower levels of the outcome space. For example, an education student who holds the 'facilitator' conception continues to accept that the experience of the literature review as a survey is an essential part of the process:

To me a literature review is a survey of disciplines involved in my research to find out the historical and present day (and possibly future) directions. Thinking about it–it puts my research in its proper context–helps me find a suitable topic and to decide if it's worth pursuing... (Transcript 1)

It is also likely that it is through holding the higher level conceptions that the other ways of experiencing the literature review become more meaningful and manageable. It would, therefore, be important to encourage students to adopt the higher level conceptions of the six described, that is the literature review as an opportunity for learning, as a research facilitator and as a report.

The 'list', 'search' and 'survey' conceptions are inadequate for a student if he or she is to complete a review which demonstrates "a fully professional grasp of the background theory" (Phillips & Pugh, 1987, p. 53). These authors also explicitly state "It is important to emphasise that a mere encyclopedic listing in which all the titles are presented with only a description of each work and no reasoned organisation and evaluation would not be adequate". Nevertheless this view was elaborated by a student of mathematics who was experiencing the literature review as a list:

A list of articles relevant to the topic being researched. This should be in the form of a bibliography so that dates, authors and titles can be readily examined. Keywords to be used in the search should also be included. Any journals that are particularly useful should be noted. These could be monitored for future developments...

A literature review would contain a list of current articles, with bibliographic details, a list of keywords that could be used for searching, a list of journals that are particularly concerned with covering a topic. (Transcript 5)

Such a conception may be a function of the early stages of research work where students are often engaged in gathering citations, collecting articles and creating bibliographies or annotated bibliographies. This means that students' thinking needs to be challenged as early as possible in their research programme so that it is clear that the final product of the literature review is a coherent synthesis of past and present research. It is not a list or annotated bibliography on the area of interest, although these may represent early stages in progress towards the end product.

Students consider both the literature search and writing as simply different aspects of the same phenomenon. The search conception is integral to the overall experience of the literature review. In fact, Cooper (1989) argues that a literature review should contain a clear statement of the search processes undertaken. However, the search needs to be experienced as subservient to the more advanced conceptions such as 'learning', 'research facilitator' and 'report'. The search, and also the survey experience, need to be seen as both contributing to the research being undertaken and being directed by the tentative parameters of the research problem.

The three higher level conceptions, therefore, are closer to what a supervisor might wish the student to move towards. The literature review as a vehicle for learning' was not uncommon amongst students across a range of disciplines, but is rare in the literature. In the form in which it is represented here, however, it is difficult to discern much about how students are conceiving learning. Students seem to be primarily concerned with themselves, and their knowledge, rather than with their research. These students wish "to obtain more knowledge regarding anatomy, physiology, etc." (Transcript 2) or "to understand the dimensions of a subject" (Transcript 35).

The role of the literature review as a 'research facilitator' is frequently cited in the literature and lends itself to moving towards a synthesis of the state of the art, and a justification of the research to hand as associated with the report conception. The report conception of the literature review ideally represents the synthesis of the content of literature in the field, and the earlier experiences the researcher has engaged in.

Students' conceptions are not new in that they are all reflected in the literature to varying degrees. They are, however, somewhat impoverished in that the little theory existing about literature reviews is not reflected in students' experience. Aspects of Cooper's taxonomy (Cooper, 1988, 1989), the computer-assisted literature review (Brent, 1986), integrative reviews (Jackson, 1980) and meta-analysis (Glass, 1976) are nowhere present in their writing. Students also need to attain significant shifts in understanding

in order to conceive of the literature review as a tool for demonstrating a "professional grasp of background theory" (Phillips & Pugh, 1987). Inherent limits in students' conceptions may be due to the early stages of postgraduate study represented by the participants. However, some of the participants in this research have been studying for more than 6 months and others are working on a second higher degree.

Because this study does not trace changes in students' conceptions during their progress it is unclear whether unfolding experience is sufficient to trigger shifts to more sophisticated conceptions. The extent to which supervisory intervention may also be required is therefore also uncertain. However, many supervisors will wish to ensure that students learn to conceive of or experience the literature review in a way which will ensure that they gain maximum benefit from their experience. My own experience, outside the confines of this study, suggests intervention is often necessary. Students can proceed a number of years into higher degree study without understanding the nature or role of a literature review. This may be due to the writing of a literature review not falling within their thesis requirements, or to a reluctance on the student's part to face the psychological barrier of writing. One student commented that "the writing up of the literature review seems very daunting".

These observations have been corroborated by supervisors from faculties of education and humanities who have given me anecdotal feedback on their own experiences with students. One observed that a student who had not been working at an acceptable standard on her literature review expressed surprise when, at the thesis presentation stage, she finally understood that her literature review comprised a significant section of her thesis. Another supervisor has indicated to me that in his experience many students, even upon completion of a doctoral thesis, have not attained high levels of achievement with respect to their literature review. It is likely that students do not achieve adequately in this area because they have inadequate understandings of what actually constitutes a literature review.

Supervisors have a responsibility to clarify their own conceptions of a literature review and to guide their students' understandings of this part of the research process. It is more important that they adopt this role than they meet students' expectation in providing personal contacts and important references. Marton & Ramsden (1988, p. 26) suggest a range of strategies for assisting students to change their conceptions of a phenomenon, including making students' conceptions explicit to them. Students could also be introduced to the idea of reflecting on the 'state' of their literature review, using the various conceptions as a framework. They could systematically ask themselves, from time to time, questions founded on each conception, such as:

- What is the present state of my list of references? Is it up to date in my areas of present interest? Is it adequate?
- What literature searching have I done this fortnight? Are there any new areas that I have become interested in which I may need to search on?
- What have I read recently? Have I found time to read recently?
- What have I learned from the literature this fortnight? Have I changed, in any way, my understanding of the area in which I am working?
- Is what I have read going to influence my research in any way? Has it given me any ideas which I need to consider and incorporate?
- Have I been writing about what I have read? Do I need to reconsider how what I have been reading fits into my research?

Conclusions

This study has investigated a broad interdisciplinary picture of research students' early conceptions of a literature review. The results suggest that students' conceptions may not always be the most productive in the early stages of their research. How this matter could be addressed where similar problems are encountered requires further investigation. A comparison with the existing literature about literature reviews, despite its limited nature, also suggests that students' experiences of the literature review are somewhat impoverished.

Further research is also required to identify distinctive conceptions within particular discipline areas. Because this study was 'interdisciplinary' it has not investigated qualitatively different conceptions held by students in individual discipline areas. It may be that individual disciplines may have ways of seeing the literature review which differ from those of other disciplines. Scientists and applied scientists, for example, may hold conceptions which differ from those of social scientists.

The literature review is but one of many facets of the research process which postgraduate students need to master. Focusing on their understanding of different facets of the research process may assist in both improving the calibre of the research students as well as reducing completion times and drop-out rates. Applying the principles of 'phenomenographic pedagogy' to this area of postgraduate study and supervision will help students gain maximum benefit from their experience.

REFERENCES

ANDERSON, J., DURSTON, B & POOLE, M. (1970) Thesis and Assignment Writing (Brisbane, Wiley).
BORG, W.R. & GALL, M.D. (1989) Educational Research: an introduction, 5th edn (New York, Longman).
BOWDEN, JOHN A. (1990) Curriculum development for conceptual change learning: a phenomenographic pedagogy, Occasional Paper 90.3 (RMIT, Victoria University of Technology, Educational Research and Development Unit).
BENT, E.E. (1986) The computer-assisted literature review, Computers and the Social Sciences, 2, pp. 137-151.
COOPER, H.M. (1988) The structure of knowledge synthesis, Knowledge in Society, 1, pp. 104-126.
COOPER, H.M. (1989) Integrating Research: a guide for literature reviews, 2nd edn (Newbury Park, CA, Sage).
GLASS, G.V. (1976) Primary, secondary and meta-analysis research, Educational Researcher, 5(10), pp. 3-8.
JACKSON, G. (1980) Methods for integrative reviews, Review of Educational Research, 50(3), pp. 438-460.
LEEDY, P. (1989) Practical Research: planning and design, 4th edn (New York, Macmillan).
MARTON, F. (1981) Phenomenography: describing conceptions of the world around us, Instructional Science, 10, pp. 177-200.
MARTON, F. (1986) Phenomenography–a research approach to investigating different understandings of reality, Journal of Thought, 21(5), pp. 28-49.
MARTON, F. (1988) Phenomenography–exploring different conceptions of reality, in: D. FETTERMAN (Ed.) Qualitative Approaches to Evaluation in Education (New York, Praeger).
MARTON, F. & RAMSDEN, P. (1988) What does it take to improve learning? in: P. RAMSDEN (Ed.) Improving Learning: new perspectives (London, Kogan Page).
MARTON, F. & SALJO, R. (1984) Approaches to learning, in: F. MARTON, D. HOUNSELL & N. ENTWISTLE (Eds) The Experience of Learning (Edinburgh, Scottish Academic Press).
MERRIAM, S.B. (1988) Case Study Research in Education: a qualitative approach (San Francisco, CA, Jossey-Bass).
NIGHTINGALE, P. (1984) Examination of research theses, Higher Education Research and Development, 3(2), pp. 137-150.
PHILLIPS, E.M. & PUGH, D.S. (1987) How to Get a PhD (Milton Keynes, Open University Press).
RENSTROM, L, ANDERSSON, B. & MARTON, F. (1990) Students' conceptions of matter, Journal of Educational Psychology, 82(3), pp. 555-569.
SALJO, R. (1979) Learning about learning, Higher Education, 8, pp. 443-451.
SALJO, R. (1988) Learning in educational settings: methods of enquiry, in: P. RAMSDEN (Ed.) Improving Learning: new perspectives (London, Kogan Page).

Correspondence: Christine Susan Bruce, School of Social, Business and Environmental Education, Queensland University of Technology, Kelvin Grove Campus, Victoria Park Road, Locked Bag No. 2, Red Hill, Queensland 4059, Australia.

THE BEST KEPT SECRET IN COUNSELING: SINGLE-CASE (N=1) EXPERIMENTAL DESIGNS

By Duane A. Lundervold and Marilyn F. Belwood

Counselor education has been repeatedly faulted for failing to adequately train counselors in research methodology, generally, and practice-relevant methods, specifically. Continued emphasis and education in the use of group experimental design methodology, which is by definition insensitive to the exigencies of everyday practice, will have little effect on counseling practice. It is ironic that single-case (N = 1) design developed for use in practice settings continues to be the "best kept secret" in counseling. Single-case (N = 1) designs offer a scientifically credible means to objectively evaluate practice and conduct clinically relevant research in practice settings. A 7-component model for establishing the use of single-case design research methods in counseling programs is presented.

As recent evidence attests, there is agreement that several problems related to training in research methodology exist in counselor education (Fong & Malone, 1994; Garcia, 1995; Hashmond, 1994; Heppner, Carter, et al., 1992; Woolsey, 1989). The conclusions are that (a) counselors are ill-prepared to conduct research; (b) the research methods taught are irrelevant to practice settings, thus contributing to the ever-growing gap between research and practice; (c) skills in conducting research and objectively evaluating treatment outcomes are antithetical to the "helping" profession of counseling; (d) the problem resides in who teaches research methodology; and (e) the content of the research methods course is the culprit.

A number of proposals have aimed at addressing these weaknesses in training. These include preconvention workshops on research methods, calls for methodological diversity, altering curricula to enable counselors-in-training to be consumers of research, increasing research involvement of students, and having counseling faculty teach research methods courses (Council for Accreditation of Counseling and Related Educational Programs [CACREP], 1994; Garcia, 1995; Heppner, Carter et al., 1992; Heppner, Kivlighan, & Wampold, 1992; Robinson, 1994). Still, problems remain with respect to increasing the relevance and integrity of research training in counseling. Counseling's historical tradition of equating research methods with group experimental design and statistical analysis is an overly narrow research approach with little direct relevance to practice settings. Improving education and training in group experimental design methodology will continue to have little impact on practitioner behavior in practice settings, because counselors frequently work with individual clients who have unique problems with living. Until education and training in counseling focus on instruction in practice-relevant evaluation and research methods, counselors-in-preparation and practitioners will continue to be hampered intellectually and pragmatically.

Group experimental design methodology by definition is insensitive to the exigencies of everyday practice. Although group experimental design methodology is appropriate for technique testing, counseling practice is primarily concerned with the development of techniques that are effective for the individual case or technique building. Consequently, it is ironic that a research methodology, single-case (N = 1) design, developed for use in practice settings and capable of evaluating counseling process, evaluating counseling intervention outcomes, and demonstrating experimental control, continues to be the "best kept secret" in counseling. In this article, we discuss historical and contemporary contextual factors that need to be addressed with respect to teaching students research methods that

From Journal of Counciling and Development, Winter 2000, pp. 92-103. ©2000 by the American Counciling Association. Reprinted by permission.

bridge the research-practice gap. Next, a brief summary of the critical features, single-case (N = 1) designs, and analysis of data are presented. We end with some clinical case examples and a description of a seven-component model for establishing the use of single-case design methods in counseling.

HISTORICAL AND CONTEMPORARY CONTEXTUAL FACTORS

There are many objections to conducting research in counseling. Some counseling professionals have suggested that counseling is an expressive act of caring and that the counseling process is its own justification or that counseling is an "art form" that defies scientific analysis. In either case, empirical evaluation is precluded (Halmos, 1966; Storr, 1990). Similarly, others have suggested that it is simply not possible to define and quantify the processes and outcomes of counseling and that doing so results in distortion of information and the counselor-client relationship (Ruckdeschel & Farris, 1982; Saleeby, 1979).

If one eschews the scientific method as a way of knowing, then appeals to intuition, authority, and tenacity serve as alternate ways of knowing and are used to make decisions affecting clients (Buchler, 1955). Such traditional methods of decision making are collectively known as "clinical judgment." Research over the past 45 years has shown that such methods of evaluation suffer from serious problems of reliability and validity (e.g., Arkes, 1981; Chapman & Chapman, 1967; Garb, 1998; Meehl, 1954; Nisbett & Ross, 1980). Moreover, in the present context, this method of evaluating progress and client outcome in practice settings is likely to carry little weight. Faith that change will (has) occur(red) is no longer a substitute for accountability in behavioral health care services because practitioners are now responsible for providing objective evidence on counseling outcomes on a case-by-case basis (Browning & Browning, 1994; Giles, 1993; Todd, 1994). Single-case designs provide a quantitative, objective, inferential aid on which evidence-based clinical decision making may occur, thus delimiting the bias and inaccuracy of decisions based solely on clinical judgment (Garb, 1998).

The scientific method as a way of knowing is applicable to the practice of counseling. Unfortunately, group experimental design and related statistical analyses, which are not directly relevant to everyday practice, have been the primary research methods taught in counselor education. Such approaches rely on large sample sizes, random assignment, fixed research protocols, and the use of inferential statistics to determine statistically significant differences between groups on mean scores of dependent variables. The application of group research designs is seldom possible in clinical settings for a number of reasons, including the fact the most counselors frequently work with one individual at a time. As the inclusionary criteria for participation in the research narrows, the gap between research and practice grows and the problem of external validity is enhanced. Use of heterogeneous groups increases the likelihood of failing to reject the null hypothesis, that is, obtaining nonsignificant results. Widening the gap further is the lack of research directly relevant to effective counseling intervention for the individual case. A group mean score does not represent the individual case. It is not surprising, then, that research is viewed with scorn, deemed irrelevant to practice, believed to be only conducted by academics who are "far from the trenches" (and are in it only for the purposes of getting tenure), and consequently is described as irrelevant by students, faculty, and counseling practitioners (Gelso, 1979; Heppner, Kivlighan, et al., 1992).

What has been lacking in counselor education and training is instruction in an existing research methodology capable of scientific inquiry yet flexible enough to be used in practice settings: single-case (N = 1) research design. It has been suggested that a diversity of research methods be taught to counselors, yet on closer scrutiny the diversity discussed is restricted to diversity of group design methods (Garcia, 1995).

Our analysis suggests that the failure to use single-case research design methods is due to traditional views of scientific methodology being equated with group experimental design, a lack of understanding of the contributions of group and N = 1 design methodologies, ways of knowing, and the inherent irrelevance of group experimental methods to clinical practice settings. Counselors need scientific methods that are directly applicable to practice settings and that can be used with a single individual or group. Single-case (N = 1) research designs are amenable to such a task (Bloom, Fischer, & Orme, 1995; Kazdin & Tuma, 1982). Instruction of students and practitioners in the use of single-case research design and statistical tests used with such designs as needed provides a scientifically acceptable and clinically feasible method of demonstrating the effectiveness and validity of counseling and the means for incorporating the scientific method into day-to-day counseling practice (Heppner, Kivlighan, et al., 1992). Given the contingencies of practice and disaffection with current instructional models, the time is ripe for counseling to lead the way in the application of practice-based research and evaluation methods using single-case designs.

SINGLE-CASE (N = 1) DESIGN

Single-case (N = 1) experimental design, a methodology in which information on a single individual or several individuals is obtained concurrently, has been specifically developed for use in practice settings (Barlow & Hersen, 1984; Bloom et al., 1995). A more general term, single-system design, encompasses single-case design and refers to a design that gathers information on any system treated as a single unit (Bloom et al., 1995). The unit of analysis may be a fourth-grade classroom, one child in the classroom, or a group of children in the classroom. At the heart of single-case research methodology is graphical analysis of data patterns, yet single-case research design is much more than simple charting. Data depicted on graphs are used to make evidence-based treatment decisions and as a means of demonstrating causality and generalizability. (See Bloom et al., 1995, and Barlow & Hersen, 1984, for a thorough discussion of single-case design methodology.)

Single-case (N = 1) designs used in counseling research and practice are theory-free; the use of such designs is not the province of one school of thought or theoretical orientation. In fact, single-case (N = 1) designs have been advocated and used by marriage and family therapists, practitioners of transactional analysis, and phenomenological as well as behaviorally oriented professionals (Bentley, 1990; Dean & Reinherz, 1986; Greene, 1988; Jacobson, 1979a; Kolko & Milan, 1983; Slonim-Nevo & Vosler, 1991). For example, single-case designs have been used to evaluate the effects of levels of counselor empathy on within-session client behavior (Nugent, 1992). Single-case designs are also applicable to evaluation and experimental analysis of the effects of group counseling (Edelson, Miller,

Stone & Chapman, 1985; Kelly, 1980; Vera, 1990). Finally, single-case designs are directly applicable to counseling applications and present a flexible and viable scientific methodology useful for counseling research and practice, regardless of theoretical orientation.

Phases of Intervention

A phase is a period of time during which a specific counselor action is taking place. The effectiveness of counseling is based on comparisons of the client's behavior across varying phases of counseling, for example, before, during, and after (follow-up). In single-case designs there are two generic phases: baseline and treatment.

Baseline. Ideally, a "baseline" phase, established before implementing a systematic counseling intervention, is conducted. Baseline assessment is consistent with CACREP standards regarding appraisal of the client, followed by counseling geared toward addressing targeted areas (CACREP, 1994). This phase has several benefits, such as allowing the counselor to (a) conduct an assessment to determine the targets of change, (b) specify corresponding relevant measures for evaluating change, (c) evaluate the severity or frequency of the client's problem before implementing any specific counseling intervention (other than simply listening to the client), and (d) establish rapport. The primary function of baseline assessment is to provide the counselor with feedback regarding the target of change in order to make clinical decisions as to whether intervention is necessary. Baseline assessment continues until a stable pattern of behavior is obtained.

Baseline is labeled "A." The client's behavior during the baseline period is used as the standard by which subsequent improvement is judged. A minimum of three observations is recommended (Barlow & Hersen, 1984). Less than three observations make interpretations of the data and causal statements regarding change difficult. Clinically, client self-recording of the target over a 1-week period provides a reasonably accurate estimate of the pattern of behavior and representative pretreatment baseline.

Baseline serves as the "no treatment control condition" analogous to a no treatment control group used in between-groups nomothetic research methods. However, in single-case design methodology, comparisons of change in the target are idiographic. In clinical practice it is unethical to withhold treatment. However, in such cases, standard appraisal and generic counseling skills (e.g., empathy) function as the "baseline" condition (Egan, 1998).

Treatment. After baseline data are obtained, the intervention or treatment phase (B) is initiated. A change in counselor actions (independent variable), such as the use of confrontation or challenging the client, represents movement out of baseline and into an intervention phase. Ongoing assessment of the target during the intervention phase allows comparison of data obtained during the baseline phase during which, for example, empathic listening was used. If the frequency or intensity of the target changes as a function of implementation of the counseling intervention, there is strong evidence that the counseling intervention was responsible for such change. Treatment phases may have many components because therapy changes as a function of the pattern of data regarding the target. These changes in phases are labeled alphabetically, depending on the extent to which previous treatment components are included in subsequent treatment phases (e.g., BC, C, CD). As with baseline, phase changes are made after establishing a period of stability in the target (i.e., limited variability) or when target performance is worsening.

Specifying the Target(s) of Change: Dependent Variables

The fundamental requirement of a scientific approach to understanding is defining variables. To establish the construct validity of the dependent variable means to translate the client's complaints into behavioral targets, which are the focus of change and which brought the client to counseling in the first place. Behavior is broadly defined and includes overt speech, scores on self-report questionnaires, daily self-ratings, motoric behavior, or physiologic responses. The most relevant target, determined by the counselor and client, is selected as the target of change. Direct measures, such as crying, are more precise and preferred over indirect measures, for example, mood (Bloom et al., 1995). Directly observable targets decrease the level of inference regarding the occurrence of the target and enhance construct validity (Heppner, Kivlighan, et al., 1992). Multiple targets are selected whenever possible due to issues regarding response covariation and construct

validity (Heppner, Kivlighan et al., 1992; Lang, 1968). Regardless of theoretical orientation, these targets serve as the dependent variable(s) that are expected to change as a function of counselor actions.

Quantification

A means of indexing targets is needed. Standard behavioral dimensions of measurement include duration, intensity, and frequency. All behaviors occur and are thus amenable to measurement using a simple frequency count. Targets may be assessed using standardized inventories, such as self-rated depression, that provide a summary score (Beck, Ward, Mendelssohn, Mock, & Erbaugh, 1961). However, these measures are amenable for use on a weekly basis and may not be practical due to the need to establish a baseline of at least 3 data points (3 weeks in this case) and the rapid delivery of services. A viable alternative is self-observation and recording by using individualized rating scales constructed to quantify emotional states, for example, a daily mood rating using a 0- to 9-point scale. The Subjective Unit of Distress (SUD) rating scale, a client self-recording instrument, is widely used for assessing client emotional distress (Lundervold & Perez, 1998; Wolpe, 1991).

Consider marital counseling. The wife complains about her husband being cold and unaffectionate. The couple has agreed that they would like to communicate more frequently and be more intimate. To address the effectiveness of counseling for this couple, it may be useful to quantify and measure the frequency of reciprocal positive statements or physical touch, and the degree of satisfaction in daily communication (Jacobson, 1979b). Each target is defined and a self-recording procedure developed for use in data collection. Other targets may be relevant and may need to be assessed as well.

Systematic Data Collection

To make sense of the pattern of the target and the effect of counseling on the target, systematic methods of observation are required. Specifying the nature of the data to be collected is necessary. These specifications include how, by whom, how often, and under what circumstances the data will be gathered. For example, daily self-reports of ounces of alcohol consumption provide precise information about "real world" actions of the client outside the artificial confines of the therapy room. These data also serve as direct indicators to the client (and the counselor) of success in achieving desired counseling outcomes.

Repeated Observation

Repeated measurement of the target(s) of interest over time is obtained, for example, client self-recording of the intensity of emotional distress associated with flashbacks occurring each day. Repeated observation of the target(s) over time, that is, before and during counseling intervention, allows the counselor to determine if change has occurred and what factors are likely responsible for such change.

Specifying the Independent Variable: Counselor Actions

Counselor actions are the independent variables. The assumption of all theories of counseling is that the presence or absence of certain counselor actions result in a change in client behavior. This is analogous to the manipulation (i.e., presentation or removal) of the independent variable in basic science or laboratory-based clinical research.

As independent variables, counselor actions must have construct validity and require precise behavioral descriptions to increase internal validity (Heppner, Kivlighan, et al., 1992). For example, a counselor using a person-centered counseling approach would demonstrate warm, genuine, and empathic behaviors while in session. Collectively, these counselor actions serve as the independent variable. Further specification of these counselor actions is needed, however, to establish construct validity, to establish change in the target, and to rule out alternative explanations that may be responsible for a change or lack of change in the dependent variable. At a more pragmatic level, precise description and definition of counselor actions enable the counselor to replicate the effects of counseling interventions. Imprecision and vagueness in terms of counselor actions render this outcome unlikely and ultimately harms other clients by not being able to precisely specify the conditions leading to effective intervention. Similarly, a counselor using Gestalt methods may use the "empty chair" technique (Yontef & Simkin, 1989). In this case, speaking to the empty chair is the independent variable. To determine the effect of the empty chair technique on the target, several sessions during which only this technique is used must be implemented concurrent with data collection on the target.

As is often the case, the counselor simultaneously engages in a set of actions, or, in other words, multiple independent variables are manipulated at the same time. This is referred to as a "treatment package" (Barlow & Hersen, 1984) and is often seen in clinical practice. There is no inherent problem with package treatments. The primary weakness lies in establishing causality with respect to a change in the dependent variable. Because multiple independent variables are manipulated simultaneously, it is unclear which one is the active ingredient responsible for change in the target. When a treatment package is used, all treatment components must be described and defined. Moreover, the treatment package must then be implemented within each session until a stable pattern in the target is observed; failure to do so constitutes a phase change and renders the data uninterpretable.

Design Choices

Experimental designs. Experimental control of the dependent variable is elegantly demonstrated in single-case designs based on time series and replication logic (Barlow & Hersen, 1984; Bloom et al., 1995; Cook & Campbell, 1979; Sidman, 1960). The skilled evidence-based counselor may be capable of using single-case experimental designs in everyday practice (Lundervold & Enterman, 1989; Perez, Lundervold, & Gonzalez, 1998; Terrazas & Lundervold, 1999). (For a more complete discussion of the types of experimental designs and related issues refer to the sources cited.)

Evaluation designs. Single-case evaluation designs used in counseling practice aid in determining the effects of counselor actions on the target of change. Demonstrations of experimental control are not the priority; weak or no attempt at demonstrating experimental control occurs. Such designs consist of a sequence of phases, with each new phase corresponding to implementation of a different (set of) independent variable(s) in an effort to change the target and meet the goals of the client. However, phase changes still rely on the pattern of data observed. Single-case evaluation design might have three phases: A, B, and C. For example, "A" consists of empathic listening; Phase "B" is problem solving; and "C" represents coping skills. When appropriately used, single-case (N = 1) evaluation designs are capable of ruling out most threats to internal validity, and a strong causal statement related to the changes observed in the target can be made (Kazdin, 1981).

Analysis of Data

Visual analysis. The traditional method of evaluating outcomes using single-case research designs has been visual inspection of graphed data to determine a pattern in the data (Barlow & Hersen, 1984; Parsonson & Baer, 1978). Five primary concepts are used in data analysis: slope, trend, stability, level, and overlap. A trend in the data indicates a pattern where the target is increasing (upward trend), decreasing (downward trend), or staying the same (stable). A change in trend may also indicate improvement or deterioration in the target. *Slope* is the magnitude or steepness of the trend. Level refers to the relative magnitude of change observed and can be assessed at any point during baseline or intervention. The final determination of a change in level occurs at the point immediately after intervention ends. A large change in level between baseline and intervention phases is an important indicator of a change in the target and is consistent with the hypothesis that intervention is responsible for the change. *Overlap* is the extent to which data patterns across phases overlap with each other. The less the degree of overlaps between adjacent phases the stronger the argument for the functional effect of the independent variable on the dependent variable.

Intervention effects are most easily observed when there is a large and immediate change in the slope and level of target after manipulation of the independent variable. Large and obvious effects are viewed as clinically significant (Parsonson & Baer, 1978). When the characteristics act in concert, rather clear inferences of causality can be drawn (Barlow & Hersen, 1984; Bloom et al., 1995).

Drawing valid conclusions based on visual analysis of graphed data are hampered by variability in the data (Furlong & Wampold, 1982; Matyas & Greenwood, 1990; Wampold & Furlong, 1981). Statistically significant autocorrelation in the data increases the likelihood of Type II errors occurring when visual inspection is the sole criterion used to judge intervention outcomes (Matyas & Greenwood, 1990). Autocorrelation, in general, refers to serial correlation or a correlation between data

points "n" steps apart, or a lack of independence among observations. In the context of single-case design, the issue of autocorrelation is specific to a correlation among the residuals or error terms of the model used in the analysis. In addition, small but important effects may be overlooked due to the criterion of "bigger is better." Finally, like it or not, professional and scientific credibility is based on obtaining clinical outcomes that are clinically as well as statistically significant (Huitema, 1986). Fortunately, statistical approaches and the use of single-case designs are compatible and complementary.

Statistical analysis. Although it has subjective aspects, statistical analyses of behavioral data provide a systematic and scientifically agreed on "yardstick" for evaluating counseling effectiveness. Statistical tests are especially useful when visual analysis is difficult because of complex patterns in the data. Statistical analysis is also useful in determining whether obtained changes in the target are reliable (i.e., beyond that expected from variability in the target and measurement error). When small but important change occurs, as in the initial stage of development of counseling intervention, statistical tests serve as a guide to the counselor regarding further use of such procedures.

Statistical tests do present a uniform method and set of criteria by which to judge effects. Thus, similar results from independent sources lend credibility to the findings reported. Presently there is no general consensus as to the appropriate statistical approach for the analysis of data obtained from a single-case, and a variety of techniques are advocated. The primary reason for this confusion has been concern with autocorrelation (Huitema, 1985). Consequently, nonstatisticians are left with the difficult decision of how to analyze data from a single case. Huitema's (1985) meta-analysis of 300 individual single-case design experiments and recent research by Belwood (1997) further clarifies the issue of autocorrelation in the context of data obtained from N = 1 designs and supports the use of inferential statistics to analyze such data.

An equally important impediment to the use of statistical tests for single-case research designs has been the lack of graduate training in this research method and the application of statistical tests with such data. Related to this is the belief that the process is too complicated and time consuming to be of value. These presumed disadvantages are likely to diminish with training, practice, and increasing availability of desktop computers and user-friendly statistical analysis software.

Finally, statistical significance does not mean clinical significance. Clinical significance refers to change that has substantial and meaningful effect on the functioning of the individual. It has been recommended that evaluation of treatment outcome should be based on both clinically significant and statistically reliable change (Jacobson, Follette, & Revensdorf, 1984). *Statistically reliable change* refers to change that is greater than that which would be expected to occur due to behavioral variability and measurement error. Statistical reliability is a necessary condition for determining *clinically significant change.*

Case Examples

Two case examples are presented, each using single-case (N = 1) research designs. In each case, specific counseling interventions were used to address client targets, with change in counseling intervention based on objective evidence obtained in the context of single-case research design methods.

Case 1. Judith, a 67-year-old woman, sought services because of emotional distress associated with severe, unilateral essential tremor (ET), an idiopathic neurological movement disorder. Tremor affected her entire right arm. ET is the most prevalent movement disorder and is associated with significant emotional and physical disability (Lundervold, 1997). Emotional arousal is known to exacerbate tremor, which, in turn, increases disability. This process has been described as a self-activating feedback loop (Lundervold, 1997).

Judith reported that her tremor became worse in situations in which a person with whom she had a history of negative interactions was present. Frequently, the tremor would worsen when Judith was in a stressful situation and the person was present. Negative interactions between them may or may not have occurred. In either case, Judith experienced increased emotional distress (anger) and more tremors. She would then flee the situation and the tremor would eventually subside.

An A-B single-case evaluation design, with multiple targets including client ratings and physiologic measures, was used to evaluate the effects of counseling interventions. In the

baseline phase LA), Judith was instructed to imagine the situation that elicited distress. The counselor provided a verbal description of the stressful situation to enhance the vividness of the scene. During the guided imaginal exposure to the stressful situation, measures of electromyographic (EMG) activity from four muscle sites, mid-deltoid, biceps, forearm flexor, and extensor, were obtained. EMG represents a quantitative measure of tremor (Delwaide & Gonce, 1988). At the end of each imaginal exposure trial, Judith was asked to provide a rating of her emotional distress.

Figure 1 displays self-reported distress and electromyographic activity on a trial-by-trial basis. As can be seen in the lower panel of the figure, with each subsequent exposure to the stressful situation self-rated emotional distress declined.

EMG data, displayed in the upper panel, conveys a much different picture. Here, each subsequent exposure trial resulted in significantly higher EMG levels. Based on this evidence and direct observation of increased tremor by the counselor, a change in counseling intervention was taken. Judith was taught relaxation and self-instructions to guide her relaxation while coping with the stressor (Poppen, 1998). After implementation of the coping skills intervention, self-rated distress continued to decline and declined further than in the previous phase. Variability in EMG activity across all four muscle sites substantially decreased, demonstrated synchrony across sites, and stabilized at low levels. Despite the A-B design used, this pattern of response covariation and use of multiple measures that change in a systematic manner after intervention strongly suggests that the coping skills intervention was responsible for the counseling outcome obtained (Kazdin, 1981).

Case 2. Sexual assault can be a very traumatizing experience often resulting in a diagnosis of post-traumatic stress disorder (PTSD). Juanita, a 24-year-old African American woman, was raped by an acquaintance. She reported frequent assault-related flashbacks and nightmares, which served as individual targets. Juanita met with the counselor approximately every 2 weeks during baseline assessment. During this time, Juanita was instructed to record her subjective unit of distress (SUD), using an 11-point scale (0 = *none*, 10 = *extreme*) associated with the occurrence of each target (Wolpe, 1991).

A multiple baseline across targets single-case experimental design was used to evalu-

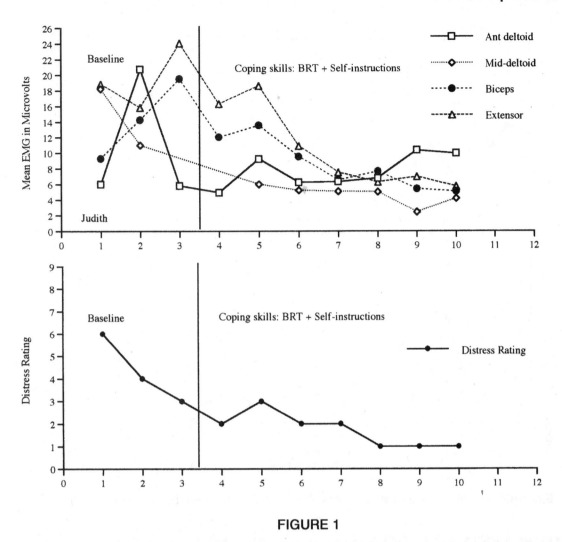

FIGURE 1

Example of an A-B Single-Case Design With Multiple Targets for Change, Self-Reported Distres
and Four Channels of Electromyographic (EMG) Activity

ate the effects of the counseling intervention on each target and to demonstrate experimental control of the dependent variables (Bloom et al., 1995). Consistent with multiple baseline logic, eye movement desensitization (EMD), the counseling intervention was implemented in time-lagged fashion—first for flashbacks and subsequently for nightmares (Barlow & Hersen, 1984; Montgomery & Allyon, 1994). Implementation of the counseling intervention for the second target did not occur until (a) a treatment effect was observed for the first target, and (b) the pattern of the data for the second target was stable.

Figure 2 displays the frequency of the targets. During baseline (supportive counseling) the frequency of flashbacks declined slightly; however, SUD ratings remained high. Nightmares continued regularly. After the implementation of EMD, a systematic decline in the frequency of flashbacks and

intensity of SUD ratings was observed. A slight downward trend in the frequency of nightmares also occurred during this phase, but SUD ratings remained high. Frequency of nightmares then stabilized. EMD was then implemented for nightmares. The frequency of nightmares declined to zero and remained at this level for 7 weeks. SUD ratings also declined.

After a stable baseline and implementation of the counseling intervention, a systematic treatment effect was observed for the first target. Some initial generalized effect of EMD to the untreated target (nightmares) was observed, followed by a period of stability. Demonstration of experimental control of the dependent variable was replicated when EMD was implemented for the second target. Only after manipulation of the independent variable did the frequency of nightmares decline to below baseline levels.

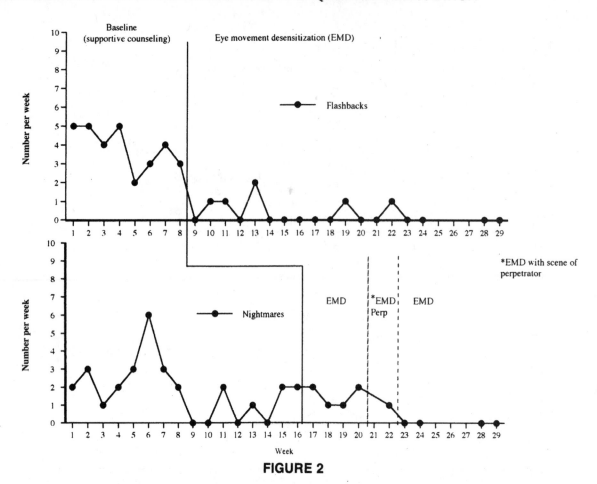

FIGURE 2

Example of a Multiple Baseline Across Targets Single-Case Experimental Design

COMPONENTS FOR SUCCESS: COUNSELOR EDUCATION

How can we, that is, counselor educators and researchers, make practice-relevant research methods a reality in counseling programs? We offer a 7-component model implemented to address this problem that is consistent with the suggestions of others concerned with the quality and integrity of instruction in practice-relevant research methods.

Establishing Entry-Level Conceptual Skills

Analytic and systematic problem-solving skills are the heart of the scientific way of knowing and are prerequisite to any research model (Heppner, Carter, et al., 1992; Kerlinger, 1973). These skills represent a way of approaching the subject matter of counseling both inside and outside the therapy room. As Falvey (1989) pointed out,

> Any clinician becomes engaged in the process of framing an initial client encounter, which parallels the thought involved in formulating a research question. A clinician

then reflects on the presenting issues (e.g., generates hypotheses) and uses heuristic guides of his or her orientation (e.g., methodology) to gather facts (e.g., data collection) and assess (e.g., analyze) relevant information in order to develop a specific treatment plan (e.g., conclusion) . . . research and psychotherapy are. . . similar endeavors. (pp. 97–98)

To establish this way of conceptualizing counseling, concepts such as independent and dependent variable, problem statement, hypotheses, and hypothesis testing are introduced in Theories of Counseling, a required course in all graduate counseling programs. Used as part of the criteria in conducting a scholarly and critical evaluation of theoretical models (Tzeng & Jackson, 1990), students are required to select, review, and evaluate published treatment outcome articles representative of the theory.

Learning Practice Relevant Assessment Methods

Identification and repeated assessment of targets are critical to the use of single-case design methodology. Instruction in these basic skills requires a shift from traditional vaganotic to idemnotic assessment procedures and has profound implications for counselor education, practice, and research. *Vaganotic* (e.g., trait) measurement refers to the creation of scales and measures on the basis of variability in a set of underlying characteristics, for example, neuroticism. The units of measurement are defined in terms of statistical variability with mean scores and standard deviations derived from nomothetic samples and applied to individual performance on tests or questionnaires. The assumptions of vaganotic methods include measurement of traits and abilities that are stable over time and largely unaffected by contextual variables. In addition to being time consuming and cumbersome to administer, repeated measurement using vaganotic measures is rare or deemed to be unnecessary because of the stability of the trait. Furthermore, in the context of statistical measurement theory, differences in scores are attributed to "measurement error," rather than change in the target as a function of counseling intervention. Consequently, such measures are not amenable to evidence-based clinical decision making and single-case research design methods.

In contrast, *idemnotic* or *idiographic* measurement denotes a type of measurement that incorporates absolute and standard units for the individual whose performance is established independent of variability within a group (Johnston & Pennypacker, 1980). Idiographic assessment focuses on the use of practice-relevant measurement procedures assessing individual behaviors or a cluster of behaviors that covary and are specific to the individual and problem situations (Hawkins, 1979; Nelson, 1981). (See Bellack & Hersen, 1998, and Chapters 4–6 and 8–9 in Bloom et al., 1995, for a description of selecting clinically relevant dependent variables. Nelson & Hayes, 1986, provide an excellent theoretical account of behavioral assessment as it relates to construction of dependent variables.) Consequently, behavioral assessment must be included as a core area class in graduate programs, or, at the very least, a substantial portion of current assessment courses must be devoted to instruction in behavioral assessment procedures. The course, Clinical Assessment in Counseling, at the University of Texas at El Paso addresses issues of reliability and validity relative to standardized tests, direct observation, and self-report measures. Multi-

behavior-multimethod assessment procedures are emphasized including the use of brief, structured self-report questionnaires and individualized rating scales. Finally, students are required to conduct clinical interviews using a standard assessment protocol and develop a direct observation coding procedure. A minimum of two targets for observation is required, complete with behavioral definitions. Next, systematic direct observations are conducted, and the data are graphed and interpreted. Interrater reliability on direct observation is also calculated.

Creating A Supportive Environment

Development of a student special interest group (SSIG) is a functional mechanism to establish interest and entry-level research skills by providing a context where the application of single-case research design is modeled by advanced graduate counseling students. Within the Counseling Program at the University of Texas at El Paso, an SSIG in Behavioral Medicine and Therapy has been established. The group meets twice per month under faculty supervision. Each student member presents and discusses a journal article related to behavioral or cognitive intervention for biomedical or behavioral disorders. Students preparing theses, research projects, or completing practicum or internships describe cases and present intervention data obtained in the context of single-case research methods.

Instruction in Single-Case Design Methods

One of the single most important components is offering a research methods course in single-case (N = 1) experimental design to graduate counseling students. Here, students acquire the necessary analytical, conceptual, and procedural skills to use single-case designs in practice and research. Basic (A-B) and complex (e.g., alternating treatments, repeated pre-post training assessment) designs are presented (Barlow & Hersen, 1984; Bloom et al., 1995). The use of descriptive and inferential statistics for single-case design is also addressed. As part of the single-case experimental design course taught at the University of Texas at El Paso, students are required to develop a research project using a single-case experimental design. The written product includes an introduction, method, and results section. Results based on hypothetical data are displayed on graphs and the data are interpreted in the results section of the manuscript. This project may function as a minithesis prospectus or as a draft of a proposed master's research project.

Experimental Design Taught by Practicing Counselors

As advocated by Garcia (1995), the single-case experimental design course is taught by a counseling faculty member who is also a practitioner. One significant benefit of having a practicing counselor teach the experimental design course is the individual's skill in bridging the gap between research and practice through the use of clinical examples. Moreover, because a scientist-practitioner is facile with single-case design, multiple design examples that have been used in the practice setting can be provided. Because clinical practice is not always a mirror of a textbook example (i.e., perfect), positive and negative (i.e., confounded) teaching examples of research design are used. These teaching examples serve as excellent instructional aids to establish concepts and rules related to manipulation of independent variables, construct validity, and data analysis.

Shaping Emergent Skills

To move from conceptual to practical applications of single-case research design, students must have the opportunity to apply the methodology in practice settings. Students have the opportunity to enroll in practicum and internship sections where such methods are regularly used. Faculty work closely with students and shape students' analytical, conceptual, clinical, and research skills in the context of providing services. Depending on the case and student skills, basic evaluation or experimental single-case designs are used.

Promoting Research and Scholarship

Research and scholarship are vital components of any master's- or doctoral-level graduate counseling program. Students must also have the opportunity to conduct controlled single-case research for thesis and nonthesis research projects. Research and scholarship take place at several levels. Faculty-student application of single-case evaluation and research designs in counseling are presented at regional and national conferences and submitted for publication in scholarly professional journals (Lundervold & Perez, 1998; Perez et al., 1998; Terrazas & Lundervold, 1999). For

thesis research projects, single-case designs are used to address specific research questions regarding treatment efficacy or mechanisms of change with a focus on demonstrating experimental control.

SUMMARY

There are several advantages to teaching counselors-in-preparation and practitioners single-case research design methodology. First, single-case research methodology is theory free. Counselors of any orientation may use single-case research designs as long as he or she adheres to the basic tenants of scientific methodology with respect to construct and internal validity and measurement. Second, single-case research designs are flexible, evidence-based methods designed for use in practice settings. As such, there is a greater likelihood that practitioners will actually use the research methods because they were designed for that purpose. Third, single-case research designs provide practitioners with an evidence-based decision making tool, thereby improving counseling effectiveness. Treatment decisions are data based. The fourth advantage is that single-case designs are directly relevant to counseling practice and to the science of counseling. Consequently, such designs bridge the scientist-practitioner gap that is so frequently bemoaned and as frequently ignored. Practitioners can directly engage in clinically relevant research and evaluation. Fifth, the "statistical bogeymen" is not an issue. Analysis of data obtained from single-case (N = 1) designs does not require necessarily the use of statistical methods. As a result, single-case research methods are more user-friendly because strong quantitative skills, which are unlikely to be observed given the diversity of backgrounds of counseling students, are not required. (Garcia, 1995). For those so inclined, statistical analysis of data from N = 1 designs can be conducted (Chung, Poppen, & Lundervold, 1995; Kazdin, 1984). *Single-case* research methods generate scientifically acceptable evidence that leads to professional credibility. Finally, the use of *single-case* designs is consistent with CACREP standards calling for increased emphasis on research, accountability, and diverse research methodologies in the scientist-practitioner model of counselor preparation (CACREP, 1994)

REFERENCES

Arkes, H. R. (1981). Impediments to accurate clinical judgment and possible ways to minimize their impact. *Journal of Consulting and Clinical Psychology, 49*, 23–330.

Barlow, D. H., & Hersen, M. (1984). Single-case experimental designs. Strategies for studying behavior change. Elmsford, NY: Pergamon.

Beck, A. T., Ward, C. H., Mendelssohn, M., Mock, J. E., & Erbaugh, J. K. (1961). An inventory for measuring depression. *American Journal of Psychiatry, 142*, 559–563.

Bellack, A. S., & Hersen, M. (1998). Behavioral assessment. A practical handbook (3rd ed.). Boston: Allyn & Bacon.

Belwood, M. E (1997). A Monte Carlo study of the relationship between linear model specification and estimates of lag-one autocorrelation in data from a single-case (N = 1) design. Unpublished doctoral dissertation, Southern Illinois University, Carbondale, IL.

Bentley, K. J. (1990). An evaluation of family-based intervention using single system research. *British Journal of Social Work, 20*, 101–116.

Bloom, M., & Fischer, J., & Orme, J. G. (1995). Evaluating practice: Guidelines for the accountable professional (2nd ed.). Upper Saddle River, NJ: Prentice–Hall.

Browning, C. H., & Browning, B. J. (1994). How to partner with managed care. Los Alamitos, CA: Duncliff's International.

Buchler, J. (1955). Philosophical writings of Pierce. New York: Dover.

Chapman, L. J., & Chapman, J. P. (1967). The genesis of popular but erroneous diagnostic observations. *Journal of Abnormal Psychology, 74*, 271–280.

Chung, W., Poppen, R., & Lundervold, D.A. (1995). Relaxation training for tremor disorders. *Biofeedback and Self–Regulation, 20*, 123–135.

Cook, T. D., & Campbell, D. T. (1979). Quasi-experimentation: Design and analysis issues for field settings. Chicago: Rand McNally.

Council for Accreditation of Counseling and Related Educational Programs. (1994). CACREP accreditation standards and procedures manual. Alexandria, VA: Author.

Dean, R. G., & Reinherz, H. (1986). Psychodynamic practice and single system design. *Journal of Social Work Education, 22*, 71–81.

Delwaide, P. J., & Gonce, M. (1988). Pathophysiology of Parkinson's signs. In J. Jankovic & E. Tolosa (Eds.), Parkinson's disease and movement disorders (pp. 59–73). Baltimore–Munich: Urban & Schwarzenberg.

Edelson, D. M., Miller, D. M., Stone, G. W., & Chapman, D. E (1985). Group treatment for men who batter. *Social Work Research and Abstracts, 21*, 18–21.

Egan, G. (1998). The skilled helper (6th ed.). Pacific Grove, CA: Brooks/Cole.

Falvey, E. (1989). Passion and professionalism: Critical rapprochement for mental health research. *Journal of Mental Health Counseling, 11*, 86–105.

Fong, M. L., & Malone, C. M. (1994). Defeating ourselves: Common errors in counseling research. *Counselor Education and Supervision, 33*, 356–362.

Furlong, M. J., & Wampold, B. E. (1982). Intervention effects and relative variation as dimensions in experts' use of visual inference. *Journal of Applied Behavior Analysis, 15*, 415–421.

Garb, H. N. (1998). Studying the clinician. Judgement research and psychological assessment. Washington, DC: American Psychological Association.

Garcia, S. K. (1995, Fall). Counselor education and training in research: Are counseling students being short–changed? *TCA Journal*, 12–19.

Gelso, C. J. (1979). Research in counseling. Methodological and professional issues. *Counseling Psychologist, 8*, 7–36.

Giles, T. R. (1993). Managed mental health care. A guide for practitioners, employers and administrators. NY: Plenum.

Greene, G. (1988). Analysis of research on the effectiveness of transactional analysis for improving marital relationships: Towards close encounters of the single kind. *Transactional Analysis Journal, 18*, 237–248.

Halmos, P. (1966). The faith of counselors. New York: Schocken Books.

Hashmond, L.T. (1994). Supervision of predoctoral graduate research: A practice-oriented approach. *The Counseling Psychologist, 22*, 147–161.

Hawkins, R. P. (1979). The functions of assessment: Implications for selection and development of devices for assessing repertoires in clinical, educational, and other settings. Journal of Applied Behavior Analysis, 12, 501–516.

Heppner, P. P., Carter, J. A., Claiborne, C. D., Brooks, L., Gelso, C. J., Fassinger, R. E., Holloway, E. L., Stone, G. L., Wampold, B. E., & Gallassi, J. P. (1992). A proposal to integrate science and practice into counseling psychology. *The Counseling Psychologist, 20*, 107–122.

Heppner, P. P., Kivlighan, Jr., D. M., & Wampold, B. E. (1992). Research design in counseling. Pacific Grove, CA: Brooks/Cole.

Huitema, B. E. (1985). Autocorrelation in applied behavior analysis: A myth. *Behavioral Assessment, 7*, 107–118.

Huitema, B. E. (1986). Statistical analysis and single subject designs: Some misunderstandings. In A. Poling & R. W. Fuqua (Eds.), Research methods in applied behavior analysis: Issues and advances (pp. 209–232). New York: Plenum.

Jacobson, N. E. (1 979a). Increasing positive behavior in severely distressed marital relationships: The effects of problem solving training. *Behavior Therapy, 10*, 311–326.

Jacobson, N. E. (1979b). Marital therapy: Strategies based on social learning and behavior exchange theory. New York: Bruner/Mazel.

Jacobson, N. E., Follette, W., & Revensdorf, D. (1984). Psychotherapy outcome research: Methods for reporting variability and evaluating clinical significance. *Behavior Therapy, 15*, 336–352.

Johnston, J. M., & Pennypacker, H. 5. (1980). Strategies and tactics of human behavioral research. Hillsdale, NJ: Erlbaum.

Kazdin, A. E. (1981). Drawing valid inferences from case studies. *Journal of Consulting and Clinical Psychology, 49*, 183–192.

Kazdin, A. E. (1984). Statistical analysis. In D. H. Barlow & M. Hersen (Eds.), Single-case experimental designs. Strategies for studying behavior change (pp. 285–324). Elmsford, NY: Pergamon.

Kazdin, A. E., & Tuma, A. H. (1982). New directions for methodology of behavioral and social science, Vol. 13. Single-case research design. San Francisco: Jossey-Bass.

Kelly, J. A. (1980). The simultaneous replication design: The use of a multiple baseline design to establish experimental control in a single group social skills treatment study. *Journal of Behavior Therapy and Experimental Psychiatry, 11*, 203–207.

Kerlinger, E (1973). Foundations of behavioral research (2nd ed.). New York: Holt, Rinehart and Winston.

Kolko, D. J., & Milan, M. A. (1983). Reframing and paradoxical instruction to overcome "resistance" in the treatment of delinquent youths. *Journal of Consulting and Clinical Psychology, 51*, 655–660.

Lang, P. J. (1968). Fear reduction and fear behavior: Problems in treating a construct. In J. M. Schlein (Ed.), Research in psychotherapy, Volume 3 (pp. 90–102). Washington, DC: American Psychological Association.

Lundervold, D. A. (1997). Behavioral medicine interventions for older adults coping with essential tremor. *Directions in Rehabilitation Counseling, 3*, 3–11.

Lundervold, D. A., & Enterman, M. (1989). Antecedent and consequent control of medical regimen adherence skills in an adult with developmental disabilities. *Education and Training of the Mentally Retarded, 24*, 126–132.

Lundervold, D. A., & Perez, L. (1998). Brief counseling intervention for incest related post traumatic stress disorder: A single-case analysis. Manuscript submitted for publication.

Matyas, T. A., & Greenwood, K. M. (1990). Visual analysis of single-case time series: Effects of serial dependency and magnitude of intervention effects. *Journal of Applied Behavior Analysis, 23*, 341–351.

Meehl, P. E. (1954). Clinical vs. statistical prediction. A theoretical analysis and review of the evidence. Minneapolis, MN: University of Minnesota Press.

Montgomery, R.W., & Allyon, T. (1994). Eye movement desensitization across subjects: Subjective and physiological measures of efficacy. *Journal of Behavior Therapy and Experimental Psychiatry, 25*, 2 17–230.

Nelson, R. O. (1981). Realistic dependent measures for clinical use. *Journal of Consulting and Clinical Psychology, 49*, 168–182.

Nelson, R. O., & Hayes, S. C. (1986). Conceptual foundations of behavioral assessment. New York: Guilford.

Nisbett, R., & Ross, L. (1980). Human influence. Strategies and shortcomings of social judgment. Englewood Cliffs, NJ: Prentice Hall.

Nugent, W. R. (1992). The affective impact of a clinical social worker's interviewing style: A series of single-case experiments. *Research on Social Work Practice, 2*, 6–27.

Parsonson, B. S., & Baer, D. M. (1978). The analysis and presentation of graphic data. In T. R. Kratochwill (Ed.), Single-subject research: Strategies for evaluating change (pp. 101–165). New York: Academic Press.

Perez, L., Lundervold, D. A., & Gonzalez, J. (1998, April). Effectiveness and acceptability of behavioral parent training with Hispanic parents. Paper presented at the Texas Association for Behavior Analysis Conference, Houston, TX.

Poppen, R. (1998). Behavioral relaxation training and assessment (2nd ed.). Thousand Oaks, CA: Sage.

Robinson, E. H. (1994). Critical issues in counselor education: Mentors, models, and money. *Journal of Counseling and Development, 67*,491–492.

Ruckdeschel, R., & Fans, B. E. (1982). Science: Critical faith or dogmatic ritual? *Social Casework, 63*, 272–275.

Saleeby, D. (1979). The tension between research and practice: Assumption of the experimental paradigm. *Clinical Social Work Journal, 7*, 267–284.

Sidman, M. (1960). Tactics of scientific research. New York: Basic Books.

Slonim-Nevo, V., & Vosler, N. R. (1991). The use of single system with systemic brief problem solving therapy. *Families in Society, 72*, 3 8–44.

Storr, A. (1990). The art of psychotherapy (2nd ed.). London: Routledge.

Terrazas, A., & Lundervold, D. A. (1999, May). Health counseling: Behavioral relaxation training and coping self-instructions for hypertension. Paper presented at the Association for Behavior Analysis Conference, Chicago.

Todd, T. (1994). Surviving and prospering in the managed mental health care marketplace. Sarasota, FL: Professional Resources Press.

Tzeng, O. C. S., & Jackson, J. W. (1990). Common methodological framework for theory construction and evaluation in the social and behavioral sciences. *Genetic, Social and General Psychology Monographs, 1 17*, 38–44.

Vera, M. I. (1990). Effects of divorce groups on individual adjustment. A multiple methodology approach. *Social work Research and Abstracts, 26*, 11–22.

Wampold, B. E., & Furlong, M. J. (1981). The heuristics of visual inference. *Behavioral Assessment, 3*, 79–92.

Wolpe, J. (1991). The practice of behavior therapy (4th ed.). Boston: Allyn & Bacon.

Woolsey, L. K. (1989). Research and practice in counseling: A conflict of values. *Counselor Education and Supervision, 26*, 84–94.

Yontef, G. M., & Simkin, J. 5. (1989). Gestalt therapy. In R. J. Corsini & D. Wedding (Eds.), Current psychotherapies (4th ed., pp. 323–362). Itasca, IL: Peacock.

Duane A. Lundervold was an assistant professor in the Counseling Program in the Department of Educational Psychology at the University of Texas at El Paso and is now in the Department of Psychology and Counselor Education at Central Missouri State University, Warrensburg. **Marilyn F. Belwood** is an assistant professor in the Math Department at Missouri Valley College, Marshall. The first author thanks Norma Hernandez for her intellectual and moral support for this project. The authors thank Helen Hammond for her help. Each author contributed equally to this project. Correspondence regarding this article should be sent to Duane A. Lundervold, Department of Psychology and Counselor Education, 117 Lovinger Hall, Central Missouri State University, Warrensburg, MO 64093 or Marilyn F. Belwood, 1480 S. Grant, Marshall, MO 65340 (e-mail: Lundervold@cmsu1.cmsu.edu).

ISSUES IN TEACHING PARTICIPATORY ACTION RESEARCH

PAULE MCNICOLL

This article discusses participatory action research, a methodology that incorporates subjects in the research and indexes results to transforming the lives of those involved. The approach is gaining momentum and recognition in academic circles but still often limited to specialized training centers. The author discusses two years of experience teaching participatory action research at a school of social work, focusing on the challenges that educators planning courses in action-oriented research are likely to meet.

PARTICIPATORY ACTION RESEARCH is gaining momentum and recognition in academic circles, but it has not been well integrated into regular university curricula. Schools of social work, however, would be ideal sites for such courses, as they are mandated by their accrediting bodies (the Council on Social Work Education in the United States; the Canadian Association of Schools of Social Work in Canada) to work toward social justice. Participatory action research courses would provide social work students with needed training in non-oppressive and social change–oriented research strategies, which are consistent with the pursuit of emancipation and equity.

Because education in participatory research, as it is also known, has not been widely offered in universities, researchers are often left to fend for themselves. Maguire (1993) described the obstacles she encountered doing participatory research in her doctoral dissertation, while others first developed their participatory research in their field work (Mason & Boutilier, 1996). Although there are notable exceptions (Martin, 1996a; Meulenberg-Buskens, 1996; Tolley & Bentley, 1996), relatively little has been written on the particular difficulties, challenges, and pleasures of teaching

PAULE MCNICOLL is assistant professor, School of Social Work, University of British Columbia.
This article is based on a paper presented at the Fourth International Social Science Methodology Conference at the University of Essex, July 1996, Colchester, UK.

participatory research. My objectives in this article are to share my experiences based on two years of teaching, alert those who are planning similar courses about expectant challenges, and reassure them that it is both possible and deeply satisfying to prepare students for research that furthers the goals of social justice.

Definition and Critique

Participatory action research puts "research capabilities in the hands of the deprived and disenfranchised people so they can transform their lives for themselves" (Park, 1993, p. 1). It is what happens when researchers are both part of the population to be researched and beneficiaries of the findings. These participants are involved in all stages of the research project, which includes education, reflection, research, and action. Academic and professional researchers serve not only as experts, but as co-learners who share their research skills and also recognize and benefit from the skills and knowledge of the other group members.

The emergence of participatory action research stems from the development of critical perspectives and practices "in the countries of the South" and the recent expansions of perspectives on knowledge in the Northern hemisphere (Tandon, 1996, p.20). Participatory action research has the power to revolutionize the way social scientists do research, that is, by working "*with* and *for* people rather than *on* people" (Reason, 1988, p. 1). It has been linked to empowerment and social awareness (Martin, 1996b; Park, 1993; Ristock & Pennell,

1996), counter-hegemonic practice (Hall, 1993), and the breaking of the "academic monopoly" on knowledge production (Hall, 1979; Hall, Gillette, & Tandon, 1982).

Participatory action research does have its critics. Stanley and Wise (1983) fear that using traditional science techniques, even when working *with* women and oppressed people, will further their exploitation. In a similar vein, Maguire (1987) warns that the progressive character of participatory action research should not prevent us from seeing the androcentric bias it conceals—by which she means that participatory action research has not completely rejected this approach to science. Other researchers report the difficulties of real power-sharing among research partners (Kent, 1996; Mason & Boutilier, 1996). The current popularity of participatory research is also perceived as a potentially dangerous trend by some who fear that it will become the only acceptable way to do research and, therefore, could stifle the vitality of progressive work (Duelli Klein, 1983). Advocates for participatory action research, however, surely recognize that other approaches could also lead toward liberatory knowledge and progressive action.

Notwithstanding their cautions, most critics are also proponents of participatory research for several reasons. First, such research leads directly to action because it arouses the motivation of those directly involved. Second, it sets in motion a permanent process of reflection that leads to subsequent and continuous actions (Comstock & Fox, 1993). Colorado (1988) sees a good fit between participatory action research and aboriginal culture and science because both focus on alliance rather than on separation and hierarchy. Participatory action research has been used in health promotion (Ritchie, 1996), community planning and development (Comstock & Fox, 1993), land use studies (Jackson, 1993), needs assessments (Gould, 1994; Jackson & McKay, 1982), feminist studies (Reinharz, 1992), and evaluation research (Morrell-Bellai & Boydell, 1994), among other purposes. Its use is increasing in Latin America (Fals-Borda & Rahman, 1991), Asia (Hall, Gillette, & Tandon, 1982; Kassam & Mustafa, 1982), Africa (Mwansa, Mufune, & Osei-Hwedie, 1994), Australia (Ritchie, 1996), the United Kingdom and Europe (Callaway, 1981; Dubell, Erasmie, & deVries, 1980) and North America (Park, Bryden-Miller, Hall, & Jackson, 1993).

Experiences

When I first undertook to teach participatory action research to a group of undergraduate students, I searched the literature in vain for guidelines and advice. I knew in advance that the experience would be unlike any other introductory research methodology courses I had taught, but remained unaware of the potential hurdles I would meet along the way. Nevertheless, I share my experiences to reassure colleagues that the task is feasible, worthwhile, and, at times, even exhilarating.

The students who took the course were in their last year of the bachelor's degree in social work. They had already successfully completed one course on research methodology and one on statistical analysis. With one last research course remaining, they were allowed to choose between a course on participatory research and one on practice evaluation. The group split about equally, which resulted in classes of approximately 25 students. The participatory action research group was very diverse in terms of life experiences, ages, races, cultures, and social classes. Most students (80%), as is typical of schools of social work, were women. Thirty-five percent were from visible minority groups, mostly students of Chinese and South Asian descent and including a few American Indian students. About half of the remaining students came from cultural backgrounds other than British: Eastern and Western European, French-Canadian, as well as several from mixed heritage. Their ages ranged from 24 to 60 with a median of 30. Statistics on social class and life experiences were not kept, but interests and experiences shared by the students in class evidenced much diversity.

Case Examples

In two years, 60 students completed 14 projects, using either qualitative or quantitative methods, sometimes both. The following are some of the projects.

- One action project on dating violence involved 15 volunteer interviewees using feminist qualitative research principles. The interview data were analyzed, and women who had experienced dating violence on campus integrated the research findings in a play.
- Euro- and Chinese-Canadians talked about their mutual views of each others' com-

munity during two focus group sessions and challenged the news media to stop feeding misconceptions. Transcriptions of the focus groups were analyzed using the constant comparative approach, and the results were disseminated through a 10-minute videotape.

- A group of self-advocates expressed their displeasure at being labelled mentally disabled. Three participants in this group surveyed their peers using a questionnaire that contained both closed- and open-ended questions. In a second stage of the project, participants present a huge collage exhibition, which seemed to have more impact on the community than the mostly quantitative findings of the survey. Through the exercise, the participants found the motivation, interest, and hope to fight the stereotypes that affected them.

Many students used the university or the school as their action research turf.

- A study of barriers faced by visually impaired university students led to the formation of a self-help group and the installation of at least one new safe street crossing. The students used an observation participant approach, where notes were collated, audiotaped, and analyzed in collaboration with blind participants.
- Documentation of instances of racism on campus provided the impulse for a university-wide study sponsored by the student association. This was done through a survey containing closed- and open-ended questions.
- A satisfaction survey of the social work student body culminated in a multimedia exhibition of findings and an open forum, followed by a community enhancement project and an assessment of day care needs.
- One group of friends who did a self-study of their own group dynamics by content analysis of taped meetings and comparative analysis of standard educational and personality tests came close to a breaking point before finding greater appreciation for one another and for difference.

In this article, I use the case of youth who painted graffiti and vandalized their community center but gained new appreciation and services after presenting a video and an art display of their needs. Most of the challenges

encountered in training for participatory action research will be illustrated. Three social work students established rapport with these adolescents from a poor neighborhood (called here East City) who were angry to be the only group ignored by their local community center. They were labelled "delinquents" by community workers and were somewhat feared locally. Some reconciliation between the adolescents and staff of the center occurred during the project, and the adolescents of East City eventually got their own community social worker and own space in the community center.

Teaching Challenges

The special challenges of teaching action-oriented research, as contrasted with other research courses, can be summarized via six main issues: (1) the need to adopt a new research perspective; (2) the tension between grading and modeling; (3) the realization that ethical considerations sometimes hide social control elements; (4) the limitation of the time frame; (5) the tension between research and action; and (6) the need to pay attention to group process. How instructors attend to these issues will make a huge difference: either participatory action research will be perceived as 'just another fad,' or we will see the emergence of researchers with the necessary attitude and skills to exploit the full transformative potential of this approach.

A New Perspective on Research

A first hurdle instructors face is the blank stare of students who do not grasp the difference between a traditional research approach and research oriented toward action. They do not immediately perceive the action component; for them, participatory action research is just another method of acquiring knowledge. Therefore, they can be confused as to how to do such research.

There are two main areas of confusion. First, many students have an experimental view of research. They tend to ask comparison questions, such as "Is this group more politically aware than this other group?" The jump to action-oriented and participatory types of research is enormous, and most students initially wonder if they are even in the right class. They do not recognize the validity of other types of research questions, especially broad ones such as "What does the experience of becoming politically aware look and feel like?" I have found it helpful to start from students' own research questions, or from the comparative questions they think they should be asking. I then pose the many different ways these questions may be phrased. For example, "Are adolescents from East City (a poor neighborhood) more delinquent than those of West City (an affluent neighborhood)?" can become "How does it feel like to be 13 to 16 years old, poor, and offered no services by your own community center?"; "Are adolescents of East City 'delinquent'?" can become "What do East City adolescents say they need?"

After three or more examples of this type, students are generally surprised by how relevant and flexible research can be. At this point, they may well be more prepared to see their own seeking as legitimate and to think in terms of action as well as inquiry. Students' research questions are often ignored in research methodology courses in favor of the textbook's and instructor's examples, but it is crucial for students of participatory action research to be open to their own and others' tacit research desires and motivations. Researchers who fail to recognize their own research questions as valid can hardly help a community generate a full complement of alternative questions that can be used to solve a given problem. With participatory action research, theory and social skills need to work hand in hand.

The second type of confusion has to do with the predominant desire of students to study other people, or situations that have nothing to do with their own. Part of this stems from the positivist code of objectivity: only those people who are disinterested in a topic can research it. But choosing to explore unknown territories in participatory research means cutting yourself off from a strong source of motivation toward action, much contextual knowledge of the situation, and important allies in the effort to promote change. This distant attitude toward research may also be objectionable on ethical grounds; it has encouraged a kind of voyeurism, particularly in the predominantly white middle-class students who have traditionally come to colleges and universities. As Noel (1993) puts it, those who benefit from being perceived as "mainstream" cannot see themselves as subjects of research.

Students from increasingly multicultural backgrounds are leading us toward a con-

sciousness of their higher visibility as potential study subjects. Their feedback, and the feedback of many overstudied communities, help us also to realize that studies not followed by information and action are both exploitative and no longer wanted. Study populations increasingly want to be integral participants from beginning to end, from phrasing the original questions to interpretation and diffusion of the results. They are suspicious of academic researchers' motives, which they correctly see as influential on the findings and outcome. They want to understand the motivation of those who plan to study their community. As Lili Walker, an Australian aboriginal woman, put it:

> If you are here to help me, then you are wasting your time. But if you come because your liberation is bound up in mine, then let us begin. (in Schutzman & Cohen-Cruz, 1994, pp. 183–184)

To help students deal with this second type of confusion, one may teach them to ask questions about their own communities and identify the resources for change they could involve in various phases of a project. In the process, they will realize the full relevance of research in their own lives and be prepared to face the responsibilities that come with knowledge of research methods.

Grading versus Modeling

Traditional research methods fit well within academic structures. One can teach survey and/or experimental techniques; students set their own projects, write reports, and are graded. Beyond teaching the techniques, little instructor involvement is required for training the students to work in the field. Students become professionals who know how to keep their distance and do "objective" research. Without much instructor involvement, the better-prepared students produce better papers, and vice versa. This scenario produces reliable grading because a student's intellectual capabilities, effort, and life challenges are relatively stable characteristics.

Preparing students to do participatory action research requires more than teaching research methods. The instructor must call on students' group work and community organization skills. Because the relationship between researcher and study participants will be a major determinant of the study outcome, students have to learn what this relationship entails. This is best done through modeling by the instructor. Ideally the instructor in the class—and the researcher in the community— takes the role of coach, someone who instills and helps maintain motivation, clarifies matters when the research project gets muddy (as it often does), and provides methodological guidance and encouragement. Unfortunately, such involvement comes at the price of reliable grading, since not everyone needs, and therefore receives, the same level of instructor support.

In my opinion, the increased validity more than adequately compensates for the loss of reliability. An instructor who takes into account students' ability to take full advantage of resources and consultation may be grading the *real* ability of students to do field research, rather than solely the ability to follow instructions received during class lectures.

I received some evidence of the necessity for instructor/principal researcher involvement when I was consulted by a community researcher who had been given traditional training (accompanied by modeling of a "hands-off' approach to research). The problem presented was the loss of enthusiasm for a project that had started in high spirits. Participants, in this case pregnant women addicted to drugs and alcohol, got discouraged by the difficulties encountered during their evaluation project. When asked what she had suggested to solve these difficulties, the researcher said she had made no suggestions and that she had refrained from warning the other women of the coming pitfalls, although she knew their plans were leading to trouble. She had not shared her knowledge, "because to empower people, you have to let them do their own mistakes." Believing that knowledge equals power, the researcher feared that the women participants would be at a disadvantage if she showed she knew more than they did. Fortunately, if knowledge can be shared, so can power, and this situation soon improved after the researcher started to share her knowledge and resources with the research team.

This community researcher was right in thinking one can disempower people by showing greater knowledge. The know-how to share knowledge effectively is not something that instructors can assume is learned automatically; rather, the best way I know of teaching this is through modeling, discussion, and feedback. The price to pay is having to grade a final project which has often benefited from instructor input.

Ethics versus Social Control

Universities require that all research projects involving people, whether conducted by students or faculty, be pre-approved by university ethics committees to ensure that respondents are protected from abuse and exploitation. This protective function is extremely important and is not problematic for participatory action research. However, ethics committees have developed their criteria and procedures based upon traditional forms of research, with an emphasis on consent, confidentiality, and lack of deception. Recommendations to equalize the power differential between researchers and respondents, such as informing participants of the results of the study, are gradually being added. With growing interest about academic research in the media, and the possibility of media outrage and even legal complications, some university ethics committees have moved to protect the interests of the university as well as those of research participants. This new role as safeguard of institutional reputation often results in more rigid regulations and increased processing time.

For researchers involved in participatory action research, it is hard to know the appropriate moment to enter the ethics committee procedure, because the research itself starts with the first contact with the community partners. One either files the ethics form at this stage, and gets it back for lack of a defined research question, or files the form when the question is fully formulated. The person then has to explain to the community partners that the process must stop for a month or two while the ethics of the project are being evaluated.

It can also be tough to tell whether one needs to seek approval of the university ethics committee at all. When one's research methodology mainly uses adult education techniques (Freire, 1970; Nadeau, 1996) as data gathering, is it research? Take, for instance, the case of adolescents interested in identifying the needs of other adolescents in their neighborhood. They put huge blank wall posters in the local schools and invited their peers to write graffiti, ideas, slogans, and jokes on them. If this action is merely perceived as a step toward meeting students' needs, the adolescent researchers require only the permission of the school principal. If they call it research, however, they might have multiple hurdles to clear: not only do they need the approval of the university ethics committee, but they must get local school board and parents' permissions.

Participatory action research is a relatively new form of research on campuses and has yet to be fully recognized by university procedures. As such, it requires more flexible treatment by ethics committees. The fact that the university researcher has less control over the research process may worry ethics committee members. Moreover, the transformative nature of the work may be unwelcome in some powerful quarters that may have influence on university affairs. To the extent that participatory action research is about "breaking the monopoly of the university" over knowledge (Hall, 1979; Hall, Gillette, & Tandon, 1982), those who challenge the academic institution are likely to encounter opposition (Heany, 1993). Thus, those who want to work at empowerment have first to create the conditions of empowerment for themselves. They can do so by sensitizing their respective ethics committees to the special requirements for participatory action research, possibly with the support of their school, faculty, and/or professional associations (e.g., CSWE).

Limited Time Frame

As mentioned earlier, the best way to learn participatory action research is to do it firsthand. Unfortunately, 13- to 26 week sessions are very unnatural time frames for the completion of such projects. By and large, it takes longer to complete participatory action research than other types of research. Maguire addresses the problem of not knowing where to start (1987, pp. 111–112) and points at the unlikelihood of being "requested" by a community to do participatory research. At first, a researcher faces the time-consuming and uncertain task of gaining the trust of a community. Then comes the task of getting them interested in inquiry. Once this is done, discovering the right questions in a collective way takes much more time than a single researcher or group of academic researchers would need. Groups have their own dynamics, timings, and priorities; research activities should ideally intersperse among the activities and events of their daily lives. This is real time—as opposed to a university's rigid time

frame—and if we are to work with marginalized people, it needs to be respected. On the other hand, one advantage to a limited time frame is that students are compelled to be realistic and choose projects with their own communities.

This issue of time is first contextual, but also has important ramifications in the essential shift in a researcher's attitude. A major distinction between traditional and participatory research concerns the continuity of the

---

Either participatory action research will be perceived as 'just another fad,' or we will see the emergence of researchers with the necessary attitude and skills to exploit the full transformative potential of this approach.

---

relationship. Traditional researchers leave the field after completion of the project; no ongoing involvement exists because no real relationship was established in the first place. But this disappearance can be perceived as abandonment by communities that have worked closely with a researcher to promote change in their locale. A mutually respectful relationship may become more distant over time, of course, but should not be broken altogether. The rapid opening and closing of relationships is a cultural trait of the nonmarginalized, one which others may not understand.

The students who worked with the adolescents of East City had to leave the neighborhood because they found jobs in other cities at the completion of the project. They kept an interest and some communication with the youth with whom they worked, but they left before meeting the community worker who was hired on a temporary contract. Ideally, they would have remained until permanent services were in place.

Tension between Research and Action

Participatory action research is used sometimes to signify an accent on action and other times to emphasize research goals. In the first instance, a process of information gathering, group discussion, and soul searching leads to greater awareness and action in some communities. In all research projects, however, it is important to ensure against bias of the results. The critical point is to be clear at the onset what the goals are and to keep a proper balance between research and action goals during the course of the project. This brings to the fore the issue of objectivity. Although, like many critics of positivist research methods, I do not believe in the objective insularity of the researcher, I do believe that bias and subjectivity exist and can be problematic.

In our case example, a few co-researchers were more eager to express themselves than to provide a space for the youths' expression. Although these co-researchers found camera work and interviewing to be empowering, the principal researchers took the time to confront the playing of jokes on interviewees and ensure that all neighborhood youth could truly be heard during the remainder of the project. In this instance, the action goals (empowerment for the interviewers) threatened to supersede and negate the research goals (knowledge of the needs and desires of neighborhood youth). This tension between research and action goals is present in most projects, and needs to be discussed and clarified repeatedly. Members of the community who are not directly involved in the study, classmates working on different projects, and the instructor all can provide useful feedback to researchers and co-researchers in this respect. An additional strength can be the timely integration of other social work courses, particularly in community development and group work, either before or alongside participatory research courses.

Attention to Group Process

Because of the complex human relationships at play, attention to group process, at both class and community levels, is especially important for those teaching participatory action research. Group process is always an issue for students whenever they have to produce a collective product. Although most are ill-prepared for the difficulties in group dynamics that arise, students are often left to fend for themselves with their group assignments. Some students cannot find a way to participate equitably, some coast on the work of their peers, and others believe that they

carry the whole project on their shoulders. Many say that they have been "burned" during the completion of collective assignments and avoid further courses requiring group work. In these cases, not only are the benefits expected from group exercises (e.g., preparing practitioners for collaborative practice) lost, but indifference is replaced by fear and loathing.

Group dynamics determine, in great part, the success or failure of participatory research. Because students are involved in projects with community members, the importance of group dynamics is more crucial here than in other cases where students simply complete group projects with one another. How does one, for instance, handle in-fighting in the participating community? In the East City project, students found themselves disparaged by community center workers because of their alliance with "delinquent" local youth. Regaining the trust of these workers and creating opportunities for cooperative exchanges took more than theoretical and methodological preparation; students needed support, critical feedback, and their own group work skills. Instructors teaching participatory action research have the opportunity to model the relationship between professional and community researchers. The power differential between instructor and students can be used to illustrate the crucial mistake of assuming equality of power and equality of input (Bryceson & Mustafa, 1982).

Anyanwu (1988, p. 15) cites "willingness to learn from and with the people, sensitivity, adaptability, patience, empathy and a flexibility of attitude" among the attitudes and skills needed by participatory researchers. To these, Meulenberg-Buskens (1996, pp. 42–43) adds "an attitude of and a capacity for critical reflection on the participatory-research process . . . and the commitment to stimulate that attitude and capacity in others who are involved in the research." Without these skills, which are not emphasized in traditional research, students risk becoming disenchanted with collaborative research; worse, projects aimed at social justice may result in disempowerment and exploitation. Here again, one may be reminded of the need to see participatory research as only one of many courses that provide the skills and attitudes for empowerment work.

Other Difficulties

Not all the projects completed as course requirements were truly participatory because the impetus sometimes came from the students rather than the community. Once the process was initiated, however, the original research questions and goals for action were vastly modified, and in most cases the community took ownership of the process. People with psychiatric illnesses who were approached by students in a drop-in activity center and who ended up playing an active part in a provincial health consultation did not remember who had approached whom; they felt they were acting on their own agenda.

Some students encountered insurmountable difficulties and could not complete a project. Those instances generally involved an institution protecting itself against criticism, loss of funding, or both. In all cases, students were not well connected (or not well enough) to the community with which they wanted to work. Asian students focusing on the mental health needs of their local high school counterparts may have had the support of the student association and teachers, but not the clout necessary at the administration level. Even in cases where official permission was obtained, it was not always sufficient. Administrators of a host program for new immigrants realized the thoroughness of the students' research investigation and balked at publicizing the results. One central person in a second-stage transition house for women dragged her feet so much that the feedback from the women was not available in time for class presentation. Students who could not complete a project were then asked to critically analyze the situation, the process, their own strategy, and the impact on the community of their attempt at action research.

Rewards

As the instructor leading a class through uncharted waters, I feared being overwhelmed by students' needs and demands. Both years, however, I was surprised at their self-sufficiency. After an initial period of anxiety, when students were scrambling for ideas and checking and rechecking their plans, came a period when I felt almost neglected. I was consulted for major hurdles, but mostly students kept busy solving problems where and with whom they arose. If gratification can be summarized in a brief instant, this moment for me—observing a group of bright-eyed students in hot discussion about a point I cannot remember, but that had to do with social action and research—was it.

Conclusion

Participatory action research is too important a tool to be ignored by schools of social work, especially those that have adopted programs with a focus on structures of oppression, the fight for social justice, and embracement of diversity. If social work truly means to break its legacy of alliance with and legitimization of institutional power, the profession will have to develop new research and intervention approaches. As Hall, Gillette, and Tandon (1982) write:

> Research and research institutions play an important role in the development of national and international strategies for social transformation. Research is used by the ruling classes to justify or maintain unfavorable or exploitative positions. But, by the same measure, if research is playing an increasing role in the development of new strategies of control, it can at the same time be used to provide both an alternative analysis and a means of expanding the base of analysis to include the most exploited sectors of society. (p. 6)

Participatory action research approaches require a major shift in attitudes and behaviors related to power relations. The relative novelty of these approaches in university settings will doubtless cause trepidation for some instructors, but I hope this account of the difficulties and joys I have encountered will be instructive and will encourage those who contemplate teaching participatory action research to take the initial plunge. Instructors who take the challenge will find the experience rewarding.

REFERENCES

Anyanwu, C. N. (1988). The technique of participatory research in community health. *Community Development Journal, 23*(1), 11–15.
Bryceson, D., & Mustafa, K. (1982). Participatory research: Refining the relationship between theory and practice. In Y. Kassam and K. Mustafa (Eds.), *PR.: An emerging alternative methodology in social science research* (pp. 87–109). New Delhi: Society for Participatory Research in Asia.
Callaway, H. (Ed.). (1981). *Case studies in participatory research.* Amersfoort, The Netherlands: Netherlands Centre for Research and Development in Adult Education.
Colorado, P. (1988). Bridging native and western science. *Convergence, 21* (2/3), 49–68.
Comstock, D. E., & Fox, R. (1993). Participatory research as critical theory: The North Bonneville, USA, experience. In P. Park, M. Bryden-Miller, B. Hall, & T. Jackson (Eds.), *Voices of change: Participatory research in the United States and Canada* (pp. 41–46). Westport, CT: Bergin and Garvey.

Dubell, F., Erasmie, T., & de Vries, J. (Eds.). (1980). *Research for the people, research by the people.* Likoping, Sweden: Likoping University Press.

Duelli Klein, R. (1983). How to do what we want to do: Thoughts about feminist methodology. In C. Bowles & R. Duelli Klein (Eds.), *Theory of women's studies* (pp.88–104). Boston: Routledge, Kegan and Paul.

Fals-Borda, 0., & Rahman, M. A. (Eds.). (1991). *Action and knowledge: Breaking the monopoly with participatory action-research.* New York: Apex.

Freire, P. (1970). *Pedagogy of the oppressed.* New York: Seabury.

Gould, K. (1994). *Ideas about health care from very marginalized women from all over Vancouver.* Unpublished manuscript prepared for the Vancouver Health Board.

Hall, B. (1979). Participatory research: Breaking the academic monopoly. In J. Niemi (Ed.), Viewpoints on adult education (pp. 43–69). De Kalb: Northern Illinois University Press.

Hall, B. (1993). Introduction. In P. Park, M. Bryden-Miller, B. Hall, & T. Jackson (Eds.), *Voices of change: Participatory research in the United States and Canada* (pp. xiii–xxii) . Westport, CT: Bergin and Garvey.

Hall, B., Gillette, A., & Tandon, R. (Eds.). (1982). *Creating knowledge: A monopoly?* New Delhi: Society for Participatory Research in Asia.

Heany, T. (1993). If you can't beat 'em, join 'em: The professionalization of participatory research. In P. Park, M. Bryden-Miller, B. Hall, & T.Jackson (Eds.), *Voices of change: Participatory research in the United States and Canada* (pp. 41-46). Westport, CT: Bergin and Garvey.

Jackson, T. (1993). A way of working: Participatory research and the aboriginal movement in Canada. In P. Park, M. Bryden-Miller, B. Hall, & T. Jackson (Eds.), *Voices of change: Participatory research in the United States and Canada* (pp. 47-74). Westport, CT: Bergin and Garvey.

Jackson, T., & McKay, G. (1982). Sanitation and water supply in Big Trout Lake: Participatory research for democratic technical solutions. *Canadian Journal of Native Studies, 2* (1), 129–145.

Kassam, Y., & Mustafa, K. (Eds.). (1982). *PR: An emerging alternative methodology in social science research.* New Delhi: Society for Participatory Research in Asia.

Kent, J. (1996, July). Group inquiry: A democratic dialogue? Paper presented at the Fourth International Social Science Methodology Conference, Colchester, UK.

Maguire, P. (1987). *Doing participatory research: A feminist approach.* Amherst: Center for International Education, University of Massachusetts.

Maguire, P. (1993). Challenges, contradictions and celebrations: Attempting participatory research as a doctoral student. In P. Park, M. Bryden-Miller, B. Hall, & T. Jackson (Eds.), *Voices of change: Participatory research in the United States and Canada* (pp. 157–176). Westport, CT: Bergin and Garvey.

Martin, M. (1996a,July). *Teaching and learning in participatory research: Issues and experiences from practice.* Paper presented at the Fourth International Social Science Methodology Conference, Colchester, UK.

Martin, M. (1996b). Issues of power in the participatory research process. In K. de Koning & Martin (Eds.), *Participatory research in health: Issues and experiences* (pp. 82–93). London: Zed Books.

Mason, R., & Boutilier, M. (1996). The challenge of genuine power-sharing in participatory research: The gap between theory and practice. *Canadian Journal of Community Mental Health, 15(2),* 145–152.

Meulenberg-Buskens, I. (1996). Critical awareness in participatory research: An approach towards teaching and learning. In K. de Koning & M. Martin (Eds.), *Participatory research in health: Issues and experiences* (pp. 40–49). London: Zed Books.

Morrell-Bellai, T., & Boydell, K. (1994). The experience of mental health consumers as researchers. *Canadian Journal of Community Mental Health, 13(1),* 97–110.

Mwansa, L. K., Mufune, P., & Osei-Hwedie, K. (1994). Youth policy and programmes in the SADC countries of Botswana, Swaziland and Zambia: A comparative assessment. *International Social Work, 37(3),* 239–263.

Nadeau, D. (1996). *Counting our victories: Popular education and organizing.* Vancouver: Repeal the Deal Productions.

Noel, L. (1993). *Intolerance: A general survey.* Montreal: McGill-Queens University Press.

Park, P. (1993). What is participatory research? A theoretical and methodological perspective. In P. Park, M. Bryden-Miller, B. Hall, & T. Jackson (Eds.), *Voices of change: Participatory research in the United States and Canada* (pp. 1-19). Westport, CT: Bergin and Garvey.

Park, P., Bryden-Miller, M., Hall, B., & Jackson, T. (Eds.). (1993). *Voices of change: Participatory research in the United States and Canada.* Westport, CT: Bergin and Garvey.

Reason, P. (Ed.). (1988). *Human inquiry in action: Developments in a new paradigm of research.* London: Sage.

Reinharz, S. (1992). Feminist action research. In S. Reinharz (Ed.), *Feminist methods for social research* (pp. 175–196). New York: Oxford.

Ristock, J. L., & Pennell, J. (1996). *Community research as empowerment: Feminist links, postmodern interruptions.* Don Mills, ON: Oxford University Press Canada.

Ritchie, J. E. (1996). Using participatory research to enhance health in the work setting: An Australian experience. In K. de Koning & M Martin (Eds.), *Participatory research in health: Issues and experiences* (pp. 204–215). London: Zed Books.

Schutzman, M., & Cohen-Cruz, J. (Eds.). (1994) *Playing Boal: Theatre, therapy, activism.* New York: Routledge.

Stanley, L., & Wise, S. (1983). *Breaking out: Feminist consciousness and feminist research.* London: Routledge, Kegan and Paul.

Tandon, R. (1996). The historical roots and contemporary tendencies in participatory research: Implications for health care. In K. de Koning & M. Martin (Eds.) , *Participatory research in health: Issues and experiences* (pp. 19–26). London: Zed Books.

Tolley E. E., & Bentley, M. E. (1996). Training issues for the use of participatory research methods in health. In K. de Koning & M. Martin (Eds.), *Participatory research in health: Issues and experiences* (pp. 50–61). London: Zed Books.

Accepted 5/98

Address correspondence to: Paule McNicoll, University of British Columbia, School of Social Work, 2080 West Mall, Vancouver, BC V6T 1 Z2.

Practical Issues for Teachers Conducting Classroom Research

Marilyn K. Rousseau
Brian Kai Yung Tam

We have found many barriers and benefits associated with conducting classroom research (see accompanying boxes on following pages)—but in our view, the benefits outweigh the barriers, and we would like to encourage teachers to engage in research. *The most important benefit is the increased learning of students—which is the object of classroom research.*

In this article, we discuss practical issues regarding some of the controls necessary for successful classroom research. We discuss how to select a research topic, choose an appropriate research design, and maintain a sufficient number of participants. In addition, we discuss management and logistical problems of maintaining appropriate student behavior, creating classroom conditions favorable to research, and scheduling time for research. We focus on *single-subject* research because it is more easily incorporated into daily classroom instruction than in most group-design research.

Identifying a Practical Research Topic

Your research topic should address a realistic classroom problem (Mohr, 1994), such as an academic problem or a question about better ways to teach or manage student behavior. Research topics might include lengthening a student's attention span, increasing the amount of work a student completes in a given time period, determining the best pacing of lesson presentation, or determining whether a student has a motivational problem or a learning problem (Rousseau & Poulson, 1989).

By reviewing the research literature, you can identify a topic and get background information for developing a research project. Your literature review might uncover a study that could be systematically replicated in your classroom. A procedure that has been effective in a different setting or with a different group of participants could provide solutions to the problem you have identified.

Selecting an Appropriate Research Design

Single-subject research is concerned with the functional (cause and effect) relationship between an intervention of an individual participant's response over time in which the person serves as his or her own control (Baer, Wolf, & Risley, 1968). In most single-subject designs used in classroom research, baseline data consisting of ongoing daily records are collected on the response under study for several days or weeks to provide a record of the response before the intervention is introduced. Baseline data enable you to evaluate the performance of each student with and without the intervention.

The following description of single-subject research designs show how each type of design might be used in classroom research. This section will give you an idea of the types of practical questions that can be answered by classroom research.

Reversal Design

The reversal design is a single-subject design in which experimental control is demonstrated if the response increases or decreases only when the intervention is introduced or removed (Baer, Wolf, & Risley, 1968). The

sequence of introducing experimental conditions is usually baseline, intervention, baseline, in an *ABA* sequence where *A* represents baseline and *B* represents intervention. A more complete reversal design is *ABAB,* in which a successful intervention is reintroduced after the second baseline. The reversal design is useful when the response under study is reversible. In other words, when the intervention is removed, the response returns to near-baseline levels.

Examples of a reversal design include classroom management problems such as out-of-seat, talk-outs, and arguing, and "motivation" problems such as being late to class, not submitting homework on time, or not completing assignments.

Multiple-Baseline Design

The multiple-baseline design (Baer, Wolf, & Risley, 1968) is useful when the response under study is not reversible. This design is often useful in studying the acquisition of academic skills. In a multiple-baseline across-subjects design, in which the response to be changed (increased, in this case) is the percentage of words read correctly during 1 min of oral reading, for example, baseline data are recorded on several participants' correct oral reading rates simultaneously.

When all participants' baselines are stable, the intervention is introduced to the first participant only, and baseline is continued for the other participants. When the first participant's correct oral reading rate increases, the intervention is introduced for the second participant, and baseline is continued for the other participants. This procedure is repeated until all participants have experienced both the baseline and intervention conditions *(AB)*. As with the reversal design, experi-

Barriers to Conducting Research

Teachers and researchers often want to find effective instructional methods to enable students to acquire and retain knowledge under realistic classroom conditions. Certain barriers, however, often discourage educators from applying or conducting research in the classroom:

- Much educational and psychological research in education is conducted in controlled laboratory environments instead of classrooms (Olejnik & Doeyan, 1982: Snyder, 1992).
- Many studies cannot be implemented in the classroom because of lack of support or poor participation by schools (Bennett, 1993; Olejnik & Doeyan, 1982).
- According to Duckett (1986), school administrators and teachers are often skeptical about the importance of educational research and are reluctant to participate.
- Many believe that most educational research is done by college professors who do not know much about real-life classrooms (Duckett, 1986).
- Unfortunately, many teachers suffer from "research mystique"—the misconception that research is beyond the understanding of classroom teachers (Gable & Rogers, 1987).
- Many teachers probably do not realize the parallels between teaching and research (Tawney & Gast, 1984).
- Although some teachers might read research journals to improve their teaching skills and to stay abreast of current instructional information, most are not well trained in incorporating research findings into classroom applications (Duckett, 1986).

Despite these problems, classroom research can be a valuable tool for teachers who are interested in finding better ways to teach and who are willing to learn research techniques.

---

mental control is demonstrated if the correct oral reading rates change only with the introduction of the intervention. The multiple-baseline design can be used:

- Across settings (e.g., to determine whether free time is an effective reinforcer in different classrooms).
- Across students (e.g., to determine whether an instructional method works with different students).
- Across responses (e.g., to determine whether self-recording will increase the rate of correct answers by the same student on written assignments in math, spelling, and reading).

Changing-Criterion Design

A third type of design is the changing-criterion design (Hartmann & Hall, 1976). This is a baseline-intervention *(AB)* design in which the criterion for reinforcement during intervention is increased in small steps over time until the responses reach an acceptable level. This design is useful, for example, if you want to change a student's performance level on responses such as the percentage correct of increasingly difficult spelling words, or the number of words read aloud correctly by a child who is reluctant to try.

Alternating-Treatments Design

The alternating-treatments design is used to evaluate the effectiveness of two or more treatments or interventions (Barlow &

Hayes, 1979). For example, this design has been used to determine which of two treatments (silent or listening previewing) is more effective in increasing the oral reading rates of bilingual students with speech and language impairments in a special education class (Rousseau & Tam, 1991). Usually, in this design, baseline data are collected, then two or more interventions are introduced for each participant and are alternated in random order across research sessions or days.

Maintaining Sufficient Numbers of Participants

You can use the whole class, a small group, or individual students as participants, or subjects, in single-subject research, depending on the research question. Regardless of the number, single-subject research requires collecting individual data on each participant to demonstrate a functional relationship between the intervention and the participant's responses. (Johnston & Pennypacker, 1993).

All Students as Participants

Using too few participants can cause difficulties when you conduct research in your classroom. Sometimes a participant might be unable to complete the study because of chronic absences or because he or she moves to another school district. You can handle such attrition in several ways. One is to include all the students as participants, so that

if one student cannot complete all sessions, it will not adversely affect the study.

In some cases, an entire class can serve as the participant, or subject, in single-subject design. For example, to determine whether a particular procedure will increase the number of students who submit their homework papers on time, you might report data for two or more groups in a multiple-baseline design (Rousseau, Poulson, & Salzberg, 1984).

Students with Good Attendance Records

Another way to handle problems of participant attrition is to consider only those students with good attendance records as research participants. Those students not considered participants, nevertheless, should be included in all research sessions on the days they are present to allow them the benefit of the intervention. Thus, all students in the class would benefit from the procedures to the maximum extent possible. If you maintain records on those students with poor attendance records, you might discover the effects of the intervention on low-attending students. Of course, you might discover an appropriate additional research topic—ways to increase school attendance.

Depending on the policies of your school district, you might be required to submit a research proposal to a review committee to ensure that students' rights are protected. These rights include confidentiality regarding the use of students' names, a statement of any potential risks to students, informed consent of the parents and other safeguards. Formal approval of the research by the school district also helps ensure cooperation by administrators, supervisors, and parents. Parental approval and cooperation might increase students' attendance rates because their children are receiving recognition by participating in a special project.

Creating Classroom Research Conditions

You should gather enough copies of materials and check equipment used in the study each day to avoid delays and malfunctions during research sessions. Use a daily checklist as a reminder of tasks to perform before and during each research session, to help minimize wasted time and provide data for establishing the reliability of the procedures you use (Cooper, Heron, & Heward, 1987; Johnston & Pennypacker, 1993).

Proper arrangement of space can affect the participants' performance, as well as your performance. If necessary, you can use a chalkboard, bookshelf, or cabinet to cordon off an area for research sessions. The research area should allow good visibility so you can monitor the entire classroom; and it should contain few distractions for participants engaged in research sessions (Minner & Prater, 1989).

Maintaining Appropriate Participant Behavior During Research

Classroom Management

Maintaining student behavior in the classroom during research sessions might well be the most important practical issue you face as you conduct classroom research. An effective classroom management plan should be in effect *before* the research begins. If you introduce a behavior management plan to control behavior problems *after* the research study has begun, it might affect participants' performance on the research task, thus confounding the results. You cannot conclude that the intervention produced an effect on the response because another variable was introduced. On the other hand, if the behavior management plan is in place before the study begins and is maintained consistently throughout, it will not confound the results of the study because it was in effect throughout baseline and intervention (Cooper et al., 1987).

Inclusion of All Students

An excellent part of a behavior management plan to maintain interest and on-task responding is to include *all* the students as participants in the research sessions—even if some are not included as subjects in the research. Further suggestions for classroom organization and management are provided by Alberto and Troutman (1995).

Positive Feedback

Effective classroom management can be affected by your own attitude. Participants might give up easily if they think they are not performing well, or if they think you disapprove of their performance (Bargar & Hoover, 1984). Maintaining a pleasant nonjudgmental attitude despite possible disappointing performances can help you avoid giving discouraging feedback to the participants (Bargar & Hoover, 1984). Positive feedback at the end of the session for trying hard can help maintain participants' efforts because increasing success helps build confidence (Schunk, 1989).

Benefits of Classroom Research

Classroom research can benefit teachers and students in many ways:

- Classroom research can be a means for teachers to identify and differentiate the educational needs of their students, to test teaching methods and materials, and to evaluate ongoing programming (Gersten, Morvant, & Brengelman, 1995; Kamps, Carta, Delquadri, Arreaga-Mayer, Terry, & Greenwood, 1989; Kyle, Linn, Bitner, Mitchener, & Perry, 1991).
- Classroom-based research can become a means of bridging the gap between research and practice (Eiserman & Shisler, 1987).
- Cross (1987) proposes that classroom research can help teachers evaluate the effectiveness of their teaching and provide information about student performance in their classrooms.
- Teachers who collect and maintain student data make instructional decisions more effectively than those who do not (Minner, Minner & Lepich, 1990).
- Through classroom research, teachers may identify effective intervention strategies to increase students' acquisition and fluency rates and document their progress. When asked about a student's performance, it is not enough for a teacher to simply say, "He is doing fine" or "She has not made any progress," without basing such statements on reliable data.
- Classroom research can provide program accountability by documenting changes in student performance as a direct result of curricular and methodological interventions.
- Some teachers have reported feeling more positive about themselves in relation to their jobs after engaging in classroom research (Bennett, 1993). As a result, many perceive themselves as professionals whose opinions are valued and respected (Oja & Pine, 1987).
- Teachers who are problem-solvers typically maintain good records and consistently seek better teaching and classroom management procedures (Miller & McDaniel, 1989). Despite similarities between research and teaching, research demands tighter controls than teaching to ensure that the intervention alone produces changes in the response under study.

Scheduling an Optimal Time for Research

Time of Year

Although there is no research reporting the optimal time of the school year for beginning a research study, you should start early enough in the school year to allow time for making adjustments in the procedures if an intervention does not prove effective. You need time to implement an alternative intervention and evaluate its effects before the school year ends.

In addition, if you start classroom research too near the end of the school year, hot weather can cause participants to become restless (Badger & O'Hare, 1989); and it might decrease their attending to the research task. Conversely, neither should you begin research too near the beginning of the school year. Participants need sufficient adaptation time (Catania, 1992), possibly a few weeks, to adjust to the new classroom environment; and you need time to establish a classroom organization and management plan.

Time of Day

Research sessions should be held at the same time of day throughout the study to ensure

that all conditions are the same for all participants (Cooper et al., 1987; Johnston & Pennypacker, 1993). If individual sessions within the designated research time are necessary, as might be the case with oral reading, you should counterbalance the order in which the participants read aloud so that a participant is not always the first or the last to read (Tawney & Gast, 1984). If the focus of the research is a behavior such as off-task that might occur at a high rate immediately after lunch, for example, it would make sense to schedule research sessions after lunch to provide more opportunities for changing the behavior when the intervention is introduced. You might decrease off-task behavior by differentially reinforcing an incompatible behavior (on-task), thus allowing you to use positive reinforcement instead of punishment to decrease the inappropriate response (Deitz & Repp, 1983).

Problem-Solving as a Way of Life

If you are a problem-solver, you have the potential to become a classroom researcher. Finding solutions to classroom problems is similar to conducting classroom research; for both, you must try an intervention and observe its effect on participant behavior. Single-subject research is ideal for use in classrooms because it requires frequent measurement and the use of systematic teaching. Classroom research can solve problems for the teacher-researcher—such as how to increase appropriate social interaction skills or how to improve reading proficiency. Classroom research can help you identify effective intervention strategies to increase students' acquisition and fluency rates and document their progress.

References

Alberto, P. A., & Troutman, A. C. (1995). *Applied behavior analysis for teachers* (4th ed.). Columbus, OH: Charles E. Merrill.

Badger, B., & O'Hare, E. (1989). Disruptive behaviour and weather in a West Cumbria secondary school. *British Education Research Journal, 15,* 89–94.

Baer, D. M., Wolf, M. M., & Risley, T. R. (1968). Some current dimensions of applied behavior analysis. *Journal of Applied Behavior Analysis, 1,* 91–97.

Bargar, R. R., & Hoover, R. L. (1984). Psychological type and the matching of cognitive styles. *Theory Into Practice, 23*(1), 56-63.

Barlow, D. H. & Hayes, S. C. (1979). Alternating treatments design: One strategy for comparing the effects of two treatments in a single subject. *Journal of Applied Behavior Analysis, 12,* 199–210.

Bennett, C. K. (1993). Teacher-researchers: All dressed up and no place to go? *Educational Leadership, 51,* 69–70.

Catania, A. C. (1992). *Learning* (4th ed.). Englewood Cliffs: Prentice Hall.

Cooper, J. O., Heron, T. E., & Heward, W. L. (1987). *Applied behavior analysis.* New York: MacMillan.

Cross, P. K. (1987). The adventures of education in wonderland: Implementing education reform. *Phi Delta Kappan, 68,* 496–502.

Deitz, D. E. D., & Repp, A. C. (1983). Reducing behavior through reinforcement. *Exceptional Education Quarterly, 3,* 34–36.

Duckett, W. (1986). An interview with Robert Eaker: Linking research and classroom practice. *Phi Delta Kappan, 68,* 161–164.

Eiserman, W. D., & Shisler, L. (1987). Research in your classroom. *Childhood Education, 64* (2), 105–108.

Gable, R., & Rogers, V. (1987). Taking the terror out of research. *Phi Delta Kappan, 68,* 690–695.

Gersten, R., Morvant, M., & Brengelman, S. (1995). Close to the classroom is close to the bone: Coaching as a means to translate research into classroom practice. *Exceptional Children, 62,* 52–66.

Hartmann, D. P., & Hall, R. V. (1976). The changing criterion design. *Journal of Applied Behavior Analysis, 9,* 527–532.

Johnston, J. M., & Pennypacker, H. S. (1993). *Strategies and tactics of behavioral research* (2nd ed.). Hillsdale, NJ: Lawrence Erlbaum Associates.

Kamps, D. M., Carta, J. J. Delquadri, J. C., Arreaga-Mayer, C., Terry, B., & Greenwood, C. R. (1989). School-based research and intervention. *Education and Treatment of Children, 12,* 359–390.

Kyle, W. C., Jr., Linn, M. C., Bitner, B. L., Mitchener, C. P., & Perry, B. (1991). The role of research in science teaching: An NSTA theme paper. *Science Education, 75,* 413–418.

Miller, R., & McDaniel, E. A. (1989). Enhancing teacher efficacy in special education through the assessment of student performance. *Academic Therapy, 25,* 171–181.

Minner, S., Minner, J., & Lepich, J. (1990). Maintaining pupil performance data: A guide. *Intervention in School and Clinic, 26 (1),* 32–37.

Minner, S., & Prater, G. (1989). Arranging the physical environment of special education classrooms. *Academic Therapy, 25 (1),* 91–96.

Mohr, M. M. (1994). Teacher-researchers at work. *English Journal, 83,* 19–21.

Oja, S. N., & Pine, G. J. (1987). Collaborative action research: Teachers' stages of development and school contexts. *Peabody Journal of Education, 64,* 96–115.

Olejnik, S. F., & Doeyan, D. J. (1982). Soliciting teacher participants for classroom research. *Journal of Education Research, 75,* 165–168.

Rousseau, M. K., & Poulson, C. L., (1989). Motivation problem or learning problem? *TEACHING Exceptional Children, 21,* 18–19.

Rousseau, M. K., Poulson, C. L., & Salzberg, C. S. (1984). Naturalistic behavioral intervention with inner-city middle school students. *Education and Treatment of Children, 7,* 1–15.

Rousseau, M. K., & Tam, B. K. Y. (1991). The efficacy of previewing and discussion of key words on the oral reading proficiency of bilingual learners with speech and language impairments. *Education and Treatment of Children, 14,* 199–209.

Schunk, D. H. (1989). Self-efficacy and cognitive achievement: Implications for students with learning problems. *Journal of Learning Disabilities, 22,* 14–22.

Snyder, I. (1992). "It's not as simple as you think!" Collaboration between a researcher and a teacher. *English Education, 24,* 195–211.

Tawney, J. W., & Gast, D. L. (1984). *Single subject research in special education.* Columbus, OH: Charles E. Merrill.

Marilyn K. Rousseau *(CEC Chapter #742), Professor of Special Education, The City College and the Doctoral Faculty in Psychology (Learning Processes) and Educational Psychology, the Graduate School of the City University of New York.* **Brian Kai Yung Tam,** *former teacher and Educational Evaluator, New York City Board of Education, New York, and currently doctoral candidate, Special Education and Applied Behavior Analysis, The Ohio State University, Columbus.*

Address correspondence to Marilyn K. Rousseau, The City College of New York, Department of School Services, Room 3/227 NAC, Convent Avenue at 138th Street, New York, NY 10031.

Unit Selections

Key Points to Consider

❖ What influences affect the reliability and validity of studies that use videotaped observations?

❖ Compare the benefits of using telephone interviews and self-administered diaries for daily data collection.

❖ How have focus groups been misused?

❖ State and explain the four advantages of the use of self-report methods.

❖ What are the advantages and disadvantages of using electronic mail surveys?

❖ Discuss the merits and limitations of the following daily reporting methods of data collection; daily diaries; daily telephone initiated by the subjects; daily telephones initiated by the researcher.

❖ Outline the process of questionnaire development and validation.

 **Links** | **www.dushkin.com/online/**

14. **Journal of Undergraduate Research Paper**
    http://www.clas.ufl.edu/CLAS/jur/0001/stanfordpaper.html
15. **Oregon Survey Research Laboratory**
    http://darkwing.uoregon.edu/~osrl/relatdlnks.html
16. **Social Research Update 19: Focus Groups**
    http://www.soc.surrey.ac.uk/sru/SRU19.html
17. **Using E-mail to Survey Internet Users in the United States**
    http://www.ascusc.org/jcmc/vol4/issue3/sheehan.html
18. **Using the Internet for Quantitative Survey Research**
    http://www.swiftinteractive.com/white-p1.htm

These sites are annotated on pages 4 and 5.

There are many means by which researchers systematically collect data and make sense out of it. Although no research method or study is perfect, each method has a profile of strengths and limitations. The strengths are what make one method better suited to a particular research question than the next. The limitations are the drawbacks about which every responsible researcher must be keenly aware.

In Unit 4 we highlight some of the data collection methods that have gained greater acceptance in research involving human subjects. The social sciences pose particular challenges to researchers because they routinely deal with people rather than with things and with complex processes rather than with simple, linear sequences. Although research methods may appear to newcomers to be static and codified, the truth is that they are constantly evolving and changing in response to the perplexing yet interesting task of answering worthwhile questions formulated by researchers. Numbered among the research methods that are currently in wide use are focus groups, the subject of the article by Richard Krueger, and videotaped behavioral observation, the topic of Jennifer Harrison Elder's article. Unit 4 concludes with other types of data collection, including self-evaluation, in "Self-Assessment at Work: Outcomes of Adult Learners' Reflections on Practice," by Catherine Marienau; e-mail surveys in "Using Electronic Mail to Conduct Research," by Liz Thach; and a comparison of three daily data collection methods in an article by Diane Morrison,

Barbara Leigh, and Mary Rogers Gillmore. Unit 4 concludes with Lei Chang's research on college students' attitudes toward quantitative research methods, which illustrates the process of survey design and validation procedures.

Videotaped Behavioral Observations: Enhancing Validity and Reliability

Jennifer Harrison Elder

Observing and quantifying behaviors in natural or clinical settings has long produced challenges for researchers and clinicians. Although nurses are uniquely positioned to conduct behavioral research, they may not be well acquainted with behavioral observation strategies. The author identifies several problems commonly encountered while studying behavior in natural settings and suggests methods for enhancing validity and reliability through videotaped observations. Results of a newly developed calibration procedure are discussed with implications for rater training. Nurse clinicians and researchers should find this information useful for evaluating interventions in clinics, homes, and other applied settings.

EASY ACCESS TO and the relatively low cost of videotaping have contributed to its increasing use in studying human behavior in clinical and home settings. Yet, the systematic development of research procedures related to videotaping has not kept pace. Several problems with this type of data collection methodology can adversely affect validity and reliability, including (a) subject reactivity, (b) environmental extraneous variables, (c) ambiguous behavioral definitions, and (d) low inter-rater agreement in videotape interpretation.

SUBJECT REACTIVITY

"Subject reactivity" is defined by Johnson and Bolstad (1975) as the subject's knowledge

From the College of Nursing, University of Florida, 100187 JHMHC, Gainesville, FL 32610.

Jennifer Harrison Elder, PhD, RN, College of Nursing, University of Florida, 100187 JHMHC, Gainesville, FL 32610.

that he is being observed. Ethical considerations and environmental constraints often prohibit observing subjects without their knowledge; therefore, it is possible that videotaping may threaten the validity of research findings because subjects recognize they are being videotaped. In the most basic sense, "validity" refers to how true or accurately claims or important concerns are measured (Burns & Grove, 1997).

Surprisingly, little has been reported regarding reactivity effects. Well-controlled clinical trials are needed to empirically evaluate whether videotaping influences subject behavior. The author's experience suggests that although subjects may initially be camera-conscious, they become habituated with repeated observations (three to four sessions). Thus, it is likely that reactivity effects are minimized as subjects become accustomed to the observers and/or cameras (Elder, 1995).

"Mock taping sessions" are often useful in familiarizing participants with the videotaping process and reducing reactivity bias. With

From *Applied Nursing Research*, November 1999, pp. 206-209. © 1999 by W. B. Saunders Co. Reprinted by permission.

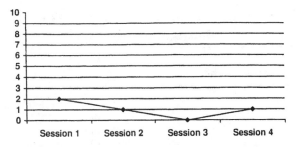

Figure 1. Sample showing stabilization.

this approach, videotaping takes place for several sessions but data obtained from these sessions are not analyzed. This also gives raters opportunities to rehearse the procedure, check for light and sound quality, and determine the most advantageous camera positions. Another method is to conduct numerous baseline sessions where behaviors are coded and analyzed before an intervention is introduced. This method is commonly used in single-subject experimental designs (Elder, 1997). Ideally, baseline data should stabilize, and not show any trends or unusual graphical spikes. An example of stable baseline data is noted in Figure 1, which graphically depicts frequencies of a target behavior recorded during four 10-minute baseline sessions (i.e., sessions that occurred prior to the introduction of the intervention). The line is almost flat, indicating that the behavior occurred with similar frequency across the four baseline sessions.

In sharp contrast to the data in Figure 1 are the unstable rates for another target behavior as depicted in Figure 2. When baseline instability is observed, as in this case, it is critical for investigators to closely examine videotapes and look for confounding (extraneous) variables and/or signs that participants may be overly aware of or distracted by the videotaping procedures.

ENVIRONMENTAL EXTRANEOUS VARIABLES

Polit and Hungler (1997, p. 459) define "internal validity" as "the degree to which it can be inferred that the experimental treatment (independent variable), rather than uncontrolled, extraneous factors, is responsible for the desired effects." In behavioral research, internal validity can be threatened by environmental extraneous variables (e.g., noise from surrounding areas, the presence of other individuals other than research subjects), which may confound findings. It is critical for investigators to consider possible extraneous variables prior to data collection.

Once identified, potential confounds can be eliminated, controlled, or even isolated for study within the context of the treatment. However, even with optimal preparation and planned control, natural settings may offer unexpected interference. Videotape methodology usually surpasses direct behavioral observations with regard to detecting extraneous variables. One reason for this is that raters present in the environment may be so focused on the target behavior(s) that they fail to notice environmental influences. Videotapes can be paused as needed and carefully studied. In addition, because videotapes can be viewed repeatedly, they provide opportunities for more accurate pictures of the actual target behaviors.

Such was the case in Elder's (1997) report of an autistic child engaging in self-stimulatory behavior. Data indicated wide variability across the sessions, and this variability was difficult initially to explain. However, repeated viewing of videotapes indicated the presence of environmental noises from an adjacent room that clearly affected the child's behavior. Because the videotaping method afforded numerous data points over time, it was possible to analyze the graphed data and identify and eliminate the environmental confounding variables.

AMBIGUOUS BEHAVIORAL DEFINITIONS

Ambiguous behavioral definitions present a threat to "construct validity," which is described as the instrument's ability to measure the constructs of interest (Polit & Hungler, 1997). In behavioral research it applies most directly to how targeted behaviors are defined. When determining frequencies of behaviors, it is critical that observers recognize when the targeted behavior begins and ends

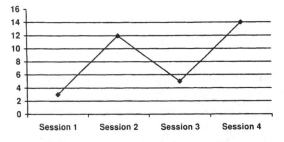

Figure 2. Sample showing instability.

Table 1. Summary of Potential Threats to Validity and Reliability and Their Management

Videotaping Problem	Potential Threat	Management
Subject reactivity	Internal validity	Subject habituation through repeated videotaping; mock taping sessions; extended baseline periods
Environmental extraneous variables	Internal validity	Careful preplanning to minimize chances of environmental extraneous variables; repeated viewing of video-tapes with close visual inspection of graphed data
Ambiguous behavioral definitions	Construct validity reliability	Clear behavioral definitions that address duration
Low Interrater agreement	Reliability	Initial group practice and discussion sessions; ongoing calibration activities

Table 2. Written Behavioral Definitions Given to Raters Prior to Training

Target Behavior	Operational Definition
Tantrum	Clearly audible crying sounds emitted by the child, associated with kicking and/or flailing arms (and bounded by a 5-s pause).
Mother initiating	Movement cycle beginning with a clearly observable or audible maternal action or prompt indicating an attempt to engage/instruct the child (verbal or physical), directed toward the child (e.g., pushing a toy, verbal directive).
Child initiating	Movement cycle beginning with a clearly observable or audible child action or prompt (verbal or physical) directed toward the mother indicating that the child wants to engage the parent (e.g., showing an object to the parent), verbal directive.
Child responding	Movement cycle that begins with the occurrence of a parental prompt and ends after the child initiates the requested movement or vocalizations within 5 s.
Mother responding	Movement cycle that begins with the occurrence of a child behavior and ends after the mother initiates the requested movement or offers a comment that indicates that the mother acknowledged, understands, and/or approves of the child initiation within 2 s.

as well as what constitutes the behavior. For example, "tantrum" has a variety of meanings. In earlier work, this author found that the definition of "tantrum" needed clarification. The following operational definition was developed: "tantrum is clearly audible crying sounds emitted by the child, associated with kicking and/or flailing arms (and bounded by a 5-second pause)". This definition not only provides observers with a "behavioral picture" of a tantrum but also a time parameter necessary to differentiate one tantrum from another.

LOW INTER-RATER AGREEMENT

A reliable instrument should yield the same results repeatedly; if it does not, the meaning and applicability of findings are in question (Burns & Grove, 1997). In behavioral research, the instruments are often the observers (raters). Consistency among raters is critical. Two methods for enhancing inter-rater reliability—initial group practice/discussion sessions and ongoing "rater calibration" activities—are noted in Table 1. "Rater calibration" is a term derived from a process described by

Johnston and Pennypacker (1986) whereby observational instruments are kept finely tuned to ensure that the targeted behaviors are captured accurately. When behavioral instruments are human observers, similar care must be taken to facilitate consistency among the raters.

EVALUATION OF A NEW CALIBRATION PROCEDURE

The author conducted a pilot project to quantify mother–child interactions. Child subjects ranged in age from 3 to 6 years old and were diagnosed with "pervasive developmental delay." This broad diagnostic category includes children who have impairments in social interaction and communication and ex-

Table 3. Mean Interrater Reliability Scores* Before and After Training Sessions

Type of Observation	Noncalibrated[†]	Calibrated
Mother initiating	0.79	0.93
Child responding	0.82	0.90
Child initiating	0.70	0.90
Mother responding	0.74	0.86

N = 11 videotapes, 4 raters.
*Calculated by (number of agreements)/(number of agreements + disagreements).
†Using only written behavioral definitions.

hibit restricted, stereotyped patterns of behavior (American Psychiatric Association, 1994). Mothers ranged in age from 23 to 35 years old and were videotaped playing with their children in a clinic playroom setting during a standard intake procedure. Concerned about issues related to validity and reliability, the author developed written behavioral definitions (Table 2).

Procedure

Coding Using Only Written Definitions. Following the development of written behavioral definitions, four raters, who were members of an honors nursing research class, were instructed to independently code (without consulting one another) preadmission videotapes of 11 children and their mothers. Even though the raters initially commented that the behavioral definitions "seemed clear" and were easy to understand," inter-rater agreement was less than optimal (Table 3), particularly for behaviors that occurred infrequently. For example, a child displayed a brief tantrum on one occasion during a 15-minute segment. Two of the four raters correctly coded the tantrum, while the other two did not record the incident at all. This resulted in an inter-rater reliability score of .50, far below the desired .80 to 1.0.

Initial Group Practice and Discussion. A need for more rater training and opportunities to discuss behavioral occurrences was noted. Practice videotapes of children who were not subjects in the current project were coded, with coders "calling out" their responses to the group. In cases where discrepancies occurred, discussions commenced. Raters coded the videotapes repeatedly until 100% (1.0) agreement was obtained.

Ongoing Rater Calibration. After viewing a number of videotapes, raters began to describe "drifting effects"; that is, concern that they were losing focus because of fatigue. In addition, inter-rater reliability was still not consistently within the acceptable range. They also noted extreme individual differences among the children that suggested tailoring some of the behavioral definitions. For example, one child's "initiating" did not include direct eye contact, yet he was clearly attempting to interact with his mother in the session. In response to this concern, calibration sessions were implemented. These involved a procedure similar to the previously described training sessions, but instead of using practice tapes from children not in the project, raters used 5-minute segments from each of the mother-child sessions. These 5-minute segments were later discarded and not part of the analysis.

RESULTS

Pre- and post-calibration scores of four behaviors: (1) mother initiating, (2) child responding, (3) child initiating, and (4) mother responding are presented in Table 3. Although the sample size was too small to claim statistical significance (11 videotapes and 4 raters), these preliminary findings suggest that the calibration sessions implemented in this study enhanced inter-rater reliability. By using practice tape segments that were not part of the data analysis, scientific integrity of the project was maintained. In addition, raters reported a much clearer understanding of behavioral response categories and an absence of drift effects.

DISCUSSION AND IMPLICATIONS

Videotaping offers new opportunities for nurse researchers and clinicians to empirically evaluate client behavior and intervention efficacy in a variety of natural settings. However, there are a number of potential problems associated with this type of inquiry that must be addressed to facilitate reliable and valid findings. Clearly there is a need for additional work in this area. This research project illustrates the type of procedural inquiry that can provide answers to methodological questions raised in behavioral research. Informed nurses are uniquely positioned to lead the way in advancing this methodology while ensuring quality research and empirically based clinical practice.

ACKNOWLEDGMENTS

I acknowledge the following honors nursing research students for their participation as raters in this project: Alicia Anderson, Melissa Beauchamp Spurrier, Jonathan Decker, and Mitzi Tucker. I am also grateful for Dr. Kathlean Long's suggestions regarding the preparation and submission of this manuscript.

REFERENCES

American Psychiatric Association (1994). *Diagnostic and Statistical Manual of Mental Disorders. 4th Ed. Revised.* Washington, DC: American Psychiatric Association.

Burns, N., & Grove, S. (1997). *The Practice of Nursing Research: Conduct, Critique and Utilization.* Philadelphia, PA: WB. Saunders..

Elder, J. H. (1995). In-home communication intervention training for parents of multiple handicapped children. *Scholarly Inquiry for Nursing Practice, 9,* 71–92.

Elder, J. H. (1997). Single subject experimentation for psychiatric nursing. *Archives in Psychiatric Nursing, 11,* 1–7.

Hartmann, D. P., & Gardner, W. (1979). On the not so recent invention of interobserver reliability: A commentary on two articles by Birkimer and Brown. *Journal of Applied Behavior Analysis, 12,* 559–560.

Johnson, J. M., & Bolstad, O. D. (1975). Reactivity to home observation: A comparison of audio recorded behavior with observers present or absent. *Journal of Applied Behavior Analysis, 8,* 181–185.

Johnston, J., & Pennypacker, H. (1993). *Strategies and Tactics of Human Behavior Research,* 2nd Ed. Hillsdale, NJ: Lawrence Erlbaum Associates.

Polit, D. F., & Hungler, B. P. (1997). *Essential of Nursing Research: Methods, Appraisal, and Utilization.* Philadelphia, PA: Lippincott.

THE FUTURE OF
FOCUS GROUPS

by Richard A. Krueger

For over a decade I have had the opportunity to learn about focus groups. Through study; research, observation, coaching, teaching, and advising I have learned about how they work, when they work, and what makes them successful. I have observed their use in a wide variety of situations and have had exposure to many different moderator strategies. During that time I have seen changes in how focus groups are used and in who uses focus groups. As I reflect on these experiences, I would like to share some trends that are currently occurring with focus groups, and speculate on the future development of these trends, particularly within the public and nonprofit sectors.

MORE USE

Over the past decade we have regularly conducted electronic database searches on focus group interviewing. Ten years ago there were few citations and articles, largely appearing in advertising and marketing publications. Since the 1980s the number of citations has increased exponentially and references to focus groups appear not only in academic and trade journals, but also have been discussed on talk radio, television, serials, in movies, and by Doonesb™ characters.

The pervasiveness of the term focus groups in the media is one indicator of the mushrooming use of focus groups, particularly in the public and nonprofit sectors. Ten years ago few studies were conducted within the public/nonprofit sectors and those that were done were conducted by market research professionals. Largely, focus groups were conducted with white, middle-class adults who were consumers in the American marketplace. Many of these focus group studies were conducted to find out about consumer behavior and product characteristics.

MORE MISUSE

With this huge increase in use has come an increase in misuse. For a number of years the term focus group has been applied to a broad array of group experiences. Likely, this will continue as group experiences are mislabeled or inadvertently called focus group interviews. Mislabeling has occurred with virtually all social science research procedures and one should not be surprised that it occurs with focus group interviews. Although many mislabeled groups are beneficial and yield helpful results, reasonably often the mislabel is an indicator that the individual organizing the focus group is confused on the acceptable protocol. This confusion can lead to sloppy procedures and bad data.

Individuals have used focus group procedures for purposes unrelated to research, such as improving morale, providing feelings of involvement, conveying the impression that the organization is listening, or simple public relations. Although these topics can be legitimately studied using focus groups, the sole intent of these abusive studies is to create an impression of listening without actually doing so. In these situations the sponsoring organization is flying under false colors because they convey the impression of being research-based but in fact they exist for other reasons. As a social scientist, this is a bit unsettling because it conveys the impression that researchers are gathering data for beneficial uses but later they disregard that information.

ACADEMIC RESPECTABILITY

Focus group research has gained increased acceptability within academic institutions. Up until the early 1980s, focus groups were often not deemed suitable for dissertations and focus group interviewing was not taught in graduate schools across the nation. Focus groups were troubling to academics because interaction between participants was interpreted as respondent contamination. The prevailing thinking in academic circles was that the proper way to conduct interviews was to keep subjects isolated and unaware of the thoughts and ideas of other participants. Also, the complexity of analyzing focus group results was a daunting task and considerably more difficult and subjective than analysis of

From *Qualitative Health Research*, November 1995, pp. 524-531. © 1995 by Sage Publications, Inc. Reprinted by permission.

individual interviews or written materials. As the academic community gained more exposure to focus groups, many academics have eagerly embraced it, in part because of the potential insight it offers on the human experience.

MORE COLLABORATIVE STUDIES

A decade ago it was not acceptable to suggest that nonresearchers could be helpful in conducting focus groups studies. In recent years we have realized that nonresearchers can be enormously helpful in conducting focus group research when they are carefully selected, properly supervised, and adequately prepared for the experience. Indeed, nonresearchers actually improve the quality of the data when they are part of a team that includes knowledgeable researchers. In these collaborative studies, the researcher works as a teacher, coach, and guide to a team of nonresearchers. Nonresearchers can be employees of the organization, volunteers, or even customers. I have had the opportunity to work with scores of volunteers ranging from teens to senior citizens in focus group projects. These nonresearchers often assist in areas where they have special expertise, unique credibility, or background essential to the success of the study. In some studies it is critical that the moderator be of the same gender, age, or ethnic background as the participants. It may be impossible to have adequate diversity among the professional researchers but it is feasible to include diversity through individuals who assist on the research team. In other studies the planning, recruiting, or analysis is greatly enhanced when nonresearchers are members of the total team.

These individuals possess special insights that may be essential to understanding the participants or the topic of study and designing appropriate recruiting processes, incentives, and questions. In addition, a secondary benefit is that the nonresearchers participating on the research team develop a special commitment to the success of the study and the application of results.

This trend of involving nonresearchers who often volunteer their time will continue because it improves the usefulness and credibility of the information. But it does not reduce costs as some expect. Indeed, when all factors are considered, the cost savings may be minimal. It often takes more time and much more effort to coordinate a collaborative study than a study completed by professional moderators.

CHANGING ROLE OF THE RESEARCHER

The involvement of nonresearchers in focus group studies demands additional researcher skills. In the old role, the researcher would plan and conduct the study alone or perhaps with a team of fellow researchers. Community members were subjects. In the new paradigm, the community or sponsoring organization is considered a partner in the research process as opposed to the recipient of the results. As a result, the research takes on the role of teacher, coach, and mentor to a team of nonresearchers. This changing role demands different skills from researchers such as group decision making, communications, and community organizing which, incidentally, are rarely taught in graduate education.

ANALYSIS OPTIONS

Analysis has been a headache for many focus group researchers. Analysis is time consuming, tedious, and difficult. Of all the time allocated to a focus group study, analysis can easily demand the greatest share. Over the coming years focus group analysis will be approached in a variety of ways. We will continue to see the careful and rigorous analysis strategies that are based on focus group transcripts. Yet this strategy of using transcripts is sometimes overrated and may be impractical in many situations. Viable options include using abridged transcripts that contain only the most pertinent data and real-time transcripts of fast typists with laptop computers who sit in on the focus groups. Faster strategies for analysis are essential and the challenge is to develop an analysis protocol that is defensible, systematic, and appropriate to the problem. The analysis task is one of understanding and this inherently takes time.

The public and nonprofit sectors have approached analysis differently than market research. Within market research, the standard procedure calls for clients to observe and interpret focus groups from behind the one-way mirror.

As a result, analysis is a shared responsibility between the moderator and client. This strategy allows organization employees involved in marketing, research and development, sales, or other key aspects to experience firsthand the comments of customers. This opportunity to observe the focus groups also enhances the credibility of results. By contrast, the public and nonprofit sectors have conducted most of their studies outside of these special focus group rooms where client observation is impossible or could jeopardize the quality of the discussion. As a result, communications, reporting, and analysis are of greater importance in these studies. This trend within the public and nonprofit sectors to emphasize analysis will continue.

HIGH TECH WILL OFFER NEW OPTIONS

Developments in technology have ushered in new options that were not possible just a few years ago. Focus group facilities offer an array of impressive features. Focus group participants have been allowed to express their views using buttons, rheostats, and computer keyboards. Interactive videoconferencing allows clients to observe on a television set a focus group conducted in another city miles away. With interactive conferencing, clients can send questions and requests to the focus group moderator for follow-up or clarification. This has allowed clients to watch the focus group in the comfort and convenience of their headquarters.

In the market research tradition, considerable value has been placed on the physical features of the focus group room. Indeed, if a client were to make a decision about which research firm to used based on promotional materials, it would be easy to assume that the special interview room is the most critical feature. Research firms often describe at length the benefits of their physical facilities, but interestingly enough, do not describe the qualities or experiences of the moderator, which is far more likely the critical ingredient of quality.

NATURAL ENVIRONMENTS WILL CONTINUE

Focus groups within the public and nonprofit environment have traditionally placed less emphasis on technology and more on obtaining convenient locations conducive to conversations. Natural environments with familiar surroundings were originally used in the public/non-profit sectors because of the cost and limited availability of special focus group facilities. Over time many researchers have learned to prefer these options because of the enhanced quality of data resulting from these comfortable surroundings.

FOCUS GROUPS MOVE BEYOND THE WHITE MIDDLE CLASS

Focus groups emerged in a consumer-oriented, white, middle-class, western society. This has changed dramatically in recent years. Focus groups are an effective means of gathering information in other cultures and among all demographic categories. Focus groups can be used successfully with highly educated professions and people who have very limited educations. Furthermore, focus groups work with non-whites and people with few economic resources. However, careful thought must be given to how the process needs to be adapted to gain the trust and cooperation of participants. Critical factors in conducting successful focus groups are the attitude of the moderator and the circumstances of the study. A condescending moderator attitude, which is a problem in any focus group, is a fatal flaw in these focus groups and a surefire way to discourage open communication. In addition, the circumstances surrounding the study (who sponsors the study); for what purpose, how people were selected, etc.), which are often of minimal importance in most focus group studies, can take on major importance in these studies. Power differentials between the moderator (or sponsor) and the participants can

stifle discussion and must be taken into consideration. These focus groups must be conducted in a respectful way that sees culture and tradition as assets.

SOME MYTHS ABOUT FOCUS GROUPS ARE BREAKING DOWN

Several myths about focus groups will be increasingly challenged.

Myth: Focus groups should have 10–12 participants.

Fact: Increasingly, the most effective focus groups are composed of 6 to 8 participants. Serious thought should be given to using smaller groups when topics are complex (as they are in the public environment) or when participants have expertise on the topic.

Myth: Focus groups are best conducted in special focus group rooms.

Fact: Focus group rooms have served market research well but are generally ill-suited for focus groups in the public and nonprofit sectors. These rooms are expensive, often in the wrong location, and lack the casual and natural environment that is sometimes essential.

Myth: Focus groups are cheap.

Fact: Focus groups are time intensive and require skilled researchers. The visible time spent in the focus group is the tip of the iceberg, with planning and analysis consuming considerable amounts of time. Administrators in the public sector are often shocked at the price tag for a focus group study.

Myth: Focus groups should be conducted with strangers.

Fact: In many communities it is impossible to find strangers. Virtually everyone in the community knows each other, yet focus groups in these

areas have been successful.

Myth: Focus groups in the work environment should be avoided.

Fact: Another area of increased focus group use is within the work environment. These focus groups have successfully explored topics such as morale, benefits, salary, training needs, quality control, and a host of others.

Myth: Focus groups should be conducted with respondents who have not participated previously in focus groups.

Fact: There is no sound reason why focus group participants should not be invited to future groups. This has proven effective and is at times the most desirable strategy when a time-series study is being used.

SUMMARY

Focus groups will continue to receive considerable use because they fill a unique niche. Focus groups allow participants to hear ideas and use those concepts in formulating their opinions. Focus groups capture the complexity of the human experience and provide valuable information to decision makers. People will continue to modify and adapt focus group interviews. The change will be driven by emerging opportunities, technology; resources, changes in thinking, and the desire for descriptive information. These changes will have an impact on the rigor or usefulness of future focus group studies.

Richard A. Krueger is a professor at the University of Minnesota. His work in focus groups is well known, and he has conducted numerous workshops in training moderators of focus groups. He is also interested in exploring the development of this methodology.

SELF-ASSESSMENT AT WORK: OUTCOMES OF ADULT LEARNERS' REFLECTIONS ON PRACTICE

CATHERINE MARIENAU

ABSTRACT

This qualitative study examined the outcomes of engaging in self-assessment as perceived by students in an experience-based graduate program. Self-assessment is one of the elements of experiential learning that provided the framework for this study. Fifty students in three groups participated in an iterative process of focus group interviews and follow-up surveys over 12 months. An additional 30 students generated data upon graduation. Fifteen themes representing specific outcomes of self-assessment emerged from an inductive analysis of the data within and across groups. The findings indicated that self-assessment serves as a powerful instrument for experiential learning, strengthens commitment to competent performance in the workplace, enhances higher order skills for functioning in the workplace, and fosters self-agency and authority. The findings were interpreted within frameworks concerning experiential learning, workplace performance, and personal development. Self-assessment was found to offer profound benefits to participants and to earn an integral place in the curriculum.

A hallmark of an educated person is the capacity to reflect on and learn from experience such that the learning yields meaningful interpretations of life occurrences and informs future action. When that educated person is also a practicing professional, the ability to reflect on and learn from practice becomes paramount. Reflective practice is "the process of bringing past events to a conscious level and of determining appropriate ways to think, feel, and behave in the future" (Caffarella & Barnett, 1994, p. 38). Reflective practice may also involve reflecting-in-action, the

CATHERINE MARIENAU is Professor, School for New Learning, DePaul University. The author would like to acknowledge the contribution to this study of the following individuals: Drs. Jean Knoll, John Rury, David Shallenberger, and Morry Fiddler. The study was supported by a grant from the National Center on Adult Learning, Empire State College, New York.

capacity to think about and change what one is doing while doing it (Schon, 1983). These capabilities are cornerstones of effective practice in the complex and uncertain worlds encountered by most practitioners today. A critical dimension underlying reflective practice is the capability of self-assessment, the focus of the research reported here.

Self-assessment may be examined in terms of its structure, process, or outcomes. This study examined the latter by focusing on students' perceptions of the outcomes derived from iterative self-assessment activities in both their academic and work settings. Findings are reported as themes that emerged from data analysis, illustrated by representative quotes from the participants. The study is set in the larger context of experiential learning. Implications of the findings are discussed from the perspectives of learning, performance at work, and personal development.

Learning from Experience

Dewey (1938) advocated engaging in experience with purpose and urged that "every experience should do something to prepare a person for later experiences of a deeper and more expansive quality" (p. 47). Dewey's concept of purposefulness is reflected in Kolb's (1984) cycle of effective learning that links reflection on concrete experience to the formation of generalizations or abstract principles that, in turn, inform action. The reflection element of the cycle "implies a conscious consideration of experience and ideas . . . [that involves] more than recollection" (Maclean, 1987, p. 131). It also involves developing frameworks and generalizing from them. Recognizing the potentially self-limiting character of reflection, Brookfield (1987) insists that future action be guided by critical reflective thinking which involves recognizing, judging, and justifying one's ideas and actions (p. 13). Watkins and Marsick (1993) add that the demands of critical reflection include "taking the time to look deeply at one's situation to identify values, assumptions, and beliefs that cause us to interpret the situation as we do" (p. 33).

These convergent views on the complexities of learning from and through experience are captured in Mezirow's definition of learning. According to Mezirow (1996), "Learning is understood as the process of using a prior interpretation to construe a new or revised interpretation of the meaning of one's experience in order to guide future action" (p. 162).

Situated in the center of the learning process is a self as the interpreter of experience and the agent of future actions. Implicitly, the individual is engaged in the act of self-assessment where, sitting beside herself and in conversation with herself, she judges and justifies her ideas and actions within the context of her beliefs and values as well as in interactions with others. She interprets meaning from her experiences and sets direction for future experiences.

In spite of the centrality of self-assessment in learning and meaning-making processes, it has occupied relatively little space in the research literature of adult learning. Noted exceptions include the work of Boud (1986) which focuses on implementing self-assessment. In addition, MacGregor (1993) describes self-evaluation as a tool for learning and offers illustrations of various educational program practices. Yet other related fields recognize the importance of self-assessment and depend upon it to contribute both to individual growth and development and to effective performance in the workplace. As human developmentalists, Chickering and Reisser (1993) see self-assessment as a necessary skill for intellectual and interpersonal growth. Haswell (1993) suggests that self-assessment may be an inducer of individual development. In the workplace learning literature, self-assessment is emphasized for its part in monitoring and correcting one's behaviors (Sheckley, Lamdin, & Keeton, 1993). In the literature on organizational learning, self-assessment is linked to guiding individuals' continuous learning and improvement in their work (Kline & Saunders, 1993; Schon, 1983).

The Context: Practicing Self-Assessment at School and Work

This research was conducted with students in the Master of Arts in Integrated Professional Studies (MAIPS) program in the School for New Learning (SNL) at DePaul University. The program strives to enable practitioners to become more reflective on their learning and practice, thereby prompting integration of thought and action that leads to more effective performance. The program's design is supported by Schon's (1983) epistemology of practice that engenders in practitioners a capacity for reflection on their intuitive knowing in the midst of action . . . [that will equip them] to cope with the unique, uncertain and conflicted situations of practice" (pp. viii–ix). Guided by a common set of criteria, practitioners in diverse fields tailor an area of focus that is connected to their world of work (e.g., managing strategic change in non-profit organizations, developing models for zoo conservation, or advocating holistic health care practices). Students' specialized studies are complemented by a set of liberal learning skills and abilities that are developed through intensive liberal learning seminars (see Marienau & Fiddler, 1996b).

As one of the liberal learning skills, self-assessment involves "reflecting critically on one's experience, assessing the quality of one's work, and incorporating feedback from others" (School for New Learning, 1996–97). Self-assessment is built into processes for admission, mid-program, and graduation reviews as well as into the assessment of students' performance in the prescribed liberal learning curriculum. In addition, at regularly scheduled assessment sessions, students reflect (in writing and in group discussion) on how they are applying their learning and skills in the workplace, on what changes they are experiencing as a result, and on specific areas for further development (Marienau & Fiddler, 1996a). Thus, the curriculum design, in Haswell's (1993) terms, "coerces" students to engage in self-assessment, leaving "no way out but to think and take a stand about themselves" (p. 90).

Purpose and Methods

The study intended to add new elements to the research on self-assessment. The participants represented a wide range of professional fields. The study focused on participants' own perceptions of their experiences with self-assessment, particularly as conducted in their workplaces. Their perceptions were based on actual, rather than hypothetical, situations that occurred over a 12 month period. As the focus of their reflections, they drew on multiple rather than single situations.

In my role as co-designer of the MAIPS program and director for the first eight years, I advocated rigorous attention to self-assessment; as a practitioner scholar, one of my goals has been to examine its appropriate place in the curriculum. Recognizing the program's insistence on self-assessment, this study explored what outcomes graduate students in the MAIPS program perceived they were deriving from this activity.

Data Collection Procedures

Two questions provided the organizing framework for this study: What do practicing professionals see as the important outcomes, if any, of engaging in self-assessment? What connections do they make between self-assessment and their learning and performance in the workplace?

Data were collected from December 1991 through March 1993 from two different sources. The primary source was first-year students enrolled in three different clusters (N=50), all of whom agreed to participate in the study. The enrolled students constituted 40 percent of the total student body at that time and were representative of the larger student body with regard to gender (54% male, 46% female), age (27 to 55), ethnic minorities (14%), work experience (5 to 30 years), and diverse fields of study. The second, more limited, source was 30 graduating students who represented 35% of the total number of graduates at that time.

Data were collected through an iterative process. The enrolled students engaged in focus group interviews to explore open-ended questions and follow-up surveys to verify emerging themes and patterns. The graduating students contributed a one-time essay.

The focus group interviews were conducted during each cluster's assessment sessions occurring three to four times over a 12 month period. The cluster's faculty mentor facilitated the 90 minute discussion, while I acted as recorder and occasional questioner. Interviews were tape-recorded with permission of the participants. The essays from graduating students were collected during quarterly graduation review sessions over a 15 month period.

Data were analyzed inductively within and across the three clusters, and were corroborated by data obtained from graduating students. Each of the first three rounds of data collection from the enrolled students generated new data that were folded into the next round. In the first round, members in each cluster responded to the same open-ended questions: How do you define self-assessment and what does it involve? What value, if any, do you place on self-assessment? What links, if any, do you make between self-assessment and your learning and performance at work?

Each cluster's responses were analyzed separately to discern patterns within the group. In the second round, each cluster received a report on its preliminary patterns and provided further interpretation of that data in a focus group interview. In addition, each cluster responded to a major theme that had emerged from another cluster. For example, Cluster B had generated responses concerning how their values informed their decision-making. Cluster C had highlighted the importance of setting and carrying out goals, while Cluster A had emphasized aspects of self-authorship. Each of these themes was cross-checked with at least one other cluster, using a written survey, to discriminate idiosyncratic responses from common patterns across clusters. During the third and final rounds of data collection and analysis, existing themes and patterns were examined in more depth within each cluster, using a combination of survey and focus group interviews.

As noted, the role of graduating students was limited to corroborating emerging patterns from the clusters of enrolled students. The graduating students wrote one essay concerning what links they saw, if any, between self-assessment and their learning and performance at work. Their written responses were analyzed for common themes that were then compared to the results of the within cluster analysis as well as to the cross-cluster analysis.

Findings consisted of patterns that were (a) supported by 50% or more of the respondents within a given cluster of students, (b) validated by at least two of the three clusters, and, (c) corroborated in the responses of the graduating students.

Findings

Participants defined self-assessment as both a process and a capability. Over 75% of all participants defined self-assessment as an "internal process of evaluating oneself." Commonly used metaphors were "looking in on oneself," and "sitting beside oneself." Fifty percent of the participants also referred to self-assessment as a capability—the "ability to make authentic, objective judgments about oneself." The multiple dimensions of self-assessment are reflected in this student's description:

> Self-assessment means looking critically at one's performance or work efforts and then *acting* upon areas that display personal strength or a need for improvement. It relates not only to post-effort reflection and action, but also to the prior process of first setting an appropriate personal standard and then measuring one's effort against that standard. In this way, self-assessment involves personal standards and expectations, task performance, reflection and critique, and then usually a corrective action for improvement. Such a process becomes an ongoing personal cycle.

The outcomes of engaging in self-assessment are represented in 15 themes, grouped under four attributes, that emerged from the analysis of participants' responses. The selected quotes best represent the expressed views of half or more of the participants.

Learning From Experience

The first four themes are instrumental in fostering an individual's ability to learn from her or his experiences. As one student noted, "My increasing ability to engage in self-assessment has become the strong foundation upon which all other learning has been built."

Stimulates reflection and introspection. As a prerequisite to learning from experience, participants reported becoming more open to reflecting on their experience. As one participant explained, "I've been stimulated to be more of a 'learner' in work activities and have pushed myself to be more introspective."

Heightens awareness of own ways of learning. Self-assessment has helped many participants become more aware of themselves as learners. Students who, as one person said, are "forced to *engage* with the learning process so personally" find themselves, in the words of another person, becoming more "aware of my own processes of cognition."

Fosters shifts in perspectives. Participants reported gaining flexibility in changing their perspectives, particularly with regard to making mistakes. Statements from two people illustrate: "As a result of doing self-assessment, I no longer view making mistakes as a character flaw." Said another, "Self-assessment is gradually giving me the sense that success doesn't mean doing everything perfectly all the time; but rather, that one can grow and improve through setbacks."

Whets appetite for feedback. Participants reported that feedback, both from oneself and others, became an especially important aspect of reflecting on and learning from their experience. One participant described himself as "becoming more intentional about seeking out the ideas of others as well as offering more frequent feedback."

Functioning More Effectively

The next three themes focus on skills and habits that, sharpened by self-assessment, help participants function more effectively, both collaboratively and independently, in the workplace.

Enhances interpersonal communication. The single most important set of skills, cited by nearly 90% of all participants, concerned interpersonal communication. On the top of their list was the positive impact of employing good listening skills, followed by seeking feedback (as represented in the fourth theme). Participants also linked listening to collaboration. As one student described, "I listen better to others . . . and my supervisors have noticed and supported my own self-assessment of my increased ability to work independently, consult with co-workers in an appropriate manner, and use co-workers as resources, and employ teamwork."

Promotes goal-directedness. For nearly two-thirds of the participants, self-assessment focused their attention on establishing, executing, and evaluating their goals. Self-assessment helped them know what goals to set. For example, "Self-assessment helps me identify what the gap may be between the present and desired states of what I'm trying to achieve." Another student added the element of developing her strengths: "I use self-assessment to determine what I see as realistic goals for myself at work. Once I decide upon these goals, I work to lessen my shortcomings and to utilize my assets."

Reinforces critical reflection in problem-solving and decision-making. Participants noted that critical reflection leads to better problem-solving and decision-making. One person explained:

> Work provides a more structured environment for allowing one to step back and evaluate a particular procedure, an approach to a problem or one's interpersonal skills. The work environment allows for immediate feedback. By assessing any of these areas, an understanding of one's limitations becomes evident. It may also become evident that the limitations may be false self-perceptions. All of this should work toward improving confidence in decision-making.

Other participants pointed to the role of emotions in critical decision-making. One student explained, "Self-assessment involves trying to eliminate the emotions one might attach to a particular action or reaction. Although I do not desire to be void of emotion when making decisions, emotions can cloud issues."

Strengthens Commitment To Competent Performance

The next four themes center on how self-assessment heightens participants' striving for competent performance in the workplace.

Promotes monitoring of one's performance. Participants reported that self-assessment has stimulated them to more consciously monitor their work. They described the monitoring as developing an ongoing, critical view of one's work, and identifying the need for corrective action. One student offered this metaphor: "Self-assessment is like taking the blood pressure of my own performance. This shouldn't be considered a 'good' reading or a 'bad' reading; instead, I consider it a reading that does or does not require corrective action."

Enhances motivation for better performance. The self-conscious monitoring of one's performance has enhanced the participants' motivation to do even better. As one student said, "A necessary component of successful [self] assessment is the discipline and commitment to adjust one's path so as to notice measurable progress upon the next assessment." Another student identified other elements of motivation: "By performing self-assessment at work, I make myself a better employee. . . . It gives me a sense of satisfaction and self-confidence. Even when my assessment isn't positive, I know what improvements can be made."

Targets areas for improvement and development. Supported by the motivation to improve their performance, participants were able to target specific areas for improvement and development. For some, the task was to broaden their skills base. One student reported: "My ongoing self-assessment on the job led to the identification of a need to broaden my skills as a supervisor of staff and as a planner." Others noted the need for specific behavior changes. For example: "Self-assessment allows me to pinpoint areas where work habits or behavior changes are needed to better meet the objectives my boss and I have agreed upon." For others, perspective changes were in order, as this student reported: "By self-assessing problems and self-diagnosing solutions an important balance is achieved, and although it sometimes is a sobering experience, it results in the objectivity I need."

Enhances contributions. The cumulative effect of monitoring their performance, striving to do better, and targeting specific areas for improvement enabled participants both to see themselves as contributors and to contribute more effectively. "Through ongoing self-assessment, I have learned to use a different approach to management for each of my staff." And, others are contributing more effectively as leaders, as one student reported: "Self-assessment has helped me to improve my own leadership by motivating others and using informal channels of communication."

Fosters Self-Agency and Authority

The final cluster of themes centers on the role of self-assessment in fostering individuals' greater awareness of self and self in relationship with others.

Increases self-acceptance and self-confidence. Participants reported having developed a keener sense of competence in their work, contributing to greater self-acceptance and self-confidence in their abilities. As one person shared, "My performance as a professional is much less inhibited and guarded by virtue of the fact that self-assessment has revealed someone that I like and accept." Another person said, "Instead of looking for the universal 'right' way to do things, I now feel confident in trusting my own instincts to perform my career responsibilities."

Complements internal frame of reference with external feedback. Participants indicated that self-assessment has helped them develop an internal frame of reference, particularly with regard to meeting standards. As one student said, "By assuming responsibility for my own assessment, I must also develop the criteria by which I will measure my progress and achievements." Participants indicated that their source for standards had become, on balance, more internal than external. One student said simply, "Since all who judge us are not wise . . . the inner judge helps us to maintain our direction and self-esteem." This emphasis on the internal frame of reference represents a shift for some students: "Presently, my main source of assessment is internal; a year ago I would have thought differently. . . . I have had to base my assessment on what I determine from the environment, but the ultimate assessment comes from within me."

At the same time, recognition of the importance of external reference points was noted. One student explained his approach: "My self-assessment and improvement cycle (plan/do/assess/reflect/plan again/re-do/etc.) is an ongoing 'doing and checking' set against my personal goals and the 'looking glass' reaction received from others." Another student elaborated:

In the context of work, the standards by which I assess myself are self-generated, usually to reach and surpass mine and the organization's expectations. . . . I rely on my superiors and peers for essential feedback and internalize this information. However, their standards belong to them, not me.

Incorporates values in measuring performance. Participants noted that their values influence their criteria for judging performance. Among the many values identified, those named most consistently included quality of the process or product, integrity in self-conduct, making a difference, and honesty. One student said, "The recognition of values, I feel, makes it easier to assess myself." Another said, "The values seem to give a direction in which to go."

Enhances sense of identity. Self-assessment helped participants see themselves as developing professionals who are reflective about their life journeys. One person noted, "I came face-to-face with a discovery that has since caused me to fundamentally rethink my whole role . . . to come to terms with my own limitations." Another person revealed, "My personal development has deeply influenced my professional abilities by altering my self-image, which has impacted not only how I see myself as an individual, but also my self-perception as a practitioner."

Discussion

This exploratory research succeeded in four major respects. First, the findings provided feedback to the program regarding the significant role of self-assessment in its curriculum. Second, the study generated themes that represented specific positive outcomes of individuals' conscious reflections on practice. Third, the findings are congruent with experiential learning theory and related schemes of meaning making. Finally, the findings offer directions for further research into other dimensions of self-assessment.

Given the program's emphasis on self-assessment it is not surprising that students were conscious, reflective, and articulate about their experiences with self-assessment. It is surprising, however, that all of the participants indicated that doing self-assessment had some positive impact on their capabilities concerning both learning and performance. Only mildly negative concerns were expressed about the challenge of doing "honest" self-assessment and the tendency to be "too hard on [oneself]." None of the participants indicated that doing self-assessment was not worth the effort. Thus, the participants strongly endorsed self-assessment as an integral component of the curriculum wherein students engage in self-assessment intentionally, regularly, and with consistent reinforcement from the program.

Emerging from the themes are four key attributes of self-assessment. The first attribute is that intentional self-assessment serves as a powerful instrument for learning from experience. Participants reinforced the notion that attention and reflection are key components in converting experience into a source for learning. The models of Jarvis (1992) and Kolb (1984) make clear that little or no learning takes place without conscious attention to one's experiences. Indeed, Dewey (1938) advocated that learning from experience requires purposeful engagement with the experience. Boud, Keogh, and Walker (1985) emphasize reflection as the necessary companion to attention. Reflection makes possible "creating and clarifying the meaning of experience (past or present) in terms of self (self in relation to self and self in relation to the world)" (Boyd & Fales, 1983, p. 101).

Participants in the study reported that self-assessment helped them to exercise keener attention to and reflection on their experience. They appear to have gained enhanced perceptual capacities (Kolb, 1984), making them less likely to ignore the familiar or avoid the unfamiliar, and more likely to expand their repertoire of experiences for critical reflection. Outcomes of their reflective process have included greater awareness and understanding of the self, new perspectives on their experience, changes in behavior, and deeper commitments to action—all elements of learning from experience.

The second attribute of self-assessment is that it strengthens commitment to competent performance in the workplace. The participants, all of whom exercised self-assessment in their work settings, expressed a strong desire to continuously improve their work and contribute to their organizations. They reported becoming more motivated to monitor their attitudes and behavior and to identify areas for improvement. Assuming this kind of responsibility for one's work involves the complex capacities of being self-initiating, self-correcting, and self-evaluating (Kegan, 1994). Further, it demands an internal standard (Kegan, 1994) which participants tended to describe as judging themselves in light of their own standards and values, mediated by feedback from external sources.

The participants also illustrated the observation of Kline and Saunders (1993) that "as we perceive ourselves more realistically, we become better able to guide our own learning and thus continuously improve our work" (p. 17). The improvements participants made in their interpersonal relations, in setting and achieving goals, and in monitoring their work performance are indications of increased behavioral complexity (Kolb, 1984). Participants found self-assessment to be a gauge for initiating, evaluating, and correcting their performance. Through an iterative process, they have gained greater confidence in their levels of competence as employees and leaders.

The third attribute of self-assessment is that it enhances higher order skills for functioning in the workplace. As a subset of the second attribute, these skills are highlighted because they were voiced repeatedly by the participants as being developed or refined through self-assessment. The higher order skills involve goals, interpersonal relations, critical reflection, and value-based decision making.

With regard to goals, participants indicated that self-assessment made them more attentive to the cycle of setting goals, monitoring progress toward them, evaluating results of goal achievement, and establishing the next goal or set of goals. In the interpersonal domain, self-assessment has assisted participants in developing deeper levels of competence. Their interpersonal skills were evidenced in particular by more consciously seeking feedback from others, as well as from offering it to others. They became more open to learning from mistakes in a public way;

they came to view "mistakes as stepping stones to continuous learning" (Kline & Saunders, 1993, p. 17).

Participants also indicated that self-assessment contributed to aspects of their intellectual competence as problem-solvers and decision-makers. For example, self-assessment helped to sharpen their skills in critical reflective thinking and heightened their awareness of their values. They attributed becoming more adept at problem-solving and decision-making to incorporating values in their reflective thinking process.

Participants' reported changes in these higher order skills seem illustrative of the three-to-four shift in Kegan's (1994) orders of consciousness. These shifts involved taking greater responsibility for their actions, engaging multiple perspectives, and defining themselves as active constructors of meaning rather than as reactive recipients.

The fourth attribute of self-assessment is that it fosters self-agency and authority. Participants reported that engagement in self-assessment engendered a sense of self-agency or personal agency, as referred to by Merriam and Yang (1996). Evidence of personal agency is seen in the participants' shifts toward an internal frame of reference, which educators consider a "preferred developmental outcome"(Merriam and Yang, 1996, p. 66). Participants exhibit self-authoring potential (Kegan, 1994) as seen in their work. Another dimension of personal agency is seen in a growing interdependence with others as co-learners in the workplace.

Participants also spoke of their increased self-acceptance and self-esteem, that "generalized judgment about personal value or merit" (Chickering & Reisser, 1993, p. 199). Their sense of competence was heightened through self-assessment as was evident in their increased confidence in abilities to communicate, work with others, make decisions, and pursue realistic goals. They spoke of feeling more in charge of their personal and professional lives and of having clearer life direction, thus expressing a growing sense of personal agency.

The various shifts in perspective reported by participants bring to mind Mezirow's emancipatory paradigm, a key component being a "meaning scheme which is constructed by a cluster of specific beliefs, feelings, attitudes, and value judgments that accompany and shape an interpretation" (Mezirow, 1996, p. 163). Participants expressed more awareness of their own meaning schemes, thereby possibly enhancing the capacity to transform these schemes or perspectives (i.e., transformative learning).

Represented among the attributes of self-assessment are two areas of competency identified by Mezirow. First, participants reported growth in "instrumental competence . . . [the] attainment of task-oriented performance skills that may involve reflective problem-solving and sometimes problem-posing" (Mezirow, 1996, p. 164). They also reported growth in an aspect of their internal worlds, in "communicative competence [which] refers to the ability of the learner to negotiate his or her own purposes, values, and meanings rather than to simply accept those of others" (p. 164). These two areas of competence address Schon's (1983) call for an epistemology of practice which "places technical problem solving within a broader context of reflective inquiry" (p. 69).

Based on the findings of this research study, self-assessment can equip individuals to navigate learning from experience and master attitudes and skills for effective functioning in the workplace. Self-assessment may also open the door to transformative and continuous learning, and personal development.

Future Inquiry

The four attributes of self-assessment that emerged from the 15 themes and were interpreted within various frameworks suggest intriguing avenues for future research. First, what is the nature of the interactions between and among the themes found in this study? What might be the core outcomes that are most integral to self-assessment? Second, what frameworks might best be used to examine further the developmental potential of self-assessment? For example, is there a relationship between developmental level and ability to do meaningful self-assessment? Third, recognizing this study's reliance on self-reports, what constitutes authentic self-assessment? How do individuals actually achieve it? Fourth, is there a defining structure to self-assessment? Are there individual styles of self-assessment, much like different styles of learning? If so, how might individuals be oriented to self-assessment and helped to adapt it to their own styles and situations? Investigations into these kinds of questions can further elevate the significance of self-assessment in promoting learning and development in individuals and their effective performance in the workplace.

References

Boud, D. (1986). *Implementing student self-assessment.* Sydney: Higher Education Research and Development Society of Australia.

Boud, D., Keogh, R., & Walker, D. (Eds.). (1985). *Reflection: Turning experience into learning.* London: Kogan Page.

Boyd, E. M. & Fales, A. W. (1983). Reflective learning: Key to learning from experience. *Journal of Humanistic Psychology, 7*(4), 261–284.

Brookfield, S. (1987). *Developing critical thinkers: Challenging adults to explore alternative ways of thinking and acting.* San Francisco: Jossey-Bass.

Caffarella, R., & Barnett, B. (1994, Summer). Characteristics of adult learners and foundations of experiential learning. In L. Jackson and R. Caffarella (Eds.), *Experiential learning: A new approach.* New Directions for Adult and Continuing Education, no. 62 (pp. 29–42). San Francisco: Jossey-B ass.

Candy, P. (1991). *Self-direction for lifelong learning.* San Francisco: Jossey-Bass.

Chickering, A. & Reisser, L. (1993). *Education and identity,* 2nd ed. San Francisco: Jossey-Bass.

Dewey, J. (1938). *Experience and education.* New York: Collier Books.

Haswell, R. (1993). Student self-evaluations and developmental change. In J. MacGregor (Ed.), *Student self-evaluation: Fostering reflective learning.* New Directions for Teaching and Learning, 56 (pp. 83–99). San Francisco, Jossey-Bass.

Jarvis, P. (1992). *Paradoxes of learning.* San Francisco: Jossey-Bass.

Kegan, R. (1994). *In over our heads: The mental demands of modern life.* Cambridge: Harvard University Press.

Kline, P., & Saunders, B. (1993). *Ten steps to a learning organization.* Arlington, VA: Great Ocean Publishers.

Kolb, D.A. (1984). *Experiential Learning: Experience as the source of learning and development.* Englewood Cliffs, N.J.: Prentice Hall.

Maclean, H. (1987). Linking person-centered teaching to qualitative research. In D. Boud & V. Griffin (Eds.), *Appreciating adults learning: From the learners' perspective* (pp. 127–136). London: Kogan Page.

MacGregor, J. (Ed.). (1993, Winter). *Student self-evaluation: Fostering reflective learning.* New Directions for Teaching and Learning, 56. San Francisco: Jossey-Bass.

Marienau, C., & Fiddler, M. (1996a). Case 14: Assessment colloquia, Master of Arts Program. In T. Banta, J. Lund, K. Black, & F. Oblander (Eds.), *Assessment in practice: Putting principles to work on college campuses* (pp. 121–124). San Francisco: Jossey-Bass.

Marienau, C.,& Fiddler, M. (1996b). Diminishing distinctions. *Ocotillo: The Journal of Adult Learning, 1,* 20–22.

Merriam, S. (1994). Learning and life experience: The connection in adulthood. In J. Sinnott (Ed.), *Interdisciplinary Handbook of Adult Lifespan Learning* (pp. 74–89). Westport, CT.: Greenwood Press.

Merriam, S. & Yang, B. (1996, Winter). A longitudinal study of adult life experiences and developmental outcomes. *Adult Education Quarterly, 46*(2), 62–81.

Mezirow, J. (1996, Spring). Contemporary paradigms of learning. *Adult Education Quarterly, 44*(3), 158–173.

School for New Learning. (1996–1997). *Master of Arts in Integrated Professional Studies Program Handbook.* Chicago: DePaul University.

Schon, D. (1983). *The reflective practitioner.* New York: Basic Books.

Sheckley, B., Lamdin, L., & Keeton, M. (1993). *Employability in a high performance economy.* Chicago: CAEL.

Watkins, K., & Marsick, V. (1993). *Sculpting the learning organization.* San Francisco: Jossey-Bass.

Using Electronic Mail to Conduct Survey Research

Liz Thach

Electronic mail (Email) has revolutionized communication processes by allowing users to transmit and receive information from virtually anyplace in the world with a computer node connected to an online service. No longer bound by the slower rate of traditional mail, people can receive mail at the rate of electricity—almost instantly and at a relatively low cost. This type of information system obviously has other applications, such as private discussion groups or listservs, public announcements, access to expert opinion, group work, and even socioemotional applications where company employees use electronic mail as a type of "gripe board" to discuss issues (Steinfield, 1990; Zuboff, 1988). However, one application which hasn't been discussed as widely is the use of electronic mail for survey research, even though it has been utilized for this purpose since the late 1970s (Kiesler & Sproull, 1986).

Email Survey Research is the systematic data collection of information on a specific topic using computer questionnaires delivered to an online sample or population. Respondents receive, complete, and return their questionnaires via Email. With the growth of online networks around the world, it is feasible to see an increase in the use of Email survey research.

With this in mind, the purpose of this article is to review the literature on the topic of survey research via electronic mail in order to understand the key issues in design, implementation, and response using this medium. To begin, however, a brief description of several online networks, as well as the characteristics of electronic mail, will be provided.

Descriptions of Online Networks

Online networks can be divided into the two major categories of private and public. Private networks are closed to all but a select group of users. These are characterized by the private Email networks operated by corporations to provide a business communication system for employees. They can be small local area networks (LANs) within one or two departments connected by Ethernet or Token Ring protocols, or wide area networks (WANs) connecting multiple sites of one corporation through transmission mediums of cable, fiber optics, or even satellite for global connections. Access to these private networks is restricted to a specific group of users, who must have permission and a password to communicate on the network. Often, however, these private networks have access to public networks.

Public networks are open to anyone who is willing to pay a user fee to join the network. Examples of public networks include CompuServe, Prodigy, America Online, Delphi, and similar service companies which provide access to their online networks as long as the user pays a monthly and sometimes hourly fee. Once connected to one of these public networks, users can send electronic mail messages to other users on the network. In addition, they are often given the option of paying additional fees in order to have access to large databases of information on specific topics of personal interest.

The largest, international online network offering users access to massive databases of information is the *Internet.* First established as a mechanism for U.S. military and scientific researchers to communicate with each other, it has since become the largest educational online network in the world. Primarily for university and research use, it is now attracting more and more corporate interest.

Obviously, with the multitude of networks available on a global basis, there is much room for survey research. However, it is first necessary to examine the characteristics of electronic mail and determine how these impact survey research.

From *Educational Technology,* March/April 1995, pp. 27-31. © 1995 by Educational Technology Publications. Reprinted by permission.

Characteristics of Electronic Mail

Sproull (1986) lists four characteristics of electronic mail that make it useful for communication, and specifically for survey research. These are: (1) *Speed*—messages can be transmitted in seconds to any location in the world, depending on the scope of the network. (2) *Asynchronous Communication*—messages can be sent, read, and replied to at the convenience of the user. It is not required that the participants communicate synchronously, but instead can take their time to think about their response and answer when ready. (3) *No Intermediaries*—Email messages are generally only read by the receiver. In general, there are no secretaries or other clerical staff to open and sort the mail (though this is changing in large corporations where high level managers can receive over 100 Emails per day and therefore have their secretaries sort them). Due to this characteristic, Email messages have a better chance of being "opened" and read by the receiver than a traditional letter might. (4) *Ephemerality*—Email messages appear on screen and can easily be deleted with no trace of a hard copy. This lends an ephemeral quality to electronic mail that cannot be matched by traditional mail. However, users still have the option of saving Email messages in electronic folders and printing them out in hard copy if so desired.

These four characteristics relate directly to the success of Email survey research, in that the speed of the message transmission could result in faster response rates; asynchronous communications allow the users time to think about their answers (though this may not always be desirable); lack of intermediaries will increase the chances of the respondent receiving the survey immediately, rather than have it relegated to a lower priority pile of mail; and, finally, the ephermal quality of the messages may encourage the user to respond in a more candid fashion—as in fact it does, according to research findings (Kiesler & Sproull, 1986; Sproull, 1986; Synodinos & Brennan, 1988). These characteristics can be seen again in some of the key issues mentioned in the review of the literature.

Issues in Design, Implementation, and Response to Email Survey Research

The review of the literature illustrates **eleven key issues** in regard to the design, implementation, and response to Email survey research. Each of these issues can be categorized under one of the three headings: design issues, implementation issues, and response findings. The following describes the issues in more detail.

Design Issues

When discussing the design of surveys, it is useful to review the major steps for questionnaire development outlined by Borg and Gall (1989). Specifically these are "defining objectives, selecting a sample, writing items, constructing the questionnaire, pretesting, preparing a letter of transmittal, and sending out your questionnaire and follow-up" (p. 423). Defining objectives is simply determining the type of information you hope to obtain as a result of your questionnaire. This includes deciding what you will do with the information once you have collected it and how each item on the questionnaire contributes to meeting specific objectives. This type of activity is necessary in all types of survey research, and has not been shown to be any different with Email survey research.

Selecting a sample, however, does figure as a key issue in Email survey research, because the **demographics (issue No. 1)** of the sample are limited to those people who have access to online networks. Kiesler and Sproull in their 1986 research described the population as follows (p. 411):

> The population of interest for an electronic survey will be a community of organization with access to and familiarity with computers or computer networks. These groups will tend to be relatively well-educated, urban, white collar, and technologically sophisticated.

Obviously, if the population or sample to be surveyed does not fit this description, then Email survey research may not be a viable option. However, with the rapid spread of technology and falling costs for equipment and online fees, it is feasible that more diverse populations will have access to Email in the future.

Related to the demographic issue is one of self-selection and bias. Walsh *et al.* (1992) conducted a research study wherein they administered an Email survey to a random sample of users on a private oceanographic network, and at the same time made it available to the complete listserv on a volunteer basis. Respondents who self-selected to complete the electronic survey were found to be much more experienced with networks, responded more rapidly, gave higher quality responses, and had more positive attitudes towards the complete process. This illustrates the need to carefully consider population background and the potential bias effects that can result from self-selection. Indeed, Synodinos and Brennan (1998), in some earlier research, caution that "the relationship of basic demographic variables to computer survey responses must be systematically investigated" (p. 132).

Other design considerations, such as writing items and constructing the questionnaire, raise the issue of **layout and presentation (2)** of the electronic survey. Carr (1991) found that it took much longer to create a computer survey that was distributed to users on a floppy disk than it would take to type and print a paper survey. He states (p. 37):

> The paper medium is well understood and straightforward to complete. I was neither a novice nor an expert at survey creation or programming, but writing a computer-based survey program took three months.

In addition, he found that the use of technology made users more critical of format issues such as color, spacing, and location of items. On the other hand, with advances in technology, it is now possible to send beautiful colored surveys complete with graphics to users on online networks for a much lower cost than it would be to reproduce and mail colored copies of a paper survey. Due to this, there is much potential for developing effective questionnaire layouts and presentations in the future. Also, with time and practice, the increased design time to which Carr alluded should decrease.

The design steps of pretesting, preparing a letter of transmittal, sending out the questionnaire, and follow-up also raise two issues for electronic surveys. The first of these is **user orientation and instructions (3).** For less technically sophisticated users, an orientation and instructions on how to complete the survey electronically may be necessary (Carr, 1991; Synodinos & Brennan, 1988), especially if the user has to copy and paste the questionnaire into a reply mode. America Online advises its users to copy questionnaires and assignments for its electronic university classes to a file in order to save users money for online time. The users can access the file later—off-line at no charge and complete the survey. When they are ready to return the survey, they can copy the file, log online again, and submit the completed document through Email. These types of additional orientations and instructions are often necessary when administering a survey electronically.

Related to this issue are potential technical problems the user may have with either the survey or their computer equipment. Data can be lost due to software or hardware problems, and therefore it is prudent to make back-up copies (Synodinos & Brennan, 1988).

A second, more positive, issue with pretesting, transmittal, and follow-up is the **ease of editing and analysis (4)** with electronic surveys. Pretests can be sent directly to a small pilot group of users at virtually no cost with online networks, and returned with suggested revisions in the same manner. Editing and revisions are much quicker, since the questionnaire is already developed in a computer format, and changes can be made readily on the screen (Kiesler & Sproull, 1986; Synodinos & Brennan, 1988). Follow-up reminders with a copy of the questionnaire can be sent with a touch of a few buttons.

Related to this is ease of data analysis when information is collected in an electronic format. Tedious retyping and re-entry of data are usually not necessary, since the researchers can just save and copy the responses to an analysis file. From there data can be coded, organized, and sorted according to the research methodology. Ferrara and Nolan (1974) report that:

> 20–40 percent of the total computing costs of conducting a survey may derive from transforming data collected off-line into a form which can be processed by the computer (p. 27).

With this in mind, it is obvious that editing and analysis are much more cost-effective and time-saving than the traditional paper method.

Implementation Issues

Implementation of the electronic survey illuminates four new issues. The first of these is **confidentiality (5).** Due to the open nature of electronic networks, it is more difficult to guarantee anonymity or confidentiality to respondents (Price, 1975). Most online systems will automatically send the respondent's Email address (name) along with the electronic survey response. Therefore, the researcher will know who responded and how. This eliminates anonymity, but doesn't necessarily preclude confidentiality. According to Berdie *et al.* (1986), anonymous questionnaires are those that no one—not even the researcher—can determine who responded to them, but confidential questionnaires are those that promise to keep the name and responses of the respondent confidential to all but the researcher. Given this definition, anonymity cannot be promised, but confidentiality can. However, the researcher will probably want to define Berdie's definition of confidentiality in the Email cover letter.

On the topic of the Email cover letter, the additional issue of an **Email invitation to participate (6)** is useful. By sending the random sample an advance Email invitation to participate in an online survey and requesting a response as to whether or not the participant would prefer to complete the survey online or in paper format, the researcher can obtain an initial estimate of how many people will actually respond to the online survey. This type of approach is especially useful in large networks such as the Internet where there are many "dead" addresses—those that have not been deleted, or the person never looks at their mail (Eastman, 1993). If a low response is received with the initial invitation, then the researcher can choose new names for the random sample. A side benefit to using the invitation approach is the building of commitment to participate. If the user agrees to participate, they are much more likely to actually follow through and complete the questionnaire.

The issue of **faster transmission (7)** when implementing the online survey is noted by researchers (Sproull, 1986; Synodinos & Brennan, 1988). Instead of waiting for surveys to arrive by traditional postage mail, the online questionnaire can be delivered—and redelivered if lost—in virtually seconds.

Finally, **cost-saving (8)** in implementing the online questionnaire is also an obvious advantage. Postage fees are avoided, and if online charges are made (educational users on the Internet are not charged for *personal* use time, though their schools do pay), they are usually much less than traditional postage. McBrien (1984) reported that computer administered interviews at the First National Bank of Chicago resulted in a 33–40% sav-

Table 1

Advantages and Disadvantages of Electronic Mail Surveys

Advantages	Disadvantages
Cost-savings—less expensive to send questionnaires over online network than to pay postage for paper questionnaires or interviewers' salaries.	*Sample demographic limitations*—population and sample are limited to those with access to a computer and online network.
Ease of editing/analysis—simpler to make changes to questionnaire after pretesting and easier to copy and sort data, since it doesn't have to be re-typed.	*Lower levels of confidentiality*—due to the open nature of most online networks, it is difficult to guarantee anonymity and confidentiality.
Faster transmission time—questionnaires can be delivered to recipient in virtually seconds, rather than days as with traditional mail.	*Layout and presentation issues*—constructing the format of a computer questionnaire can be more difficult the first few times, due to lack of experience for some researchers.
Easy use of preletters (invitations)—invitations to participate can be sent and responded to in a very short time, thus providing the researcher with an estimate of the participation level.	*Additional orientation/instructions*—extra instructions and even orientation to the computer and online system may be necessary in order for respondents to complete the questionnaire online.
Higher response rate—research shows that response rates on private networks are higher with electronic surveys than with paper surveys.	*Potential technical problems with hardware and software.*
More candid responses—research shows that respondents will answer more honestly with electronic surveys than with paper surveys or in interviews.	
Potentially quicker response time with wider magnitude of coverage—due to the speed of online networks, participants can answer in virtually minutes or hours, and coverage can be global.	

ings in costs compared to traditional methods. General Foods and Xerox reported similar cost-saving advantages (Steinfield, 1990; Synodinos & Brennan, 1988). Kiesler and Sproull (1986) believe that the cost-savings benefits of Email surveys will be one of the major reasons for its growth in the future:

> If only because it seems to reduce research costs, the electronic survey may become widespread. Once respondents have access to a computer or to a network, relatively lower marginal costs of collecting and communicating data electronically can be substituted for the substantial costs of interviewing, telephoning, and sending questionnaires through the mail (pp. 403–404).

Response Findings

Response findings for Email research surveys are, on the whole, very positive. Three key issues are found in this category. The first of these is **faster response rates (9)**. Sproull (1986) found that response rates to electronic mail surveys were more than 20% higher than the typical 20 to 50% rate of hard-copy mail questionnaires. However, he also found that face-to-face interviews had a

higher response rate than electronic surveys, due mainly to the social presence of the researchers.

In a second study, Kiesler and Sproull (1986) found that in addition to higher response rates, electronic mail respondents also completed more items and made fewer mistakes on their questionnaire. Walsh *et al.* (1992) achieved a 76% response rate to their electronic mail survey with a random sample, and an amazing 96% response rate with a self-selecting group. It must be noted, however, that all of the above studies were with private online networks where the researchers had access to Email addresses. When conducting research on large public networks, such as the Internet, this type of response may not be as high due to the proliferation of "dead" addresses (Eastman, 1993) and the difficulty in obtaining Email addresses for a random sample. Self-selecting surveys could be conducted, but modification for bias would need to be estimated.

Another interesting issue with response findings is the proclivity for **candid responses (10)** with electronic survey research. In the above referenced studies, the researchers found that respondents answered much more honestly and with more socially undesirable responses than comparison groups completing paper questionnaires and/or face-to-face interviews (Kiesler & Sproull, 1986; Sproull, 1986; Synodinos & Brennan, 1988; Walsh *et al.*, 1992). It is suggested that this type of candid response results from the fact that the computer effectively shields the respondent from the social context of traditional communication. Indeed, many users have the option of using alias Email address names which allow them to disguise their gender, age, and nationality. Ironically, these same attributes are true of paper questionnaires, but they don't ellicit the same degree of candor (Sproull, 1986; Synodinos & Brennan, 1988).

The last issue related to response finding is the **speed and magnitude (11)** of the responses. Because of the large number of people on private online networks and the ability to send a large number of questionnaires out very quickly, response rate speed combined with magnitude of coverage is much better than traditional paper questionnaires and interviews. Steinfield (1990) cites an example of an Email survey that was administered at Xerox in the following passage:

> They broadcast a message throughout the company asking for advice.... The message included a description of the options, and what they saw as the strengths and weakness of each.... This message was sent in the morning, and by the late afternoon, they had received several hundred replies. The group then tallied up the replies, and sent a message back to everyone the same afternoon. ... Without electronic mail, this same activity simply could not have occurred without great cost and effort, and yet in this instance was completed all in the same day (p. 288).

The magnitude of an Email network is something which should not be taken lightly, as many networks can now reach remote locations around the world in seconds, and receive responses just as quickly. Though respondents do have the option of waiting and delaying their response due the asynchronous nature of the network, the fact that participants can be accessed in the remote mountains of New Zealand, or even the cold depths of the Arctic (Walsh *et al.*, 1992) gives tribute to the large magnitude and response time potential of Email survey research.

Summary and Conclusion

In conclusion, it can be said that there are many advantages to Email survey research over traditional paper questionnaires and interview formats, but also some disadvantages. Table 1 outlines some of these based on the review of literature and issues described in the preceding passages. Some drawbacks include the sample demographic limitations, lower levels of confidentiality, additional orientation/instructions, layout and presentation issues, and potential technical problems with hardware and software. Advantages include cost-savings, ease of editing/analysis, faster transmission time, easy use of pre-letters (invitations), and the three major response findings: (1) higher response rates, (2) more candid responses, and (3) potentially quicker response time with wider magnitude of coverage.

References

Berdie, D. R., Anderson, J. F., & Neibuhr, M. A. (1986). *Questionnaires: Design and use* (2nd ed). Metuchen, NJ: Scarecrow Press.

Borg, W. R., & Gall, M. D. (1989). *Educational research* (5th ed). New York: Longman.

Carr, H. H. (1991). Is using computer-based questionnaires better than using paper? *Journal of Systems Management* September, 19, 37.

Eastman, P. (1993). Response rates to electronic mail questionnaires, personal phone interview.

Ferrara, R., & Nolan, R. L. (1974). New look at computer data entry. In S. Kiesler & L. S. Sproull (1986). Response effects in the electronic survey. *Public Opinion Quarterly, 50,* 402–13.

Kiesler, S., & Sproull, L. S. (1986). Response effects in the electronic survey. *Public Opinion Quarterly, 50,* 402–13.

Manes, S. (1988). *The complete MCI mail handbook.* New York: Bantam Books.

Price, C. R. (1975). Conferencing via computer. In H. A. Linston & M. Turoff (Eds.), *The Delphi method: Techniques and Applications.* Reading, MA: Addison-Wesley.

Sproull, L. S. (1986). Using electronic mail for data collection in organizational research. *Academy of Management Journal, 29,* 159–69.

Steinfield, C. W. (1990). Computer-mediated communications in the organization: Using electronic mail at Xerox. In C. W. Steinfield (Ed.), *Organizational and communication theory.* Newbury Park, CA: Sage.

Synodinos, N. E., & Brennan, J. M. (1988). Computer interactive interviewing in survey research. *Psychology & Marketing, 5*(2), 117–137.

Walsh, J. P., Kiesler, S., Sproull, L. S., & Hesse, B. W. (1992). Self-selected and randomly selected respondents in a computer network survey. *Public Opinion Quarterly, 56,* 241–244.

Zuboff, S. (1988). *In the age of the smart machine.* New York: Basic Books, Inc.

Daily Data Collection:
A Comparison of Three Methods

Diane M. Morrison, Barbara C. Leigh, and Mary Rogers Gillmore
University of Washington

This paper compares three methods for daily data collection to examine the co-occurrence of intoxication and unsafe sex at the incident level. Sexually transmitted disease clinic clients and sexually active college students were randomized to complete either written daily diaries, daily telephone interviews they initiated, or daily telephone interviews initiated by project staff for a period of 4 weeks. The three methods are compared on rates of retention, number of days missed, number of items missed, and respondents' self-assessments of ease and accuracy of their responses. Dropout rates were low in all conditions. Respondents who initiated daily phone calls had the highest rate of missing days, and those in the written diary condition had the highest rate of missed items.

Intoxication, from use of alcohol or other drugs, is commonly thought to be a cause of unsafe sex, particularly of the failure to use condoms conscientiously. Research on this association has yielded mixed findings. A number of studies document general associations between high rates of substance use and high rates of sexual behavior risk (e.g., Anderson & Dahlberg, 1992; Biglan et al., 1990; Penkower et al., 1991; Rolfs, Goldberg, & Sharrar, 1990). Other studies have gone further to demonstrate links between substance use in conjunction with sexual activity and sexual risk-taking (cf., Cooper, Peirce, & Huselid, 1994; Hingson, Strunin, Berlin, & Heeren, 1990). As Leigh and Stall (1993) point out, associations of substance use and unsafe sex may be attributable to a number of causes, including confounding personality or situational characteristics. The crucial data needed to answer the question of whether intoxication has a causal relationship to sexual risk-taking are reports of several sexual encounters, varying by levels of intoxication, from the same individuals.

Such an analysis would control for personality characteristics and lifestyle characteristics.

One method for gathering such data is a daily diary, three variants of which are described in this paper. Data from daily diaries can be used to examine the co-occurrence of intoxication and unsafe sex intra-individually, at the incident level; that is, to answer the question of whether the same person is less likely to use protection when intoxicated than when sober. Diaries have been used successfully to track both alcohol consumption (e.g., Hilton, 1989; Poikolainen & Karkkainen, 1983) and sexual behavior (e.g., Harvey & Beckman, 1986; Hornsby & Wilcox, 1989; Reading, 1983). They have also been used to assess the co-occurrence of intoxication and sexual behavior (Harvey & Beckman, 1986; Leigh, 1993; Weatherburn et al., 1993) and to assess condom use (Leigh, 1993; McLaws, Oldenburg, Ross, & Cooper, 1990; Weatherburn et al., 1993).

Using a daily diary methodology in this context presents some novel challenges. There are several behaviors to assess each day: use of alcohol, use of other drugs, occasions of sexual intercourse, and condom use. There may be multiple instances of each behavior, and all must be captured. The temporal order of, and lag between, substance use and sexual intercourse is important, since substance use after intercourse, or a long time before intercourse, would not lead to intoxication at the time of intercourse. The quantity of the substance used will also influence the level of intoxication. The number of ques-

Data collection was supported by a grant from the Alcohol and Drug Abuse Institute, University of Washington, and preparation of this paper was supported by research grant R01 AA09701 from the National Institute of Alcohol Abuse and Alcoholism.

Correspondence to Diane M. Morrison, University of Washington, 4101 15th Ave. N.E., Seattle, WA 98105-6299; e-mail: DMM@uwashington.edu

From *The Journal of Sex Research*, February 1999, pp. 76-81. © 1999 by the Society for the Scientific Study of Sexuality. Reprinted by permission.

tions asked to elicit all this information results in a daily questionnaire that is considerably longer than those used in previous research. In addition, many potential respondents have already been exposed to public health messages that teach that "high = high risk." Such a belief might influence respondents' recollections of condom use, or affect the perceived social desirability of reporting condom use. A potential solution to this problem is to embed questions about substance use, sexual intercourse, and condom use in a larger daily questionnaire, disguising the hypothesis that underlies the questions. This leads to an even longer daily diary, however, and greater respondent burden.

Both substance use and intercourse are typically sporadic, rather than daily, behaviors. This necessitates a fairly long data collection phase to ensure that most respondents will record at least a few instances of both target behaviors (intercourse and substance use). Respondents must therefore complete daily diaries over a long period of time, further increasing respondent burden.

In addition, the respondents of interest for such a study are individuals whose sexual behavior puts them at risk for unintended pregnancy or disease, and who drink alcohol or use substances at least occasionally. This subject population may be more transient or have less stable or less predictable lives, which may make it more difficult for them to incorporate a new daily ritual into their habits.

There are multiple reporting modes available for daily diaries. Three methods are written diaries, daily phone calls to the respondent from project staff, and daily phone calls from the respondent to the project staff. Each of these modes has advantages and disadvantages. A written diary does not demand frequent contact with the project staff, and allows the respondent maximum flexibility in time and location for filling out the diary. However, there is no *time stamp* on the data (i.e., no independent verification of the time when the responses were recorded), and it is possible for a respondent to fill out diaries for several days retrospectively. There is also no daily reminder to subjects to fill out that day's diary, and no daily check on the diary for completeness. Daily phone calls from the respondent allow flexibility of location but less flexibility of time, unless the project phones are staffed round-the-clock (which is expensive and difficult to implement). Because the respondent is talking to an interviewer, missing data due to respondents overlooking questionnaire items is minimized but there is the potential for missing entire days when the respondent forgets to make the phone call. Daily phone calls to the respondent allows the least flexibility for the respondent, who needs to be at the phone at a specific time each day. The respondent does not need to remember to make a phone call each day, but does need to be where she or he is expected to be at that time, and that place must have a phone with a known number. A major advantage of both phone methods is that each daily diary can be time stamped, and use of well-trained interviewers

can minimize missing data due to overlooked questions or ambiguities.

This paper describes a study undertaken to assess the feasibility of collecting daily diaries of substance use and risky sexual behavior in two high-risk samples composed of individuals who may be difficult to recruit, track, and retain. The study was designed to test three strategies—self-administered written diaries, respondent-initiated telephone interviews, and project-initiated telephone interviews—for collection of daily data on substance use and risky sexual activity, and to assess these three strategies in terms of feasibility, subject compliance, and data quality. The results of this study were used to inform choice of diary collection for a larger study investigating the relationship of intoxication to sexual safety in a variety of populations (Gillmore, Leigh, & Morrison, 1993).

METHOD

Respondents

Respondents were 79 adolescents and adults (35 males and 44 females), aged 16 to 38 (mean age 24; median age 22). Twenty-four percent were aged 16–20, 49% were 21–25, 8.9% were 26–30 and 18% were 31 or older. The majority were White (64%), with 25% African American, 5% Asian American, 1% Hispanic, and 5% of other racial/ethnic backgrounds. A question about marital status found that 61 participants (77%) had never been married, 11(14%) were married, 6 (8%) were separated or divorced, and 1 (1%) was widowed.

Recruitment

Respondents were recruited in three ways. First, clients of a sexually transmitted disease (STD) clinic who had previously taken part in a study of condom use were sent letters inviting them to participate in the study. Second, a sample of 191 college student names was randomly drawn from the student directory at the University of Washington. The sample was limited to third-year students, in order to increase the probability that the prospective respondent (a) drank alcohol and (b) was not graduating during the time of the study. Third, additional college students were recruited from two undergraduate sociology classes. The study was described to all potential respondents as a study of general health habits.

Potential respondents received a letter inviting them to contact the project staff to find out if they were eligible to participate. The letter stated that participants would be paid $20 a week for the four weeks of the study. Stamped postcards addressed to the project office were enclosed for recipients to return if they were interested in participating.

Screening

Those who returned postcards were contacted by telephone and administered a screening questionnaire, which assessed the respondent's age, ethnicity, marital status, alcohol use, and sexual activity during the last 3 months. Respondents were ineligible if they had not had sex or drunk alcohol in the previous 3 months, or if they were planning to leave the area and be out of contact for more than 3 days in the next month. Eligible respondents were sent consent forms to sign and return. Upon receipt of the consent form, respondents were randomly assigned to one of the three experimental conditions, stratified by gender and sample: college students, adult STD clinic clients (over 20 years old), or adolescent STD clinic clients (aged 16–20). Sexual orientation was not assessed, as it had no substantive bearing on the research and the expected numbers of homosexual and bisexual respondents in this the sample would be too small to allow analysis by subgroup.

Experimental Conditions

Project-initiated telephone interview condition. Respondents in this condition were contacted daily by an interviewer, who administered the interview checklist by telephone. At the end of each interview, the time and phone number for the next day's interview was scheduled, to increase the likelihood that the respondent could be reached.

Respondent-initiated telephone interview condition. In this condition, respondents were instructed to call the research office every evening between 6 and 10 p.m. Respondents in this condition were sent $7.00 at the beginning of the study to cover the cost of 28 local phone calls (at $.25 per call).

Self-administered written diary condition. Each participant in the self-administered written diary condition was sent a four-week supply of daily logs, along with four stamped envelopes addressed to the project office. Participants were instructed to fill out the logs daily, preferably at the end of the day but no later than the following morning, and to send a completed log booklet to the project office at the end of each week.

Respondents in all three conditions were told that they would be sent $20 for each week that they completed the procedures, prorated for missing days.

Materials

The daily log was identical for all respondents, differing only in the method of administration. Each daily log was a simple checklist on a single, double-sided sheet of paper, labeled with the respondent's study ID number and the day of the week it was to be used. The log included 12 questions about a variety of health-related behaviors, in which items about substance use and sexual activity were embedded, in order to reduce sensitivity to the items of interest. Respondents checked *yes* or *no* to questions asking them whether, since the time they completed the log the day before, they had eaten fresh fruit, eaten fresh vegetables, eaten sweets, drunk alcohol, smoked cigarettes, smoked marijuana, taken other drugs not prescribed by a

doctor, ridden a bicycle, driven a car, had sex, and exercised hard for 20 minutes or longer. They were also asked how many hours they had slept the night before. The last items on the log were a set of 14 adjectives describing both positive (warm, happy, calm) and negative (frustrated, sad, afraid) moods; respondents were instructed to check all the adjectives that described how they felt that day in general. Completing the log took about 5 minutes or less in all three conditions.

For several items, a yes answer led to a branching question with further information requested. Respondents who showed that they had drunk alcohol were asked how many cans of beer, glasses of wine, and shots of liquor they had consumed; respondents who had smoked cigarettes were asked how many; respondents who drove a car were asked if they had worn a seatbelt, had been drinking, or had used drugs before driving; and respondents who reported having sex (vaginal or anal) were asked if they had used a condom, had been drinking, or had used drugs before or during sex.

RESULTS

Recruitment Success

For the college student sample, 191 recruitment letters were sent out, of which 37 were undeliverable. Of the 154 recipients who received the letters, 88 (57%) returned postcards indicating interest in participating in the study. Of these potential respondents, 45 people (51%) were ineligible for participation (27 had not had sex in the last 3 months, 9 had not drunk alcohol in the last 3 months, 2 had neither had sex nor drunk alcohol in the last 3 months, and 7 were leaving the area in the succeeding 4 weeks), leaving 43 participants.

For the STD clinic sample, 300 recruitment letters were sent to potential respondents, of which 118 were undeliverable. Of the 182 recipients who received the letter, 58 (32%) returned postcards. Of these 58, 16 (28%) were ineligible (4 had not had sex in the last 3 months, 11 had not drunk alcohol in the last 3 months, and 1 had neither had sex nor drunk alcohol in the last 3 months), leaving 42 participants.

Retention

Of the 85 respondents who agreed to participate in the study, two (one male college student, one female STD adolescent) never returned the consent form and thus were not assigned to an experimental condition. Three respondents dropped out in the first 2 days, and one dropped out after 2.5 weeks. All of the dropouts were in the respondent-initiated telephone interview condition. Seventy-nine respondents (93%) participated throughout the four weeks of data collection: 29 in the project-initiated telephone interview condition, 23 in the respondent-initiated telephone interview condition, and 27 in the written diary condition.

Table 1. Mean Number of Missing Days, by Condition and Gender

Condition	n	Respondent sex		
		Male	Female	Both sexes
Project-initiated telephone interview	29	2.6	2.9	2.8
Respondent-initiated telephone interview	23	8.0	3.3	5.4
Written diary	27	0.1	0.0	0.0
All conditions	79	3.3	3.1	2.6

Rates of Target Behaviors

Because potential respondents who had not had intercourse of who had not drunk alcohol in the previous 3 months were excluded from the study, the rates of intercourse and of substance use are not readily generalizable but are of importance to provide a context for the findings related to missing data and retention. The number of instances of vaginal and/or anal intercourse during the 28 days of daily data collection ranged from 0 to 23, with a mean of 7.90 ($SD = 5.77$). The mean proportion of condom use was .20 ($SD = .35$). The number of days alcohol was used ranged from 0 to 26, with a mean of 6.67 ($SD = 6.12$), and the quantity consumed at a drinking occasion ranged from 1 to 9 drinks, with a mean of 2.62 ($SD = 1.52$). Seventeen respondents reported use of marijuana or other recreational drugs during the period. The mean proportion of sexual encounters (vaginal or anal intercourse) that included drinking was .11 ($SD = 23$).

Missing Data

Missing days. Among the 79 participants, there was a total of 205 missing days of data (9.3% of total days). The range of missing days per person was 0–19. The percent of days missing differed by condition: 81 of 812 days (10%) were missing in the project-initiated telephone interview condition, 123 of 644 days (19%) were missing in the respondent-initiated telephone interview condition, and only 1 of 756 days (<1%) was missing in the self-administered written diary condition. The number of partici-

pants who had no missing days differed significantly by condition: 5 of 29 in the project-initiated telephone interview condition, 1 of 23 in the respondent-initiated telephone interview condition, and 26 of 27 in the written diary condition ($\chi^2_{(2\ df)} = 53.9$; $p < .001$).

Table 1 shows the mean number of days missing, per person, by condition and gender. A 3 X 2 X 3 analysis of variance (Condition, Gender, and Sample) showed main effects of Condition ($F = 24.76$, 2 and 61 df, $p < .001$) and Gender ($F = 4.27$, 1 and 61 df, $p = .043$), and a significant Condition X Gender interaction ($F = 5.69$, 2 and 61 df, $p = .005$), but there were no significant differences for sample, nor interactions of sample with condition or gender. The respondent-initiated telephone interview condition yielded nearly twice as many missing days as the project-initiated telephone interview condition, with virtually no missing days in the self-administered written diary condition. Scheffé tests for the entire sample showed that each of the conditions differed significantly ($p < .05$) from each of the other conditions. Overall, men had more missing days than women, but this effect was limited to the respondent-initiated telephone interview condition.

Item-level missing data. The amount of missing data on particular items was small, ranging from missing an item on 2 days (cigarette use) to missing on 17 days (amount of sleep), representing from 0.1% to 0.8% of all nonmissing days. Table 2 presents the mean number of missing values, per person, for selected items by condition (the table includes nonmissing days only). One-way analyses of variance showed that the self-administered written diary condition resulted in the most item-missing data. The items with the most missing data were marijuana use, followed by the number of drinks consumed.

Participant Feedback

At the completion of the daily reporting period, each respondent completed a self-administered exit questionnaire. A plurality of the respondents (42%) reported that they did not think that participating in the study changed their behavior; 24% were not sure whether it changed their behavior; 27% thought that it may have changed

Table 2. Mean Number of Missing Values for Selected Items, Per Person, by Condition

Condition	n	Topic of the item					
		Alcohol Use	Number of Drinks	Marijuana Use	Drug Use	Cigarette Use	Sexual Intercourse
Project-initiated telephone interview	29	0.00	0.03	.07	0.00	0.00	0.00
Respondent-initiated telephone interview	23	0.00	0.04	0.17	0.09	0.00	0.00
Written diary	27	0.11	0.33	0.37	0.19	0.07	0.15
F (2, 78 df)		3.13*	1.73 (ns)	2.30 (ns)	3.09*	2.00 (ns)	2.74*

Notes. ns = not significant.
*$p < .05$.

Table 3. Participant Opinion of Ease of Remembering to Report, by Condition

Condition	n	How easy to remember[a]	Correlation with missing days
Project-initiated telephone interview	29	1.82	.22 (ns)
Respondent-initiated telephone interview	23	2.56	.48*
Written diary	27	1.68	.10 (ns)

Notes. = not significant.
[a] = east, 5 = hard.
*$p < .05$.

their behavior; and 6% thought that it definitely did change their behavior. Only one respondent (1%) reported that the information provided for the past 4 weeks was *not at all correct*; 3% thought it was *somewhat correct*, 37% said *pretty correct*, and 59% said that it was *very correct*. There were no differences between the three conditions in these responses.

Participants' reports of how easy it was to remember to participate in the study (i.e., to remember to call in for an interview, to be available for an interview, or to fill out the diary each day) differed significantly by condition ($F = 8.35$, 1 and 75 df, $p < .001$). As shown in Table 3, participants rated the written diary condition as easiest to remember, and the respondent-initiated telephone interview condition as the hardest. Scheffé tests showed that the means for the two telephone conditions differed significantly from the written diary condition, but not from each other ($p < .05$). In addition, ratings of difficulty were significantly ($p = .022$) correlated with the number of missing days only in the respondent-initiated telephone interview group, such that respondents with more missing days found it more difficult to remember to call in for their interviews.

DISCUSSION

Dropout Rates

Only six of the 85 people who agreed to be in the study did not complete the study; two of these dropped out before data collection began. This 7% dropout rate compares favorably to rates in other studies, although many studies using diaries do not report dropout rates. In a study of record-keeping of drinking occasions and sexual encounters, Leigh (1993) reported a 16% dropout rate. In other studies of sexual behavior, Reading (1983) reported that 34% of those in a diary condition failed to complete the study, and McLaws et al. (1990) lost 30% of their respondents to dropout. Sudman and Lannom (1980), in a study of general health behavior, reported a 40% dropout rate for participants who returned diaries by mail. Despite fears that retention of respondents in diary studies is problematic, the present study demonstrates that

most respondents can be retained even in a relatively lengthy study (see Bolger, 1991, and Stone, Kessler, & Haythornthwaite, 1991, for strategies for maximizing retention).

Missing Data

Missing data can stem from missed days or missed items on reported days. None of the three conditions was lowest on both types. With regard to missing days, the respondent-initiated telephone interview condition, which placed the burden of making daily telephone calls on the respondent, was the most problematic. All four of the participants who dropped out during the course of the study were in this condition. Since dropouts inevitably introduce sample bias of unknown magnitude and effect, this condition is clearly the least acceptable. Respondents in this condition missed reporting on an average of 19% of the days, and 83% of participants in this condition missed at least 1 day. The greatest number of missing days in this condition is attributable primarily to days missed by male respondents. These men missed an average of 8 days, compared to 2.6 days for men in the project-initiated telephone interview condition and less than 1 day for men in the written diary condition. Women missed only 3.3 days in the respondent-initiated telephone interview condition.

In the project-initiated telephone interview condition, fewer days were missed overall but, as in the respondent-initiated telephone interview condition, 83% of the respondents missed at least 1 day. Gender was not a factor in number of days missed in the project-initiated telephone interview condition: Men missed only fractionally fewer days than women did. Project-initiated phone calls are clearly preferable to respondent-initiated calls in minimizing gender bias of missing data, as well as for overall level of missing data.

Self-administered written diaries resulted in the fewest missing days. However, there was no way to ensure that these respondents had actually filled out their diaries each day. Since diaries were mailed in only once a week, filling out several days of the diary at one time was possible for respondents in this condition. The daily telephone interview conditions resulted in somewhat more missing days than the written diary condition, but we could be sure that the data were collected on the day that the events occurred. If participants fill out the diary forms at a later date, the advantages of daily data collection in terms of accurate recall are compromised. Clearly there is a trade-off between telephone and self-administered written methods in missing days versus certainty about the time diaries are completed. One way to maximize both would be to require more frequent mailing of self-administered questionnaires. Although this would add to respondent burden and to project cost, it would help ensure daily reporting. In previous studies of sexual behavior diaries, a range of collection periods have been used, from every 3 days

(Reading, 1983) to weekly (Hornsby & Wilcox, 1989) or monthly (Kunin & Ames, 1981; McLaws et al., 1990).

In the two telephone conditions, there were practically no item-missing data, because interviewers were careful to ask every question and were available to clarify any ambiguities. The self-administered written diary condition had higher levels of item-missing data. Item-missing data was still quite low, however, with even the most sensitive items. Items about drinking and drug use, for example, averaged less than one missing item per person, over the 4 weeks of the study. Because we were interested in highlighting differences between the data collection methods, we did not follow up with calls to written-diary participants who missed particular items. Phone reminders in these cases may decrease this already low rate even further.

Sampling Issues

Studies of participation bias in sex surveys have demonstrated that volunteers and nonvolunteers differ in sexual attitudes and behaviors, with volunteers being more liberal and permissive (see Catania, Gibson, Chitwood, & Coates, 1990, for a review). The members of this sample who volunteered to disclose their sexual behavior over a month's time, and who were screened for recent intercourse and substance use, may represent an unusual group. Because reliability coefficients vary with different distributions of the measures (Armstrong, White & Saracci, 1992), the generalizability of the findings of this study is not assured.

Although the participants in this study were selected on the basis of their levels of alcohol use and frequency of sexual activity, the behavior of sample members is quite similar to that of estimates from general population surveys of drinking behavior (Midanik & Clark, 1994) and sexual behavior (Leigh, Temple, & Trocki, 1993). Respondents in the present study were more frequent drinkers; 40% reported usually drinking at least once a week, compared to 28% of the general population. However, average quantity consumed per drinking occasion was approximately 2.5 drinks in both the general population and the study sample. In the general population, 60% report having sex at least once a week, compared to 67% of the study sample. The similar distributions of these variables give more confidence in the generalizability of the results from the present study.

In summary, the results of this pilot study suggest a clear choice between the two telephone methods. Respondent-initiated telephone calls resulted in more missing days than project-initiated telephone calls, particularly among males, and had no compensating advantage in cost or number of missing items. We therefore would not recommend this method. Between project-initiated telephone calls and self-administered written diaries there are trade-offs, and neither emerges as clearly preferable. Self-administered written diaries resulted in the fewest missing days, but the most missing items per day; project-initiated phone calls resulted in more missing days, but fewer missing items per day. Overall, the written diaries resulted in the least missing data.

The quality of the data obtained from written diaries is not as good as that obtained by trained interviewers over the phone. It is almost impossible to guarantee that the data were collected on the day intended. How serious this problem is may depend on the frequency of the target behaviors. For behaviors engaged in with high frequency (e.g., smoking), this longer period of retrospection may result in greater errors of recall. For lower frequency behaviors, filling out diaries for a few days at the same time may not result in greater error, because recall is likely to be reasonably good for distinctive salient behaviors. Thus, for populations who engage in sex less than daily, the self-administered diary may well provide reasonably accurate data, even if diaries for 2 or 3 days are sometimes completed at once. Because it is far less expensive to implement than daily phone calls, this may be a good method to use for populations with infrequent sex occasions. For populations with high frequencies of sexual behavior (e.g., sex industry workers), project-initiated telephone calls may produce higher quality data, though more missing days. Given the trade-offs among the methods, researchers need to consider whether missing days or missing items are more problematic to their studies, the frequencies of the target behaviors among the population of interest, and the higher cost of administering daily phone calls.

REFERENCES

Anderson, J. E., & Dahlberg, L. L. (1992). High-risk sexual behavior in the general population: Results from a national survey, 1988–1990. *Sexually Transmitted Diseases, 19,* 320–325.
Armstrong, B. K., White, E., & Saracci, R. (1992). *Principles of exposure measurement in epidemiology.* New York: Oxford University Press.
Biglan, A., Metzler, C. W., Wirt, R., Ary, D., Noell, J., Ochs, L., French, C., & Hood, D. (1990). Social and behavioral factors associated with high-risk sexual behavior among adolescents. *Journal of Behavioral Medicine, 13,* 245–261.
Bolger, N. (1991, August). Using diaries to study personality in everyday life. In H. Tennen (Chair), *Daily events and experiences—research challenges and directions.* Symposium conducted at the 99th Annual Meeting of the American Psychological Association, San Francisco, CA.
Catania, J. A., Gibson, D. R., Chitwood, D. D., & Coates, T. J. (1990). Methodological problems in AIDS behavioral research: Influences on measurement error and participation bias in studies of sexual behavior. *Psychological Bulletin, 108,* 339–362.
Cooper, M. L., Peirce, R. S., & Huselid, R. F. (1994). Substance use and sexual risk taking among black adolescents and white adolescents. *Health Psychology, 13,* 251–262.
Gillmore, M. R., Leigh, B. C., & Morrison, D. M. (1993). *Daily event analysis of alcohol/drug use and risky sex.* Unpublished manuscript.
Harvey, S. M., & Beckman, L. J. (1986). Alcohol consumption, female sexual behavior and contraceptive use. *Journal of Studies on Alcohol, 47,* 327–332.
Hilton, M. E. (1989). A comparison of a prospective diary and two summary recall techniques for recording alcohol consumption. *British Journal of Addiction, 84,* 1085–1092.
Hingson, R. W., Strunin, L., Berlin, B. M., & Heeren, T. (1990). Beliefs about AIDS, use of alcohol and drugs, and unprotected sex among Massachusetts adolescents. *American Journal of Public Health, 80,* 295–299.

Hornsby, P. P., & Wilcox, A. J. (1989). Validity of questionnaire information on frequency of coitus. *American Journal of Epidemiology, 130,* 94–99.

Kunin, C. M., & Ames, R. B. (1981). Methods for determining the frequency of sexual intercourse and activities of daily living in young women. *American Journal of Epidemiology, 113,* 55–61.

Leigh, B. C. (1993). Alcohol consumption and sexual activity as reported with a diary technique. *Journal of Abnormal Psychology, 102,* 490–493.

Leigh, B. C., & Stall, R. D. (1993). Substance use and risky sexual behavior for exposure to HIV: Issues in methodology, interpretation, and prevention. *American Psychologist, 48,* 1035–1045.

Leigh, B. C., Temple, M. T., & Trocki, K. F. (1993). Sexual behavior of adults: Results from a U.S. national survey. *American Journal of Public Health, 83,* 1400–1408.

McLaws, M-L., Oldenburg, B., Ross, M. W., & Cooper, D. A. (1990). Sexual behavior in AIDS-related research: Reliability and validity of recall and diary measures. *The Journal of Sex Research, 27,* 265–281.

Midanik, L. T., & Clark, W. B. (1994). The demographic distribution of US drinking patterns in 1990: Description and trends from 1984. *American Journal of Public Health, 84,* 1218–1222.

Penkower, L., Dew, M. A., Dingsley, L., Becker, J., Satz, P., Schaerf, F., & Sherican, K. (1991). Behavioral, health, and psychosocial factors and risk for HIV infection among sexually active homosexual men: The multicenter AIDS cohort study. *American Journal of Public Health, 81,* 194–196.

Poikolainen, K., & Karkkainen, P. (1983). Diary gives more accurate information about alcohol consumption than questionnaire. *Drug and Alcohol Dependence, 11,* 209–216.

Reading, A. E. (1983). A comparison of the accuracy and reactivity of methods of monitoring male sexual behavior. *Journal of Behavioral Assessment, 5,* 11–23.

Rolfs, R. T., Goldberg, M., & Sharrar, R. G., (1990). Risk factors for syphilis: Cocaine use and prostitution. *American Journal of Public Health, 80,* 853–857.

Stone, A. A., Kessler, R. C., & Haythornthwaite, J. A. (1991). Measuring daily events and experiences: Decisions for the researcher. *Journal of Personality, 59,* 575–607.

Sudman, S., & Lannom, L. B. (1980). *Health care surveys using diaries.* National Center for Health Services Research Report Series (DHHS Publication No. PHS 80-3279). Washington, DC: Department of Health and Human Services.

Weatherburn, P., Davies, P. M., Hickson, F. C. I., Hunt, A. J., McManus, T. J., & Coxon, P. M. (1993). No connection between alcohol use and unsafe sex among gay and bisexual men. *AIDS, 7,* 115–119.

Manuscript accepted August 3, 1998

QUANTITATIVE ATTITUDES QUESTIONNAIRE: INSTRUMENT DEVELOPMENT AND VALIDATION

LEI CHANG
Chinese University of Hong Kong

This article reports on the development and validation of the Quantitative Attitudes Questionnaire (QAQ), a 20-item instrument measuring graduate students' attitudes toward quantitative research methodology. The QAQ was developed in a sample of 90 graduate students in education and was cross validated in 3 additional samples of similar size. The QAQ was found to correlate positively with quantitative exams and self-reported GRE-Math scores, and to differentiate doctoral versus master's students and students from research- versus teaching-oriented universities.

Assessing social science graduate students' attitudes toward quantitative research methodology is an important step in fostering appreciation of research and its methodology among these students. Such assessment results are also useful for curriculum development and instructional evaluation, because attitude change can be an important indicator of instructional success. However, there is currently no instrument assessing quantitative attitudes of graduate students in the social sciences. Existing attitude instruments that are most closely related to quantitative methodology include the Attitude Toward Statistics Scale developed by Wise (1985), the Statistics Attitude Survey by Roberts and Bilderback (1980), the Attitude Toward Education Research Scale (Napier, 1978), and the Mathematics Attitude Scale (McGalion & Brown, 1971). Most of these instruments target the undergraduate population. This article reports on the development of the Quantitative Attitudes Questionnaire (QAQ), a short survey prepared for graduate students in education and other social science disciplines.

The author thanks Robert Baker, Cecilia Barron, Susan Cohen, Gerry Ledford, Angela McBride, and Catherine McBride-Chang for their help with instrument development, and Larry Daniel and two anonymous reviewers for their helpful comments on the manuscript. Correspondence regarding this article should be addressed to Lei Chang, Department of Educational Psychology, Chinese University of Hong Kong, Shatin, N.T., Hong Kong. This study was conducted while the author was at the University of Central Florida.

From *Educational and Psychological Measurement*, December 1996, pp. 1037-1042. © 1996 by Sage Publications, Inc. Reprinted by permission.

Development of the QAQ

For this instrument, quantitative attitudes were defined as consisting of four components: (a) utility (the extent to which one finds quantitative methodology useful in his or her work), (b) value (how important one thinks quantitative methodology is in social science research), (c) efficacy (one's belief in one's quantitative abilities), and (d) knowledge (how much one thinks or feels he or she knows about quantitative methodology).

These four related attitudes were believed to have an impact on graduate students' performance in research methodology and other quantitative areas. They were derived by six faculty judges representing the fields of education, psychology, nursing, and business administration from four universities. These four constructs were subsequently translated into test items that were intended to duplicate the constructs. An initial pool of 65 items was developed and was reviewed by the same judges for content validity. Forty-five items receiving consensus endorsements from the judges were retained.

These 45 items, together with nine filler items measuring acquiescence or overall positive opinion, were administered to a convenience sample of 90 master's students in education from three sections of a research methods course and a statistics course taught by the author. The items were administered at the beginning of the semester using a 6-point Likert-type scale anchored by the commonly used *disagree* and *agree* designations. Students were asked to comment on the items. Based on their comments, some items were eliminated or revised. The revised items were administered 1 week later to the same students using a 4-point scale. Students were again asked to comment on the items and to indicate which of the two scales, 4-point versus 6-point, they preferred.

Five criteria were used in the subsequent item analyses, Specifically, satisfactory items were expected to have (a) few negative comments from the students, (b) high test-retest correlations over the two administrations, (c) high loadings on respective factors, (d) low correlations with filler items, and (e) positive correlations with a composite score made up of the midterm and final exams of the two quantitative courses the students were taking at the time. Not all criteria were equally adhered to. For instance, for some items that were not retested, the test-retest criterion did not apply.

These item analyses resulted in two test forms. The long form contained 30 items and the short form contained 20 out of 30 items. Both forms

used the 6-point scale, which most students preferred. The following validation studies were based on the 20-item QAQ.

Validation Studies

The 20-item QAQ was subsequently administered to three convenience samples. The first sample contained 120 master's students in education who were enrolled in different sections of a research methods course and a statistics course taught by the author. The second sample included 92 Ed.D. and counseling specialist students. Both samples were taken from a regional teaching university in the United States. The third sample contained 60 Ph.D. students and 14 faculty in psychology from a major research university in the United States. Gender composition of the sample of master's students was 80% female. There was no significant gender difference on any of the four QAQ factors. Gender information was not gathered for the other samples. However, the two departments from which the samples were taken were about 70% female.

Confirmatory factor analysis (CFA) using LISREL-7 was conducted within each of the three samples. In all three samples, the four-factor QAQ structure was identified and shown to be superior to two alternative (one-factor and five-factor) structures. Although chi-square tests of goodness of fit were statistically significant, other goodness-of-fit indexes indicated acceptable fit. For example, the average chi-square to degree of freedom ratio was 1.7. Interfactor correlations were .30 on average. The average standardized factor loadings were above .70. Internal consistency reliability estimates were similarly high. (CFA results are available from the author.) Reliability and validity information is included in Table 1.

Criterion-related validity was investigated in Sample 1 by correlating the four QAQ scores with a composite made up of the midterm and final exams of the two quantitative courses the students were enrolled in. The midterms for the two courses each had 76 multiple-choice items. The finals for the two courses each had 40 multiple-choice items. The four exams had internal consistency reliabilities above .80. Because of the different item difficulties, z scores were used to compute the criterion composite. The average correlation between the four QAQ scores and the criterion was .34. Among the four factors—utility, value, efficacy, and knowledge—utility correlated lowest at .22 and knowledge correlated the highest at .46. It seems that quantitative performance is more reflective of how much one thinks one knows about quantitative methodology than how important one thinks the methodology is. Similar but stronger validity evidence was observed in Sample 2, where self-reported GRE-Math scores were used as the criteria. The average correlation was .41. Efficacy and knowledge had the highest correlations with GRE-Math at .57 and .59, respectively. Overall, these correlations showed that this attitude instrument could differentiate graduate students of high versus low quantitative performance. These results support a criterion-related validity inference of the QAQ's application.

Mean differences among the three samples on four scales were investigated using MANOVA. Hotelling's test was statistically significant, approximate $F(8, 558) = 36.68$, $p < .01$. As expected, Sample 3, which included Ph.D. psychology students and faculty from a major research university, had significantly higher means than either of the other two samples on all QAQ factors except for utility, where the difference between Sample 3 and Sample 2 was not statistically significant. These results strengthen the validity inference of the use of QAQ. Doctoral students from a research university, who were heavily engaged in research, were expected to show more positive attitudes toward quantitative methodology than students from a teaching university, who had almost no research experience. Between the two samples of Ed.D./counseling specialist students (Sample 2) and master's students (Sample 1), both of which were taken from the teaching university, the former was expected to have higher means than the latter, because there was more methodological training in the Ed.D. and specialist programs than in the master's program. On utility and knowledge, Sample 2 had significantly higher scores than Sample 1. However, Sample I had a higher mean on the value factor. This last finding could be due to the fact that, because Sample I students were enrolled in the quantitative courses at the time, they could be more positive than usual about the research value of quantitative methodology.

Table 1

Descriptive Statistics and Reliability and Validity Estimates for QAQ Scores Across Samples

Scale	M	SD	α	Validity Estimate[a]
Sample 1 ($n = 120$)				
Utility	4.07	0.87	.81	.35
Value	4.69	0.72	.77	.22
Efficacy	3.33	1.12	.84	.33
Knowledge	3.18	0.81	.80	.46
Total score	3.82	0.55	.85	.35
Sample 2 ($n = 92$)				
Utility	5.18[b]	1.11	.77	.29
Value	4.13[c]	0.97	.86	.20
Efficacy	3.61	1.13	.75	.57
Knowledge	3.60[c]	0.99	.78	.59
Total score	4.14	0.67	.80	.39
Sample 3 ($n = 74$)				
Utility	5.35[d]	0.68	.82	
Value	5.00[e]	0.79	.74	
Efficacy	4.17[e]	1.01	.87	
Knowledge	4.70[e]	0.76	.80	
Total score	4.85	0.62	.89	

Note. Sample 1 contained master's students in education enrolled in two quantitative courses. Sample 2 contained Ed.D. and specialist students. Both samples were drawn from a teaching university. Sample 3 contained faculty and Ph.D. students in psychology from a major research university. Mean comparisons were made on the four scales but not on the total score; familywise error rate exceeds the reported p value.
a. Correlations with quantitative course exam for Sample 1 and GRE-Math for Sample 2.
b. Higher than Sample 1, $p < .01$.
c. Lower than Sample 1, $p < .01$.
d. Higher than Sample 1, $p < .01$.
e. Higher than Samples 1 and 2, $p < .01$.

Appendix
The Quantitative Attitudes Questionnaire Items

1. Knowledge of quantitative research methods is useful for my job.
2. The "truth" or falsity of a research question has to be tested by empirical data.
3. I need to know research methodology in order to do my own research.
4. I'm confident in my quantitative ability.
5. Any theory "worth its salt" has to be subjected to data-based quantitative tests.
6. I understand the basic principles of hypothesis testing and statistical inference.
7. A sound methodology is essential for quality research.
8. I see the usefulness of quantitative research methodology in my life.
9. I enjoy working with numbers.
10. I have a thorough understanding of quantitative research methods.
11. I understand the basic principles of classical test theory.
12. I'm good with numbers.
13. Quantitative research methodology is useful for my career.
14. I understand the interrelations among measurement, statistics, and research design.
15. Math has been one of my favorite subjects in school.
16. I need to keep up with quantitative development to do my job well.
17. I know which statistical procedure to use to test my hypothesis.
18. A good researcher must have a strong background in quantitative methodology.
19. Compared to others I know, I'm very good in quantitative subjects.
20. Statistical tools are invaluable for understanding and interpreting one's data.

Note. The scale Perceived Utility for Oneself comprises items 1, 3, 8, 13, and 16; the scale Perceived value in Research comprises items 2, 5, 7, 18, and 20; the scale Quantitative Efficacy comprises items 4, 9, 12, 15, and 19; the scale Perceived Quantitative Knowledge comprises items 6, 10, 11, 14, and 17.

Conclusion

The present study reports on 2 years of properly planned and implemented instrument development and validation procedures. Data presented here provide evidence that the 20-item QAQ is an efficient instrument to assess graduate students' attitudes toward quantitative methodology. However, there are two limitations. First, one of the criterion measures—the GRE-Math score—was based on self-reports that could contain errors. Second, gender information was incomplete. Although one of the degree programs showed no gender difference, and a similar gender composition was expected in the three programs, the mean differences found across programs could still have been confounded by potential gender differences. Validation is an ongoing process. Further research is needed to draw a stronger validity inference in the use of this new instrument.

References

McGallon, E. L., & Brown, J. D. (1971). A semantic differential instrument for measuring attitude toward mathematics. *Journal of Experimental Education, 39*(4), 69–72.

Napier, J. (1978). An experimental study of the relationship between attitude toward and knowledge of education research. *Journal of Experimental Education, 47*(2), 131–134.

Roberts, D. M., & Bilderback, E. W. (1980). Reliability and validity of a statistics attitude survey. *Educational and Psychological Measurement, 40*, 235–238.

Wise, S. L. (1985). The development and validation of a scale measuring attitudes toward statistics. *Educational and Psychological Measurement, 45*, 401–405.

Unit 5

Key Points to Consider

❖ What is the relationship between treatment effect, sample size and errors of statistical significance, as stated by Matt Wilkerson and Mary Olson?

❖ What special considerations need to be addressed when writing qualitative research at its various stages?

❖ What are the basic steps for conducting a survey?

❖ Discuss the new arts-based research approaches proposed by Elliot Eisner.

❖ What is action research? Why is it beneficial for teachers to become researchers in their own practice?

 **Links**   **www.dushkin.com/online/**

These sites are annotated on pages 4 and 5.

Research. Researcher. What mental images do those words create in your mind's eye? If you are anything like most students, you pictured researchers as white-coated males in labortory settings conducting experimental research. Perhaps the words "research" and "researcher" remind you of the sound bytes that are reported in the media (e.g., "A _____ University study found that . . ."). Where do you fit in this picture of research and researcher? Perhaps you find it hard to imagine yourself in this world of contradictions where research is sometimes respected to the point of dramatically altering beliefs and, at other times, dismissed for being esoteric; and where researchers can be regarded as the new pioneers or, conversely, portrayed as out of touch with the "real world"; or, worst of all, as charlatans who use the power of statistics to persuade and deceive.

Each of the articles selected for Unit 5 looks at a broad genre of research. The first article, coauthored by Matt Wilkerson and Mary Olson, deals with more traditional experimental and quasiexperimental designs and the most commonly held misconceptions about sample size, statistical significance, and treatment effect. In contrast to this genre, Donna Alvermann, David O'Brien and Deborah Dillon explore qualitative research methods and how those methods are used to study growth in literacy. Survey research is the topic of the third article by Susan Watson. In article four, Elliot Eisner, an articulate spokesperson for nontraditional forms of research, discusses the new frontier in qualitative research. Unit 5 concludes with

an article on action research by Mary Gove and Connie Kennedy-Calloway that is a type of "everyday" research conducted by professionals as they work together to achieve common goals.

MISCONCEPTIONS ABOUT SAMPLE SIZE, STATISTICAL SIGNIFICANCE, AND TREATMENT EFFECT

By MATT WILKERSON AND MARY R. OLSON,
Department of Continuing Education, George Fox University, Boise Center

Researchers' interpretations of statistical significance relative to sample size were obtained and analyzed. Fifty-two graduate students responded to a 6-question instrument designed to measure interpretations of the relationships between sample size and treatment effect, sample size and Type I error, and sample size and Type II error. Respondents placed more confidence in results of studies with large sample sizes than in results of studies with small sample sizes, regardless of the criterion on which that confidence was based. A discussion of the mathematical procedure for significance testing shows that respondents were not justified in these interpretations. An improved understanding of the relationship between treatment effect, sample size, and errors of statistical inference is suggested.

THE STATE OF KNOWLEDGE in the social sciences is advanced by conducting and reporting research (American Psychological Association, 1994). One commonly used tool for reporting research results, the significance test, has enjoyed great popularity and acceptance within the social sciences (Nelson, Rosenthal, & Rosnow, 1986). Despite this popularity and acceptance, literature suggests widespread misunderstanding regarding the use and interpretation of the significance test (Bakan, 1966; Carver, 1978; Cohen, 1990; Morrison & Henkel, 1970). Evidence has suggested that researchers place more confidence in the statistical significance of studies in which large samples have been used than in studies employing small samples (Bands & Boen, 1972; Rosenthal & Gaito, 1963; Stone & Bodner, 1969). An understanding of the mathematical procedures

of the significance test demonstrates that such confidence is misplaced (Bakan, 1966).

A correct interpretation of the significance test requires knowledge of the relationship between sample size and treatment effect. Because sample size (n) is in the denominator of the formula for deriving statistical significance, small samples demand a larger treatment effect than large samples to reach an equal level of statistical significance. This inverse relationship between treatment effect and sample size is often misunderstood (Bands & Boen, 1972).

A correct interpretation of the significance test also requires knowledge of two types of inferential error, Type I error and Type II error. A Type I error is the error of rejecting the null hypothesis when it is, in fact, true. The probability of making a Type I error is equal to the

selected value for alpha (a). A Type II error is the error of accepting the null hypothesis when it is, in fact, false. Whereas increasing the sample size reduces the probability of committing a Type II error, decreasing the alpha level is the only means of reducing the probability of committing a Type I error. For identical p values, given equal alpha levels, the probability of committing a Type I error is the same regardless of sample size. The reason the probability of a Type I error is the same is that the mathematics of the significance test takes into account the sample size (Bakan, 1966; Rosenthal & Gaito, 1963).

The literature in the field of psychology has failed to clarify the relationship between sample size and treatment effect, sample size and Type I error, and sample size and Type II error (Beauchamp & May 1964; Rosenthal & Gaito, 1963;

From *Journal of Psychology Interdisciplinary and Applied,* November 1997, pp. 627-632. © 1997 by Heldref Publications, 1319 Eighteenth St., NW, Washington, DC 20036-1802. Reprinted by permission.

Stone & Bodner, 1969). If the criterion for valuing research results is inferred treatment effect, researchers are incorrect in placing more confidence in studies using larger sample sizes (Bands & Boen, 1972). If the criterion for valuing research results is the probability of committing a Type I error, researchers are incorrect in placing more confidence in studies using larger samples (Bakan, 1966; Rosenthal & Gaito, 1963). If, however, the criterion for valuing research results is the probability of committing a Type I error, researchers are justified in placing greater confidence in studies using larger samples (Bakan, 1966; Rosenthal & Gaito, 1963).

This study was designed to obtain data on the following questions: How do researchers interpret the relationship between sample size and treatment effect, given equal statistically significant findings? How do researchers interpret the relationship between sample size and Type I error? How do researchers interpret the relationship between sample size and Type II error?

Method

Participants

Our participants were 52 graduate students attending the University of Idaho, Boise Center. Twenty (39%) were pursuing a PhD, 14 (27%) were pursuing an EdD, and 16 (31%) were pursuing a master's degree. Two respondents (4%) did not respond to the question regarding degree being pursued. Twenty-one of the 52 respondents (40%) reported that they had, or were currently, engaged in conducting original research.

Procedure

Questionnaires were distributed to the participating students in three classes during the 1996 summer session. They were given approximately 5 min of class time to complete and return the questionnaires. The instrument was a 1-page questionnaire regarding the relationship between sample size and treatment effect, the relationship between sample size and Type I error and the relationship between sample size and Type II error. After answering the questions, the students were asked to explain the reasoning behind their responses.

Results

Only 1 of 52 respondents (1.9%) recognized that, given two different studies, both reporting a p value of .05, the study with the smaller n provides better evidence for treatment effect. Chi-square analysis indicated that a significant number of respondents incorrectly answered this question, $Chi[sup 2](3, N = 51) = 29.70, p < .05$. The most common reason respondents gave for their answers was that increasing sample size decreases the amount of statistical error.

Six of 52 respondents (11.5%) recognized that the probability of Type I error does not depend on sample size. This result reached statistical significance, $Chi[sup 2](3, N = 52) = 45.84, p < .05$. The most common reason respondents gave for their answers was similar to that received for the first question, that increasing sample size decreases the amount of statistical error. Those who responded correctly to this question commented that statistical significance at the .05 level is statistical significance at the .05 level, regardless of sample size.

Twenty-five of 52 respondents (48%) demonstrated an understanding that the probability of Type II error decreases with a larger sample size. A significant number of respondents answered this question correctly, $Chi[sub 2](3, N=48) = 19.66, p < .05$. The most frequently obtained comment again was that increasing the sample size decreases the amount of statistical error.

Discussion

Despite the widespread use of the significance test, there is misunderstanding associated with its interpretation. The results of this study support the existence of misunderstanding as to the relationship between sample size and statistical significance. Respondents placed more confidence in the results of studies with large sample sizes than in studies with small sample sizes, regardless of the criterion on which that confidence was based.

A significant number of respondents failed to recognize that a small sample requires a greater treatment effect than a large sample to obtain an equal level of statistical significance. For two different studies—one employing a sample of 25 and the other employing a sample of 250—the treatment effect for the smaller sample must be more than three times as large as the treatment effect for the larger sample to reach an equal level of significance (Bands & Boen, 1972). That is because the sample size (n) is in the denominator of the formula for deriving statistical significance. Readers of research results need not adjust obtained significance levels according to sample size, for sample size has already been taken into consideration in the computation of the obtained significance levels (Bakan, 1966).

Results of the question concerning the relationship between Type I error and significance level were statistically significant at the .05 level. Fewer respondents answered this question correctly than would nave been expected by chance; 88.5% of respondents answered this question incorrectly. With four responses available, 13 respondents (of 52) would be expected to guess the correct answer, given no knowledge of these matters. Responses to this question suggest that close to 90% of the respondents did not realize that statistical significance at the .05 level is statistical significance at the .05 level, regardless of sample size.

The reason for this misunderstanding may be due to the adage "If we wish to reduce the possibility of both types of error, we must increase N" (Siegel, 1956, p. 9). Although it is true that increasing the sample size reduces the probability of committing a Type II error, decreasing the alpha level is the only means of decreasing the probability of committing a Type I error (Bakan, 1966; Rosenthal & Gaito, 1963). Because the sample size is taken into consideration in the formula for determining statistical significance (Bakan, 1966), judging the probability of a Type I error by sample size leads to inaccurate interpretations of research results.

The finding that a significant number of respondents recognized that a larger sample decreases the probability of committing a Type II error is consistent with the literature (Stone & Bodner, 1969). Although more respondents answered this question correctly than would have been expected by chance, the majority of respondents (52%) answered this question incorrectly. Respondents employed the same line of reasoning used for the previous questions (i.e., that a larger sample size decreases the probability of error, regardless of the type of error in question).

This study provides information about the level of understanding of graduate-level researchers regarding fundamental issues of interpretation of research results. Although we recognize the limited scope of this sample, we believe that such misinterpretations are widespread throughout the social sciences. Replications of this study are necessary to determine the degree to which results may be generalized.

The interpretation of research results is critical to the advancement of knowledge in the social sciences. Although previous studies have provided evidence suggesting that researchers place greater confidence in the results of studies employing larger sample sizes (Beauchamp & May, 1964; Nelson, Rosenthal, & Rosnow, 1986; Rosenthal & Gaito, 1963), the criteria used for defining respondent confidence were not documented.

In this study, we separated the criteria by which respondents valued the relationships between sample size, evidence of treatment effect, Type I error, and Type II error. Our findings support the existence of a misunderstanding of the relationship between sample size and treatment effect. Furthermore, our findings support the existence of a misperception that to decrease both types of inferential error, the sample size must be increased. A better understanding of the relationship between sample size and statistical significance would lead to more accurate interpretations of research results, and the state of knowledge in the social sciences will benefit from such improved interpretations.

REFERENCES

American Psychological Association. (1994). Publication manual of the American Psychological Association (4th ed.). Washington, DC: American Psychological Association.

Bakan, D. (1966). The test of significance in psychological research. *Psychological Bulletin, 66*, 423–437.

Bandt, C. L., & Boen, J. R. (1972). Prevalent misconceptions about sample size, statistical significance, and clinical importance. *Journal of Periodontology, 43*, 181–183.

Beauchamp, K. L., & May, R. B. (1964). Replication report: Interpretation of levels of significance by psychological researchers. *Psychological Reports, 14*, 272.

Carver, R. R (1978). The case against statistical significance testing. *Harvard Educational Review, 48*, 378–399.

Cohen, J. (1990). Things I have learned (so far). *American Psychologist, 45*, 1304–1312.

Morrison, D. B., & Henkel, R. B. (1970). The significance lest controversy—A reader. Chicago: Aldine.

Nelson, N., Rosenthal, R., & Rosnow, R. L. (1986). Interpretation of significance levels and effect sizes by psychological researchers. *The American Psychologist, 11,* 1299–1301.

Rosenthal, R., & Gaito, J. (1963). The interpretation of levels of significance by psychological researchers. *The Journal of Psychology, 55,* 33–38.

Siegel, S. (1956). Nonparametric statistics for the behavioral sciences. New York: McGraw-Hill.

Stone, L. A., & Bodner, G. (1969). Concern-worry associated with commission of Type I and II errors as a function of prescribed alpha level. *The Journal of General Psychology 80,* 163–169.

Address correspondence to either Mary R. Olson, 2900 Sheffield Court, Boise, ID 83702 or Matt Wilkerson, 1925 Priest Place, Boise, ID 83706.

Received July 22, 1966

Donna E. Alvermann
University of Georgia, Athens, Georgia, USA

David G. O'Brien

Deborah R. Dillon
Purdue University, West Lafayette, Indiana, USA

On writing qualitative research

This article began with a conversation that included just the three of us, but from the start we have envisioned a greatly expanded dialogue—one that would embrace the thinking of many of you, should you accept our invitation to join the discussion. We think the need for a dialogue about writing qualitative research has never been greater. We say this because we are aware through our continuing conversations and readings that literacy researchers, like others in the social sciences, are beginning to push in exciting and new ways at boundaries that once separated quite clearly the genres of qualitative writing (e.g., ethnographies and life histories) from other genres such as narratives of the self, fiction, poetry, and performance texts.

In the wake of such activity have come critiques of writing formats which, admittedly, the three of us have grown quite comfortable in using over the years. It was through examining the substance of these critiques in relation to our own work that this article began to take shape. To focus our conversations, we assigned ourselves the task of thinking about the writing of qualitative research from three perspectives: as a writer, as a reviewer for refereed journals, and as a reader of published articles.

Working separately, we each generated a written list of issues or challenges that we face in writing up our own qualitative research findings. Next, we examined the reviews we had written for journal editors to identify the struggles other writers faced, and we made a separate list for them. Then, we selected published qualitative literacy research articles that we found particularly appealing in terms of how they were written, and we created a list of things we liked about each piece. Finally, we each made copies of our

three lists and exchanged them. Prior to our next meeting we analyzed the lists to identify patterns and overlapping issues in our responses. We also indicated works in the literature on qualitative research that would be helpful in addressing those issues. Four key issues were identified: (a) problems in distinguishing between levels of theory, (b) holistic and microlevel issues in methodology, (c) crises in representation and legitimation, and (d) differences in the writing and write-up processes.

In talking through these issues, we collaboratively discussed a plan for writing about them. That was the easy part. The struggle came in deciding how we would maintain the spirit of our conversations on paper. We wrote our first drafts in the first-person singular and shared them. Although we agreed it would be easy enough to change every *I* to *we* and write as one voice (except in the few instances where we differed in our views), this approach didn't work. Not surprisingly, the attempt to merge our three voices into one produced a voice that none of us recognized. Consequently, to be more fully present in our writing (as we were in the lively talks that shaped this piece), we retain our individual identities even though the ideas we express reflect our collective thinking.

Theory

David:

The importance and role of theory in writing qualitative research are confusing. According to Wolcott (1992), "ultimately, everything can be subsumed under theory, even the theory implicit in empiricism that holds sensory experience to be the only source of knowledge" (p. 16). This statement highlights the

From *Reading Research Quarterly*, January/February/March 1996, pp. 114-120. © 1996 by the International Reading Association.

irony of using traditional notions of theory in qualitative studies, many of which generate theories. I have often wondered how much I should be depending on theory to direct a study versus hoping that theory will evolve from my ongoing data analysis. Anxiety is my constant companion when I wonder how much I should write about theory directing the questions, data collection, and analysis.

I have always considered my work to be theoretical in terms of the substantive theory to which my questions and purposes have been linked. Before I do research, I demonstrate that I understand relevant work and have formulated a problem based upon a corpus of research in a discipline. I started to think differently, albeit more ambiguously, about the role of theory in writing qualitative research when I read Glaser and Strauss's (1967) discussion of grounded theory. They discuss substantive theories, which inform a given field or embody conceptual work. They also give licence to well-established and fledgling researchers alike to generate theories.

Eleven years after reading my first pieces on theory and theorizing in qualitative research, I find it difficult to distinguish among levels of theorizing. From my early reading until the present, I have adhered to two rules when doing qualitative research and writing it up. First, I have tried to embed my research in the substantive work of a discipline (e.g., the predominant ideas, connections among those ideas, and ways of representing them). Second, I have strived to include a theoretical framework or lens that ultimately influences topic selection and methodological issues such as research design and analysis (LeCompte & Preissle, 1993). I have typically based my work on symbolic interactionism because I study the social organization of classrooms and how students and teachers work within the organizational structure of secondary schools.

In order to include both levels of theory, I have sometimes viewed them as equally necessary but serving different functions. Lately, I have thought and read more about how the two levels reciprocally influence each other. Wolcott (1992) caused me to think more about how useful and friendly theories can be. He noted theories shouldn't be moral imperatives that take the form of the question, "What is your theory?" An expected response like "symbolic interactionism" shows that I am familiar with big theories, paradigms (Patton, 1990), or traditions (Jacob, 1988). Wolcott freed me from using theoretical frameworks in this perfunctory way. He grants researchers their rights to more genuine theories like "little theories" or "hunches" (1992, p. 8). I look at my hunches as my personal angles on more formal substantive theories that are also compatible with my theoretical lens. For example, my current study of at-risk high school students is informed by substantive theories including work on achievement motivation, goal and attribution

theory, affective perspectives on literacy learning, and historical and cultural research on schooling. My personal hunch is that, to a large extent, the failure of so-called at-risk students can be attributed to the organizational culture of secondary schools. Using symbolic interactionism and phenomenology as my theoretical lenses, I write about how students construct their culture within the larger school culture and how they view their experiences within the system. I am working to generate a grounded theory that elaborates on how the students' school lives set them up for academic failure.

When I review qualitative articles, I look for substantive theories ranging from widely articulated and formally researched theories (e.g., schema theory) to simply stated concepts or "ideas of all shapes and sizes" (Wolcott, 1992, p. 11). Formal labels are useful if researchers understand how the traditions behind the labels inform their research. I like informal theories if researchers state clearly what their hunches are and where they come from. I like to see papers in which researchers show the role of theory in shaping their ideas, design, and methods.

For about 10 years, through two revisions of their qualitative methodology book, LeCompte and Preissle (1993) have provided guidance for incorporating theory and theorizing in qualitative work. I query myself based on the reasons they state for why theory is important. Do I use theory to help me sort out my worldview and to guide how I study people and settings? Do I show how my background, disciplinary bent, and biases are related to the design of my research? Is it clear in my research report how my work is embedded in substantive theory in my field and how my hunches and biases might have influenced how I conducted the study?

I do not use the above questions to establish hard criteria for theory in my research. There are always thorny issues surrounding the questions. Here are a few I ask myself when looking at the role of theory in the write-up: If I have chosen to generate a theory, how can I represent it and clarify its relationship to existing theory? To what extent do I need to write about substantive theory if I generate a theory? Finally, and perhaps most crucial, does my theoretical bent slant my perspective too much? This last question makes me think of Eisner's (1993) statement that theory "not only reveals, it conceals" (p. viii).

Methodology

Deborah:

When I read a piece of qualitative research, I read the text on two levels, asking myself the following questions: From a microlevel, are the important components of a qualitative research study discussed in enough detail to indicate that the study was carefully constructed and rigorously carried out? From a holistic perspective, is the information written in a complete, coherent, and interesting manner? In short, is the piece insightful? When a piece does not address both the microlevel and holistic perspective, I have reservations about the credibility of the work.

At the *microlevel,* one of the first things I look for is the author's statement of purpose and the questions that guided the study. Does the author wish to help a reader understand descriptive processes and relationships, interpret old knowledge in new ways, verify existing theories, or assist in the evaluation of a given policy or practice (Peshkin, 1993)? Further, when I examine the research questions, I expect to see that there is an emphasis on understanding the phenomena under study as a complex whole. In sum, the purpose statement and questions serve to focus the reader. They also serve as springboards for conducting and writing about the study's design, methodology, analysis, and interpretation.

In reading about the design of a study, I want to know if the researcher has spent an extended time in the field, has had personal contact with the participants in the study, and has not attempted to manipulate the phenomena under investigation (acknowledging, of course, that all researchers influence events and actions merely by their presence). One aspect of qualitative research designs that I do not often see addressed in articles, and one that I find problematic in my own work, is an explanation of when and why the original research questions may have shifted during the study and how this shift may have affected the design, methods, and findings.

As I continue reading a manuscript, I look for evidence that an author has attended to the research questions concerning decisions about appropriate data collection and analysis strategies. For example, if the research questions focused on reading groups as opposed to individual readers, were data collected and analyzed in ways that provide an understanding of group processes and products as well as individual efforts within the group? Other methodological concerns that I expect to see addressed include site and sampling rationales. I am especially interested in knowing the criteria a researcher used in selecting the site and the participants, and how these criteria helped to address the research questions.

One neglected component of methodology sections in many qualitative studies is an explanation of the role, perspectives, and biases of the researcher. As Denzin and Lincoln (1994) remind us, qualitative researchers can never overlook the fact that they are gendered, multiculturally situated, and theoretically inclined to view phenomena in ways that influence what questions get asked and what methodology is used to answer those questions. It is important to know what perspective the researcher used to capture the participants' experiences and perspectives in the various social, historical, and temporal contexts (Patton, 1990) in which they occurred. I am also interested in knowing how daily events and interactions with participants shape the lenses used by researchers as they engage in ongoing data collection, analysis, and interpretation. Incorporating this information in a written report is critical to a reader's understanding of the research, yet I have found it is difficult to accomplish. For example, I remember my own struggles when my co-researchers and I (Dillon, O'Brien, & Ruhl, 1989) tried to build a collaborative relationship and then write about how our evolving relationship shaped certain research events and the interpretation of those events.

Finally, in looking over a methodology section that I have written, I like to ask myself this question: Have I fallen victim to "methodolatry—a preoccupation with selecting and defending methods to the exclusion of the actual substance of the story being told?" (Janesick, 1994, p. 215). Or have I merely mentioned the data collection and analysis strategies used (e.g., "I used constant comparative analysis"), with little explanation of the specific processes I engaged in when constructing categories or patterns of findings? What I look for is a thorough description of the researcher's analytic processes throughout the study and how these processes shaped the patterns generated from the data. For example, I appreciate authors who allow me, as the reader, to shadow them as they detail how they grappled with understanding events. I have no rule of thumb that I can offer here in terms of balance between too little or too much detail. However, in the qualitative pieces that I enjoy reading, approximately the first third of an article is devoted to the rationale and methodology. That leaves the other two thirds for the presentation of the data, interpretation, discussion, and conclusions.

From a *holistic perspective,* merely having all the components of a qualitative study in place does not ensure that the article will read as a credible, coherent, insightful, or interesting piece. What matters is how the author approaches the writing of the article—including the formulation of an argument with threads that run throughout the piece and hold it together. As a writer, and later as a reader, I often move backward and forward through a manuscript to determine if I have accomplished several goals. First, I want to provide a clear outline of what information will be presented in the manuscript and the order of presentation. With complex and interrelated findings, it is crucial to assist readers with structural overviews as they move through the material. Second, it is important to present clearly the overall assertions and supporting categories and then provide evidence in support of them. It is also useful to revisit the assertions and categories after the entire case has been presented. To help the reader with this process, I encourage researchers to use maps and charts to show the big picture (assertions), the parts (categories), and how everything fits together (e.g., see Moje, 1994). By developing maps and moving backward and forward through a manuscript, I can see where my story is incomplete, or where it doesn't hold together. I can also see where transitions between sections are needed, or where I have tried to tell too much or too little.

Beyond demonstrating that a manuscript is coherent and that all of the important components of the study are discussed, writers of qualitative research are faced with the Catch-22 of trying to write in a manner that is both interesting and credible. I believe that it's not a matter of being one or the other—both are important. To achieve both, authors of qualitative studies need flexibility in crafting a compelling story. In support of this notion, Janesick (1994) states that writers of qualitative research are like choreographers who make statements by creating dances: "For the researcher, the story told is the dance in all its complexity, context, originality, and passion" (p. 218). What is clear to me as a reader and writer is that researchers must construct a well-designed story that involves the reader along the way and results in a compelling message. This message may strike an important chord in readers that influences them to nod in agreement, pause in reflection, or take action. My goal is to make a difference in an intellectual and emotional way. Perhaps this is my attempt to integrate art and science.

Representation and legitimation

Donna:

One of the principal things researchers do is write. We write to represent what we have come to understand through our research. What we write, of course, is an incomplete or partial translation of the reality of others' lived experiences. In fact, some (e.g., Brodkey, 1987; Denzin, 1994; Lather, 1991) would argue that we create those experiences through the texts we write. In a nutshell, this argument and the assumptions that underlie qualitative researchers' attempts to make a direct link between the texts they write and others' lived experiences is what poststructuralists refer to as the *crisis of representation*. It is accompanied by a second *crisis of legitimation*, which involves challenges to many of the criteria (e.g., credibility, comprehensiveness, and coherence) that qualitative researchers use in evaluating the trustworthiness of their own writing and that of others. The importance of these intersecting crises centers on the tensions they produce for us as writers and readers of qualitative research.

As a writer or reviewer of qualitative research I struggle with issues of representation. How do I represent the actions and interactions of the individuals I study, how do I position myself, and how do both of

these figure into the interpretations I construct? As a writer of my own research or a reader of someone else's, I am continuously interpreting or (re)presenting earlier representations of the data. To write (or to read) is to interpret, to tell stories. As I have come to learn, like it or not, the interpreting I do as a writer (or reviewer) tells as much about me as it does about the *others* whose stories are being told. Why is this so?

Because I write (or read) from perspectives informed by my personal history, by what I believe counts as knowledge, and by how willing I am to accept a text on its own terms, I can never separate my own experiences of those I write (or read) about. Nor would I want to, mainly because I believe that the more multiple experiences represented, the more meaningful the text. This belief leads me to treat every text I create or review as partial and in the process of becoming.

For example, I am currently collecting and analyzing data for a study that explores how four teachers, including myself, come to know and alter discursive practices that are counterproductive to students' engagement in discussions of their assigned texts. As part of this process, I am writing multiple narratives about each teacher's experiences. One narrative is titled "Donna's story about Sally." The other two narratives are titled "Donna's story about 'Michelle's story about Sally' " and "Donna's story about 'Josephine's story about Sally.' " Sally is also keeping a journal of her experiences. While these multiple layerings of interpretation can enrich the research process and guide further data collection and analysis, they do not permit us to make any final statements about Sally. For in writing about our own and others' experiences, we create (rather than simply mirror) those experiences. Clearly, then, as Denzin (1994) argues, "there can never be a final, accurate representation of what was meant or said, only different textual representations of different experiences" (p. 296).

Issues of representation and legitimation invariably lead to questions of practical concern for me as a writer and a reviewer. For example, under what circumstances does the convention of situating the researcher-as-writer in the text become a problem? When are multiple examples necessary and when are they too much? How can I present the many complexities of a qualitative study in a cogent manner and still stay within a journal's editorial guidelines on manuscript length? As a writer, I take these concerns seriously and force myself to make difficult decisions, knowing full well that if I don't, journal reviewers and editors will make them for me.

First of all, situating myself in qualitative studies that I write up is not as straightforward or easy as it might seem. In struggling to account for the influences that shape my role as researcher and writer, a tension is created as I strive for a balance between inserting myself in the text and preserving the spotlight for other participants. Even if I am successful in achieving such a balance, there is a tension in knowing that disclosures about my personal self, the problems I encountered in doing the research, and the contingencies I dealt with in writing it up do not vouch for the text's credibility. As I have argued elsewhere (Alvermann, 1993), one simply cannot count on such behind-the-scenes prose to neutralize the power differentials that exist between the knower (the researcher) and the known (the researched).

A second concern—that of knowing when multiple examples are necessary and when they are too much—can be traced to the tension I feel as a writer when I attempt to be comprehensive without inundating or boring my readers. Achieving a balance between giving space to participants' firsthand (re)presentations of their experiences and making room for my own interpretations of those experiences becomes less problematic when I recall Geertz's (1973) advice that "it is not necessary to know everything in order to know something" (p. 20). Still, I find myself vacillating when it comes to making decisions about which examples to include and which to exclude. For instance, I tend to include too many examples to illustrate a particular point because I see important nuances in multiple examples of the same event. At the same time I know from experience that what may seem like a subtle, but important, difference to me is often lost on those who review my work. More than once I have had a reviewer tell me that I should cut back on the number of examples I give. One way of doing that, I find, is to keep the purpose of the study foremost in mind when making decisions about what stays and what gets cut. Focusing on the purpose helps me to do more than just limit the number of examples; it also provides guidance in determining which examples are the most salient of those that pertain to the purpose.

Third, presenting the complexities of a qualitative study in a cogent manner while staying within a journal's editorial guidelines on manuscript length is another tension that I experience, both when I write and when I review the writings of others. Although I know of no hard and fast rule on how to resolve this tension, I like the common sense appeal of Wolcott's (1990) oft-quoted aphorism, "Do less, more thoroughly" (p. 62). It reminds me that emphasis is important, that in featuring certain descriptive accounts of the data I will necessarily be downplaying others. What matters is that I am thorough in reporting the data I choose to emphasize. Among other things, this involves presenting triangulated evidence in support of the points I am trying to make as well as any discrepant cases that might provide greater insight into the phenomena under study. As a reviewer, I am especially interested in knowing how an author attempted to make sense of the data that did not fit an evolving interpretation. This does not mean that I expect to be informed of all discrepant details, but rather just those that have the potential to influence my interpretation of the event being emphasized.

I do not need to read lengthy descriptions of procedures used in conducting member checks to establish a written report's credibility. As a reviewer and writer, I find myself agreeing with Riessman (1993) who questions the legitimacy of relying too heavily upon participants and other informants to affirm the interpretations we draw as researchers. If we have learned anything from the crisis of representation, it is that personal accounts can change over time as consciousness is raised and new meanings are attached to old experiences. Having said as much, I still value the opportunity to learn from member checks, especially if they are written concisely and presented in a manner that achieves balance in reporting. Achieving this balance means including information that reveals differences as well as similarities in the participants' and researchers' perspectives. Tightly woven interpretations that show little sign of human differences are less interesting and believable to me than those that are less impeccably portrayed.

Writing and write-up

David:

I find it helpful to think of *writing* before *write-up*. When writing research reports, I typically think about the product of my efforts and the appropriate audience for the product. I ask myself, "Where should I send the manuscript? Which journal has reviewers on the review board who are most interested in my thesis and the methods portrayed in the manuscript?" *Write-up* focuses on final representation. I am concerned about how I represented the participants and setting, or a slice of life or culture that supports my themes or assertions. Ironically, the focus on the final product, the manuscript, neglects the more important issue of how writing shapes the representation.

The tenet that supports this shaping aspect of writing in qualitative research is familiar to literacy researchers: "Writing is a form of thinking" (Wolcott, 1990, p. 21). When I first encountered the quote in Wolcott (who cites Becker [1986], who in turn cites Flower [1979] and Flower and Hayes [1981]), I reacted with a combination of enthusiasm and embarrassment. Of course, but literacy scholars *know* that writing is a form of thinking. Yet, up to the point of encountering Wolcott's reminder, I thought of my qualitative research in terms of write-up. Now I follow Wolcott's advice and write early—I write as soon as I find something interesting to say. If I am not writing, I don't have anything interesting to say and I think about why. As I write to shape various representations of a study, I can see ultimately how the pieces fit together, but I keep changing them.

For example, I have been collecting fieldnotes for about 400 hours of participant observation on a current project. As I write fieldnotes, or in most cases write via dictation into my tape recorder on my way back to the university, I write description, commentary, thoughts about my role and methods, or memos about a theory I am working on. As I transcribe the tapes, I write extended discourse, which has taken the form of some individual cases of at-risk students. However, as I write the cases, I am thinking about various ways of constructing them and reasons for constructing them. They have evolved from surface descriptions of interesting at-risk students to more purposefully constructed commentaries on the disengagement from learning that support the evolving theory. Writing is clearly a way to shape the eventual representation. What is more, it may be the only way to flesh out things that may otherwise elude me. Van Manen (1990) amplified my excitement about writing as thinking to shape representation. He stated that writing is method: Writing is reflection; writing is a way to separate the knower from the known; writing enables us to move out beyond the immediate study to universals as the text takes on a life of its own. We use writing to distance ourselves from the participants and their world so we can use the write-up to bring us back into the participants' world. Van Manen reminds us that *research report* suggests a contrived separation between the process of research and the report that makes it public.

In sum, the writing process shapes the representation in the write-up because it provides us with a way to reflect on what our research means. Moreover, as method, writing allows us to think about how we will make public both the representation of the participants we study and the way we study them. Like many researchers, I used to focus on write-up because I viewed it as the object that will be scrutinized by reviewers, editors, and other colleagues. What I've learned is that if I use writing to shape the representation, the final product will be much improved as an embodiment of my reflection about the data and how I want to represent my method.

Summary

The intent of this article is to extend a conversation we began several months ago in response to issues we identified in our own work as writers of qualitative research and in the work of others that we read. If in considering how writing up your own work is influenced by these or similar issues you are moved to enter the discussion, our purpose in writing this article will have been achieved. More importantly, however, by joining the conversation literacy researchers stand to enrich their own and others' understandings

of how writing as a method of inquiry—as a way of *knowing* the human experience in all its complex and diverse representations—constantly creates and recreates that experience. This point is not lost on Richardson (1990) who reminds us, therefore, that "how we write lives is important, theoretically and practically" (p. 63).

Editors' note: We see this as the beginning of a Conversation. We hope you agree and join the discussion.

JER
DMB

REFERENCES

ALVERMANN, D. E. (1993). Researching the literal: Of muted voices, second texts, and cultural representations. In D. J. Leu & C. K. Kinzer (Eds.), *Examining central issues in literacy research, theory, and practice.* 42nd yearbook of the National Reading Conference (pp. 1–10). Chicago, IL: National Reading Conference.

BECKER, H. S. (1986). *Writing for social scientists: How to start and finish your thesis, book, or article.* Chicago, IL: University of Chicago Press.

BRODKEY, L. (1987). Writing ethnographic narratives. *Written Communication, 4*(1), 25–50.

DENZIN, N. K. (1994). Evaluating qualitative research in the poststructural moment: The lessons James Joyce teaches us. *Qualitative Studies in Education, 7,* 295–308.

DENZIN, N. K., & LINCOLN, Y. S. (1994). *Handbook of qualitative research.* Thousand Oaks, CA: Sage.

DILLON, D. R., O'BRIEN, D. G., & RUHL, J. (1989). The evolution of research: From ethnography to collaboration. In J. Allen & J. P. Goetz (Eds.), *Teaching and learning qualitative traditions: The second yearbook of the International Qualitative Research in Education Conference* (pp. 1–20). Athens: University of Georgia.

EISNER, E. W. (1993). Foreword. In D. J. Flinders & G. E. Mills (Eds.), *Theory and concepts in qualitative research* (pp. vii–ix). New York: Teachers College Press.

FLOWER, L. (1979). Writer-based prose: A cognitive basis for problems in writing. *College Composition and Communication, 41,* 19–37.

FLOWER, L., & HAYES, J. R. (1981). A cognitive process theory of writing. *College Composition and Communication, 32,* 365–387.

GEERTZ, C. (1973). *The interpretation of cultures.* New York: Basic Books.

GLASER, B. G., & STRAUSS, A. L. (1967). *The discovery of grounded theory.* New York: Aldine.

JACOB, E. (1988). Clarifying qualitative research: A focus on traditions. *Educational Researchers, 17,* 16–24.

JANESICK, V. J. (1994). The dance of qualitative research design: Metaphor, methodolatry, and meaning. In N. K. Denzin & Y. S. Lincoln (Eds.), *Handbook of qualitative research* (pp. 209–219). Thousand Oaks, CA: Sage.

LATHER, P. (1991). *Getting smart.* New York: Routledge.

LECOMPTE, M. D., & PREISSLE, J. (1993). *Ethnography and qualitative design in educational research* (2nd ed.). San Diego, CA: Academic.

MOJE, E. B. (1994). *Using literacy to learn chemistry: An ethnography of a high school chemistry classroom.* Unpublished doctoral dissertation, Purdue University, West Lafayette, IN.

PATTON, M. Q. (1990). *Qualitative evaluation and research methods* (2nd ed.). Newbury Park, CA: Sage.

PESHKIN, A. (1993). The goodness of qualitative research. *Educational Researchers, 22*(2), 23–29.

RICHARDSON, L. (1990). *Writing strategies: Reaching diverse audiences.* Newbury Park, CA: Sage.

RIESSMAN, C. K. (1993). *Narrative analysis.* Newbury Park, CA: Sage.

VAN MANEN, M. (1990). *Researching lived experience.* Albany, NY: SUNY Press.

WOLCOTT, H. F. (1990). *Writing up qualitative research.* Newbury Park, CA: Sage.

WOLCOTT, H. F. (1992). Posturing in qualitative research. In M. D. LeCompte, W. L. Millroy, & J. Preissle (Eds.), *The handbook of qualitative research in education* (pp. 3–52). San Diego, CA: Academic.

Received February 16, 1995
Accepted February 22, 1995

A Primer in Survey Research

By
Suzanne C. Watson

Introduction

Adult educators are not ivory tower recluses. Adult educators are uniquely anchored in the "real" world of literacy, health care, industrial training, correctional facilities, volunteerism, workers' education, and professional education. Our theoreticians are doers as well as thinkers—Horton, Dewey, Lindeman, Knowles, Coady, Kozol, and Freire, to mention a few.

Many terminal degrees in the adult education field are D.Ed. or Ed.D. rather than Ph.D., another reflection of the practical, practitioner orientation to which we subscribe. Coorough and Nelson (1991), in a content analysis of 1,007 Ph.D. and 960 Ed.D. dissertations, concluded that the Ed.D. dissertation includes more survey research and a substantial portion of this research (42 percent) is done on the local level (institution, state, or region).

While the choice of research method to pursue is, of course, based on the research questions to be answered as well as the resources available, survey research is particularly well adapted to the pragmatic world of adult education. "Descriptive research is the most common form of research used in adult education" (Merriam and Simpson, 1995, p.71), and the survey is "the most common technique used for gathering data in descriptive research" (p. 70).

This paper provides a short primer on survey research. Topics include: when to use survey research, types of survey research, methods of survey research, steps involved in conducting survey research, and improving response rates.

When To Use Survey Research

Babbie (1995) proposed that "survey research is probably the best method available to the social scientist interested in in collecting original data for describing a population too large to observe directly" (p. 257). Babbie also recommended survey re-

From *The Journal of Continuing Higher Education,* Winter 1998, pp. 31-40. Reproduced by permission of the Association for Continuing Higher Education, Inc.

search to measure "attitudes and orientation in a large population" (p. 257). Salant and Dillman (1994), in discussing the appropriateness of survey research, stated: "If your goal is to find out what percentage of some population has a particular attribute or opinion, and the information is not available from secondary sources, then survey research is the only appropriate method" (p. 9).

When conducted properly, survey research will provide information about *what is*; what are "the characteristics, behavior, or opinions of a particular population" (Salant and Dillman, 1994, p. 10). A caveat to survey research, however, is that people's behaviors cannot be measured with a survey. A survey "can only measure their perceptions of those behaviors" (J. C. Sherblom, C. F. Sullivan, and E. C. Sherblom, 1993, p. 58). This caution should be considered during the construction of the survey instrument so that precise wording will capture the information desired.

Survey research is appropriate not only for large, well funded projects, such as that conducted by Aslanian and Brickell under the auspices of the College Entrance Examination Board to explore Americans in transition (1980), but also for the smaller, more focused action research encouraged by Quigley (1995) and Rose (1992). Practitioners in adult and continuing education need to examine their practices systematically and share their findings with others in the field. Carefully designed survey research can be an excellent tool in this endeavor.

Once the decision has been made to conduct survey research, the researcher must make every attempt to perform ethically. This includes encouraging participation but not pressuring participation (Salant and Dillman, 1994, p. 9). Anonymity and confidentiality of participants are issues that must be addressed well before actual administration of the survey. The scope of this paper does not include ethics in research, but a perusal of the chapters in Merriam and Simpson (1995) or Babbie (1995) on ethics in social research is strongly encouraged for any researcher before embarking on a research project, whatever its size or scope.

Types of Survey Research

The literature in adult and continuing education is replete with references to *programs*. Part Three of the *Handbook of Adult and Continuing Education* (1989) lists eleven providers of educational *programs* for adults. These providers include four-year colleges and universities, cooperative extension services, armed forces, correctional facilities, public libraries and museums, and religious institutions, to mention just a few.

In *Planning Programs for Adult Learners*, Caffarella (1994) identifies eleven tasks to be completed in planning a program for adult learners. Information gleaned from carefully constructed surveys could be useful in completing many of these tasks. Before a program is initiated, the planner must be fully aware of existing conditions both within and without the organization, information that surveys can gather. Identifying program ideas, sorting and prioritizing program ideas, and developing program objectives can be expedited by a survey of potential participants. Information on participant preferences for learning strategies and instructors can be acquired through surveys. Evaluations may include participant surveys to gain feedback on the program conducted as well as ideas for future programs. Information gleaned from participant surveys can provide data for communicating the value of programs conducted to sponsoring or other appropriate individuals and committees.

Salant and Dillman (1994) described three general types of survey research which the adult and continuing educator may employ:

- A *needs assessment survey* to solicit opinions about problems and possible solutions.
- A *marketing survey* to evaluate the nature and level of demand for particular programs.
- An *evaluation survey* to learn about the impact of public or private programs and policies. (p. 10)

Each type of research provides information often sought by adult or continuing education practitioners that may be gathered through various survey research methods.

Methods of Survey Research

This section provides a description of five survey research methods: mail, telephone, face to face, drop-off, and electronic. Each method is evaluated as to its best use. "No single method can be judged superior to the others *in the abstract*. Instead, each should be evaluated in terms of a specific study topic and population, as well as budget, staff, and time constraints" (Salant and Dillman, 1995, p. 33). More than one type of survey may be employed in a research project to test the same finding and thus strengthen the validity of the conclusions. For example, face-to-face surveys may be followed by telephone surveys to individuals not previously interviewed.

Mail Surveys

The simple method for conducting a survey through the mail includes sending a questionnaire with a letter explaining the purpose of the study to participants in a selected sample. A self-addressed, stamped envelope is enclosed to facilitate return of the survey. Follow-up letters and reminders may be sent a specified period of time after the original mailing.

According to Salant and Dillman (1994), mail surveys are best suited for:

- surveys of people for whom reliable addresses are available and who are likely to respond accurately and completely in writing
- surveys in which an immediate turnaround is not required
- projects in which money, qualified staff, and professional help are all relatively scarce (p. 37)

The definitive work on conducting mail surveys remains Dillman's text, *Mail and Telephone Surveys* (1978). The Total Design Method (TDM) expounded by Dillman includes detailed steps for construction of the survey instrument and implementation of the survey. Each detail, from preparation and printing of the questionnaire and cover letter; through font, point, and paper size; to the exact timing of follow-up mailings, is covered with precise rules for implementation of the TDM.

Example: Gardner-Sass (1995) used a three-page mailed questionnaire to examine employer attitudes toward hiring individuals trained through welfare training programs, gleaning valuable data about employer perceptions and practical suggestions for improving training programs.

Telephone Surveys

Telephone surveys are lauded for their ease of administration and follow up. A sample drawn from a telephone directory or other listing of phone numbers is easy to access. Interviewers record the answers to the survey instrument either by hand onto a survey form or directly into a computer. The advantages of random-digit dialing with its access to all telephone listings, not just those published in directories, and add-a-digit sampling[1] have been mitigated by the popularity of telephone answering machines to screen unwelcome calls (Babbie, 1995, p. 271).

[1] This technique involves drawing a random or systematic sample from the directory and then adding a randomly chosen number from 1 to 9 to the last digit of each number in the sample. One way to accomplish this is to add the same digit to each phone number (Salant and Dillman, 1994, p. 67).

Salant and Dillman (1994) recommended telephone surveys when:

- members of the population are very likely to have telephones
- questions are relatively straightforward
- experienced help is available
- quick turnaround is important (p. 40)

The Total Design Method (TDM) by Dillman is also applicable to telephone surveys. Again, attention to detail is the distinguishing feature of the method. Sending an advance letter may increase response rates and improve data quality while facilitating respondent cooperation (Dillman, 1978, p. 245). Dillman's meticulous method for telephone surveys also covers instrument creation and staff training. Even with the innovations in communications since 1978 when Dillman's book was published, his methods continue to be relevant and effective.

Example: In a study of the perceptions and expectations for a portfolio assessment program, Fisher (1993) effectively used a telephone survey to confirm the findings that emerged from face-to-face interviews and to probe for additional insights. The telephone survey was administered to students and faculty who had not participated in the interviews.

Face-to-Face Surveys

In a face-to-face survey, an interviewer asks the respondent questions and records the answers. In this type of survey, the interviewer plays a very visible, important role. The ideal interviewer is a neutral individual whose appearance, personality, demeanor, and opinions do not influence the respondent. The interviewer must be a trained individual, familiar with the survey instrument, skilled in recording responses verbatim, and able to probe intelligently for full answers.

Salant and Dillman (1994) recommended the use of face-to-face surveys for:

- surveying populations for whom there is no list
- collecting information from people who are not likely to respond willingly or accurately (or cannot be reached) by mail or telephone
- complex questionnaires
- well-funded projects for which experienced interviewers and professional help are available (p. 42)

The interview survey is expensive to administer, but the presence of a trained interviewer encourages greater depth in data collection than is possible with other techniques. However, while trained interviewers are costly to employ, untrained interviewers may compromise the integrity of the research project.

Example: Askov and Brown (1995) utilized pre- and post-interview surveys in a major study of four workplace literacy projects funded by the U. S. Department of Education's National Workplace Literacy Program. "Students, teachers, industry trainers, supervisors, and plant managers or CEOs" (p. 23) were interviewed for their reactions to the programs being evaluated.

Drop-off Survey

A drop-off survey is delivered by hand to the intended recipient. The individual completes the instrument at his/her leisure. The survey is either returned by mail or picked up by a study employee. This survey method is personalized by the hand delivery and/or pickup and is most appropriate for:

- a small community or neighborhood survey in which respondents are not spread over a large area
- relatively short and simple questionnaires
- projects with a small staff but relatively large sample size (Salant and Dillman, 1994, p. 43)

Example: Watson (1997) used this survey method in a study of the responses of institutions of higher education to adult students. Key informants at participating institutions completed a questionnaire describing their institutions and their perceptions of the institutional response to adult students.

Electronic Survey

Using electronic mail to conduct survey research is a natural result of the phenomenal growth in private and public electronic networks as well as increased accessibility of the Internet. Thach (1995) defined this survey method as "the systematic data collection of information on a specific topic using computer questionnaires delivered to an on-line sample or population. Respondents receive, complete, and return their questionnaires via E-mail" (p. 27).

E-mail surveys are inexpensive to administer, as paper questionnaires, telephone line charges, or interviewer salaries are not necessary. Questionnaire changes are easy to make and transmission is almost instantaneous. An estimate of participation level may be quickly adduced by extending an invitation to participate in a study. In some instances response rates may be higher with electronic surveys than with paper surveys, and respondents are more candid in their answers than with paper surveys or interviews (Thach, 1995, p. 31).

The most glaring disadvantage of E-mail survey research is the limitation to a population with access to an electronic network. Anonymity and confidentiality, while always a consideration in survey research, are particularly difficult to maintain in the open climate that pervades most networks. The intricacies of constructing an effective computer questionnaire and developing instructions for respondents to successfully complete the instrument on-line may intimidate some researchers. A final obstacle, and one familiar to those who work with any computer technologies, is that of potential technical problems with hardware and software.

In light of the peculiar characteristics of E-mail surveys, they may be most appropriate when:

- members of the population have E-mail access
- the researcher has access to the targeted networks
- the researcher has the technological experience to create and administer the instrument

Adult and continuing educators interested in conducting an electronic survey have access to several active listserves dedicated to the interests of subscribers. AEDNET (listproc@pulsar.acast.nov.edu), CPAE (listserv@tamvm1.tamu.edu), EDINFO (listproc@inet.ed.gov), LEARNER (listserv@nysernet.org), and LITERACY (listserv@nysernet.org) are a few of those available.

Steps Involved in Conducting Survey Research

Whether the adult or continuing educator is conducting a needs assessment, marketing survey, or evaluation survey, the basic steps to follow in designing, implementing, analyzing, and evaluating the survey are rather standard. J. Sherblom et al. (1993) enumerated five questions to answer to assure significant and useful study results:

1. What do we want to know?
2. About whom do we want to know it?
3. How do we word the questions?
4. How do we elicit appropriate and adequate responses?
5. How do we interpret the results?

While these questions provide very simple starting points and seminal concepts, Salant and Dillman (1994, p. 11) delineate "Ten Steps for Success" which form the basis of the chapters of their book, *How to Conduct Your Own Survey.*

1. *Understand and avoid the four kinds of error.* While it is impossible to remove all errors in a survey, an understanding of the four kinds of errors and how to mitigate their influence is invaluable.

   • Coverage error occurs when the list from which a sample is drawn does not include all elements of the population that researchers wish to study (p. 16).

   • Sampling error occurs when researchers survey only a subset or sample of all people in the population instead of conducting a census (p. 17).

   • Measurement error occurs when a respondent's answer to a given question is inaccurate, imprecise, or cannot be compared in any useful way to other respondents' answers (p. 17).

   • Nonresponse error occurs when a significant number of people in the survey sample do not respond to the questionnaire and are different from those who do in a way that is important to the study (p. 20).

   Again, it is impossible to remove all errors in a survey. However, careful selection of the target population with close attention to their characteristics, their motivation, their accessibility, and their ability to respond will enhance participation in the survey (Queeney, 1995).

2. *Be specific about what new information you need and why.* Survey objectives must be defined very specifically before the study can be designed. This includes stating exactly what problem is to be solved and what information is needed to solve it. Thinking in terms of results and utilizing focus groups may be helpful in refining survey objectives.

   While speaking of needs assessment, Queeney (1995) emphasized the importance of this step. "By specifying the objectives that incorporate the needs assessment purpose, the scope of the proposed study, the target population, the resources to be allocated to the endeavor, and the level of complexity, it is possible to bring broad goals into sharper focus" (pp. 27–28).

3. *Choose the survey method that works best for you.* The various types of survey research were described above. A researcher is always constrained by staff size and expertise, time, facilities, and money. The research questions being pursued and the mix of constraints will determine the survey method. Dillman (1978) provided a definitive chapter of choosing among mail, telephone, and face-to-face surveys which is required reading for the novice researcher.

Queeney (1995) also provided a "must-read" chapter for adult or continuing researchers devoted to methods of research for beginners. Limited access to ideal methodology and plentiful resources should not deter a neophyte researcher from plunging ahead and using the methodology and resources available and appropriate for the prevailing circumstances.

4. *Decide whether and how to sample.* If querying everyone in a population is too expensive or unrealistic, sampling is a viable alternative. Sampling involves precisely identifying the target population, assembling a list of the target population, and selecting the sample from the list. Simple random sampling, where each member of the population has an equal chance of being included, is the most elementary sampling method. (See Chapter 2, pp. 186–228, of Babbie [1995] for a more comprehensive discussion of sampling methods.)

   Some types of research, such as action research may preclude sampling. Kemmis and McTaggart (1984), quoted in Quigley (1995), defined action research as:

   • Trying new ideas in practice as a means of improvement and as a means of increasing knowledge about the curriculum, teaching, and learning. The result is improvement in what happens in the classroom and school, and the better articulation and justification of the educational rationale for what goes on. Action research provides a way of working which links theory and practice into one whole: ideas-in-action (p. 64).

   • One of the characteristics of this practical research methodology is that "participants are not systematically sampled or selected; they are part of a natural 'flow' of human activity" (Merriam & Simpson, 1995, p. 123).

5. *Write good questions that will provide useful. accurate information.* There have been many guidelines written for formulating survey questions. Dillman (1978) stated general principles for question construction. Determination of the *kind* of information being sought (attitudes, beliefs, behavior, attributes) is elemental to question construction. Dillman also offered guidance in question structure and precise wording.

   Pilot testing of the questionnaire is strongly recommended "to ensure that the questions asked are clear and the response options are comprehensive and appropriate" (Queeney, 1995; p. 146). Individuals comparable to the targeted population are asked to complete the pilot questionnaire and comment on the clarity and suitability of the directions and questions.

6. *Design and test a questionnaire that is easy and interesting to answer*. Mail, telephone, and interview surveys rely on different methods of communicating. In the mail survey, the questionnaire is seen by the respondent and must be regarded as worthwhile to complete. This means attractive, convenient presentation with concise directions. Dillman's (1978) initial, detailed instructions for a successful mail survey have been revised slightly in Salant and Dillman (1994, pp. 102–121).

While mail surveys are created to please the eye of respondents, telephone and interview surveys must be understood orally. This necessitates attention to the convenience of the interviewer in recording responses as well as attention to the burden of listening put upon the respondent. Questions should be short and simple. Again, Dillman's (1978) initial, detailed instructions for the construction of effective telephone and interview surveys have been updated in Salant and Dillman (1994, pp. 121–135).

7. *Put together the necessary mix of people, equipment, and supplies to carry out your survey in the necessary time frame*. This last step in survey design involves different procedures for each survey method. A detailed schedule and timeline for supervision, clerical help, equipment, and supplies must be carefully constructed to fully utilize the resources available. A precise plan for follow-up mailings, telephone calls, or interviews must be determined. Guidance through the administrative minutiae is readily available in Dillman (1978) and Salant and Dillman (1994).

Suskie (1996) emphasized the need for a comprehensive, detailed list of all things that must be done to complete the project. "For each item, note (1) when it must be completed, (2) how long it will take to do, and (3) when it must be started" (p.21). This is the beginning of a formal timeline for the research project. Whether the adult or continuing educator is conducting a small action research project within a classroom or administering a large, university sponsored research project, creation of and adherence to a timeline is a vital component in the successful completion of any research project.

8. *Code, computerize, and analyze the data from your questionnaires*. With the growth in personal computers and the advent of statistical packages (e.g., SPSS, Excel), data analysis is no longer the formidable task it once was. Software documentation provides background on basic statistical concepts needed to perform most data analysis. However, the researcher must still design an appropriate coding system for each answer on the survey instrument, make a master list of all the codes, edit and code the questionnaires, and enter the data into the computer.

If careful attention has been taken by the researcher from the onset of the project in the development of the objectives and methodology, this step should not be an issue. Long before the data is entered, detailed procedures have been devised that will yield the information needed and desired.

9. *Present your results in a way that informs your audience, orally or in writing*. Once the sought-after information has been collected and analyzed, it must be presented in a way that conveys the data while maintaining the interest of the audience. Salant and Dillman (1995) suggested preparing both written and oral presentations while cautioning that "It is critical to understand that what makes an effective written report usually makes a dreary and boring verbal presentation, and vice versa" (pp. 202–203).

Identifying the audience for the survey results is a crucial step to be taken prior to writing up results. The following points are considerations from an institutional perspective:

• What is your readers' frame of reference? Do they have a broad understanding of your institution, or do they see everything only in terms of their own responsibilities? Do they understand and appreciate your institution's history, values, culture, and environment? Are they aware of the relative strengths and weaknesses of your students, your programs, and your resources?

• What are their needs? What kind of support and help would they like from you? Is their most pressing need for more resources, more attention, or more respect? Do they want support for the status quo or for initiating change?

• Are they already familiar with what you have been doing, or will they need a complete description of what research was done?

• Do they have time to study an extensive report, or will they want only a short summary?

• Will they want only your findings and recommendations, or will they want to know how you arrived at your conclusions?

• Are they knowledgeable about empirical research methodology, or will you need to explain what you did in layperson's language?

• Are they likely to criticize the study? Will you need to anticipate their criticism and incorporate responses into your report?

• Are they likely to be questioned about the study by others? Will they need sufficient details to respond to others' concerns? (Suskie, 1996, pp. 115–16)

Preparing a written report ensures that a complete record of the research project will be available. An oral presentation, on the other hand, usually contains the most relevant, interesting information. Graphics are very effective in both oral and written presentations, to engage the audience and dramatize the results of a research project.

10. *Maintain perspective while putting your plans into action.* In this final step of survey research, Salant and Dillman (1994) encouraged researchers "to develop a work plan and timetable that budgets and coordinates all of your resources—including money, any volunteer efforts, and time for each activity that needs to be done" (p. 220). Researchers (Babbie, 1995; Dillman, 1978; Merriam and Simpson, 1995; Salant and Dillman, 1994) agree that survey research is a complex activity with discrete steps to be followed to a successful conclusion.

A final aspect of this last step is seeking assistance when it is needed. It is important that adult and continuing education researchers not be deterred from pursuing survey research by a perceived weakness in quantitative analysis. For beginning researchers, assistance in designing instruments and creating methodology that will yield the information desired may be essential. Salant and Dillman (1994) suggested turning to a college or university campus for advice on survey research and enumerated several organizations and publications which also provide information on survey methods (pp. 218–19).

While such a rigorous attention to planning and details may seem laborious for a novice researcher, only careful preparation will result in useful information. As Queeney (1995) noted: "A poorly conducted survey is worse than no survey at all, for it will yield bad data, possibly leading to bad decisions" (p. 143).

Improving Response Rate

When conducting survey research, a high response rate guards against response bias where nonrespondents are likely to differ from respondents in ways that affect the results of the study (Babbie, 1995, p. 261). For mail surveys, Babbie (1995) contended that at least a 50 percent re-

sponse rate is necessary for analysis and reporting, while a 60 percent response rate is considered good, and a 70 percent response rate is very good (p. 262).

Dillman spoke to this issue in terms of "social exchange;" people are motivated to act because of the rewards they anticipate receiving as a result of their actions (Dillman, 1978, pp. 12–18). "Whether a given activity occurs is a function of the ratio between the perceived costs of doing that activity and the rewards one expects the other party to provide at a later time" (p. 12). Potential program participants, therefore, may be more inclined to "buy into" a program when they have been surveyed as to their needs and preferences for programs. To encourage response, Dillman suggested that the researcher:

1. Reward the respondent by:
   • showing positive regard
   • giving verbal appreciation
   • using a consulting approach
   • supporting his or her values
   • offering tangible rewards
   • making the questionnaire interesting
2. Reduce costs to the respondent by:
   • making the task appear brief
   • reducing the physical and mental effort that is required
   • eliminating chances for embarrassment
   • eliminating any implication of subordination
   • eliminating any direct monetary cost
3. Establish trust by:
   • providing a token of appreciation in advance
   • identifying with a known organization that has legitimacy
   • building on other exchange relationships (p. 18)

As Dillman (1978) made clear throughout his text, these considerations permeate the Total Design Method for mail and telephone surveys and must be addressed throughout the construction of the survey and the cover letters or introductory remarks.

In a study evaluating data quality in mail, telephone, and face-to-face surveys, deLeeuw (1992) determined that survey methods with an interviewer (telephone survey and face-to-face survey) resulted in higher response rates and lower item nonresponse, but also produced more socially desirable answers" than did mail surveys (p. 118). Researchers did not have to rely solely on the written word to express appreciation or establish trust with respondents.

J. Sherblom et al. (1993) spoke for brevity when they stated that responses to mail surveys drop dramatically if the instrument takes more than 20 minutes to complete. They reported research studies that increased response rates by gaining management authorization for workers to complete a survey during working hours. Mention of university sponsorship, "a pre-notification letter, use of first-class postage to mail the survey, enclosure of a stamped return postage envelope, and a follow-up postcard" (p. 60) were found to increase response rates for mail surveys. A brief but comprehensive cover letter to introduce the purpose of the study and the researchers, ensure anonymity of respondents, and offer to send results also was found effective in increasing response rate (p. 60).

Hopkins and Gullickson (1992) reported an increase of 19 percent in the average response rate when a gratuity was enclosed with a mailed survey. The average increase was 7 percent when the gratuity was promised upon receipt of the completed questionnaire.

A practical note by Salant and Dillman (1994) stated that "The last few questionnaires that nudge the response rate to an acceptable level are the most expensive to secure" (p.43). This is a result of the higher expense of an interviewer returning time after time to conduct an interview, while the cost of additional mailings or follow-up phone calls is considerably less.

Salant and Dillman (1994) provided three options to achieve higher responses:

• Give potential respondents a monetary incentive to complete and return their questionnaire.
• Call nonrespondents a few days after mailing the replacement questionnaire.
• Send a fifth mailing (four mailings are suggested as the standard) by two-day priority mail.

However, Sherblom et al. (1993) summed up the response rate issue: "A survey that is well-designed, well-introduced, and one that stimulates respondents' perceptions of the value and importance of the research project will likely obtain the best overall response" (p. 60).

Conclusion

The scope of this paper was limited to a description of and introduction to survey research. Comprehensive works quoted within the paper are suggested as references for the reader who wishes to delve deeper into the subject.

References

Askov, E. N. and Brown, E. M. "Findings from Four Workplace Literacy Program Evaluation Studies." *PAACE Journal of Lifelong Learning*, 4, pp. 21–28, 1995.

Aslanian, C. B. and Brickell, H. M. *Americans in Transition: Life Changes as Reasons for Adult Learning*. New York: College Entrance Examination Board, 1980.

Babbie, E. *The Practice of Social Research* (7th ed.). Belmont, CA: Wadsworth, 1995.

Caffarella, R. S. *Planning Programs for Adult Learners: A Practical Guide for Educators, Trainers, and Staff Developers*. Jossey-Bass Inc., 1994.

Coorough, C. and Nelson, J. *Content Analysis of the Ph.D. vs. Ed.D. Dissertation*. (ERIC Document Reproduction Service No. ED 364 580), 1991.

deLeeuw, E. D. *Data Quality in Mail, Telephone and Face to Face Surveys*. (ERIC Document Reproduction Service No. ED 374 136), 1992.

Dillman, D. A. *Mail and Telephone Surveys: The Total Design Method*. New York: Wiley, 1978.

Fisher, V. A. "An Institutional Evaluation of Perceptions and Expectations for a Portfolio Assessment Program." *PAACE Journal of Lifelong Learning*, 2, pp. 27–32, 1993.

Gardner-Sass, D. "A Study of Employer Attitudes Toward Hiring Individuals Trained Through Welfare Programs." *PAACE Journal of Lifelong Learning*, 4, pp. 39–45, 1995.

Hopkins, K. D. and Gullickson, A. R. "A Meta-Analysis of the Effects of Monetary Gratuities." *Journal of Experimental Education*, 61(1) pp. 52–62, 1992.

Merriam, S. B. and Cunningham, P. M. (Eds.) *Handbook of Adult and Continuing Education*. San Francisco, CA: Jossey-Bass, 1989.

Merriam, S. B. and Simpson, E. L. *A Guide to Research for Educators and Trainers of Adults* (2d ed.). Malabar, FL: Krieger, 1995.

Queeney, D.S. *Assessing Needs in Continuing Education*. San Francisco, CA: Jossey-Bass, 1995.

Quigley, B. A. "Action Research for Professional Development and Policy Formation in Literacy Education." *PAACE Journal of Lifelong Learning*, 4, pp. 61–69, 1995.

Rose, A. "A New Age in Adult Education Research." *Adult Learning*, 4 (2), p. 6, 1992.

Salant, P. and Dillman, D. A. *How to Conduct Your Own Survey*. New York: Wiley, 1994.

Sherblom, J. C.; Sullivan, C. F.; and Sherblom, E. C. "The What, the Whom, and the Hows of Survey Research." *Bulletin of the Association for Business Communication*, 56 (4), pp. 58–64, 1993.

Suskie, L. A. *Questionnaire Survey Research: What Works* (2d ed.). Florida State University, Tallahassee, FL: Association for Institutional Research Resources for Institutional Research, Number Six, 1996.

Thach, L. "Using Electronic Mail to Conduct Survey Research." *Educational Technology*, 35 (2), pp. 27–31, 1995.

Watson, S. C. *Institutional Response to Adult Students in Higher Education*. Manuscript in preparation. 1997.

Suzanne C. Watson is a doctoral student in the Adult Education Program at Penn State University.

The New Frontier in Qualitative Research Methodology

Elliot W. Eisner
Stanford University

The past 25 years have seen an unprecedented growth in the use of nontraditional research methods in the social sciences. Interest in new approaches to research are, in part, motivated by the desire to secure more authentic information about the people and situations studied and by the realization that conventional forms of research often constrain the data in ways that misrepresent the phenomena the researcher wishes to understand. As a result of these beliefs and interests, new forms of data representation that elude conventional forms are being employed. These new forms have their promise as well as their perils. This article discusses the context in which these new forms of research have emerged and the promise and the perils they present.

First, I would like to thank the members of the Qualitative SIG for asking me to deliver this address on the occasion of the SIG's 10th anniversary. When the first meeting of the SIG convened in Washington, D.C., a decade ago, there was a small band of AERA members in attendance. Since then, the SIG, qualitative research methods, and the field of educational research in general has come a long way. You have helped make that happen. I am here this evening to help celebrate your achievements and to reflect on where we are today

The theme of my remarks focuses on the promise and perils of the new frontier in qualitative research methodology. I will be addressing the following questions: What is the new frontier and why is it being explored? What promise does it hold for improving the quality of education? What are its perils? And, finally, where do we go from here?

The new frontier in qualitative research methodology refers to research efforts that explore new assumptions about cognition, the meaning of research, and how new research

Author's Note: This is a revised version of the distinguished lecture delivered to the Qualitative Research Special Interest Group at the annual meetings of the American Educational Research Association, Chicago, March 24, 1997.

methods might broaden and complement traditional ways of thinking about and doing educational research. Conventional approaches to educational research, those employing statistical procedures and the use of correlation and experimental designs, have in the past provided the paradigmatic conditions for the conduct of research. To do research was to use such procedures. An entire technical language has been created and batteries of statistical procedures invented to draw dependable conclusions from data. These procedures and the assumptions on which they rest are quite alive and healthy, but they no longer are the exclusive—perhaps not even the dominant—orientation to educational research. But why is this exploration occurring?

The emergence of what I have referred to as the "new frontier" secured its impetus from several sources, not least of which is a dissatisfaction with the constraints of operationalism and the legacies of positivism and behaviorism. Research conducted under the influence of these theories of meaning and behavior are often extremely reductive in character. In the opinion of many researchers, they leave out more than they include. Operationalism, for example, requires the measurement of variables, and although measurement can be a precise way to describe some aspects of the world, as a form of description it by no means exhausts the ways in which the countenance of the world or its details can be represented. Increasingly, researchers are becoming aware of the fact that form and content cannot be severed; *how* one chooses to describe something imposes constraints on *what* can be described.

As for behaviorism, neither stimulus response theory rooted in Thorndike's (Joncich, 1968) legacy to American psychology nor Watson's (1925) was ever adequate for understanding how or what the world means to those who inhabit it—perhaps especially children. For humans, meaning matters and values and intentions count. Humans live in a contingent world and form purposes that shift and alter depending on the meanings those contingencies have fostered. Indeed, as constructivism has increased in saliency as a way to understand how humans made sense of the world, behaviorism as an approach to individual psychology has seemed less and less relevant. The dominant philosophical and psychological orientations of the first 50 years of the 20th century left out, in the views of

many educational researchers, too much that mattered.

Other sources of discontent developed from a growing interest in what Schwab referred to as the practical. In his classic paper (1969), given at this annual meeting in 1969, Schwab advanced a view of knowledge which at that time had little saliency among educational researchers. The view that he advanced pertained to the centrality of practical knowledge in the context of action. For Schwab, teaching and curriculum development were, above all else, practical activities. By practical he meant what Aristotle meant: Practical activities are activities aimed at making good decisions, not activities seeking truth. Practical activities dealt with contingencies, not with causal laws. Practical activities made use of theory, but as a rule of thumb, not as a rule. Practical activities required deliberation and at their best exemplified what the Greeks called *phronesis,* a concept that referred not simply to knowledge but to wise moral choice.

Schwab's emphasis on the practical adumbrated for educational researchers another way of thinking about how we come to know. As those of you who are familiar with Aristotle's theory of knowledge will know, Aristotle distinguished between three types of knowledge (McKeon, 1941). The first pertained to theoretical knowledge, knowledge that could, in principle, be secured on phenomena that were of necessity; that is, phenomena that had to be the way they were because they could be no other way. I speak here of fields such as mathematics, astronomy, physics, and other sciences whose subject matters were knowable by their necessary and sufficient conditions; subject matters whose locus of movement, Aristotle tells us, resides within themselves.

Practical knowledge, as I have indicated, is contingent knowledge; it depends on context. Perhaps its architectonic exemplification is located in the art of politics. Human activities in general cannot, in Aristotelian terms, be understood in the ways in which the stars can be.

The third form of knowledge is productive knowledge. For Aristotle, productive knowledge is knowledge of how to make something: tables, symphonies, paintings, or poems. Its most vivid manifestation is displayed in the arts.

The point that researchers derived from Schwab's presentation is that knowledge need not be defined solely in the positivistic terms that had for so long dominated the conduct of educational research and that theory itself had limited utility in the domain of practice. Theory is general, whereas action always occurs in the particular. Knowing what to do requires practical knowledge; theoretical knowledge provides a backdrop.

At about the time that Schwab presented his paper, there was also a growing interest in cognitive pluralism and cracks were beginning to appear in foundationalism. This interest was spurred by developments in philosophy—Rorty's (1979) work for example—and in feminism and multiculturalism. The traditional desiderata of "hard" data and "rigor" (the etymology of rigor refers to stiff) were both regarded as very "male" criteria, and these were criteria that were less than attractive to feminists. There was more to understanding the world than a male to take on its necessary and sufficient features. These sources of both dissatisfaction and interest led to a return to the study of cases and to attention to particularity. This attention led researchers back to schools and to the fine-grained study of educational phenomena. Among the first in education to cut new ground were Jackson (1990) in *Life in Classrooms* and Smith (1968) in *The Complexities of the Urban Classroom.*

Interest in cases, initially at least, persuaded more than a few traditional researchers to regard qualitative research as merely reconnaissance efforts that set the stage for "real" research—the kind they did. After all, they reasoned, what could you learn from a case that applied to nothing but itself? Yet, the study of cases has had a long history in human intellectual thought. Toulmin (1990), for example, pointed out with brilliant clarity that interest in the particular preceded what is usually regarded as the advent of modern science in the mid-17th century. Galileo's focus on the quantitative description of relationships helped shift our conception of what science was about. This shift in conception refocused attention from the timely to the timeless, from the local to the universal, from the oral to the written, from the particular to the general, from the qualitative to the quantitative. By the late 1940s and 1950s, according to Toulmin, interest in the timely, the local, the particular, and the oral began to reemerge. Indeed it has.

These new interests are, I think, expressed most publicly in the saliency of qualitative research in the growth of the qualitative SIG,

and in the emergence of experimental formats at the AERA annual meeting in the publication of qualitative research journals, texts, and handbooks. If you look at the subject index in the AERA annual meeting program, you will find that qualitative research is among the largest categories on that list. It is exceeded by subjects such as teacher education and school reform, but some of these domains have a timely and a temporary character to them. Indeed, one can trace the saliency of qualitative research by tracing the number of listings in each of the annual meetings over the last decade. In 1991, there were 22 papers dealing with qualitative research in the AERA annual meeting program; in 1992 there were 32, 18 in 1993, 27 in 1994, 50 in 1995, and 55 in 1996. This year there are 45.

I said that the emergence of the new frontier emanated from discontent with older paradigms, with a growing interest in cognitive pluralism, and in new ways of thinking about the nature of research itself. One of these new approaches is the more recent interest in arts-based research. As you will know, when qualitative research emerged as a viable and definable option for educational researchers, the first tendency was to look to ethnography as the form within which to do such research. This looking to ethnography is, of course, altogether understandable. Ethnography is the child of anthropology, and anthropology is a member of the social sciences. The move from one social science to another is far less wrenching than a move from a social science to an arts- or humanities-based approach to research. The idea that the arts could provide a basis for doing research is itself regarded by more than a few as an oxymoronic notion. Yet, increasingly, researchers are recognizing that scientific inquiry is a species of research. Research is not merely a species of social science. Virtually any careful, reflective, systematic study of phenomena undertaken to advance human understanding can count as a form of research. It all depends on how that work is pursued.

My point here is that this particular period in the history of the American educational research community—the period in which we are working—displays a remarkable degree of exploratory inclinations. Younger scholars especially, although not exclusively, are trying to invent new forms that they believe are better suited for studying the educational worlds they care about. Arts-based research is one of the newer developments in the educational research community, and I am happy to say that all three of the AERA-sponsored arts-based research institutes that have been offered over the past 4 years have been oversubscribed.

Thus far, my remarks have been designed to provide an overview of the evolution of qualitative research in the American educational research community. I must tell you, however, that interest in qualitative research methods and more pointedly in new ways of thinking about matters of meaning are in no way restricted to the field of education. Social scientists and others working in other domains share similar interests. Yeasty new developments are a part of our intellectual landscape. Consider, for example, the work of Schepper-Hughes (1992) in anthropology, of Becker (1990) in sociology, and of Steinberg (1988) in psychology, not to mention the newer forms that have emerged in all of the fine arts. As I said, these are yeasty times.

It is time now for us to shift our focus and to ask about the promise of these new developments in qualitative research. What might this new frontier have to offer?

One of the consequences of the new frontier in educational research methodology is so ubiquitous it might be invisible. I speak of the idea that the emergence of alternative conceptions of knowledge and method have problematized traditional views of what research entails and have escalated our consciousness of its unexamined assumptions. If the whole world were purple, we would not be able to see a thing. It is by virtue of contrast, contrast that is both qualitative and in more customary terms ideational, that helps us notice the all too familiar. When everybody is quantifying the world, it looks as though there are no other options. When everyone requires random selection of a sample from a population as a condition for generalization, it looks as though that idea is made in heaven. When almost everyone conceptualizes validity in terms of its four canonical conditions, the meaning of validity becomes a kind of catechism that novices memorize.

The fact of new ways of doing research and the presence of nontraditional conceptions of knowledge open up the debate. Such a debate was one that I engaged in with Howard Gardner at the 1996 AERA meeting regarding the possibility that a novel might be an acceptable form for a doctoral dissertation (Eisner, 1996). Gardner took the negative view, not simply to engage in debate but because he believed it. I took the positive view for the same rea-

son. The fact that there was a debate on such an issue is itself important. Who would have predicted a decade ago that fiction might be considered a legitimate form for a Ph.D. dissertation (although I must tell you that I am advised by my esteemed colleague and one of the world's leading organizational theorists, James G. March, that in his view most of what goes on at AERA is fiction!). Nevertheless, the presence of alternatives literally forces us to seek justification, and in so doing we become more conscious of the uses and limits of tradition. To the extent to which our consciousness is heightened, we will all be more likely to know what we are doing. That is no mean accomplishment.

A second promising development in the new frontier is the use and exploration of narrative. As you undoubtably know, Bruner (1985) made a distinction between paradigmatic modes of knowing and narrative modes of knowing. The former seek truth; the later seek verisimilitude, or truthlike observations. In the former, you mean what you say. In the latter you mean more than you say. Narrative relates to the telling of stories and to the sharing of experience. To the extent that experience itself can be conceived of as the primary medium of education, stories are among the most useful means for sharing what one has experienced. Narrative—which means a telling—makes it possible for others to have access not only to our own lives when our stories are about them but also to the lives of others. Narrative, when well crafted, is a spur to imagination, and through our imaginative participation in the worlds that we create we have a platform for seeing what might be called our "actual worlds" more clearly. Furthermore, when narrative is well crafted, empathic forms of understanding are advanced.

Let me say a word about empathy. Traditionally, emotion was regarded as a contaminant to understanding. To be emotional was to lose control. Rationality at its best was cool and disinterested; it did not traffic in feeling. Indeed, one of the intractable legacies of the enlightenment was the separation of body from mind, a separation that is alive and well in the subtexts of school curricula and in our conceptions of human ability. What narrative does for us is to put us there, it helps us secure a sense of how it feels to be an associate professor at 46 with a wife who nags and cajoles him about his position in the university and, indeed, in life. In *Who's afraid of Virginia Woolf?* Albee (1962) shows us, not merely tells us. The narratives of Mailer (*Armies of the night*, 1968) and Capote (*In cold blood*, 1965) give us a glimpse into the world of war and murder. Narratives "get at"—and I use that phrase consciously—what can neither be said in number nor disclosed in literal text.

I believe that schools and classrooms, families and communities, and the practice of teaching and administration need to be understood every bit as much in the terms that narrative make possible as in terms defined through correlation coefficients, *F* ratios, or *t*-tests. This assertion of mine is not to be interpreted as a rejection of statistical approaches to research. What it does reject is the view that such approaches are the only legitimate ones.

The point here is that humans have used storied forms to inform since humans have been able to communicate. In a sense, ethnography is a refinement of those stories and fine art is the quintessential achievement of creating congruence between form and content in the telling.

A third promise of the new frontier has to do with the opportunities that it provides to those engaged in the research enterprise to play to their strengths. By this I mean that methods and aptitudes interact. Not every research form is good for every player. The availability of qualitative research methods in the fullness of their possibilities offers researchers opportunities to select a way of working that fits their interests, is congruent with what they wish to study, plays to their strengths, exploits their aptitudes, and gives them a chance to find a place in the sun.

Some researchers will, of course, be happily content with calculation and statistical analysis. All the more power to them. Again, the game here concerns not the construction of our own new hegemony but the expansion of the resources considered legitimate for studying the educational world. By having available modes of inquiry that exploit the representational capacities of language and image, the possibilities for graduate students and for professors alike to find their bliss in the pantheon of research methods is increased. I am all for that. And I know that you are as well.

A fourth promise of the new frontier pertains to something not indigenous or unique to it, but which, nevertheless, has come along with it. What I am referring to is the notion of collaboration. The feminists were among the first to call our attention to status differential between researchers and teachers in the conduct of research and the cost of such differential in really finding out about the situations we wish to understand. As a result, we have been urged from many quarters to regard teachers and school administrators not as subjects (a very telling term indeed) but as partners in a common enterprise, an enterprise that recognizes the distinctive contributions that different individuals working in different sectors of the educational enterprise are capable of making. Insider knowledge, or in anthropological terms, emic knowledge, is more likely to be shared when collaboration takes place. Such collaboration, at its best, initiates with the conceptualization process and not only at the data-gathering process.

Authentic collaboration, from my perspective, will require much more than good will between researchers and teachers. It will require a redefinition of the teacher's role so that teachers have significant opportunities—especially time—to engage in collaboration. If the school is to be a center of inquiry for students, it will need to be a center for inquiry for the professional staff as well.

If the potential virtues that I have described are within the realm of possibility, what we must ask, are the perils? What do we need to look out for? Let me turn to these questions now.

Before I get to the substance of my concerns, I want to tell you first that the list of issues that I will identify is longer than the list I have just completed. Some of these concerns you may regard as ill placed or badly conceived. Nevertheless, they are my concerns and I share them with you tonight.

My aim this evening is to avoid being Pollyannish while at the same time to avoid being discouraging. My aim is to put on your plate issues that I worry about, that I have not been able to resolve, that I believe are important for the future of qualitative research. My hope is that these concerns will give you something to chew on—and to get rid of if necessary. In short, my intentions are entirely constructive.

Let me identify some practical perils that I myself have faced. The most obvious is the difficulty publishing nontext material. My own presidential address at AERA a few years ago included the playing of a videotape that was essential to the point that I was making about the cognitive functions of nonlinguistic forms. When the piece was published in the *Educational Researcher* (Eisner, 1993), as you might expect, the very form central to my case could not be included. Similar difficulties have occurred in the uses I have made of sections from films such as *Dead Poets Society* and *School Colors* and from music selections such as Beethoven's hallelujah chorus from *Christ on the Mount of Olives.* Journals have no mechanism for sharing such material. Perhaps in the future, CD-ROMS will be available to remedy this problem, but at the present it is still a problem.

Another practical concern relates to the fact that little or no tradition in the use of nonconventional forms of research exists in most universities and, as a result, there is often little faculty expertise that students can draw upon. This is not an unusual condition. Innovation, by definition, is new; and when something is new, experience is limited. Those who want to use film as a major vehicle in doing educational research not only need access to a camera; they also need an understanding of how films are made, and unless the school or department is sympathetic to such an approach and has the resources available, the prospects for such work are dim. The absence of guidance leaves students on their own without the skills needed to use the medium well. The result can be a visual disaster, even though the intention is a noble one and the display of courage beyond question. The price paid for innovation is having to pick up what you can here and there and knit it together as best you can. It is certainly a problem worth addressing, especially in a university. I mention it here because it impacts the quality of research that individuals will be able to do.

Related to the relationship between innovation and experience is the discomfort people feel from not knowing how to appraise work that does not fit conventional paradigms. How should a novel, prepared as a piece of educational research, be appraised? Who should do the appraisal? What criteria are appropriate? How should one appraise a multimedia dissertation? Are criteria pertaining to validity and reliability, generalizability and stability, appropriate? If not, what criteria are?

We can learn something about these matters from the arts. You will recall that Van Gogh sold one work in his lifetime, and Stravinsky was booed off the stage when the *Rite of Spring* was first performed in 1913. New forms may require new criteria, and new criteria evolve through the efforts of those who can help interpret the meaning of the work. Critics in the arts do this as a normal part of

their work when in those rare moments such innovative work emerges.

In addition to the foregoing more or less practical problems, there are some significant theoretical problems. Consider, for example, the fact that there are qualitative researchers who are quite reluctant to provide an analytic or theoretical interpretation of the situations they have described in their work. The argument is that works of art stand alone; after all, the author of a play does not provide a theoretical explication of the meaning of the play to the audience who beholds it. The play is manifested in language, action, and stage set. Plays are supposed to carry their own ineffable meanings, and the audience gets them or does not.

The criteria applicable to plays are analogized to educational research. I have problems with the analogy. Our work must go well beyond what a good journalist—or even a good writer—is able to do. After all, we are expected to bring to the educational situation a theoretical and analytical background in the field of education. That background must count for something in the way in which phenomena are characterized, analyzed, and assessed. It is the use of that background and the tools secured in acquiring it that provides the distinctively educational added value to our work.

In short, I am saying that I believe that except for very exceptional cases, it is unlikely that uninterpreted qualitative material will satisfy our colleagues or be optimally useful to those who work in the schools. Our challenge is learning how to make such interpretations without sacrificing the quality and character of the writing that we have done. One good model, to my way of thinking, is found in Jackson's (1993) essay describing his former algebra teacher, Mrs. Teresa Henze. In his essay, Jackson creates a remarkable rapprochement between the vividly descriptive and the philosophically analytic. The two are successfully united. I believe that we need more of that kind of work and, indeed, kinds that are yet to be envisioned. Again, good description, even very good description, is not likely to be enough.

Another concern that I have relates to the use of ambiguity in narrative and other forms of qualitative research. In literary circles, ambiguity has a positive, constructive contribution to make to the overall character of the story. At the same time, ambiguity creates uncertainty regarding the phenomena to which the story refers, hence making it difficult for readers to know with reasonable precision the point being conveyed. I feel a tension in these two pulls: the pull toward precision and the pull toward the productive consequences of ambiguity. I have no way at this moment to resolve the tension. I only want to acknowledge the dilemma that I feel in wanting to afford readers opportunities to imaginatively participate in the educational situations described without, at the same time, creating work that functions essentially as a Rorschach inkblot test.

Still another concern relates to what might be called "indefensible relativism." By indefensible, I refer to the attitude that is taken by some researchers that since interpretations are always personal, any interpretation is as defensible as any other. The logical implication of this view is that there is no basis whatsoever for making judgments about either the quality of the work or its meaning. Even if "truth" is given up as a regulative ideal in qualitative research or in a constructivist conception of knowledge, one need not be saddled by a view that provides no basis for assessing the quality of the work. Rorty (1979), for example, gives up truth but pursues what he calls "edification." Put another way, what good work should do in philosophy and elsewhere is to enrich and enliven the conversation. There should be a sense that it is moving forward, that we seem to be getting somewhere. Novelty for its own sake and relativism in assessment leaves us, I am afraid, rudderless. How should work in the new frontier be assessed? What criteria seem appropriate? How can we separate the wheat from the chaff? If a correspondence theory of truth will no longer do, what criteria will? These are some of the concerns I have about the basis for judgments about the quality of qualitative research.

What exacerbates this condition is the fact that in qualitative research—and it must also be said about most quantitative studies—the raw data upon which, say, a narrative was created are unavailable to a reader. For all practical purposes, there are no archives that house such material and even when there are, the material is at least once removed from the researcher's experience and is in fact only a pale representation of the situations or individuals it purports to describe. Thus, in qualitative studies we are at the mercy of the writer or filmmaker, at least to a large extent.

I am certainly aware of matters of triangulation, structural corroboration, referential adequacy, and other moves designed to check unwarranted conclusions or generalizations. Nevertheless, the bottom line is that the spin that is given to the description of a situation is the researcher's, and precisely how much spin is given is extremely difficult to know. These issues are ones I believe we need to think about.

Related to the issue of spin and personal interpretation is the matter of persuasiveness. All research efforts, whether in the qualitative or in the quantitative domain, seek to persuade. The question that must be addressed is the basis for the persuasiveness. Both advertising and propaganda are also aimed at persuading people to believe this or that. How shall we think about persuasiveness? What constitutes legitimate persuasiveness in qualitative research?

One answer to this question is one that Barone and I (1997) gave in our chapter on arts-based research in AERA's forthcoming *Handbook on Complementary Methods for Educational Research.* That answer was that what arts-based educational research seeks is not so much conclusions that readers come to believe but the number and quality of the questions that the work raises. Frankly, this answer—and it is our answer—is only half satisfying. Is there a way to ground persuasiveness in some kind of evidence or analysis without resorting to the same reductive procedures that motivated the move away from them? Put another way, can we have our evidentiary base and still maintain the sometime imaginative and poetic quality of well-crafted qualitative research? The questions that I have raised are by no means easy to answer, and I do not want to appear from this podium as if I had answers to them. These are issues that I worry about. They are issues that those of us working in the qualitative domain cannot afford to ignore. If we ignore them, they will be called to our attention by those who do not share our methodological proclivities.

Let me move now to another issue that is related to the troubles with relativism that I alluded to earlier. It has to do with the concept of "expertise." As you well know, we live at a time in which the notion of expertise, especially in a context that values collaboration, is regarded with suspicion. Expertise like connoisseurship seems to many to smack of elitism and to privilege the few. In an age in which so-called democratic tendencies pervade all levels of the research enterprise, the idea that someone has special competence to notice and interpret is often regarded as authoritarian. I must confess that I am not ready to give up either the concept of expertise or of authority. There is a distinction made in the sociological literature between ascribed authority and achieved authority. The former results from being assigned to a position in a hierarchy. The latter is secured through competence. Relativistic views of merit marginalize expertise because judgments about educational states of affairs are reduced to preferences or "mere" opinions.

I believe that in qualitative research, as in many other fields, expertise in knowing the subject matter that is being addressed—whether it is the Italians of Boston (Whyte, 1943), the fundamentalists of the American Midwest (Peshkin, 1986), or the young children who populated a Boston classroom (Kozol, 1968)—matters. Qualitative research designed to illuminate, for example, the quality of art or music teaching needs researchers who know something not only about art and music but about their teaching. I find that quite often matters of content quality are neglected in descriptions of classrooms. It is almost as if the content being taught and the pedagogical practices related to it do not matter. Expertise does matter, and doctoral programs preparing qualitative researchers would do well to provide opportunities for researchers to achieve the expertise they need to say something useful about the teaching of various subjects in the school.

I turn now to questions of generalization. One of the recurrent questions raised about the study of cases pertains to the generalizability of the findings. In doing case studies, are we, as Geertz (1983) would have it, simply hearing from another community or subculture, or is there something to be learned from the study of the case that generalizes to other situations?

As you well know, the canonical procedure for generalization in statistically driven studies requires the random selection of a sample from a population as a condition for determining levels of probability regarding the relationship between the findings on the sample and the population from which it was randomly selected. The logic of the enterprise is impeccable. Because in qualitative research we typically do not randomly select our populations—for the most part they are con-

venience samples—how shall we think about generalization?

It seems to me that what qualitative research yields is a set of observations or images that facilitate the search and discovery process when examining other situations, including other classrooms and schools. This is what Powell, Cohen, and Farrar (1985) give us when, in *The Shopping Mall High School,* they tell us about the treaties that are formed between high school students and their teachers that are not limited to the particular high school they studied. They provide us with a frame for not only looking at classrooms and schools but for speculating on why such agreements would be made in the first place. Given the compromises high school teachers must make to cope with the magnitude of the demands that confront them each day, such agreements between students and teachers are understandable.

The conception of "treaty" that Powell et al. (1985) advanced serves as a schema for locating similar treaties in other schools and for deepening our understanding of the kinds of interpersonal collusion that makes life bearable for both students and teachers.

Is this heuristic use of ideas and images developed from qualitative research so different from the generalizing practices of quantitative research? I think not. Although the logic of statistical generalization seems unassailable with respect to the populations from which findings on samples were drawn, that logic does not necessarily apply to other populations. First, the features of a population a researcher would need to know to determine whether the findings derived from another population are likely to apply to it are simply unavailable. Seldom are the boundary conditions for a finding or a theory specified. What we do, and wisely so, is to use findings derived from quantitative studies analogically or heuristically. In fact, we do not really know whether, for example, findings derived from a study in 1994 are applicable to a supposedly comparable population in 1997. The passage of time may matter. Furthermore, the population to which we are generalizing may or may not possess the features of the population originally studied. In short, quantitative researchers using statistical methods wind up using their findings in ways that are not unlike the ways in which qualitative researchers use theirs. Humans are not only tool-using animals, they are not only symbol-using animals; they are generalizing animals. We all generalize from N's of one and make adjustments that seem appropriate in the process. To do this we think analogically and metaphorically, and settle for plausibility.

I bring my remarks to a close by talking a bit about what the promise and perils of the new frontier mean for the future of educational research.

From my perspective, I see little likelihood that the advances that have been made, particularly in qualitative research, will be rescinded and that the world of research methodology will return to the traditional habits it displayed in the 1950s and 1960s. The practices that have emerged in the conduct of educational research are a part of a larger, more general movement, one that embraces pluralism in method and diversity in conceptions of knowledge. At the same time, I do not see the epistemological orientations that characterize our own views about inquiry widely embraced by the American public. The public continues to be goaded into a horse race view of academic performance, and for horse races, digits are much more effective than narratives. Put another way, when push comes to shove, the measurement of academic performance through testing will continue to be the way to go.

The reasons measured outcomes of schooling are attractive relate, I believe, to the fact that a meritocratic-social orientation of the kind that we have in America depends on comparison, and comparison is made very difficult when the idiosyncratic characteristics of individual performance are made salient. We prefer for purposes of comparison all students running down the same track, measured by the same tests, and whose performance is reported out to the third or fourth decimal place. I do not see qualitative forms of assessment changing that practice in our schools. Besides, quantitative methods are less labor intensive and less ambiguous. Numbers provide a false security—but a security nevertheless.

What I also see is a much greater acceptance in the research community of qualitative research than we have known before. Hardly a week goes by that I do not receive an announcement of four or five new books on qualitative research methods that have recently been published. The interest is widespread, to the point that some of our more traditionally oriented colleagues are concerned.

And with respect to our more traditionally oriented colleagues, I sense that for a significant portion, the selection of a method or orientation to the conduct of research is more than a methodological choice, it is a reflection of a personality disposition. Someone once said that the world can be divided into people who like San Francisco and those who like Los Angeles. The world might also be divided between those who prefer qualitative research and those who prefer quantitative approaches. Frankly, my hope is that the field will develop hybrid forms of research that use different approaches within the same study. As I said earlier, I have no interest in creating a new hegemony. I welcome pluralism within the field at large and, indeed, within studies themselves.

I began my remarks this evening congratulating you for the genuinely important leadership you have provided to the field. I meant what I said. I have tried this evening to identify both the promising features of the new frontier and those that seem to me to pose problems we must address. I am confident that they will be addressed. They are not only important; they are interesting. Your work has made it far easier for younger colleagues to do qualitative research in the field of education than it was for some of you when you were getting started. Cutting new ground is never easy. It takes courage and it's risky. But durability is one sign of vitality, so what better way to certify the durability of our work than to come together this evening to celebrate our 10th anniversary.

REFERENCES

Albee, E. (1962). *Who's afraid of Virginia Woolf?* New York: Atheneum.

Barone, T., & Eisner, E. (1997). *Handbook on complementary methods for educational research* (Richard Yeager, Ed.). Washington, DC: AERA.

Becker, H. (1990). Performance science. *Social Problems, 37*(1), 117–132.

Bruner, J. (1985). Narrative and paradigmatic modes of thought. In E. Eisner (Ed.), *Learning and teaching the ways of knowing: Eighty-fourth yearbook of the National Society for the Study of Education, Part II.* Chicago: University of Chicago Press.

Capote, T. (1965). *In cold blood.* New York: Random House.

Eisner, E. (1993). Forms of understanding and the future of educational research. *Educational Researcher, 22*(7), 5–11.

Eisner, E. (1996). Should a novel count as a dissertation in education? *Research in the Teaching of English, 30*(4), 403–427.

Geertz, C. (1983). *Local knowledge: Further essays in interpretive anthropology.* New York: Basic Books.

Jackson, P. (1990). *Life in classrooms.* New York: Teachers College Press.

Jackson, P. (1993). *Untaught lessons.* New York: Teachers College Press.

Joncich, G. (1968). *The sane positivist.* Middletown, CT: Wesleyan University Press.

Kozol, J. (1968). *Death at an early age.* New York: Bantam Books.

McKeon, R. (1941). *The basic works of Aristotle.* New York: Random House.

Mailer, N. (1968). *The armies of the night.* New York: New American Library.

Peshkin, A. (1986). *God's choice.* Chicago: University of Chicago Press.

Powell, A., Cohen, D., & Farrar, E. (1985). *Shopping mall high school.* Boston: Houghton Mifflin.

Rorty, R. (1979). *Philosophy and the mirror of nature.* Princeton, NJ: Princeton University Press.

Schepper-Hughes, N. (1992). *Death without weeping.* Berkeley: University of California Press.

Schwab, J. (1969). The practical: A language for curriculum. *School Review, 78*(19), 1–23.

Smith, L (1968). *The complexities of the urban classroom.* New York Holt, Rinehart & Winston.

Steinberg, R. (1988). *The triangle of love.* New York: Basic Books.

Toulmin, S. (1990). *Cosmopolis.* New York: Free Press.

Watson, J. (1925). *Behaviorism.* New York: W. W. Norton.

Whyte, W. (1943). *Street corner society.* Chicago: University of Chicago Press.

Elliot W. Eisner is professor of education and art at Stanford University. He was trained as a painter at the Art Institute of Chicago and later studied design at Illinois Institute of Technology's Institute of Design. His research interests focus on the ways in which the arts expand awareness and advance human understanding. He is also interested in the generic problems of school improvement, and especially how schools can become educative institutions for both children and the adults who work with them. His publications include Educating Artistic Vision, The Educational Imagination, Cognition and Curriculum Reconsidered, *and* The Enlightened Eye.

Gove, a reading consultant in the East Cleveland Schools (Shaw High School, 15320 Euclid Avenue, East Cleveland OH 44112, USA), is coauthor of Reading and Learning to Read, a methods text for graduate and undergraduate classes. Kennedy-Calloway is a principal in the Warrensville Heights City Schools. Both have taught at elementary, middle school, high school, and college levels.

Action research: Empowering teachers to work with at-risk students

Mary K. Gove
Connie Kennedy-Calloway

■ The staff development program in "action research" we describe here developed over a 5-year period in an urban school district in northeastern Ohio. Students in this district are in academic jeopardy as early as the fourth grade; national standardized test scores report that 36% of the fourth graders are already below grade level. The district qualifies as an "at risk" district as defined by the "30, 30, 60" Ohio State Department of Education formula: a dropout rate of 30% or more, an aid to dependent children rate of 30% or more, and an average personal income tax return figure that is less than 60% of the statewide average. With such a large number of at-risk students, we were concerned with how to have an effect on students within the regular classroom setting.

First, we will describe how we organized the program in which teachers and administrators investigated how to use reading/writing strategies to improve the learning of at-risk students within the regular classroom setting.

Second, we will describe a qualitative study we conducted of the participants. In this study our question was "What happens to participants as they work in instructional teams to conduct action research projects?" In answering this question, we will describe how we conducted the study.

Then we will describe and compare four action researchers who are examples or prototypes of real people on a continuum of professional growth. Finally, we will discuss how the professional growth of these school professionals relate to issues of teacher efficacy, or teachers' perceptions of their own ability to influence student learning, particularly the learning of low-achieving or at-risk students.

The staff development program

Twenty professionals participated in the district's 1990–1991 Action Research Staff Development Program: 16 classroom teachers, 1 elementary assistant principal, and 3 reading teachers. The classroom

Figure 1
Action research data collection by triangulation

The action researchers ask: What do I think? How will I know? Answer with 3 sources of information: behavior, written work, comments

What do I see?
Tally and/or describe what students did.
Chart interaction
Check these behaviors:
• volunteering to respond
• raising hand
• giving answers
• submitting assignment
• taking notes
• giving predictions

What does students' written work tell me?
Analyze logs, free writes, tests, essays, maps, or webs, predictions written.

What do students tell me?
Interview selected students or use a questionnaire or rating scale

teachers taught Grade 4 through 11. One of the reading teachers worked in an elementary school, one in a middle school, and one in a high school. The majority of the teachers had taught 8 years or more. All had volunteered to participate in the program and were paid a small stipend for their efforts.

All of the participants were familiar with reading/writing strategies to some extent. On a continuum of familiarity with reading/writing strategies, some had attended building level inservice sessions and were beginning to incorporate new strategies into their teaching; others had participated in four semesters of reading sequence courses taught in the school system by professors from a nearby university; one participant had a master's degree in reading and writing methods and was petitioning to be a Ph.D. candidate at a nearby university.

The action research participants worked in instructional teams with two professionals working in one classroom. Instructional team configurations included two classroom teachers, a teacher and a reading specialist, or a teacher and an administrator.

In the 1990–1991 program 10 teams participated. Four after-school organizational meetings were held during the school year in which we explained how to organize the action research studies, and the teams shared how their studies were progressing.

In organizing the individual action research projects, we asked the instructional teams to use reading/writing strategies as they taught a unit of study in science, social studies, or language arts for at least a 2-week period. The teams decided what strategies to use and who the targeted or at-risk students were.

The teams collected three types of descriptive data as they taught: (1) What do you see? The teams monitored student behavior either through a checklist or through scripting. (2) What do students tell us? Through student interviews or student surveys, the teams obtained students' perceptions of the extent the reading/writing strategies aided their learning. (3) What does written work tell us? The instructional teams analyzed both the frequency and the quality of student written work.

Figure 1 shows a chart we used to introduce data collection to the participants, and Figure 2 is an example of data collected by one team.

After studying their respective data, all the action research teams met to share their findings during this "control teaching" phase of the project. The teams then developed a hypothesis concerning how the learning of the at-risk or targeted students could be further affected.

During a second cycle of teaching in the program, the instructional teams tested their hypothesis: They put into action their theories of what could be done to increase learning, particularly for the at-risk or lowest achieving students. This teaching phase was approximately 2 weeks, with the instructional teams teaching a second unit of the same content area.

Figure 2

Outline of an action research interview with targeted students in Teacher A's class

Interviewer: Teacher B

Strategies the teacher used:

[Sample responses recorded by Teacher B]
Quiz on material read
Student devising questions and then reading orally to class and asking the class questions
Lecture/notetaking
Freewrite: What I Know...
Recitation (either class or individuals) (Example: Say the names of the bones in the skull)

Questions asked of students:

1. Which strategy helped you learn the most?
2. Which strategy helped you learn the least?
3. What is your opinion of_____? [Asked about each strategy noted above]
4. You are soon going to graduate from high school. It is very likely that later in your life you will be in an academic situation in which you will want to learn something. Which of these strategies would you use?

[Sample responses from two students]

Helen
I learned the most with the quiz on the material
I thought making up the question helped, but the oral reading did not help.
Notetaking is alright but sometimes it goes too fast.
I hate writing but it helped me 'cause it made me think.
Recitation helps. It's good.
[In a future academic situation] I'd use the one where you make up questions.

Jim
Recitation helps me the most.
The quiz helped me the least because I forgot.
I don't like making up questions. [Why?] I don't like it.
I like lecture and notetaking.
Writing–maybe I was absent. I don't remember that.
[In a future academic situation] I'd use notetaking.

Finally, the teams analyzed their data to determine the extent to which their hypothesis was confirmed, wrote a brief report, and shared their study at a final banquet.

The staff development program served to empower the participants. The individual action research studies were not administrator or even lead-teacher dominated. The teachers working in instructional teams were the collaborative decision makers. In the program, the teams solved problems and determined how to make a difference, rather than take the attitude "It's Johnny's problem. He has home problems. Johnny just can't learn!"

Studying the action researchers

As the instructional teams conducted action research projects, we conducted a study of the participants of the instructional teams to dis-

cover "What happens to the participants conducting action research?"

All of the participants in all 5 years of the program were interviewed as a team by one of the coordinators at the conclusion of each program. We then transcribed and reviewed the interviews.

During the 1988-1989 program (Gove & Roskos, 1989) the instructional teams were asked to describe their preferred reading/writing strategies, the advantages and disadvantages of using them, and their ideas about the action research project. A professor from a nearby university and one of the coordinators independently analyzed the content of transcriptions of these interviews to discern patterns of thought about the action research experience. Each independently discerned three themes recurring in the transcriptions and then jointly devised the labels for these themes, guided by the work of Goetz and LeCompte (1984) and Spradley (1979).

Figure 3

Effects that action research has on teachers' own professional lives

The following quotes taken from transcripts of the 1988–89 interviews with participating teachers illustrate major themes that appeared in their reports.

Involvement in teaching

Pat said, "I focused on a specific teaching technique and I tried to analyze how well it worked. I also came up with another idea for teaching... which is probably very important and which our students probably don't learn except by trial and error. I was also much more *involved* in working with this class than I might have been otherwise."

Collegiality

Bob said, "It changed our relationship. Louise [the administrator] worked with me and we taught and collected data together. She came in my room to work with me instead of to check up on my teaching." Louise, the administrator, noted "The teacher and students saw me in a different light because I worked with the action research project in Bob's room. I think they saw me as more helpful. This even helped when I had to discipline students from Bob's class in the office."

Focused data-based feedback

James said, "The teacher gets immediate feedback from what transpired in the classroom and on patterns of teaching which may be so natural that the teacher is not even aware of them. I also had someone to help problem solve."

In aggregate, the patterns revealed three themes which serve as broad generalizations about action research as viewed by these teachers:

1. Involvement in teaching: As a result of participation in the action research project, the teachers expressed a renewed interest and enthusiasm for teaching.

2. Collegiality: All participants commented on how they became joint decision makers while working in teams to conduct action research. The teams which included an administrator or a reading teacher indicated action research projects changed how teachers perceived the administrator/reading-teacher action researchers.

3. Focused, data-based feedback: The action research projects created a nonthreatening condition which allowed instructional teams to provide each other with focused, data-based feedback about teaching performance.

Quotes taken from the 1988–89 transcribed interviews which illustrate each of these themes can be found in Figure 3. Further examples of how these themes or areas of professional growth affected action research participants will be provided in the case studies of prototypical action researchers.

All in all, themes contributed to the answering of our research question: "What happens to teachers and administrators who participate in action research?"

In describing our action researcher cases, we used the Levels of Use of an Innovation Model (Hall, Loucks, Rutherford, & Newlove, 1975). These participants, who were all in the 1990–1991 program, are examples of school professionals on a continuum of knowledge and beliefs about the use of reading/writing strategies.

Briefly, the Levels of Use (LOU) model places teachers between Stages 0 and 5 concerning their knowledge and use of an innovation, in this case reading/writing strategies:

Stage 0 teachers know nothing about reading/ writing strategies and do not care to learn about them.

Stage 1 teachers wonder what reading/writing strategies entail and how they are useful.

Stage 2 teachers gather information in anticipation of beginning to use reading/writing strategies.

Stage 3 teachers use the strategies in a mechanical way and are interested in "how to" information.

Stage 4 teachers are concerned with how to use reading/writing strategies to further improve student learning and at times share their knowledge with colleagues. This sharing seems to be somewhat dependent on the custom of sharing about teaching that has become the norm in the schools (Little, 1982).

Stage 5 teachers have extensive understanding and are willing to help other colleagues learn reading/writing strategies. They look at how to use other innovations in conjunction with reading/writing strategies to further improve student learning.

As stated previously, all participants of the action research program had knowledge of and used reading/ writing strategies in their classrooms. Thus, they were all at Stages 3, 4, or 5.

Of the four prototypical participants we will describe, one had recently begun using reading/writing strategies and was concerned with how to conduct specific strategies (LOU Stage 3). One was knowledgeable and concerned about how to use reading/ writing strategies to further improve student learning (LOU Stage 4). The final two participants had coupled knowledge about different innovations with reading/ writing strategies in their action research projects (one at LOU Stage 4 and one at Stage 5).

While the names of the four action research participants and some details are fabricated, the cases are authentic. After a description of their action research project, and their level of use of reading/writing strategies, we discuss how the action research experience affected them in three areas of professional growth: (1) involvement in teaching, (2) collegiality, and (3) focused, data-based feedback. Then, we take a brief look at how the "results" of the four studies compare. Finally, we discuss how the action research process enhances teachers' growth at each stage of acquiring, refining, and expanding their use of reading/writing strategies.

Jill, beginning to use reading/writing strategies

In her second year of teaching ninth-grade science in a large urban high school, Jill participated in a building level inservice program which met for six afterschool sessions lasting 1½ hours. Each concluded with participants writing lessons which included prereading, active reading, postreading, and vocabulary development activities. In these sessions Jill learned strategies such as Radio Reading (Vacca & Vacca, 1989), Concept of Definition

(Vacca, Vacca, & Gove, 1991), and Prereading Plan (Vacca & Vacca, 1989).

During the baseline data-collecting part of Jill's action research project, she teamed with a reading specialist. They became aware of one student dominating the class discussion. The instructional team formulated the following hypotheses: (1) If students take a more active part in learning, then they will retain more. (2) We can encourage this if we (a) place students in small groups to complete tasks and (b) require each student to contribute to the class recitation or discussion before any student has a second turn.

In the final interview, Jill was concerned with labeling and describing two of the strategies she used: Radio Reading and Concept of Definition. When Jill was asked her reaction to action research she said, "This action research project was interesting. It made me think about what I could do to increase learning, rather than just thinking about completing my lesson plans. It made me more involved in teaching. I thought about what I could do to increase learning."

Although Jill mainly operated at LOU Stage 3 for reading/writing strategies, she had impact concerns (LOU Stage 4) as she conducted the project.

When asked if she talked to teachers other than her partner about reading/writing strategies she said, "No, I don't have many interactions with teachers about teaching."

This large urban high school tends not be a place where teachers discuss the craft of teaching; action research provided this neophyte teacher with a structured, successful experience to investigate and to talk with a colleague about her craft.

Sue, experienced with reading/writing strategies

Sue worked on a team with Judy, the building's Chapter 1 teacher. [Chapter 1 is a Federally funded U.S. program for students from disadvantaged backgrounds.] She had completed the four reading sequence courses and was well versed in reading and writing strategies.

Sue and her partner targeted as at-risk the students who were below the 36th percentile on a national standardized reading test and decided to use such comprehension-based strategies as the Directed Reading-Thinking Activity (DRTA), Webbing, Question-Answer

Relationships (QAR), and a student-devised crossword puzzle for vocabulary development.

Sue said she had often thought, "Something is wrong here. How can I change my teaching?" Thus, Sue seemed to be functioning at LOU Stage 4: She involved students in reading and writing strategies throughout her teaching *and* she was continually concerned about how to improve students' learning.

One difference for Sue was her working closely with another colleague. She said, "I usually don't like to work with others."

As they worked together on their project, they alternated the teacher and observer roles. Sue reported, "When Judy observed, she saw things I didn't see. Plus, she didn't just observe the targeted students; she saw my lesson. Once Judy said, 'Your lesson was boring.' So she helped me out in improving my teaching."

At another point in the interview Sue said, "We learned from each other. We developed a closeness and she became a resource person for me."

Sue and Judy generated several hypotheses; however, the main focus of their project was how to get more active involvement. During the control teaching, as they were collecting baseline data, students made crossword puzzles using important vocabulary terms. In planning, Sue had viewed this as a less important activity in the unit of study. However, during this activity the instructional team observed the targeted students become more engaged, more actively involved. As a result, during the experimental teaching, the instructional team asked students to devise crossword puzzles as a central activity.

In other words, the targeted students' behavior directly influenced the lesson planning in two important ways: (1) What was a peripheral vocabulary activity became a major comprehension activity for the lesson and (2) this became a student-directed learning experience for at-risk learners.

Sue and Judy concluded their report this way: "The real positive effect of this program was the professional discussion and collegiality between the project participants. We made suggestions for future lessons. We gave each other insights into the children's behaviors and the outcomes of the lessons. We hope to have more chances to do this type of team teaching."

When asked if she talked with others about their action research project, Sue said they talked with Bill and Connie, the other action research instructional team in their building, but not to other teachers.

Connie, using strategies with another innovation

Connie, a building administrator, worked with Bill, a sixth-grade teacher who had participated in the four-course reading sequence and was familiar with reading/writing strategies. Bill was functioning primarily at a LOU Stage 4. An administrator, Connie was involved schoolwide in helping teachers to reinforce prosocial skills into their daily routine.

As Bill taught his students using the DRTA, story mapping, webbing personalities in a story, and QAR, Connie observed that three male students were not participating. These same students were getting into trouble in the classroom and outside on the playground. Bill and Connie reported, "After examining our data, it became clear to us we must first change behavior before we could hope to see an improvement in the learning of the at-risk student. We were amazed at how often these students were off task!" They continued:

> We felt we would approach our project from a behavior standpoint instead of an academic focus. We believe that teachers must not only make students aware of specific behaviors that are unacceptable, but must actually teach constructive behavioral alternatives as well.

> We identified the behaviors to be changed. Next we took some baseline data for four days, had interviews with the target students, and finally decided on reinforcers or activities that the students seemed to enjoy. We agreed upon a contract with each child. In the contract they were to remain on task, participate in the classroom discussion, and complete assignments. If they met the goal of the contract, they could choose an activity for a designated number of minutes each day.

Connie talked individually to each of the boys about specific behaviors like looking at the teacher when he gave directions, raising their hands, contributing to class, and completing assignments. The students signed the contracts which included their most coveted reward, working with students in the kindergarten and first-grade rooms!

During her first observation after the contracts, Connie reported that all three targeted students had much improved behavior. Bill and Connie discussed "Would the behavior continue and transfer?" James, the first of the three targeted students, continued the prosocial behavior, supported with smiles, praise, handshakes, extra computer time, and helping in lower grade classrooms. The art, music, and gym teachers as well as his mother commented on the positive change in James' behavior.

The second targeted student, Henry, often asked to go to the lavatory when important directions were being given; then when he returned to class he did not know how to complete assignments. Connie reported this pattern to both Bill and the student. The two agreed that Henry should remain in the classroom while directions were given and complete three examples of the written work before going to the lavatory.

The third targeted student also continued the prosocial behavior throughout the contracted reinforcement period.

When asked about the benefits of the action research project, Connie said, "It helps students develop their potential. Every team had a different strategy but all the targeted children were motivated toward more learning." Furthermore, she said, "Bill and I now have a better appreciation of each other. We worked as a team. We talked about what happened in his classroom. Sometimes we disagreed. We did lots of sharing of ideas about children in his class."

Connie reported, "Bill already knew reading and writing strategies; this made him a believer in the prosocial behavior program. Our action research project created a more positive attitude toward students and learning in Bill."

Bill, too, enthusiastically commented on this change in his attitude at the final sharing of action research projects before an audience of his peers.

Jan, integrating innovations

Jan is a reading teacher in a middle school who teaches Chapter 1 classes and works with content teachers, helping them to integrate reading and writing strategies into their teaching. A doctoral student at a nearby university, Jan has had training in cooperative learning strategies with Spencer Kagan. She has also read extensively about cooperative learning (Johnson & Johnson, 1987). Thus, Jan functions at LOU Stage 5.

Jan had begun working with Mary in a peer-coaching/team-teaching arrangement before the project began. Prior to the 4-week action research project, Jan reported that they engaged the students in "class building" activities as well as teaching students the roles and behaviors associated with successful group work.

During the control teaching phase, Jan and Mary used anticipation guides, freewriting, DRTA, paired reading, reader response journals, dramatization, and story frames. Through observing the students they determined that the targeted students had on-task behaviors during the directed whole group lessons 30% of the time. Their hypotheses were: (1) If a combination of selected reading/writing and cooperative learning strategies are used with at-risk students, then the result will be increased reading achievement and improved writing skills. (2) In a cooperative learning environment, students will demonstrate a more positive attitude toward reading and writing.

During the experimental phase of the action research teaching, Jan and Mary placed students in groups based on sociogram data (elicited from students) and reading achievement scores. One high-ability, two middle-ability, and one low-ability student composed each team. Time was spent on team-building activities so that students could develop an understanding of the teaming concept.

Reading/writing strategies were coupled with a compatible cooperative learning strategy. For example, the anticipation guide was used with a Three-Step Interview (Kagan, 1990) in which students interview another member of the group and then share what they learned with the team of four. Freewriting and responses in journals were shared with team members in roundtable/round-robin format (Kagan, 1991).

Jan said working in the action research instructional team helped her in working with other teachers. Several teachers saw the two working together and said, "When are you going to work with me?" Jan received invitations to work with other teachers because of the close working relationship developed with Mary.

During Jan's interview, she discussed Mary's struggles in changing from a directed teacher role to a facilitating role and then about the power of giving data-based feedback to students:

I had the opportunity to work in the classroom with Mary, so there were two teachers in one classroom. This doesn't mean they got a double dose of teachers. What they got was a double dose of facilitating.

Mary learned how to let go. And it was hard for her. It was hard for me too when I first started using cooperative learning. But something I think teachers don't realize is that we have to help the students learn to control themselves. I think that's a very difficult part of mastering cooperative learning. You don't really give up teaching, you just take on a different function.

The teachers observe to see if what is taking place is what you want to take place. Then you give feedback to the kids and they make the adjustments. This is much better than telling them "Do this! Do that!" We told the student what on-task behaviors we observed. We gave them statistics: How many and specific on-task behaviors, also specific behaviors for helping each other. We told them how many times specific behaviors occurred in their group. The kids talked about the statistics and discussed what they needed to do next time. The next lesson we began by looking back at what they said they'd do better.

Teacher empowerment and efficacy

Our question was "What happens to participants as they conduct action research studies?" We considered four prototypical action researchers: Jill, a second-year teacher; Sue and Connie, who are very knowledgeable about reading/writing strategies; and Jan, a master teacher who has strong beliefs and knowledge about reading/writing strategies and cooperative learning strategies.

We concluded that *the impact of the experience was related to the different stage at which they were functioning concerning their knowledge and beliefs about the use of reading and writing strategies.* Teachers focusing on how to use specific strategies, like Jill, moved beyond mechanical lesson planning to begin thinking about how to improve student learning to a greater extent, at least during the time the project was being conducted. Often, insights gained about the routines they used in teaching were then incorporated into their teaching repertoire.

Participants like Sue and Connie integrated reading/writing strategies into their teaching routines and had concerns about how to use them. They became more systematic as they teamed in the action research process. Some,

like Connie, focused on coupling another innovation with reading/writing strategies to increase the impact on student learning.

Finally, some small percentage of teachers are like Jan. She has developed a high level of knowledge and beliefs about reading/writing strategies *and* has integrated these strategies with another compatible innovation, cooperative learning. She has thought through and implemented the two innovations as an integrated whole. Further, participating in the action research program aided her as she functioned as a lead teacher, helping other teachers acquire skills in using reading/writing and cooperative learning strategies. The closeness and enthusiasm she developed in the action research project with Mary was infectious. Other teachers wanted to collaborate with Jan in incorporating reading/writing and cooperative learning strategies.

The professional growth themes which emerged from talking with the participants in action research programs relate to issues of teacher efficacy. Ashton and Webb (1986) defined "teacher efficacy" as the teachers' perceptions of their own ability to influence student learning. Ashton and Webb consider teaching efficacy as a primary predictor of teacher behavior and a good indicator of the extent teachers will adopt innovations into their teaching.

Research in teaching efficacy suggests that teachers are more likely to adopt new classroom strategies if they have confidence in their own ability to control their classrooms and affect student learning (Barfield & Burlingame, 1974; Smylie, 1988). A great deal of evidence exists that teachers often behave differently in classes composed primarily of low-achieving students than in classes comprising primarily high-achieving students, and that teachers of low achievers are less likely to incorporate innovations into their teaching repertoire (Brophy & Good, 1974; Cooper, 1974).

We identified and then formulated the following statements of essential themes of professional growth which signal a paradigm shift for many classroom educators:

Involvement in teaching: I am involved in problem solving in my instructional process.

Collegiality: I am not alone. I have options and resources which are immediately available and accessible on which I can draw.

Focused, data based feedback: I have concrete, respectable evidence that I can use in deciding to make changes.

Conclusions

Bandura (1977) contended that an individual's sense of self-efficacy is derived from perceptions of both performance accomplished and social persuasion, especially as it is reinforced by organizational activities and conditions which promote individual success. Our action research staff development process created involvement in teaching by engaging teachers in joint problem solving and created a sense of collegiality by implementing instructional teaming.

The teachers emphasized "involvement" and "problem solving," themes related to ownership and its flip side, accountability. The systematic data collection led to focused, data-based feedback which gave the teachers impetus to change teaching routines that were often used, little thought through, and often ineffective. Analyzing the data collected in their classrooms in the action research process also reinforced their perceptions of task accomplishment, an important part of perceiving oneself as able to influence the learning of low-achieving children.

Thus, action research is an important staff development process. By engaging in it, teachers become empowered as they acquire and fine tune their teaching in specific and personal ways. They also integrate other innovations into their use of reading/writing strategies.

Further, the process influences their foci of control as teachers, or their teacher efficacy. They change from "Johnny has a problem. His home life is dysfunctional" to "I know I can find ways to work with Johnny." They change from "I just have to put up with Johnny" to "Johnny is a teaching challenge that I can do something about." They change from continuing to use the same teaching patterns to "Oh, I wasn't aware of that! What can I try which might be effective?"

This kind of paradigm shift is important for all teachers, but especially for those who work with low-achieving or at-risk students in the regular classroom Setting.

References

Ashton, R, & Webb, R. (1986). *Making a difference: Teachers' sense of efficacy and student achievement*. New York: Longman.

Bandura, A. (1977). Self-efficacy toward a unifying theory of behavioral change. *Psychological Review, 84,* 191–215.

Barfield, v., & Burlingame, M. (1974). The pupil control ideology of teachers in selected schools. *Journal of Experimental Education, 42,* 6–11.

Brophy, J., & Good, T. (1974). *Teacher-student relationships; Courses and consequences*. New York: Holt, Rinehart and Winston.

Cooper, H. (1974). Pygmalion grows up: A model for teacher expectation communication and performance influence. *Review of Educational Research, 49,* 389–410.

Goetz, J., & LeCompte, M. (1984). *Ethnography and qualititive design in educational research*. New York: Academic Press.

Gove, M.K., & Roskos, K. (1989). *Action research as a medium for instructional change with at-risk students*. Unpublished study. John Carroll University, University Heights, OH.

Hall, G.E., Loucks, S., Rutherford W.L., & Newlove, B.W. (1975). Levels of use of the innovation: A framework for analyzing innovation adoption. *Journal of Teacher Education, B26,* 5–9.

Johnson, D., & Johnson, R. (1987). *Cooperative learning in the classroom*. New York: Interaction.

Kagan, S. (1990). *Cooperative learning*. San Juan Capistrano, CA: Resources for Teachers.

Little, J. (1982). Norms of collegiality and experimentation: Workplace conditions of school success. *American Educational Research Journal, 19,* 325–340.

Smylie, M. (1988). The enhancement function of staff development: Organizational and psychological antecedents to individual teacher change. *American Educational Research Journal, 25,* 1-30.

Spradley, J. (1979). *The ethnographic interviews*. New York: Holt, Reinhart & Winston.

Vacca, R.T., & Vacca, J. (1989). *Content area reading*. Glenview, IL: HarperCollins.

Vacca, J., Vacca, R.T., & Gove, M.K. (1991). *Reading and learning to read*. New York, NY: HarperCollins.

Unit 6

Unit Selections

Key Points to Consider

❖ What are the guidelines for conducting and reporting research involving human subjects?

❖ Discuss possible benefits and drawbacks of alternative formats for the dissertation.

❖ Explain statistical and practical significance. How should this be reported in a research report when explaining results?

 **Links**   **www.dushkin.com/online/**

These sites are annotated on pages 4 and 5.

After researchers have conducted a study, they are expected to report their findings to the appropriate audience(s). Obviously, this aspect of research is important because it heralds the completion of the study and contributes to the storehouse of knowledge about a topic and a particular question. Reporting research is important so that others can scrutinize the study, see how the findings were obtained, and decide for themselves if the investigation was sufficiently rigorous and the findings credible. Another reason for reporting research is that it stimulates thinking and creates a network of researchers with similar interests who can build upon one another's work, thereby enriching their own. So reporting research is more than the lone researcher announcing to the world, in effect, "There! I've finished!" It is a way of participating more fully in the professional dialogue and of making a difference.

As with any type of writing, it is important when writing the research to understand the audience for whom the report is intended, to report findings accurately, to consider different outlets for the work, and to avoid common pitfalls. The first unit article, by Sonja Brobeck, explains the responsibilities of researchers as they work with their study participants and disseminate their findings with various audiences. Perhaps the type of research report that is most familiar to students in colleges and universities is the thesis or dissertation. Nell Duke and Sarah Beck's article challenges the traditional, highly structured format for the dissertation and argues instead for a wider range of possible responses, particularly those that have applicability beyond fulfilling partial requirements for the doctorate. The next article, by James Shaver, is a two-part treatment of the most prevalent misconceptions about research. Unit 6 concludes with a thought-provoking statement

coauthored by Leland Wilkinson and the Task Force on Statistical Inferences concerning the American Psychological Association's standards for reporting research.

Are You Doing Inquiry Along These Lines?

THE NEED FOR BETTER ETHICAL GUIDELINES FOR CONDUCTING AND REPORTING RESEARCH

SONJA BROBECK, *The Pennsylvania State University*

If all researchers treated their subjects as they would like to be treated, a consideration of ethics would not be necessary; however, "dissimulation, the giving of misleading information. lack of total 'openness,' deceit, and lying are a feature of many different types of social relationships, including social research."[1] People have demonstrated time and again that they will push their research to the limits of the law, and perhaps somewhat further. An extreme example is the experimentation conducted on human beings by the Nazis; a near example is studies done by researchers who ignore their university's human subjects protocol. These examples are related, and the torturous ethical path that winds between them and on into the future needs to be explored.

DEVELOPMENT OF ETHICAL GUIDELINES

At the end of World War II, when it became evident what kinds of activities had been carried out in Nazi Germany, world leaders realized we needed a code of ethics governing the kinds of research that one human being could conduct on another.

From the *Journal of Curriculum and Supervision,* Winter 1990, pp. 194-201. © 1990 by the Association for Supervision and Curriculum Development. Reprinted by permission.

The result was the Nuremberg Code of 1946, which set forth several general principles that later found their way into many modern codes of ethics.[2] The first principle is that no harm must come to the person being experimented on. Sieber uses the term *beneficence* to express this value, meaning that nothing hurtful to the person—physically, mentally, psychologically, emotionally, or socially—can be done.[3] A second principle widely embodied in codes is that a human subject must give informed consent to participating in a study, without coercion, fear, or high-pressure tactics of any kind.[4] This principle implies that a person is free and competent to make his own decisions.

Although researchers of the 1950s and 1960s might argue that they would not do research that harmed other people, their publications indicate otherwise.[5] One example of harmful research done in the 1960s is the work of a psychologist employed by a consulting firm that helped various companies keep out unions. He tested prospective employees under the guise of determining their suitability for employment, but he was actually assessing their attitudes toward unions. The American Psychological Association's Committee on Scientific and Professional Ethics and Conduct later declared his conduct unethical because his study was dishonest and showed a lack of respect for the people tested.[6]

By the early 1970s, the need for federal regulations to ensure the safety and welfare of human subjects became evident. In answer, the Privacy Act of 1974 and various regulations of the Department of Health, Education, and Welfare were enacted.[7] Because some regulations required that any institutions that received money from the Department of Health, Education, and Welfare have provisions in place to protect human subjects, universities established offices for this purpose.[8] Both the federal guidelines and the university regulations contain statements derived from the Nuremberg Code of 1946 on informed consent and freedom from harm.

RESEARCH IN GENERAL TODAY

In the 1980s, researchers routinely seek the approval of their offices to protect human subjects before beginning a study. They are finding, however, that other questions need to be answered and further guidelines established because of additional areas of potential harm and increased acceptance of cost-benefit ratios.[9]

One frequently asked question is the researcher's qualifications to do the study. Because of the risk, however slight, to the subject, an unqualified person cannot ethically "play around" trying to discover something of note. The question of how well a study is designed arises. A poorly designed study places subjects at risk, with little or no promise of benefits.[10]

Another question that needs to be addressed concerns costs and benefits, or the "justice" of research[11]—will society share the benefits of this research, or does it benefit only select groups of people? Hartley suggests doing extremely costly research may be unethical because the money might be better spent in ameliorating some of society's woes.[12]

We also need to ask about the groups under study. Is it ethical to overresearch some groups, such as undergraduates, while neglecting other groups, such as women? Are undergraduates really giving informed consent, or do they feel pressure, however subtle, to agree to participate in an instructor's study? Because undergraduates often make up convenient samples, is research involving them generalizable enough, even to other undergraduates, to be worth doing?[13] Some authors suggest that only adults from the upper levels of society should be asked to participate in research because they are the most autonomous population.

The question of whether it is ethical to reanalyze someone else's data is also open to debate. If the confidentiality of the data and the privacy of the persons are maintained, the second researcher has no way of identifying the participants or getting their consent. Analyzing from existing records tends to destroy the public trust.[14]

The question of how one researcher's work affects the studies of others needs to be considered. If a researcher violates ethical standards in such a way that further research in the area is prohibited, potential benefits to society may be sacrificed.[15]

The question of how the data is collected has many ethical ramifications. Some researchers believe that covert research is an important tool, because some information can be gotten in no other way.[16] Others believe that covert observation should be reserved for investigating criminal acts. Even those who think covert observation is acceptable disagree as to whether the observation should be done surreptitiously or whether the researcher should act as a participant-observer. Bulmer suggests, "The use of covert participant observation as a method of research is neither ethically justified nor practically necessary."[17]

QUALITATIVE RESEARCH TODAY

The path to ethical research becomes even more difficult to follow when exploring the area of qualitative research, important because it allows the researcher to see deeper, notice more, and make meaningful observations.[18] Opinions vary widely on appropriate approaches to take, as well as the methods to use. Frequently, researchers do not realize what techniques they are using in making their descriptions.[19] Even the requirements for conducting a study are seen from a different perspective.

Flinders suggests that confidentiality, as well as freedom from harm and informed consent, is a critical attribute of an ethical study.[20] This criterion may be difficult to meet, especially since Flinders argues that pseudonyms do not guarantee confidentiality.[21]

In the area of qualitative research, Wax and Glazer believe that reciprocity should be established rather than informed consent obtained.[22] Glazer defines reciprocity as the "careful formulation of agreements, the willingness to exchange goods and favors for information, the understanding that they may both assist us and attempt to use us for their own gains."[23] According to Wax and Glazer, reciprocity is more important than consent because most subjects do not really understand what they are getting themselves into by consenting to participate in a study.

How a study is reported becomes another ethical issue. Perhaps the researcher thinks that it would be advantageous to give an institution one report and the subjects involved another report, and to publish still a third report. Thornton suggests that this practice violates ethics.[24]

Barone offers certain guidelines for conducting qualitative research.[25] For example, researchers cannot use composite characters or events, the study must be told in the first person, and the thesis must be allowed to be revised "in the field" as needed.

Since some researchers believe the goal of qualitative research is "to give the richest, fullest, most comprehensive description possible," without judging or evaluating, rather than to give pages of statistics, great care must be taken to ensure an ethical description.[26] Qualitative research can be impressionistic, with little evidence of validity, and an interpretation depends as much on the point of view as the view.[27] Therefore, we must take special care in reporting results in the form of a description, keeping in mind that no two people see an event in the same way or describe it in the same terms.[28] What is significant depends on the theories, models, and values of the researcher.[29]

Other authors disagree and suggest that researchers must not be totally impartial in their descriptions, but can evaluate, criticize, appreciate, and perhaps even attempt to persuade the reader.[30] Eisner explains the difference between criticism and appreciation: "Connoisseurship is the art of appreciation; criticism is the art of disclosure.[31] Researchers' problem, then, is reconciling the goal of establishing rapport with the subjects so that they permit access to situations researchers are anxious to study and the goal of publishing results that may cause the subjects emotional distress or professional harm. Sieber sees the conflicting goals of privacy for the individual and of science's desire to know at the root of many ethical dilemmas.[32]

Some authors have suggested that studies in which subjects have shared their most private thoughts and feelings should not be published at all; it is enough that the researcher has learned. Some authors who have been privy to such information may publish it anyway, perhaps hoping that their disguise of the subjects has been good enough or that the subjects will never see a copy of the published article and so will not suffer emotional distress. Careful consideration should suggest that this "solution" to the problem of maintaining confidentiality is self-deluding at best and unethical at worst.

We must formulate answers to these questions, but to whose satisfaction? Several professional organizations have established codes of ethics for their members.[33] According to Douglas, however, "professional ethics are generally a deceit and a snare"; he believes that "it would be an irrational act of panic, possibly a form of scientific suicide, to impose professional ethics on ourselves."[34] Sieber states that "good moral intentions and adherence to a professional code of ethics are inadequate to prevent ethical dilemmas in organizational research."[35] All the pertinent questions do not yet have good answers.

SUGGESTIONS FOR NEEDED GUIDELINES

I offer here some possible answers, solutions, or guidelines. Perhaps the suggestions are best divided into two parts—those that can be legislated and those that cannot.

We could pass a law requiring that all subjects who participated in a study sign the final report before publication. A regulation could prohibit the more dominant groups from studying the less dominant groups, if these groups could be defined sufficiently well. The results of studies could also be disseminated more widely so that more people were aware of how research was done, and thus, their own consent to participate in a study would be more informed. This last suggestion could mean passing a law to require that each research institution publish an attractive, easily read bulletin of research currently being conducted.

Other suggestions, however, can not be legislated. The need to develop sensitivity,

caring, and the determination not to harm others must be emphasized to researchers. They must be educated to treat their subjects as they would be treated. Researchers need to realize that the rights of the individual are more important than science and that some research just cannot be done.[36] Qualitative researchers especially must learn to provide "sharp, accurate, *loving* descriptions, more in the line of connoisseurship than criticism."[37]

Flinders disagrees with some of these suggestions: "Ethical demands . . . move beyond academic and custodial concerns. These demands are not governed or defined by rules."[38] Rather, he suggests, the key to the ethical demands of research is flexibility and a case-by-case approach to decision making.

The need exists to know, and ethical research permits us to know, without harm to our subjects and, we hope, with benefits to society. The need also exists for clearer guidelines for doing research, especially qualitative research. If you are in the process of establishing such guidelines or know of existing ones, or have advice to offer, I would be grateful for the opportunity to learn of these and to share them with other researchers.

Notes

1. Martin Bulmer, "Ethical Problems in Social Research: The Case of Covert Participant Observation," in *Social Research Ethics,* ed. Martin Bulmer (London: Macmillan, 1982), p. 5.
2. Paul D. Reynolds, *Ethical Dilemmas and Social Science Research* (San Francisco: Jossey-Bass, 1979), pp. 234–246.
3. Joan E. Sieber, "Ethical Dilemmas in Social Research," in *The Ethics of Social Research: Surveys and Experiments,* ed. Joan E. Sieber (New York: Springer-Verlag, 1982), p. 14.
4. Paul D. Reynolds, *Ethical Dilemmas and Social Science Research* (San Francisco: Jossey-Bass, 1979), p. 110.
5. Martin Bulmer, "Ethical Problems in Social Research: The Case of Covert Participant Observation," in *Social Research Ethics,* ed. Martin Bulmer (London: Macmillan, 1982), pp. 5–8.
6. American Psychological Association, *Casebook on Ethical Standards of Psychologists* (Washington, DC: APA, 1967), pp. 1–2.
7. Paul D. Reynolds, *Ethical Dilemmas and Social Science Research* (San Francisco: Jossey-Bass, 1979), pp. 247–278.
8. Ibid., p. 251.
9. Ibid., pp. 101–102.
10. Joan E. Sieber, "Experimental Social Research and Respect for the Individual," in *The Ethics of Social Research: Surveys and Experiments,* ed. Joan E. Sieber (New York: Springer-Verlag, 1982), pp. 31–38.
11. Joan E. Sieber, "Ethical Dilemmas in Social Research," in *The Ethics of Social Research: Surveys and Experiments,* ed. Joan E. Sieber (New York: Springer-Verlag, 1982), p. 14.
12. Shirley F. Hartley, "Sampling Strategies and the Threat to Privacy," in *The Ethics of Social Research: Surveys and Experiments,* ed. Joan E. Sieber (New York: Springer-Verlag, 1982), pp. 167–189.
13. Ibid., p. 173.
14. Paul D. Reynolds, *Ethical Dilemmas and Social Science Research* (San Francisco: Jossey-Bass, 1979), pp. 214–218.
15. Ibid., p. 175.
16. Martin Bulmer, "Ethical Problems in Social Research: The Case of Covert Participant Observation," in *Social Research Ethics,* ed. Martin Bulmer (London: Macmillan, 1982), p. 10.
17. Ibid., p. 217.
18. Stephen J. Thornton, "Different Evidence for Different Audiences" (paper presented at the annual meeting of the American Educational Research Association, Washington, DC, April 1987).
19. Elizabeth Vallance, "The Landscape of 'The Great Plains Experiment,'" *Curriculum Inquiry* 7 (February 1977): 87–105.
20. David J. Flinders, "Being an Ethical Critic: A Practical Perspective" (paper presented at the annual meeting of the American Educational Research Association, San Francisco, April 1986).
21. Ibid., p. 8.
22. Murray Wax (1982) and Myron Glazer (1982), cited in David J. Flinders, "Being an Ethical Critic: A Practical Perspective" (paper presented at the annual meeting of the American Educational Research Association, San Francisco, April 1986), p. 4.
23. Myron Glazer (1982), cited in David J. Flinders, "Being an Ethical Critic: A Practical Perspective" (paper presented at the annual meeting of the American Educational Research Association, San Francisco, April 1986), p. 4.
24. Stephen J. Thornton, "Different Evidence for Different Audiences" (paper presented at the annual meeting of the American Educational Research Association, Washington, DC, April 1987).
25. Thomas E. Barone, "Research out of the Shadows: A Reply to Rist," *Curriculum Inquiry* 17 (April 1987): 453–463.
26. Vincent Rogers, "Qualitative and Aesthetic Views of Curriculum and Curriculum Making," in *Current Thought on Curriculum,* ed. Alex Molnar (Alexandria, VA: Association for Supervision and Curriculum Development), pp. 103–118.
27. Roy C. Risk, "Research in the Shadows: A Critique of an Equality Visibility and the Fine Distinction between Economic Segments," April 1987, 447–451.
28. Rene S. Harris, "Uncovering the Hidden Dimensions of Meaning in Descriptions of Educational Practice" (paper presented at the annual meeting of the American Educational Research Association, New York, March 1982).
29. Stephen J. Thornton, "Different Evidence for Different Audiences" (paper presented at the annual meeting of the American Educational Research Association, Washington, DC, April 1987).

30. Mark St. John, "Criticism and Its Use in Evaluation," *Guide Number 18, Evaluation Guide Series* (Portland, OR: Northwest Regional Educational Laboratory, 1985); Thomas E. Barone, "Research out of the Shadows: A Reply to Rist," *Curriculum Inquiry 17* (April 1987): 453–463.

31. Eliot Eisner, cited in Mark St. John, "Criticism and Its Use in Evaluation," *Guide Number 18, Evaluation Guide Series* (Portland, OR: Northwest Regional Educational Laboratory, 1985).

32. Joan E. Sieber, "Ethical Dilemmas in Social Research," in *The Ethics of Social Research: Surveys and Experiments,* ed. Joan E. Sieber (New York: Springer-Verlag, 1982), p. 4. For further information, see *The Ethics of Social Research: Fieldwork, Regulation, and Publication,* ed. Joan E. Sieber (New York: Springer-Verlag, 1982).

33. Martin Bulmer, "The Merits and Demerits of Covert Participant Observation," in *Social Research Ethics,* ed. Martin Bulmer (London: Macmillan, 1982), p. 247.

34. Jack Douglas, cited in Martin Bulmer, "The Merits and Demerits of Covert Participant Observation," in *Social Research Ethics,* ed. Martin Bulmer (London: Macmillan, 1982), p. 217.

35. Joan E. Sieber, "Experimental Social Research and Respect for the Individual," in *The Ethics of Social Research: Surveys and Experiments,* ed. Joan E. Sieber (New York: Springer-Verlag, 1982), p. 36.

36. Martin Bulmer, "The Merits and Demerits of Covert Participant Observation," in *Social Research Ethics,* ed. Martin Bulmer (London: Macmillan, 1982), p. 250.

37. Mark St. John, "Criticism and Its Use in Evaluation," *Guide Number 18, Evaluation Guide Series* (Portland, OR: Northwest Regional Educational Laboratory, 1985).

38. David J. Flinders, "Being an Ethical Critic: A Practical Perspective" (paper presented at the annual meeting of the American Educational Research Association, San Francisco, April 1986), p. 6.

SONJA BROBECK is a doctoral student in Curriculum and Instruction, College of Education, The Pennsylvania State University, University Park, PA 16802.

Education Should Consider Alternative Formats for the Dissertation

NELL K. DUKE   SARAH W. BECK

The dissertation is an enduring part of American doctoral training. The first doctorates awarded on American soil required a dissertation, and to our knowledge, so has every 'earned' doctorate awarded here since. The number of doctorates awarded, and thus the number of dissertations written each year, has grown steadily in the past several decades. Between 1960 and 1989, the number of doctoral degrees granted soared from 9,733 to 33,456 (Ziolkowski, 1990). In the 1994–1995 academic year—the most recent year for which we could obtain statistics—a total of 44,446 doctoral degrees were awarded and doctoral dissertations written (National Center for Education Statistics, 1997). And as more students are writing dissertations, more is being written about the writing of dissertations. Following this upward trend in the granting of doctoral degrees, a new niche has opened in educational publishing: the manual for writing the dissertation. Numerous manuals of this kind have been published, as a growing number of students struggle with the dissertation process and form.

The Ph.D. degree and its dissertation were imported from Germany in the mid-19th century to provide students with training in scientific methodology. Since that time, the prevailing view of the dissertation has alternated between that of the dissertation as a "training instrument" and that of the dissertation as an "original and significant contribution to knowledge" (Berelson, 1960, p. 173). Presently, the con-

sensus seems to be that the dissertation should be both of these things. In this commentary, we argue that in the field of education, the dissertation in its traditional format does not adequately serve either purpose. By "traditional format," we mean a lengthy document (typically 200–400 pages in length) on a single topic presented through separate chapters for the introduction, literature review, methodology, results, and conclusions (e.g., Mauch & Birch, 1989). We propose that the dissertation in this format is ill-suited to the task of training doctoral students in the communicative aspects of educational research, and is largely ineffectual as a means of contributing knowledge to the field.

Given the proliferation of doctoral dissertations in this country in the last several decades, and given the significant amount of time and effort that doctoral students invest in the process of designing, researching, and writing a dissertation, it is worth examining why, how, and for whom dissertations are written. We begin by examining the dissertation through the lens of genre theory, as this theory helps to elucidate what makes the dissertation both so powerful and so problematic. We briefly discuss some of the perceived advantages to the traditional dissertation format, and then discuss ways in which different fields have considered and reconsidered dissertation formats appropriate to their discipline. Finally, we argue for the acceptance of a range of alternatives to the dissertation format that currently prevails as the standard

in the field of education, and describe some alternative formats that we believe are especially promising.

The Dissertation Is a Genre

The traditional dissertation meets both classical and modern definitions of genre. In the classical sense (e.g., Aristotle, 1991), it is recognizable as a genre in terms of both *form* and *content*. The form is highly conventionalized, "a unified work with a single theme, including an introduction and literature review, a description of methods and procedures used, a presentation of results, and a concluding discussion of the meaning of the results" (Council of Graduate Schools, 1991, p. 12); and the content is restricted to an account of original research. Also following classical definitions of genre, the dissertation is written with a particular goal (or *telos*) in mind, and for a particular audience. The goal of the dissertation is to meet the requirements for receiving a doctoral degree, proving that one has mastered the skills necessary to succeed in one's chosen scholarly field while at the same time making an original contribution to that field. The audience of the traditional dissertation consists of the members of the doctoral student's committee, and perhaps the few friends, family members, and colleagues who can be persuaded to read it.

Using more modern definitions as a guide, the dissertation still constitutes a

From *Educational Researcher,* Vol. 28, No. 3, April 1999, pp. 31-36. © 1999 by the American Educational Research Association. Reprinted by permission of the publisher.

genre. According to Todorov (1976) genre is a "codification of discourse properties" (p. 162), which provides both "horizons of expectation" for readers and "models of writing" for' authors (p. 163). No one will dispute that the dissertation does both of these things: When the proposal or the dissertation does not meet the "expectations" of the readers, it is sent with readers' comments back to the author, who then revises it to fit the "model" of an acceptable dissertation. The dissertation also meets views of genre as *social action* (Miller, 1994; see also Bazerman, 1994). It is written with a clear motive—receipt of a doctorate—in a specific *rhetorical situation* in which the dissertation committee represents doctored professionals in the field, guiding and evaluating the writer's work with their standards for acceptable doctoral-level research. Another contemporary view of genre emphasizes the author's response to contextual demands (Campbell & Jamieson, 1978). This view of genre is especially appropriate for the dissertation in that it accounts for the forms within the form of the dissertation—that is, it recognizes the literature review, the research design, and so on as sub-genres, or even as genres in themselves. Here again, the dissertation meets a modern definition of genre.

But the Dissertation Is a Strange Genre

Although the dissertation is a genre, it is a strange—and, we will argue, problematic—genre in the following respects:

Limited Audience and Dissemination

The audience of the dissertation is unusual. Theoretically, the dissertation is a public document, usually available from a University library to anyone who requests it. But in fact, the readership of this "public" document is small in number and intimate in character. In most cases, the only readers of a dissertation are the three or four members of the writer's committee. Only in rare cases is a dissertation ordered from library archives for additional, albeit still limited, readership (Reid, 1978). Even if technological advances in the future facilitate more rapid retrieval of dissertations, there is no guarantee that the documents will have a significantly larger audience. However physically accessible dissertations become, the length and style associated with the traditional dissertation format make them impractical for many audiences. This is especially problematic for dissertations that are directly relevant to practitioners, whose jobs as teachers, counselors, and principals typically leave little time to seek out or read documents of this length and style.

Referring back to Aristotle's (1991) and others' inclusion of audience as a key element in the rhetorical situation that defines a genre, we must ask ourselves if the members of the doctoral student's committee are truly the only ones by whom the dissertation should be read, or for whom the dissertation should be written. Furthermore, the dissertation's limited audience makes its status as a piece of research as questionable as its status as a genre. As Halstead (1988) argues, "a piece of research is not recognized as having been completed until it is communicated, and others know about it and have enough information to enable them to test its authenticity" (p. 497). A more authentic rhetorical situation for the doctoral dissertation would allow it to be read and evaluated by a wider audience than its current limited distribution permits.

In order for dissertation material to be received by a wider audience, it must be reworked and altered from its original dissertation form. In education, this typically means either rewriting the dissertation as a book or, more commonly, rewriting the dissertation into an article or series of articles for a journal. W. Malcolm Reid (1978), in reference to the field of biology, captures the irony of this rewriting process nicely:

> Logistics of the final push toward assembling and getting approval of the traditional dissertation are wrong from the standpoint of revision for publication. The student is ending "a stylized charade in which the victim is encouraged to produce a 200-page tome, only to be told after its approval that *now* he's to operate on his teratoma for publication" (Chernin, 1975). Faced with a move to a new location and new work responsibilities, publication gets postponed for weeks, months, or indefinitely. (p. 652)

Indeed, many dissertations in our field, as in others, are never published, in the sense of being distributed widely in a public forum. We do not have current statistics as to the number for which this is the case, but as of 1973 from one quarter to one half of dissertations across fields never resulted in a published paper. In psychology, at the time, this was true of 51% of all dissertations (Boyer, 1973 cited in Reid, 1978). Moreover, as Krathwohl (1994) notes, the process of re-crafting the dissertation into publishable form(s) prevents new scholars from moving onto fresh projects and exploring the exciting possibilities afforded by their new status as doctored professionals. Not only does the traditional dissertation format have an unacceptably limited readership, but it also presents barriers to

widening that readership through publication.

Lack of Generalizability

The dissertation is also an unusual genre in its lack of generalizability for the writer. That is, except for the very rare case of someone who has multiple doctorates, one writes (at most) *one* dissertation in one's life. This is not the case with nearly all other genres we could name—letters, lists, editorials, academic papers, personal phone books, and so on. If we have written or will ever write a letter, we will probably have written and will write many; if we have written or will ever write an academic paper, chances are we have written or will write many of them. It is difficult to identify any other genre that we are likely to produce only one of in our lives. In fact, dissertation handbooks and guides (e.g., Fitzpatrick, Secrist, & Wright, 1998; Ogden, 1993) make a point of emphasizing how the dissertation is unlike every other type of writing a graduate student has done previously. Perhaps the last will and testament is similarly limited: If someone writes a last will and testament, she will probably write only one. But even then she is likely to revisit and revise the document over time, which we cannot say of the dissertation. The baby book is another possible exception—parents with only one child might produce only one baby book in their lives, but even the most enthusiastic parent won't spend nearly as much time on the baby book as a graduate student will spend on the dissertation!

With an ungeneralizable genre comes a missed opportunity for transfer of knowledge and skills that will actually be of benefit to students in the long term. Indeed, for some time, many scholars (particularly those in the sciences) have argued that the dissertation provides poor training for future academic writing (Halstead, 1988; Reid, 1978). Speaking about education, David Krathwohl (1994) agrees, and points out that students are forced to write in this very ungeneralizable genre at precisely the time when they are in the best position to receive mentorship on writing more generalizable genres, such as the journal article and proposal for funding. He explains,

> The typical four- or five-chapter dissertation structure trains students in a writing structure they will probably never again use. Equally importantly, it wastes the opportunity for students to learn writing for publication under faculty tutelage. Given the usual individual dissertation supervision, faculty are in a far better position to pass on this capacity to their students than at any other time in the graduate experience. (pp. 30–31)

Even compared to writing a book or monograph, dissertation writing is not easily generalizable. Any student who has tried to convert a dissertation into a book, or any editor of academic books who has overseen this process, would agree. For even in those relatively rare cases in which the topic of a dissertation makes it appropriate for a book rather than a journal article or series of articles, major revisions are necessary in order to turn a traditional dissertation in education into an academic book in this field. If the aim of the work is to produce a book, would it not make more sense to write the dissertation as a book proposal or manuscript in the first place?

Other Fields Have Considered Alternative Formats for the Dissertation

The field of education appears to be lagging behind other academic fields in exploring alternative formats for the dissertation. In the fields of English literature and writing, for example, the novel has become an acceptable format for the doctoral dissertation in some departments, with the stipulation that the writer submit along with his or her novel a critical introduction or appendix, as proof that he or she has conducted substantial critical and historical research as part of the process of writing—or preparing to write—the novel (Sheppard & Hartman, 1989). In at least one case that we know of, a novel was accepted as a doctoral dissertation in education at Hofstra University (Gough, in Saks, 1996). Recently, graduate students in fields as diverse as speech communication and classical archaeology have taken advantage of the affordances of computer technology by submitting their dissertations in CD-ROM format, the interactive nature of which gives readers a better appreciation of visual data such as videos of people talking and 3-D models of Celtic tombs (Mangan, 1996).

Although experimentation with alternative formats is a relatively recent phenomenon in the humanities and social sciences, the so-called 'hard' sciences have been accepting alternatives to the traditional Germanic dissertation format for decades, usually in the form of a collection of articles that have already been accepted for publication in refereed journals (Monaghan, 1989). In the 1970s a movement began among members of the scientific community to transform this tacitly condoned alternative into a requirement, and the campaign to "stop the dissertation" gathered a following on many campuses (Williams, 1971, cited in Reid, 1978). In this case, the criticism of the traditional format was based largely on the belief that writing a dissertation in the traditional style does not cultivate the writing skills necessary to succeed in the "real world" of scientific research. Strong evidence to support this argument lay in the sad fact that not a single published article had emerged from some of the best dissertations in the sciences (Reid, 1978). Even in cases in which the doctoral recipient's work was eventually published, communication of important scientific findings was often delayed because the author had to take additional time after completing the dissertation to convert the work into a publishable form. The alternative format of multiple journal articles is now used regularly by degree candidates in chemistry, geology, and physics, and to a lesser extent in departments of biology and related fields.

So the format of the dissertation, once identical for all disciplines, now varies depending on the field—and the audience—for which it is produced. The Council of Graduate Schools, in the seminal 1991 report "The Role and Nature of the Doctoral Dissertation" acknowledged this trend and supported its continuance, concluding that

> [g]raduate schools would be wise to honor the disciplinary differences . . . even to encourage them. Departments are well advised to review periodically the expectations of their discipline, the mission of graduate education, and how the dissertation serves that mission. Dissertation research should provide students with hands-on, directed experience in the primary research methods of the discipline. The dissertation should prepare students for the type of research/scholarship that will be expected of them after they receive the Ph.D. degree. (Council of Graduate Schools, 1991, p. 15)

As of this 1991 report, 9 out of 48 graduate schools surveyed—or 19%—had officially approved other options for the dissertation, allowing their departments freedom to accept alternative formats. Anecdotal reports suggest that individual departments at other graduate schools accept non-traditional dissertation formats without official sanction at the institutional level. Clearly, the appropriateness and effectiveness of the traditional dissertation format has already been called into question in a number of institutions and disciplines.

So What's a Doctoral Candidate in Education to Do?

Some individuals in the field of education have given serious thought to the problems posed by the traditional dissertation format, and how they might be addressed. The topic of the novel as a dissertation in education has been raised at AERA in recent years. In a 1996 panel, reported in *Research in the Teaching of English* (Saks, 1996), Howard Gardner argued against the acceptance of the novel as a dissertation in education, in part on the grounds that writing a novel would not provide an educational researcher with the experience of mastering education as a discipline, such that one would then be able to pass one's knowledge of the discipline on to other researchers and practitioners. But if a traditional dissertation format is not sufficiently useful for our field, and a novel is not an appropriate form either, what is a doctoral candidate in education to do?

Our answer to this question, as you might well guess, is that doctoral candidates, and departments of education that serve them, should consider other alternative formats for the dissertation. We will offer a few possible alternative formats in the paragraphs that follow, and hope that members of the field will go on to raise others. Based on our analysis of the dissertation as a genre, we recommend that those evaluating possible alternative formats for the dissertation attend to the following two questions about the dissertation, in addition to those they would traditionally ask:

- Will the format of this dissertation make it possible to disseminate the work to a wide audience?
- Will writing a dissertation in this format help prepare candidates for the type of writing they will be expected to do throughout their career?

One alternative format that would meet these criteria for many doctoral candidates was suggested by David Krathwohl in his 1994 article, "A Slice of Advice," in *Educational Researcher*. Krathwohl proposes that graduate students " . . . write the dissertation as an article (or series or set of such articles) ready for publication, [using] appendices for any additional information the committee may desire for pedagogical and examination purposes" (p. 31). While Krathwohl does not go into depth about what this might look like, as we envision it, each "chapter" of the dissertation would have its own abstract, introduction, literature review, research question(s), methodology, results, and conclusions—it would be a self-contained research article manuscript ready to be submitted for publication. As Krathwohl suggests, appendices could be used for any material that does not fit into the papers but is desired by the committee. An introductory chapter written specifically for the dissertation could be used to document the overall research program from which the enclosed papers arose.

If a doctoral student were given the option of writing the dissertation as a series of articles ready to be submitted for publication, it would address the problem of the limited readership of the traditional dissertation. From the outset the student would be writing the dissertation not solely for a small and familiar committee, but for a wider audience of professionals in the field, the same audience for whom he or she would be expected to write throughout his or her career. This would give the dissertation status as an authentic piece of research, in the sense that Halstead (1988) defines it, and would increase the potential of the dissertation to have a real impact on research and practice. Further, to the extent that the candidate would be expected to write research articles for publication throughout his or her career, writing the dissertation would support the development of a generalizable skill under the kind of close mentorship largely unique to doctoral training. Finally, writing the dissertation this way could improve the young researcher's mastery of education as a discipline in the sense that Gardner (in Saks, 1996) describes it. A doctoral recipient who has had the experience of writing multiple articles under the guidance and scrutiny of a dissertation committee will be in a much better position to train others in this skill than one who has only written a single, weighty tome now gathering dust in the archives of the library at the institution that granted his or her degree.

Notably, Krathwohl's suggestion can be extended to offer a range of alternative formats for the dissertation. In the version described above, the dissertation is a collection of articles ready to be submitted to research journals in the field. But in another version, the dissertation could be a collection of articles targeted at more practitioner-oriented publications. In yet another version, the dissertation could be a collection of policy memos intended for school districts, foundations, government agencies, and the like. Each of these offers the potential for wide readership, and all of these are potentially genres in which candidates would be expected to write throughout their career, depending on their career path. In essence, any genre that is authentic to the field could become all or part of an alternative format.

In another possible dissertation format, the dissertation could be comprised of a variety of different professional genres. For example, a dissertation could consist of one article targeted to researchers and a companion article aimed largely at practitioners, or one article for a journal in the candidate's narrow field of study and another for a journal in the candidate's broader field of study. In this format, the dissertation could offer a formal mechanism whereby students receive guided practice writing for different kinds of audiences. This offers important preparation for the nature of the field of education, in which

we are expected to be able communicate effectively with a variety of audiences (and are often, as a field, criticized for failing to do so).

Opening up the dissertation to a range of professional genres, and thus formats, offers an opportunity for individual students, committees, programs, and departments to think through their goals and mission. Individual students and committees could have fruitful discussions about what kinds of articles would best suit their research project and their particular professional development needs. Programs and departments could consider whether different kinds of degrees and programs could call for different kinds of writing skills, and thus different dissertation formats, and what kinds of writing skills are common to all career paths and programs.

Another advantage of some or all of the alternative formats we have described is that they encourage doctoral candidates to take different angles on their data. This is excellent preparation for an academic world in which scholars present and / or publish several different papers stemming from a single study. Different articles could focus on data gathered by different methodological approaches, on data that address different questions, and so on. For example, the first author of this paper has recently completed a dissertation about classroom environmental print, print resources, and print experiences offered to students in 20 first grade classrooms in two distinct socioeconomic settings. Based on this project, she wrote two different articles for the dissertation, each immediately ready to be submitted for publication in research journals. One concerns the scarcity of informational texts found across the first grade classrooms; another examines differences in the print environments and experiences offered to students in the low—as compared to the high—socioeconomic status classrooms. Although both articles stem from the same research project, they use different subsets of data, require different analytic techniques, and lead to different conclusions. While there is some overlap, as there is for any series of papers emanating from a single program of research, it is clear that these articles were best written as separate pieces. Were she to have written a traditional dissertation based on her research project, she would have had to contrive a way to write them with one literature review ("Chapter 2"), one methodology section ("Chapter 3"), and so on. The simple description of the papers above demonstrates how difficult and ultimately unproductive this would be.

A Note of Caution . . .

In adopting alternative formats for the dissertation in education, it is important that we not overlook the strengths of the tradi-

tional dissertation format. Indeed, the dissertation in its current form would not have endured as long as it has if there were not a certain amount of consensus about the value of this form and the advantages it holds for doctoral students and the community of scholars who grant doctoral degrees. For example, it has been noted that the process of writing a dissertation provides a central focus for all Ph.D. programs, and a shared experience for everyone who has achieved an academic doctorate (Isaac, Quinlan, & Walker, 1992). In accepting an alternative format for the dissertation in education, we would not want to threaten this shared experience. Departments should take care to emphasize training in processes, such as gathering and analyzing data, that are common across different dissertation formats.

Another strength of the traditional dissertation format is that it provides an explicit template for the writer to follow—in the words of Todorov, an explicit "model of writing" (1976, p. 163). Fitzpatrick et al. (1998) attempt to quell the anxieties of doctoral students in the dissertation stage with this advice: "[S]ome aspects of dissertations are rote and quite academic. . . . It doesn't take rewriting the English language to follow this type of format" (p. 8). We must be certain that whatever alternative format students choose for their dissertation, they have plenty of models to follow. This requirement should not be difficult to meet as long as the chosen alternative format meets the criterion of generalizability discussed earlier. If the format is one that is widely used in the author's field, and not just invented for the purpose of doctoral training, then the dissertation writer should have no trouble locating models, whether in research journals, among documents published by school districts, in published books, or elsewhere.

Furthermore, we should not lose sight of the fact that the traditional dissertation provides training in developing a substantial, coherent research plan through a single research study. This is an important element of dissertation training that should not be lost in adopting alternative dissertation formats. For that reason we advocate a requirement that all articles in an alternative format dissertation stem from and relate to the same study. Like Ziolkowski (1990), we are not advocating the practice endorsed in some departments in the sciences in which students are allowed to submit unrelated published articles in lieu of a traditional dissertation. Such a practice does not require the substantial, coherent research plan that educational researchers should learn to carry out as part of their training.

It is important to note that the dissertation as it is traditionally written is independent from publishing bodies, at least in the stages of data collection, analysis, and presentation of results. Decisions about acceptance of the dissertation in education are traditionally made by a student's dissertation committee, and not by outside organizations. We believe that this strength of the traditional dissertation format should also be preserved. Thus we would not advocate a model in which already-published articles are required for the dissertation, as is sometimes the case in the hard sciences. That model is problematic for two reasons. First, the publication process in education is typically quite lengthy. It is not at all unusual to wait more than 6 months for reviews of an article submitted for publication, and then to wait again when revisions of the article are submitted— revisions which themselves take time to write. And when the article is finally ready to go to press, there may be another wait, often of six months or longer if the article is to be part of a themed issue. To have dissertation approval on hold pending this process would be impractical and difficult for the student and would place substantial pressure on journal editors and others involved in the process.

A second reason we advocate a dissertation consisting of papers *ready* to be submitted for publication has to do with the content, rather than the process, of journal review. That is, there could be biases in the journal review process that prevent the publication of work that is nonetheless worthy of a doctorate. For example, there is a well-known publication bias against studies in which the null hypothesis, in effect, held true (e.g., Begg, 1994). We would not want someone to be denied a doctorate because they conducted a well-designed study that found, for example, that a particular intervention did not have a statistically significant effect. Similarly, we could envision scenarios in which an article might be ahead of its time, difficult to publish at present but publishable sometime in the future. Having a dissertation composed of articles ready to be submitted for publication lessens these potential problems.

A Final Appeal

Many fields have considered alternate formats for the dissertation appropriate to their particular discipline. It is time for education to do the same—in a comprehensive and serious way. We have tried to show here how the traditional format of the dissertation fails to prepare the doctoral candidate in education for subsequent professional work in the field on two counts: First, because it is not easily disseminated to a wide audience of professional colleagues; and second, because the format itself is not generalizable to the type of writing that the doctoral recipient will do after receiving the doctorate. We have presented a group of related alternative formats for the dissertation, but we encourage the educational community to more actively consider other alternatives suitable for the field of education. It is incumbent upon this field to adapt the dissertation to meet the professional demands faced by its members and thus to make the best possible use of this enduring institution.

Notes

We thank Courtney Cazden, Victoria Purcell-Gates, Catherine Snow, and the Harvard Graduate School of Education for supporting the first author's proposal for an alternative format for the dissertation, Marc Shell for suggesting literature relevant to this commentary, and Chris Clark for encouraging us in our writing of this piece.

Nell K. Duke is an assistant professor in the College of Education at Michigan State University in East Lansing, MI.

Sarah W. Beck is an advanced doctoral student in the Graduate School of Education at Harvard University in Cambridge, MA.

References

Aristotle (1991). *On rhetoric* (G. A. Kennedy, Trans.). New York: Oxford University Press.
Bazerman, C. (1994). Systems of genres and the enactment of social intentions. In A. Freedman & P. Medway (Eds.), *Genre and the new rhetoric*. London: Taylor and Francis.
Begg, C. B. (1994). Publication bias. In H. Cooper & L. Hedges (Eds.), *The handbook of research synthesis*. New York: Russell Sage Foundation.
Berelson, B. (1960). *Graduate education in the U.S.* New York: McGraw-Hill.
Campbell, K. K., & Jamieson, K. H. (1978). Form and genre in rhetorical criticism: An introduction. In K. K. Campbell & K. H. Jamieson (Eds.), *Form and genre: Shaping rhetorical action*. Falls Church, VA: Speech Communication Association.
Council of Graduate Schools in the U.S. (1991). *The role and nature of the doctoral dissertation*. Washington, DC: Council of Graduate Schools in the U.S. (ERIC Document Reproduction Service No. ED 331 422).
Fitzpatrick, J., Secrist, J., & Wright, D. (1998). *Secrets for a successful dissertation*. Thousand Oaks, CA: Sage Publications.
Halstead, B. (1988). The thesis that won't go away. *Nature, 331,* 497–498.
Isaac, P., Quinlan, S., & Walker, M. (1992). Faculty perceptions of the doctoral dissertation. *Journal of Higher Education, 63*(3), 241–68.
Krathwohl, D. (1994). A slice of advice. *Educational Researcher, 23*(1), 29–32, 42.
Mangan, K. (1996, March 8). Universities wonder whether to allow dissertations on CD-ROM. *The Chronicle of Higher Education,* p. A15.
Mauch, J., & Birch, J. (1989). *Guide to the successful thesis and dissertation* (2nd ed.). New York: Marcel Dekker.
Miller, C. (1994). Genre as social action. In A. Freedman & P. Medway (Eds.), *Genre and the new rhetoric* (pp. 23–42). London: Taylor and Francis. (Reprinted from Quarterly Journal of Speech, 70, pp. 151–67, 1984).
Monaghan, P. (1989. March 29). Some fields are reassessing the value of the traditional doctoral dissertation. *The Chronicle of Higher Education,* pp. Al, A4.
National Center for Education Statistics (1997). *Digest of education statistics 1997*. Washington, DC: U.S. Department of Education/Office of Educational Research and Improvement.
Ogden, E. (1993). *Completing your doctoral dissertation or master's thesis*. Lancaster, PA: Technomic.
Reid, W. M. (1978). Will the future generations of biologists write a dissertation? *Bioscience, 28,* 651–654.
Saks, A. L. (Ed.). (1996). Viewpoints: Should novels count as dissertations in education? *Research in the Teaching of English, 30,* 403–427.
Sheppard, J., & Hartman, D. (1989). Novels as Ph.D. dissertations. *AWP Chronicle, 22,* 1–3.
Todorov, T. (1976). The origin of genres. *New Literary History, 8*(1), 159–170.
Ziolkowski, T. (1990). The Ph.D. squid. *The American Scholar, 59,* 177–195.

CHANCE AND NONSENSE

A Conversation About Interpreting Tests of Statistical Significance, Part 1

Join Chris and Jean in the teachers' lounge
for some educationally significant coffee-break conversation.
Chances are you'll find this a good investment of your time.

by James P. Shaver

Chris, a special education teacher, drops his briefcase on the floor, pours a cup of coffee, and slumps into a rickety overstuffed chair in the faculty room of Sky Crest High School. The only other person in the room is Jean, seated at a small table in the corner, sipping a soda and furiously writing comments on student papers. Jean looks up, distracted by the creaking of the old chair.

JAMES P. SHAVER is a professor of education and associate dean for research in the College of Education at Utah State University, Logan. He wishes to acknowledge the helpful comments of Karl White, William Strong, James Cangelosi, and Susan Friedman on various versions of this article and its sequel.

Jean: You look tired, Chris. Still working on your master's thesis?

Chris: Yeah. [*He balances his coffee cup on the wide chair arm.*] Burning the midnight oil. But I'm pleased with how it's going.

Jean: Really? That's different.

Chris: Well, I've had tremendous cooperation from the school district, so I could do a well-designed study of a topic that interests me as a special educator. They let me select students randomly and then take them out of classes for my research. I even got to use my planning period to visit schools and administer the treatment.

Jean: Wow, that *is* cooperation! Your topic must be of interest to someone in the district office.

Chris: [*Nodding.*] Yep. There's been a lot of concern about the testing we do to decide which students need special education. We give a general screening test at the beginning of the second grade, and those students who fall below a cutoff point are tested individually. The individual test results are then used in making decisions about the type of placement for each student. So it's really important that the individual test scores indicate the students' ability and achievement, not what they know about how to take tests.[1]

Jean: Hmm. That makes sense. What did *you* do?

Chris: [*Leaning forward in his chair.*] Well, I got a list of all the students who were below the cutoff point on the general screening test and randomly selected 40 of them. Next, I randomly assigned 20 of the 40 to a treatment group and 20 to a control group. Then, for 30 minutes each day during the

> # People doing research often convey their expectations to their subjects or treat them differently, without being aware of it.

week before the individual testing, I tutored each experimental student in such test-taking skills as listening carefully to instructions and recognizing different test item formats. For the control group, I spent 30 minutes each day talking about school and how important it is to do well.

Jean: Sounds interesting. What results did you get?

Chris: [*Sitting back again.*] Well, that's part of what's so great about my study. Students in my treatment group had a higher mean score on the individually administered test, and the difference was statistically significant.

Jean: Terrific! Was the difference large enough to be important?

Chris: [*Looking puzzled.*] Well, as I said, it was statistically significant. You know, that means it wasn't likely to be just a chance occurrence. I set the level of significance at .05, as my advisor suggested. So a difference that large would occur by chance less than five times in a hundred if the groups weren't really different. An unlikely occurrence like that *surely* must be important.

Jean: Wait a minute, Chris. Remember the other day when you went into the office to call home? Just as you completed dialing the number, your little boy picked up the phone to call someone. So you were connected and talking to one another without the phone ever ringing.

Chris: [*Nodding.*] Oh yeah, that was quite a coincidence.

Jean: Okay. What do you suppose the probability would be of his picking up the phone just as you completed dialing?

Chris: Gee, I couldn't even estimate, but it would have to be minuscule.

Jean: Well, that must have been a truly important occurrence then?

Chris: [*Frowning and shifting uneasily.*] Well, no . . . I guess unlikely events aren't necessarily important.

(*A long pause ensues, during which Chris sips coffee and looks at the floor.*)

Chris: Well, when you put it in everyday terms, Jean, that makes sense. Unimportant things with a low probability of occurrence happen all the time—like running into somebody from your home town when you're visiting a city thousands of miles away. Somehow, when you do a piece of research, though, it doesn't seem so obvious. [*He leans forward, grinning slightly.*] Anyway, the statistically significant result tells me that the treatment caused the difference.

Jean: Really?

Chris: Sure. I've seen that kind of conclusion in lots of articles. Besides [*reaching for his briefcase and pulling out a book*], here in the textbook that we used in my statistics class there's this table. It presents data on rats reared in two different environments: either free or restricted. The rats reared in the restricted environment had a higher mean score on a maze performance test, and the difference was statistically significant. And right here the author says, "We conclude that the different environments have affected the maze performance of the animals."[2]

Jean: [*Hesitantly.*] That's pretty strong evidence, Chris. I don't mean to sound like a smart aleck social studies teacher, but I took my second statistics course last quarter, and that quote doesn't square with what my professor stressed about interpreting tests of statistical significance.

Chris: [*Looking uneasy again.*] What do you mean?

Jean: Ready for another homey example?

Chris: Uh-oh! I'm not sure. But fire away.

Jean: Well, remember a few Saturdays back? You and I were playing poker with Sam and Susan, and Sam had been having a bad run of cards.

Chris: Yeah, I remember.

Jean: Then, just before he dealt a hand he tapped the deck of cards with his knuckles and gave some sort of incantation?

Chris: Right, his Lady Luck thing.

Jean: And remember, he dealt himself a full house. How likely was that? Less likely than five times in a hundred, I'm sure.

Chris: Oh sure, the odds would be a lot less than that.

Jean: Then I suppose you believe that his knuckle-knocking and incantation caused that good hand?

Chris: Certainly not. [*Waving his hand in the air.*] That was just luck.

Jean: But your result wasn't just luck?

Chris: Oh, I see what you're getting at. My statistics book does refer to Type I errors: when you make the mistake of deciding that your result was not a chance happening, but it really was. With the conventional .05 level of significance, the odds of my making such an error are one in 20.

Jean: Right! Even when you draw groups randomly from the same population, they won't all be the same. And sometimes, just by chance, the difference between the groups will be large. It's like having a bowl with chips in it, half black and half red. If you shake up the bowl and pull out 10 chips without looking, you won't get five black ones and five red ones every time. You might even get all red or all black, just by chance. We could figure the probability of any particular combination in much the same way as you used the test of statistical significance to estimate the probability of the difference you found.

Chris: So I guess my result *could* have happened by chance. I can't really tell for sure, can I?

Jean: Nope. It may have been just the "luck of the draw." The test of statistical significance only tells you the probability that your result occurred by chance. It can't tell you whether it really *was* a chance occurrence—or, if it wasn't, what caused it. Like Sam's full house.

Chris: [*Chuckling.*] That *had* to be chance.

Jean: Well, you'll recall that Sam was dealing at the time. . . .

Chris: [*Looking surprised.*] You don't think Sam would cheat?

Jean: No, he wouldn't do that, I'm sure. But that thought does suggest that there might be a number of reasons for a given result.

Chris: Such as . . . ?

Jean: Well, the research books talk about experimenters' affecting the results that they get.

Chris: Looking pained.] You think *I* cheated?

Jean: Of course not! But people doing research often convey their expectations to their subjects or treat them differently, without being aware of it. That can produce results that are confused with the effect of the treatment. In your case, for example, you tutored both the experimental and the control students yourself. It *could* be that, without your knowing it, you were more enthusiastic with the treatment students. And it could be the difference in enthusiasm, not the training you gave them, that caused the difference in results on the test.

Chris: That's possible, I guess. But I do know that, by randomly assigning the students to the treatment and control groups, I avoided a common threat to the validity of educational research findings.

Jean: Oh? What's that?

Chris: Well, what the research design people call "selection" bias—that is, that the treatment and control groups were selected in such a way that they were different to begin with.

Jean: Are you sure?

Chris: [*Enthusiastically.*] You bet! I randomly assigned the students to the groups by flipping a coin to determine which group each person was going to be in.

Jean: How did that handle the problem of selection bias?

Chris: Well, according to my statistics book, random assignment insures that there will be no systematic differences between the groups that could bias the results of the experiment. [*Chris flips to a page in his statistics book and reads from it.*] "If subjects are assigned to three groups using a random method, I.Q., which may be correlated with French achievement, will not vary in any systematic way from group to group."[3]

Jean: Careful, now. What does the author mean by "systematic" variation? Is he saying that random assignment insures that the groups will be equivalent?

Chris: I'm not sure I follow you.

Jean: [*Pausing and glancing furtively at her stack of uncorrected papers.*] Well, when design experts say that random assignment is the best technique for insuring initial equivalence between groups,[4] they mean that in a purely statistical sense. They're *not* saying that there won't be any differences. They're saying that whatever differences there are will be due only to chance. In that sense, the differences are not systematic.

(*Chris looks puzzled.*)

Jean: Let's take another example. What if you had randomly selected your original group of 40 students and then randomly assigned them to two groups over and over again?

Chris: You mean, if I had just kept going back through my list, flipping my coin to assign each person to one of two groups each time?

Jean: Yes. Would everyone end up in the same group each time?

Chris: Of course not.

Jean: What if you had I.Q. scores for the students? Would the two groups that you got each time by flipping the coin always have the same mean I.Q. scores?

Chris: No—the means would probably differ somewhat each time, just by chance, although they'd usually be close to the mean I.Q. for the population.

Jean: And what if you did a test of statistical significance, using the conventional .05 level as your criterion?

Chris: Ah . . . [*His eyes brighten.*] I see what you're driving at. Five times in a hundred the difference between the group means would be so great that I'd conclude that it wasn't likely that the two groups had been selected from the same population, even though they had been. It's like the bowl of black chips and red chips.

Jean: Exactly. And you'd be making a. . . .

Chris: Type I error—as you suggested I might be doing with the mean difference in my study. Darn! I see what you mean.

(*Chris pauses, brows furrowed. He stands and walks over to pour some more coffee.*)

Chris: You know, talking about chance, there was a funny thing about the gender of my subjects.

Jean: What was that?

Chris: [*Turning to face Jean.*] Well, the split between males and females is pretty close to 50–50 in the district. But my treatment group had about 60% girls. The control group was just about right—about 50–50.

Jean: Hmm. [*Looking pensive.*] An interesting chance occurrence. Do you think it might have affected your results?

Chris: Well, girls are supposed to be more eager to please, and they may respond more to social pressure. And, with more girls than boys in the treatment group. . . . Wait a minute. Are you saying that you think my assignments weren't random?

Jean: Oh no. Randomness can't be judged by group differences or similarities. The question is, Did everyone have an equal chance of being assigned to each group? It doesn't matter what the result looked like. It's a matter of how you assigned the people, and it looks like you did a good job.

Chris: Still, a 60–40 split seems pretty strange. It almost seems like something other than chance was at work.

Jean: Not necessarily. Remember the bowl of chips. You know, it also reminds me of the time when Kim was matching dimes with you in the faculty room last week.

Chris: You're right. Ten tosses in a row! Wiped me out.

Jean: Well, how many tosses should *you* have won, assuming the coin was not biased?

Chris: Well, with no ties, five.

Jean: Right. The odds of Kim's winning 10 times in a row were less than one in a thousand. Does that mean that the coin was biased or that Kim cheated?

Chris: Heck no. That's the fun of matching. Who knows what will happen by chance?

Jean: And in research . . . ?

Chris: Yeah, I see what you mean. [*He sits back down, frowning.*] I wonder how else my groups might have differed. You know, you've sort of taken the wind out of my sails.

Jean: I'm sorry about that. But don't you think that it's better to interpret your results properly?

Chris: Sure. But, as I said before, lots of research reports make those other interpretations.

Jean: Yes. And maybe that's one reason educational research hasn't been very productive.[5]

Chris: Could be. Well, at least I can draw some inferences about one population: the group from which I drew my random sample.

Jean: For instance?

Chris: Well, take the correlation between I.Q. scores and the general screening test. For my treatment and control groups pooled, the correlation was .50. And that was statistically significant. That allows me to say that I know that the correlation in the population is .50.

Jean: Chris, I hate to say this, but have you forgotten our discussion of the meaning of statistical significance?

Chris: C'mon. Not again. . . .

Jean: That's right. The chance of a Type I error again. Even though your correlation was high, it might be due to the chance make-up of your random sample. Besides that, all your test of statistical significance did was help you to ask whether your result was a likely result if the null hypothesis was true. That is, was a sample correlation of .50 likely if the population correlation was zero? Even if the null hypothesis was not true, you could have come up with a correlation of .50 with lots of other population values. How do you know that the correlation in the population isn't .30 or .70?

Chris: [*Hand raised, palm toward Jean.*] Hold on a minute. Doesn't the correlation of .50 tell me *anything*?

Jean: Sure. Given the information you have, .50 is the best estimate of the correlation in the population from which you drew your sample. And, using basically the same procedures as for a test of statistical significance, you could set a confidence interval. That is, you could estimate a range within which the correlation in the population probably falls. But you really have no way of knowing from your one finding precisely what the population value is.

Chris: Maybe not, but it hardly seems likely that the correlation between I.Q. and test scores is zero in the population. That doesn't make sense, and other researchers have reported results pretty close to mine.

Jean: Good point! Then what gives you confidence that the correlation is about .50 is not really the statistical significance of your finding. It's the fact that your finding is consistent with the results of other research.

Chris: Okay. I'm following you. And you'd say that the same line of reasoning applies to the differences between my treatment and control groups. I mean, if the same research were carried out by others, with no reason to suspect the same design flaws from one study to the next, and the results were consistent with mine, then I'd certainly have a lot more confidence that my results could be relied on.

Jean: You bet. Scientists insist on replication. They generally won't accept a new finding until the study has been repeated independently by several researchers, with consistent results.

Chris: Well, I certainly don't recall seeing many replications reported when I did my review of the literature for my thesis.

Jean: No wonder. Replications are not very common in educational research.[6] Maybe that's another reason that educational research has not been very helpful to schoolpeople. After all, your own district-level folks won't know for sure, based on your one study, whether it is really a good idea to teach test-taking skills to kids.

Chris: But, you know, based on what you've said, I have a hunch that you'd argue that, even if I repeated the study—or if other people did—and got statistically significant results, that still wouldn't answer the question about whether the school district should adopt the procedure.

Jean: You're right. [*She looks at the stack of papers waiting to be read, then at the clock.*] But, as much as I'm enjoying our conversation, I've just got to finish reading these papers. I promised the kids I'd have them graded by next period.

Chris: Okay. But let's continue this discussion sometime. I don't want to let these ideas drop.

Jean: Sure.

Chris: How about after school today? I'll buy you a drink.

Jean: Okay. But it can't be until at least five o'clock. I'll have eager beavers in to talk about their grades on these papers, and then I've got to get organized for tomorrow.

Chris: [*Nodding.*] How about Sullivan's at 5:30?

Jean: Great.

(*Jean turns back to her stack of papers as Chris, looking thoughtful, thumbs through the statistics book.*)

---

1. The effects of test-taking skills on test scores are currently being investigated. See, for example, Cie Taylor and Karl R. White, "The Effect of Reinforcement and Training on Group Standardized Test Behavior," *Journal of Educational Measurement,* vol. 19, 1982, pp. 199–210; Cie Taylor and Thomas E. Scruggs, "Research in Progress: Improving the Test-Taking Skills of Learning-Disabled Elementary School Children," *Exceptional Children,* vol. 50, 1983, p. 277; and Robert L. Bangert-Downs, James A. Kulik, and Chen-Lin C. Kulik, "Effects of Coaching Programs on Achievement Test Performance," *Review of Educational Research,* vol. 53, 1983, pp. 571–85.
2. This quote is from George A. Ferguson, *Statistical Analysis in Psychology and Education,* 5th ed. (New York: McGraw-Hill, 1981), p. 266.
3. Ibid.; p. 225.
4. See, for example, Walter R. Borg and Meredith D. Gall, *Educational Research: An Introduction,* 4th ed. (New York: Longman, 1983).
5. See, for example, James P. Shaver, "The Productivity of Educational Research and the Applied-Basic Research Distinction," *Educational Researcher,* January 1979, pp. 3–9; and Elliot W. Eisner, "Can Educational Research Inform Educational Practice?," *Phi Delta Kappan,* March 1984, pp. 447–52.
6. See James P. Shaver and Richard S. Norton, "Randomness and Replication in Ten Years of the *American Educational Research Journal*," *Educational Researcher,* January 1980, pp. 9–15; and idem, "Populations, Samples, Randomness, and Replication in Two Social Studies Journals," *Theory and Research in Social Education,* Summer 1980, pp. 1–10.

(continued on next page)

A Conversation About Interpreting Tests of Statistical Significance, Part 2

Settle down with Jean and Chris over a cold drink after school. Their discussion is educationally (and practically) significant.

by James P. Shaver

It is 5:30 p.m. at Sullivan's Tavern, Jean and Chris, two teachers from Sky Crest High School, settle down at a small table to continue a discussion they started that morning in the faculty room.[1] Soon cold drinks are in front of them, and, after a few minutes, Jean turns the conversation back to the topic of their earlier discussion.

Jean: We left things hanging in midair this morning because I had to finish correcting my papers. But is there anything in particular about statistical significance that you'd like to discuss now?

Chris: [*Brows furrowed.*] I'd like to pick up where we left off. You said that even if my tutoring study were repeated several times and the same statistically significant results were obtained each time, it still wouldn't give the district administration much information to use in deciding whether my procedure for tutoring students in test-taking should be adopted. Frankly, I'm puzzled.

Jean: Well, it seems to me that the important question is whether your result is educationally or practically significant. And statistical significance doesn't answer that question. As we discussed this morning, results that are statistically significant can be educationally trivial.

Chris: Then how can I get at educational significance? After our discussion this morning, I checked my statistics book and couldn't find anything about educational or practical significance. As a matter of fact, most of the research articles I read refer to

"significant results." I can't recall one that made a distinction between statistical and educational significance.

Jean: [*Sighing.*] Unfortunately, you're right. It's hard to find a statistics book or research report that deals with anything other than statistical significance.[2] But we did discuss educational significance in my second statistics course.

Chris: Well?

Jean: Well, first, keep in mind that knowing that a result was statistically significant doesn't help people to know how large the difference is. A very small difference can be statistically significant if a large enough sample is used. In fact, with a large enough sample and reliably measured variables, almost any differences between means will be statistically significant. The same holds true for correlations.

My statistics professor made this point by telling us about a study done by Paul Meehl, a psychologist at the University of Minnesota.[3] Meehl had data from more than 55,000 Minnesota high school seniors. To see what the results would be, he computed correlations between 45 miscellaneous variables—such things as sex, birth order, religious preference, vocational choice, and liking for school. And guess what? Almost all of them were statistically significant—about 90%, if I remember correctly. So, if you want a statistically significant finding, just use a large sample.

Chris: [*Looking perplexed.*] But you make it sound so arbitrary, as if tests of significance just shouldn't be trusted. It seems that you should gain *something* by having

larger samples; it should make statistical significance more likely.

Jean: Sure. Especially if the sample is randomly selected, like yours. Which, by the way, isn't all that common in educational research.[4]

Chris: [*Grinning.*] Hey, that's to my credit anyway.

Jean: You bet. But maybe a good way to get at what a researcher gains from large samples is to think again about that bowl of red and black poker chips we talked about. Remember?

Chris: Sure.

Jean: Well, what if there were a thousand chips, some red and some black? But you didn't know how many there were of each color. Let's say you could reach in blind-folded and take out either 40 chips or 900 chips as a basis for guessing the percentage of black chips. How many would you draw?

Chris: Nine hundred, of course. Surely, the larger the random sample, the more likely it is to represent the total population.

Jean: Right. And that's what happens with statistical significance. The larger the samples we draw, the more likely it is in the long run that they'll resemble the population. Now, what if your hunch—what statisticians call your null hypothesis—was that there was no difference in the percentages of red chips and black chips in the bowl, but in fact there were really 40% red and 60% black?

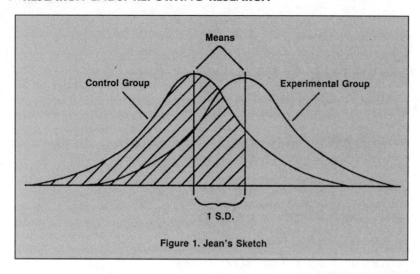

Figure 1. Jean's Sketch

Chris: Well, the larger the sample, the more likely it would be to reflect that difference. And the more likely I'd be to conclude that the null hypothesis wasn't true.

Jean: Absolutely correct! And statisticians have a name for the probability of making such a correct decision about a difference that really exists. It's called *power.* As you increase your sample size, you increase your power. That is, if there really is a difference, you're more likely to detect it, at whatever level of statistical significance, you set.

Chris: That helps me to understand why the outcome of a test of statistical significance depends on sample size—and why it really doesn't tell me whether a difference between means is large or small. If the magnitude of differences is important to educational significance, how can I get at it?

Jean: Well, there are a couple of things you might do. Researchers are beginning to report what they call *effect sizes.* One type of effect size—I'll call it *d*—is really a standardized mean difference.[5]

Chris: A what?

Jean: Let me explain. Do you remember how we can compute students' standard scores—or what are often called *z* scores? We just subtract the mean for the population from a student's raw score, then divide that difference by the standard deviation of the population.

Chris: Yeah, that rings a bell.

Jean: The principle is the same with *d.* You subtract your control-group mean from your experimental-group mean and then divide the difference by the standard deviation of the control group.

Chris: Okay, but why the standard deviation of the control group?

Jean: Good question. That standard deviation indicates the variability in scores when they haven't been affected by a treatment. For example, if tutoring students, as you did in your study, helps them all do better on a test, that may reduce variability in the test scores. So, in using the control-group standard deviation, we're really comparing the difference between two means to an estimate of the variability of scores in the untreated population.

Chris: That makes sense. But what does a *d* tell us anyhow?

Jean: Basically, it tells us the extent to which the distributions of scores for the two groups overlap.

Chris: Elaborate on that, please.

Jean: Let's say, for example, that you got a *d* of 1. We could say, then, that the means are one standard deviation apart. And, assuming normal distributions, we could go to a table that gives the values of the normal curve and estimate the percentage of the control-group distribution that is below the mean of the experimental-group distribution. In the case of a *d* of 1, for example, we could say that the mean of the experimental group was equal to or higher than 84% of the scores in the control group.

Chris: I'm having a hard time visualizing that.

Jean: [*Takes out a pencil and sketches Figure 1 on the back of a napkin.*] Try this. Here are two curves, one for the distribution of scores in an experimental group and one for a control group. The vertical line at the center of each curve represents the mean for the distribution. The *d* is 1, so the mean for

the experimental group is one control-group standard deviation above that for the control group. And the shaded area is 84% of the control-group distribution; so the average score in the experimental group is equal to or greater than 84% of the scores in the control group.

Chris: Aha! And you're saying that, if this were computed for several studies, we would have a common measure for talking about the size of the differences.

Jean: The statisticians call it a metric.

Chris: And it could be used to compare the results of different studies because it doesn't depend on the size of the samples, as statistical significance does.

Jean: Right. And there's another way to look at the whole matter of effect size. That's in terms of correlation. Ready for more?

Chris: [*Moaning in jest.*] Go on.

Jean: You know, there are lots of reasons why students don't all get the same scores. Being in the treatment or control group is only one reason for score variability.

Chris: You mean, things like how tired or rested the students are and any actual differences in how much they know about what the test measures?

Jean: Sure. And it's useful to know what percentage of the total variability in test scores is associated with whether the students were in the experimental or the control group. For example, you could ask how much of the variability in test scores for the students in your study is associated with whether they were tutored or not.

Chris: Makes sense. How can we get at that?

Jean: The point biserial correlation coefficient gives us a way. It indicates the relationship between scores on a dependent variable—such as your individually administered test—and treatment-group membership.

Chris: [*Frowning.*] Once I've computed such a coefficient, how do I interpret it?

Jean: Well, you square it to get the proportion of the variability in test scores that is associated with group membership. Let's say, for example, that for your data you got a point biserial coefficient of .40. If you squared that, you'd get .16. Multiplied by 100, that would give you 16%. You could say that 16% of the variance in test scores is associated with group membership. The other 84% would be associated with other things.

Chris: If I read you right, you're being very careful to avoid saying that 16% of the variance was *caused* by my tutoring treatment.

Jean: [*Smiling and nodding.*] Indeed, I am. That goes back to our discussion of this morning. The point biserial coefficient is an estimate of the degree of relationship between scores and membership in your tutoring and control groups. It doesn't tell us anything about what caused the relationship. Conclusions about cause and effect must be based on whether your design yielded valid results. For instance, was the difference really a result of having more girls than boys in your tutoring group?

Chris: I follow you, but how does all of this relate to statistical significance?

Jean: Well, consider this. As I recall from my statistics class, with a sample of 40, a point biserial coefficient of .30 or larger would be statistically significant at the .05 level. But with a sample of 1,000, a correlation of only .06 would be statistically significant—even though less than half a percent of the variance would be associated with group membership.

Chris: Less than 1%? That's a pretty dramatic demonstration that statistically significant results may be trivial. But I'm a little puzzled by one thing. Did your statistics professor mention how *d*'s and point biserial coefficients are related? It seems to me that they're getting at similar things.

Jean: Good conclusion! Here, look at my sketch again. The less the distributions of the treatment and control groups overlap, the higher the correlation between scores and group membership; the more the distributions overlap, the lower the correlation between scores and group membership. As a matter of fact, I've even seen a statistics book that provides a table so that, if you have *d,* you can estimate the point biserial coefficient or vice versa.[6] For example, if you had a *d* of 1, the point biserial coefficient would be about .45; with a correlation of .05, the *d* would be only .1. That is, there'd be very little spread between the two means, even though the difference might be statistically significant.

Chris: But what if you had a small sample? A difference that was quite large, with a large point biserial coefficient and effect size, might not be statistically significant.

Jean: Sure. That's the other side of the coin. And it illustrates why statistical significance tells us so little about the size of a research outcome. If nonstatistically significant differences of a similar size were found consistently in replication studies, that lack of statistical significance wouldn't be as convincing as the consistency of the results. You'd be inclined to conclude that there really was a difference even though it wasn't statistically significant in any one study.[7]

Chris: Okay. Let's go back to educational significance. I still don't see how such things as *d*'s and point biserial correlations[8] get directly at the importance of the finding—and that seems to me to be the heart of the matter.

Jean: You're right about that. Point biserials and *d*'s give us a measure of the magnitude of an effect that isn't relative to sample size. But at least a couple of other things need to be taken into account to get at educational or practical significance. One is the possible impact or benefit of the difference; the other is the cost of producing it.

Chris: I'm not sure what you mean by the "benefit" of the difference.

Jean: Okay. Let's take the difference between the means of the treatment and control groups in your study. Regardless of the size of that difference, if the tutored students' scores didn't go up enough to affect whether they would be selected for special education classes, people wouldn't be likely to say that your result had much impact or benefit.

Chris: Yeah, I see what you mean. I guess that would be a little like a store owner who put up a new sign and found that more people noticed it, but no more people came into his store.

Jean: That's the idea. But even if the research finding has some positive impact, we need to ask how much it costs.

Chris: You mean in dollars and cents?

Jean: Well, money is important, but there are other kinds of costs. New teaching materials may take a lot of teacher preparation time, or they may be difficult for teachers to use, or they may make classroom management tougher. Costs like those must be considered, too.

Chris: You know, there were quite a few complaints when I took the students out of their classrooms for tutoring. I had to sympathize with the teachers when they said that those students were the ones who could least afford to miss classwork, because they were already behind.

Jean: Loss of class time is an important cost to consider. Again, though, cost isn't important alone, any more than impact is. Both must be weighed against people's values.

Chris: I see. But I hadn't thought of research findings in that way before. Can you give me another illustration?

Jean: An example from a letter to the editor that my statistics professor had us read makes the point well, I think.[9] What if you found out about a new, proven, gas-saving gadget for your car? The gadget costs $510, and you'd have to take 17 hours of your time to install it. It would increase your average gas mileage by .68 miles per gallon, from 16 to 16.68 miles per gallon. If the variability in your mileage from one fill-up to the next resulted in a standard deviation of 1, the *d* would be .68. Would you buy the gadget?

Chris: [*Shaking his head.*] I don't think so. It'd take a long time just to pay for the cost. Besides, 17 hours for installation is a lot of time.

Jean: Okay. But what if some researchers developed a new medical treatment that cost $510, involved 17 one-hour visits, and would increase the life expectancy of a 40-year-old person by 6.8 years—from a mean life expectancy of 70 years to a mean life expectancy of 76.8 years? If the life expectancy standard deviation was 10 years, the *d* would again be .68. What's your reaction?

Chris: [*Smiling*]. Well, I know a lot of people who would be standing in line when that treatment went on the market.

Jean: Me too. And I'm sure that none of them would care whether the results were statistically significant, especially if they knew that the effectiveness of the treatment had been established through repeated studies.[10]

Chris: Hmm. I see what you mean: You know, this has been a great discussion. I'm going to go back and analyze my data differently. And the conclusions section of my thesis is certainly going to be different, too.

Jean: Just so all of this doesn't get you into trouble with your graduate committee. You know, a lot of academics are still pretty hung up on statistical significance as *the* criterion of importance.

Chris: I may need to arrange a conference between my major professor and your statistics professor. But I guess there's one problem that I really can't solve and just need to admit to in my conclusion section. I mean, everything hinges on whether the difference between my tutoring and control groups is really due to the treatment or something else, such as chance or some flaw in the design.

Jean: Yes. You're right about that.

Chris: And I suppose that the way to find out more about that is for me or someone else to repeat the study, maybe making some changes in methodology, to see if the same result occurs.

Jean: Right again. For example, one improvement would be not doing the treatments yourself.

Chris: You know, maybe I could get permission and even some help from the school district to do a replication across town. That way I could build on what I've learned.

(Jean and Chris sit looking at each other for a moment, both nodding their heads.)

Chris: [*Glancing at the clock.*] Wow, we'd both better get home before we lose our happy homes.

Jean: Right! Thanks for the drink. Good luck with the thesis.

(They push back their chairs, stand up, and head for the front door of Sullivan's, commenting on the sudden shower that is going to soak them as they run to their cars.)

---

1. For a report of that conversation, see James P. Shaver, "Chance and Nonsense: A Conversation About Interpreting Tests of Statistical Significance, Part 1," *Phi Delta Kappan,* September 1985, pp. 57–60.
2. One book that raises questions about the usefulness of statistical significance is Geoffrey R. Loftus and Elizabeth F. Loftus, *Essence of Statistics* (Belmont, Calif.: Brook/Cole, 1982), pp. 498–99.
3. Paul E. Meehl, "Theory Testing in Psychology and Physics: A Methodological Paradox," in Denton E. Morrison and Ramon E. Henkel, eds., *The Significance Test Controversy—A Reader* (Chicago: Aldine, 1970).
4. See James P. Shaver and Richard S. Norton, "Randomness and Replication in Ten Years' of the *American Educational Research Journal,*" *Educational Researcher,* vol. 9, 1980, pp. 9–15; and idem, "Population, Samples, Randomness, and Replication in Two Social Studies Journals," *Theory and Research in Social Education,* vol. 8, 1980, pp. 1–10.
5. Gene V. Glass, Barry McGraw, and Mary Lee Smith, *Meta-analysis in Social Research* (Beverly Hills, Calif.: Sage, 1981); and Jacob Cohen, *Statistical Power Analysis for the Behavioral Sciences* (New York: Academic Press, 1977).
6. See Cohen, p. 22.
7. Actually, combining the results from replications would result in a statistical test with increased power and greater likelihood that the small differences would be found to be statistically significant. See, for example, Robert Rosenthal, *Meta-analytic Procedures for Social Research* (Beverly Hills, Calif.: Sage, 1984).
8. The point biserial coefficient is used only when there are two groups.
9. Philip S. Gallo, Jr., "Meta-analysis—a Mixed Meta-phor?," *American Psychologist,* vol. 33, 1978, pp. 515–17.
10. For further medical examples, see N. L. Gage, "What Do We Know About Teaching Effectiveness?," *Phi Delta Kappan,* October 1984, pp. 87–93.

Statistical Methods in Psychology Journals: Guidelines and Explanations

Leland Wilkinson and the Task Force on Statistical Inference
APA Board of Scientific Affairs

In the light of continuing debate over the applications of significance testing in psychology journals and following the publication of Cohen's (1994) article, the Board of Scientific Affairs (BSA) of the American Psychological Association (APA) convened a committee called the Task Force on Statistical Inference (TFSI) whose charge was "to elucidate some of the controversial issues surrounding applications of statistics including significance testing and its alternatives; alternative underlying models and data transformation; and newer methods made possible by powerful computers" (BSA, personal communication, February 28, 1996). Robert Rosenthal, Robert Abelson, and Jacob Cohen (cochairs) met initially and agreed on the desirability of having several types of specialists on the task force: statisticians, teachers of statistics, journal editors, authors of statistics books, computer experts, and wise elders. Nine individuals were subsequently invited to join and all agreed. These were Leona Aiken, Mark Appelbaum, Gwyneth Boodoo, David A. Kenny, Helena Kraemer, Donald Rubin, Bruce Thompson, Howard Wainer, and Leland Wilkinson. In addition, Lee Cronbach, Paul Meehl, Frederick Mosteller and John Tukey served as Senior Advisors to the Task Force and commented on written materials.

The TFSI met twice in two years and corresponded throughout that period. After the first meeting, the task force circulated a preliminary report indicating its intention to examine issues beyond null hypothesis significance testing. The task force invited comments and used this feedback in the deliberations during its second meeting.

After the second meeting, the task force recommended several possibilities for further action, chief of which would be to revise the statistical sections of the *American Psychological Association Publication Manual* (APA, 1994). After extensive discussion, the BSA recommended that "before the TFSI undertook a revision of the *APA Publication Manual*, it might want to consider publishing an article in *American Psychologist*, as a way to initiate discussion in the field about changes in current practices of data analysis and reporting" (BSA, personal communication, November 17, 1997).

This report follows that request. The sections in italics are proposed guidelines that the TFSI recommends could be used for revising the APA publication manual or for developing other BSA supporting materials. Following each guideline are comments, explanations, or elaborations assembled by Leland Wilkinson for the task force and under its review. This report is concerned with the use of statistical methods only and is not meant as an assessment of research methods in general. Psychology is a broad science. Methods appropriate in one area may be inappropriate in another.

The title and format of this report are adapted from a similar article by Bailar and Mosteller (1988). That article should be consulted, because it overlaps somewhat with this one and discusses some issues relevant to research in psychology. Further detail can also be found in the publications on this topic by several committee members (Abelson, 1995, 1997; Rosenthal, 1994; Thompson, 1996; Wainer, in press; see also articles in Harlow, Mulaik, & Steiger, 1997).

Method

Design

Make clear at the outset what type of study you are doing. Do not cloak a study in one guise to try to give it the assumed reputation of another. For studies that have multiple goals, be sure to define and prioritize those goals.

There are many forms of empirical studies in psychology, including case reports, controlled experiments, quasi-experiments, statistical simulations, surveys, observational studies, and studies of studies (meta-analyses). Some are hypothesis generating: They explore data to form or sharpen hypotheses about a population for assessing future hypotheses. Some are hypothesis testing: They assess specific a priori hypotheses or estimate parameters by random sampling from that population. Some are meta-analytic: They assess specific a priori hypotheses or estimate parameters (or both) by synthesizing the results of available studies.

Some researchers have the impression or have been taught to believe that some of these forms yield information that is more valuable or credible than others (see Cronbach, 1975, for a discussion). Occasionally proponents of some research methods disparage others. In fact, each form of research has its own strengths, weaknesses, and standards of practice.

Population

The interpretation of the results of any study depends on the characteristics of the population intended for analysis. Define the population (participants, stimuli, or studies) clearly. If control or comparison groups are part of the design, present how they are defined.

Psychology students sometimes think that a statistical population is the human race or, at least, college sophomores. They also have some difficulty distinguishing a class of objects versus a statistical population—that sometimes we make inferences about a population through statistical methods, and other times we make inferences about a class through logical or other nonstatistical methods. Populations may be sets of potential observations on people, adjectives, or even research articles. How a population is defined in an article affects almost every conclusion in that article.

Sample

Describe the sampling procedures and emphasize any inclusion or exclusion criteria. If the sample is stratified (e.g., by site or gender) describe fully the method and rationale. Note the proposed sample size for each subgroup.

Interval estimates for clustered and stratified random samples differ from those for simple random samples. Statistical software is now becoming available for these purposes. If you are using a convenience sample (whose members are not selected at random), be sure to make that procedure clear to your readers. Using a convenience sample does not automatically disqualify a study from publication, but it harms your objectivity to try to conceal this by implying that you used a random sample. Sometimes the case for the representativeness of a convenience sample can be strengthened by explicit comparison of sample characteristics with those of a defined population across a wide range of variables.

Assignment

Random assignment. *For research involving causal inferences, the assignment of units to levels of the causal variable is critical. Random assignment (not to be confused with random selection) allows for the strongest possible causal inferences free of extraneous assumptions. If random assignment is planned, provide enough information to show that the process for making the actual assignments is random.*

There is a strong research tradition and many exemplars for random assignment in various fields of psychology. Even those who have elucidated quasi-experimental designs in psychological research (e.g., Cook & Campbell, 1979) have repeatedly emphasized the superiority of random assignment as a method for controlling bias and lurking variables. "Random" does not mean "haphazard." Randomization is a fragile condition, easily corrupted deliberately, as we see when a skilled magician flips a fair coin repeatedly to heads, or innocently, as we saw when the drum was not turned sufficiently to randomize the picks in the Vietnam draft lottery. As psychologists, we also know that human participants are incapable of producing a random process (digits, spatial arrangements, etc.) or of recognizing one. It is best not to trust the random behavior of a physical device unless you are an expert in these matters. It is safer to use the pseudorandom sequence from a well-designed computer generator or from published tables of random numbers. The added benefit of such a procedure is that you can supply a random number seed or starting number in a table that other researchers can use to check your methods later.

Nonrandom assignment. *For some research questions, random assignment is not feasible. In such cases, we need to minimize effects of variables that affect the observed relationship between a causal variable and an outcome. Such variables are commonly called confounds or covariates. The researcher needs to attempt to determine the relevant covariates, measure them adequately, and adjust for their effects either by design* *or by analysis. If the effects of covariates are adjusted by analysis, the strong assumptions that are made must be explicitly stated and, to the extent possible, tested and justified. Describe methods used to attenuate sources of bias, including plans for minimizing dropouts, noncompliance, and missing data.*

Authors have used the term "control group" to describe, among other things, (a) a comparison group, (b) members of pairs matched or blocked on one or more nuisance variables, (c) a group not receiving a particular treatment, (d) a statistical sample whose values are adjusted post hoc by the use of one or more covariates, or (e) a group for which the experimenter acknowledges bias exists and perhaps hopes that this admission will allow the reader to make appropriate discounts or other mental adjustments. None of these is an instance of a fully adequate control group.

If we can neither implement randomization nor approach total control of variables that modify effects (outcomes), then we should use the term "control group" cautiously. In most of these cases, it would be better to forgo the term and use "contrast group" instead. In any case, we should describe exactly which confounding variables have been explicitly controlled and speculate about which unmeasured ones could lead to incorrect inferences. In the absence of randomization, we should do our best to investigate sensitivity to various untestable assumptions.

Measurement

Variables. *Explicitly define the variables in the study, show how they are related to the goals of the study, and explain how they are measured. The units of measurement of all variables, causal and outcome, should fit the language you use in the introduction and discussion sections of your report.*

A variable is a method for assigning to a set of observations a value from a set of possible outcomes. For example, a variable called "gender" might assign each of 50 observations to one of the values male or female. When we define a variable, we are declaring what we are prepared to represent as a valid observation and what we must consider as invalid. If we define the range of a particular variable (the set of possible outcomes) to be from 1 to 7 on a Likert scale, for example, then a value of 9 is not an outlier (an unusually extreme value). It is an illegal value. If we declare the range of a variable to be positive real numbers and the domain to be observations of reaction time (in milliseconds) to an administration of electric shock, then a value of 3,000 is not illegal; it is an outlier.

Naming a variable is almost as important as measuring it. We do well to select a name that reflects how a variable is measured. On this basis, the name "IQ test score" is preferable to "intelligence" and "retrospective self-report of childhood sexual abuse" is preferable to "childhood sexual abuse." Without such precision, am-

biguity in defining variables can give a theory an unfortunate resistance to empirical falsification. Being precise does not make us operationalists. It simply means that we try to avoid excessive generalization.

Editors and reviewers should be suspicious when they notice authors changing definitions or names of variables, failing to make clear what would be contrary evidence, or using measures with no history and thus no known properties. Researchers should be suspicious when code books and scoring systems are inscrutable or more voluminous than the research articles on which they are based. Everyone should worry when a system offers to code a specific observation in two or more ways for the same variable.

Instruments. *If a questionnaire is used to collect data, summarize the psychometric properties of its scores with specific regard to the way the instrument is used in a population. Psychometric properties include measures of validity, reliability, and any other qualities affecting conclusions. If a physical apparatus is used, provide enough information (brand, model, design specifications) to allow another experimenter to replicate your measurement process.*

There are many methods for constructing instruments and psychometrically validating scores from such measures. Traditional true-score theory and item–response test theory provide appropriate frameworks for assessing reliability and internal validity. Signal detection theory and various coefficients of association can be used to assess external validity. Messick (1989) provides a comprehensive guide to validity.

It is important to remember that a test is not reliable or unreliable. Reliability is a property of the scores on a test for a particular population of examinees (Feldt & Brennan, 1989). Thus, authors should provide reliability coefficients of the scores for the data being analyzed even when the focus of their research is not psychometric. Interpreting the size of observed effects requires an assessment of the reliability of the scores.

Besides showing that an instrument is reliable, we need to show that it does not correlate strongly with other key constructs. It is just as important to establish that a measure does not measure what it should not measure as it is to show that it does measure what it should.

Researchers occasionally encounter a measurement problem that has no obvious solution. This happens when they decide to explore a new and rapidly growing research area that is based on a previous researcher's well-defined construct implemented with a poorly developed psychometric instrument. Innovators, in the excitement of their discovery, sometimes give insufficient attention to the quality of their instruments. Once a defective measure enters the literature, subsequent researchers are reluctant to change it. In these cases, editors and reviewers should pay special attention to the psychometric properties of the instruments used, and they might want to encourage revisions (even if not by the scale's author) to prevent the accumulation of results based on relatively invalid or unreliable measures.

Procedure. *Describe any anticipated sources of attrition due to noncompliance, dropout, death, or other factors. Indicate how such attrition may affect the generalizability of the results. Clearly describe the conditions under which measurements are taken (e.g., format, time, place, personnel who collected data). Describe the specific methods used to deal with experimenter bias, especially if you collected the data yourself.*

Despite the long-established findings of the effects of experimenter bias (Rosenthal, 1966), many published studies appear to ignore or discount these problems. For example, some authors or their assistants with knowledge of hypotheses or study goals screen participants (through personal interviews or telephone conversations) for inclusion in their studies. Some authors administer questionnaires. Some authors give instructions to participants. Some authors perform experimental manipulations. Some tally or code responses. Some rate videotapes.

An author's self-awareness, experience, or resolve does not eliminate experimenter bias. In short, there are no valid excuses, financial or otherwise, for avoiding an opportunity to double-blind. Researchers looking for guidance on this matter should consult the classic book of Webb, Campbell, Schwartz, and Sechrest (1966) and an exemplary dissertation (performed on a modest budget) by Baker (1969).

Power and sample size. *Provide information on sample size and the process that led to sample size decisions. Document the effect sizes, sampling and measurement assumptions, as well as analytic procedures used in power calculations. Because power computations are most meaningful when done before data are collected and examined, it is important to show how effect-size estimates have been derived from previous research and theory in order to dispel suspicions that they might have been taken from data used in the study or, even worse, constructed to justify a particular sample size. Once the study is analyzed, confidence intervals replace calculated power in describing results.*

Largely because of the work of Cohen (1969, 1988), psychologists have become aware of the need to consider power in the design of their studies, before they collect data. The intellectual exercise required to do this stimulates authors to take seriously prior research and theory in their field, and it gives an opportunity, with incumbent risk, for a few to offer the challenge that there is no applicable research behind a given study. If exploration were not disguised in hypothetico-deductive language, then it might have the opportunity to influence subsequent research constructively.

Computer programs that calculate power for various designs and distributions are now available. One can use them to conduct power analyses for a range of reason-

able alpha values and effect sizes. Doing so reveals how power changes across this range and overcomes a tendency to regard a single power estimate as being absolutely definitive.

Many of us encounter power issues when applying for grants. Even when not asking for money, think about power. Statistical power does not corrupt.

Results

Complications

Before presenting results, report complications, protocol violations, and other unanticipated events in data collection. These include missing data, attrition, and nonresponse. Discuss analytic techniques devised to ameliorate these problems. Describe nonrepresentativeness statistically by reporting patterns and distributions of missing data and contaminations. Document how the actual analysis differs from the analysis planned before complications arose. The use of techniques to ensure that the reported results are not produced by anomalies in the data (e.g., outliers, points of high influence, nonrandom missing data, selection bias, attrition problems) should be a standard component of all analyses.

As soon as you have collected your data, before you compute any statistics, *look at your data.* Data screening is not data snooping. It is not an opportunity to discard data or change values to favor your hypotheses. However, if you assess hypotheses without examining your data, you risk publishing nonsense.

Computer malfunctions tend to be catastrophic: A system crashes; a file fails to import; data are lost. Less well-known are more subtle bugs that can be more catastrophic in the long run. For example, a single value in a file may be corrupted in reading or writing (often in the first or last record). This circumstance usually produces a major value error, the kind of singleton that can make large correlations change sign and small correlations become large.

Graphical inspection of data offers an excellent possibility for detecting serious compromises to data integrity. The reason is simple: Graphics broadcast; statistics narrowcast. Indeed, some international corporations that must defend themselves against rapidly evolving fraudulent schemes use real-time graphic displays as their first line of defense and statistical analyses as a distant second. The following example shows why.

Figure 1 shows a scatter-plot matrix (SPLOM) of three variables from a national survey of approximately 3,000 counseling clients (Chartrand, 1997). This display, consisting of pairwise scatter plots arranged in a matrix, is found in most modern statistical packages. The diagonal cells contain dot plots of each variable (with the dots stacked like a histogram) and scales used for each variable. The three variables shown are questionnaire measures of respondent's age *(AGE)*, gender *(SEX)*, and

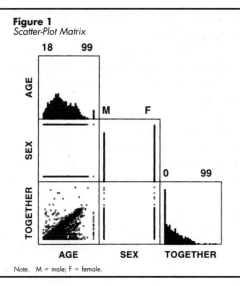

Figure 1
Scatter-Plot Matrix

Note. M = male; F = female.

The main point of this example is that the type of "atheoretical" search for patterns that we are sometimes warned against in graduate school can save us from the humiliation of having to retract conclusions we might ultimately make on the basis of contaminated data. We are warned against fishing expeditions for understandable reasons, but blind application of models without screening our data is a far graver error.

Graphics cannot solve all our problems. Special issues arise in modeling when we have missing data. The two popular methods for dealing with missing data that are found in basic statistics packages—listwise and pairwise deletion of missing values—are among the worst methods available for practical applications. Little and Rubin (1987) have discussed these issues in more detail and offer alternative approaches.

Analysis

Choosing a minimally sufficient analysis. The enormous variety of modern quantitative methods leaves researchers with the nontrivial task of matching analysis and design to the research question. Although complex designs and state-of-the-art methods are sometimes necessary to address research questions effectively, simpler classical approaches often can provide elegant and sufficient answers to important questions. Do not choose an analytic method to impress your readers or to deflect criticism. If the assumptions and strength of a simpler method are reasonable for your data and research problem, use it. Occam's razor applies to methods as well as to theories.

We should follow the advice of *Fisher (1935)*:

Experimenters should remember that they and their colleagues usually know more about the kind of material they are dealing with than do the authors of text-books written without such personal experience, and that a more complex, or less intelligible, test is not likely to serve their purpose better, in any sense, than those of proved value in their own subject. (p. 49)

There is nothing wrong with using state-of-the-art methods, as long as you and your readers understand how they work and what they are doing. On the other hand, don't cling to obsolete methods (e.g., Newman-Keuls or Duncan post hoc tests) out of fear of learning the new. In any case, listen to Fisher. Begin with an idea. Then pick a method.

Computer programs. There are many good computer programs for analyzing data. More important than choosing a specific statistical package is verifying your results, understanding what they mean, and knowing how they are computed. If you cannot verify your results by intelligent "guesstimates," you should check them against the output of another program. You will not be happy if a vendor reports a bug after your data are in print (not an infrequent event). Do not report statistics found on a printout without understanding how they are computed or what they mean. Do not

number of years together in current relationship *(TOGETHER)*. The graphic in Figure 1 is not intended for final presentation of results; we use it instead to locate coding errors and other anomalies before we analyze our data. Figure 1 is a selected portion of a computer screen display that offers tools for zooming in and out, examining points, and linking to information in other graphical displays and data editors. SPLOM displays can be used to recognize unusual patterns in 20 or more variables simultaneously. We focus on these three only.

There are several anomalies in this graphic. The *AGE* histogram shows a spike at the right end, which corresponds to the value 99 in the data. This coded value most likely signifies a missing value, because it is unlikely that this many people in a sample of 3,000 would have an age of 99 or greater. Using numerical values for missing value codes is a risky practice (Kahn & Udry, 1986).

The histogram for *SEX* shows an unremarkable division into two values. The histogram for *TOGETHER* is highly skewed, with a spike at the lower end presumably signifying no relationship. The most remarkable pattern is the triangular joint distribution of *TOGETHER* and *AGE*. Triangular joint distributions often (but not necessarily) signal an implication or a relation rather than a linear function with error. In this case, it makes sense that the span of a relationship should not exceed a person's age. Closer examination shows that something is wrong here, however. We find some respondents (in the upper left triangular area of the *TOGETHER–AGE* panel) claiming that they have been in a significant relationship longer than they have been alive! Had we computed statistics or fit models before examining the raw data, we would likely have missed these reporting errors. There is little reason to expect that *TOGETHER* would show any anomalous behavior with other variables, and even if *AGE* and *TOGETHER* appeared jointly in certain models, we may not have known anything was amiss, regardless of our care in examining residual or other diagnostic plots.

report statistics to a greater precision than is supported by your data simply because they are printed that way by the program. Using the computer is an opportunity for you to control your analysis and design. If a computer program does not provide the analysis you need, use another program rather than let the computer shape your thinking.

There is no substitute for common sense. If you cannot use rules of thumb to detect whether the result of a computation makes sense to you, then you should ask yourself whether the procedure you are using is appropriate for your research. Graphics can help you to make some of these determinations; theory can help in other cases. But never assume that using a highly regarded program absolves you of the responsibility for judging whether your results are plausible. Finally, when documenting the use of a statistical procedure, refer to the statistical literature rather than a computer manual; when documenting the use of a program, refer to the computer manual rather than the statistical literature.

Assumptions. *You should take efforts to assure that the underlying assumptions required for the analysis are reasonable given the data. Examine residuals carefully. Do not use distributional tests and statistical indexes of shape (e.g., skewness, kurtosis) as a substitute for examining your residuals graphically.*

Using a statistical test to diagnose problems in model fitting has several shortcomings. First, diagnostic significance tests based on summary statistics (such as tests for homogeneity of variance) are often impractically sensitive; our statistical tests of models are often more robust than our statistical tests of assumptions. Second, statistics such as skewness and kurtosis often fail to detect distributional irregularities in the residuals. Third, statistical tests depend on sample size, and as sample size increases, the tests often will reject innocuous assumptions. In general, there is no substitute for graphical analysis of assumptions.

Modern statistical packages offer graphical diagnostics for helping to determine whether a model appears to fit data appropriately. Most users are familiar with residual plots for linear regression modeling. Fewer are aware that John Tukey's paradigmatic equation, *data = fit + residual*, applies to a more general class of models and has broad implications for graphical analysis of assumptions. Stem-and-leaf plots, box plots, histograms, dot plots, spread/level plots, probability plots, spectral plots, autocorrelation and cross-correlation plots, coplots, and trellises (Chambers, Cleveland, Kleiner, & Tukey, 1983; Cleveland, 1995; Tukey, 1977) all serve at various times for displaying residuals, whether they arise from analysis of variance (ANOVA), nonlinear modeling, factor analysis, latent variable modeling, multidimensional scaling, hierarchical linear modeling, or other procedures.

Hypothesis tests. *It is hard to imagine a situation in which a dichotomous accept–reject decision is better than re-* *porting an actual p value or, better still, a confidence interval. Never use the unfortunate expression "accept the null hypothesis." Always provide some effect-size estimate when reporting a p value.* Cohen (1994) has written on this subject in this journal. All psychologists would benefit from reading his insightful article.

Effect sizes. *Always present effect sizes for primary outcomes. If the units of measurement are meaningful on a practical level (e.g., number of cigarettes smoked per day), then we usually prefer an unstandardized measure (regression coefficient or mean difference) to a standardized measure (r or d). It helps to add brief comments that place these effect sizes in a practical and theoretical context.*

APA's (1994) publication manual included an important new "encouragement" (p. 18) to report effect sizes. Unfortunately, empirical studies of various journals indicate that the effect size of this encouragement has been negligible (Keselman et al., 1998; Kirk, 1996; Thompson & Snyder, 1998). We must stress again that reporting and interpreting effect sizes in the context of previously reported effects is essential to good research. It enables readers to evaluate the stability of results across samples, designs, and analyses. Reporting effect sizes also informs power analyses and meta-analyses needed in future research.

Fleiss (1994), Kirk (1996), Rosenthal (1994), and Snyder and Lawson (1993) have summarized various measures of effect sizes used in psychological research. Consult these articles for information on computing them. For a simple, general purpose display of the practical meaning of an effect size, see Rosenthal and Rubin (1982). Consult Rosenthal and Rubin (1994) for information on the use of "counternull intervals" for effect sizes, as alternatives to confidence intervals.

Interval estimates. *Interval estimates should be given for any effect sizes involving principal outcomes. Provide intervals for correlations and other coefficients of association or variation whenever possible.*

Confidence intervals are usually available in statistical software; otherwise, confidence intervals for basic statistics can be computed from typical output. Comparing confidence intervals from a current study to intervals from previous, related studies helps focus attention on stability across studies (Schmidt, 1996). Collecting intervals across studies also helps in constructing plausible regions for population parameters. This practice should help prevent the common mistake of assuming a parameter is contained in a confidence interval.

Multiplicities. *Multiple outcomes require special handling. There are many ways to conduct reasonable inference when faced with multiplicity (e.g., Bonferroni correction of p values, multivariate test statistics, empirical Bayes methods). It is your responsibility to define and justify the methods used.*

Statisticians speak of the curse of dimensionality. To paraphrase, multiplicities are the curse of the social sciences. In many areas of psychology, we cannot do research on important problems without encountering multiplicity. We often encounter many variables and many relationships.

One of the most prevalent strategies psychologists use to handle multiplicity is to follow an ANOVA with pairwise multiple-comparison tests. This approach is usually wrong for several reasons. First, pairwise methods such as Tukey's honestly significant difference procedure were designed to control a familywise error rate based on the sample size and number of comparisons. Preceding them with an omnibus F test in a stagewise testing procedure defeats this design, making it unnecessarily conservative. Second, researchers rarely need to compare all possible means to understand their results or assess their theory; by setting their sights large, they sacrifice their power to see small. Third, the lattice of all possible pairs is a straitjacket; forcing themselves to wear it often restricts researchers to uninteresting hypotheses and induces them to ignore more fruitful ones.

As an antidote to the temptation to explore all pairs, imagine yourself restricted to mentioning only pairwise comparisons in the introduction and discussion sections of your article. Higher order concepts such as trends, structures, or clusters of effects would be forbidden. Your theory would be restricted to first-order associations. This scenario brings to mind the illogic of the converse, popular practice of theorizing about higher order concepts in the introduction and discussion sections and then supporting that theorizing in the results section with atomistic pairwise comparisons. If a specific contrast interests you, examine it. If all interest you, ask yourself why. For a detailed treatment of the use of contrasts, see Rosenthal, Rosnow, and Rubin (in press).

There is a variant of this preoccupation with all possible pairs that comes with the widespread practice of printing p values or asterisks next to every correlation in a correlation matrix. Methodologists frequently point out that these p values should be adjusted through Bonferroni or other corrections. One should ask instead why any reader would want this information. The possibilities are as follows:

All the correlations are "significant." If so, this can be noted in a single footnote.

None of the correlations are "significant." Again, this can be noted once. We need to be reminded that this situation does not rule out the possibility that combinations or subsets of the correlations may be "significant." The definition of the null hypothesis for the global test may not include other potential null hypotheses that might be rejected if they were tested. A subset of the correlations is "significant." If so, our purpose in appending asterisks would seem to be to mark this subset. Using "significance" tests in this way is really a highlighting technique to facilitate pattern recognition. If this is your goal in presenting results, then it is better served by calling attention to the pattern (perhaps by sorting

the rows and columns of the correlation matrix) and assessing it directly. This would force you, as well, to provide a plausible explanation.

There is a close relative of all possible pairs called "all possible combinations." We see this occasionally in the publishing of higher way factorial ANOVAs that include all possible main effects and interactions. One should not imagine that placing asterisks next to conventionally significant effects in a five-way ANOVA, for example, skirts the multiplicity problem. A typical five-way fully factorial design applied to a reasonably large sample of random data has about an 80% chance of producing at least one significant effect by conventional F tests at the .05 critical level (Hurlburt & Spiegel, 1976).

Underlying the widespread use of all-possible-pairs methodology is the legitimate fear among editors and reviewers that some researchers would indulge in fishing expeditions without the restraint of simultaneous test procedures. We should indeed fear the well-intentioned, indiscriminate search for structure more than the deliberate falsification of results, if only for the prevalence of wishful thinking over nefariousness. There are Bonferroni and recent related methods (e.g., Benjamini & Hochberg, 1995) for controlling this problem statistically. Nevertheless, there is an alternative institutional restraint. Reviewers should require writers to articulate their expectations well enough to reduce the likelihood of post hoc rationalizations. Fishing expeditions are often recognizable by the promiscuity of their explanations. They mix ideas from scattered sources, rely heavily on common sense, and cite fragments rather than trends.

If, on the other hand, a researcher fools us with an intriguing result caught while indiscriminately fishing, we might want to fear this possibility less than we do now. The enforcing of rules to prevent chance results in our journals may at times distract us from noticing the more harmful possibility of publishing bogus theories and methods (ill-defined variables, lack of parsimony, experimenter bias, logical errors, artifacts) that are buttressed by evidently impeccable statistics. There are enough good ideas behind fortuitous results to make us wary of restricting them. This is especially true in those areas of psychology where lives and major budgets are not at stake. Let replications promote reputations.

Causality. *Inferring causality from nonrandomized designs is a risky enterprise. Researchers using nonrandomized designs have an extra obligation to explain the logic behind covariates included in their designs and to alert the reader to plausible rival hypotheses that might explain their results. Even in randomized experiments, attributing causal effects to any one aspect of the treatment condition requires support from additional experimentation.*

It is sometimes thought that correlation does not prove causation but "causal modeling" does. Despite the admonitions of experts in this field, researchers sometimes use goodness-of-fit indices to hunt through thickets of competing models and settle on a plausible substantive explanation only in retrospect. McDonald (1997), in an analysis of a historical data set, showed the dangers of this practice and the importance of substantive theory. Scheines, Spirites, Glymour, Meek, and Richardson (1998; discussions following) offer similar cautions from a theoretical standpoint.

A generally accepted framework for formulating questions concerning the estimation of causal effects in social and biomedical science involves the use of "potential outcomes," with one outcome for each treatment condition. Although the perspective has old roots, including use by Fisher and Neyman in the context of completely randomized experiments analyzed by randomization-based inference (Rubin, 1990b), it is typically referred to as "Rubin's causal model" or RCM (Holland, 1986). For extensions to observational studies and other forms of inference, see Rubin (1974, 1977, 1978). This approach is now relatively standard, even for settings with instrumental variables and multistage models or simultaneous equations.

The crucial idea is to set up the causal inference problem as one of missing data, as defined in Rubin's (1976) article, where the missing data are the values of the potential outcomes under the treatment *not* received and the observed data include the values of the potential outcomes under the received treatments. Causal effects are defined on a unit level as the comparison of the potential outcomes under the different treatments, only one of which can ever be observed (we cannot go back in time to expose the unit to a different treatment). The essence of the RCM is to formulate causal questions in this way and to use formal statistical methods to draw probabilistic causal inferences, whether based on Fisherian randomization-based (permutation) distributions, Neymanian repeated-sampling randomization-based distributions, frequentist superpopulation sampling distributions, or Bayesian posterior distributions (Rubin, 1990a).

If a problem of causal inference cannot be formulated in this manner (as the comparison of potential outcomes under different treatment assignments), it is not a problem of inference for causal effects, and the use of "causal" should be avoided. To see the confusion that can be created by ignoring this requirement, see the classic Lord's paradox and its resolution by the use of the RCM in Holland and Rubin's (1983) chapter.

The critical assumptions needed for causal inference are essentially always beyond testing from the data at hand because they involve the missing data. Thus, especially when formulating causal questions from nonrandomized data, the underlying assumptions needed to justify any causal conclusions should be carefully and explicitly argued, not in terms of technical properties like "uncorrelated error terms," but in terms of real world properties, such as how the units received the different treatments.

The use of complicated causal-modeling software rarely yields any results that have any interpretation as causal effects. If such software is used to produce anything beyond an exploratory description of a data set, the bases for such extended conclusions must be carefully presented and not just asserted on the basis of imprecise labeling conventions of the software.

Tables and figures. *Although tables are commonly used to show exact values, well-drawn figures need not sacrifice precision. Figures attract the reader's eye and help convey global results. Because individuals have different preferences for processing complex information, it often helps to provide both tables*

Figure 2
Graphics for Regression

A

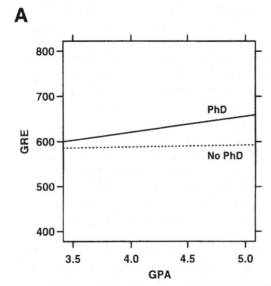

B

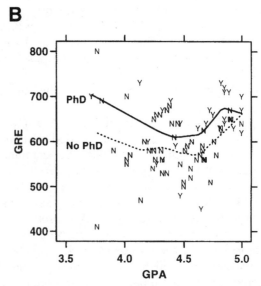

Note. GRE = Graduate Record Examination; GPA = grade point average; PhD and No PhD = completed and did not complete the doctoral degree; Y = yes; N = no.

Figure 3
Graphics for Groups

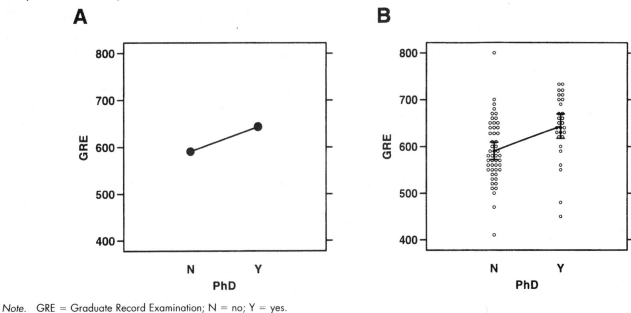

A   B

Note. GRE = Graduate Record Examination; N = no; Y = yes.

and figures. *This works best when figures are kept small enough to allow space for both formats. Avoid complex figures when simpler ones will do. In all figures, include graphical representations of interval estimates whenever possible.*

Bailar and Mosteller (1988) offer helpful information on improving tables in publications. Many of their recommendations (e.g., sorting rows and columns by marginal averages, rounding to a few significant digits, avoiding decimals when possible) are based on the clearly written tutorials of Ehrenberg (1975, 1981).

A common deficiency of graphics in psychological publications is their lack of essential information. In most cases, this information is the shape or distribution of the data. Whether from a negative motivation to conceal irregularities or from a positive belief that less is more, omitting shape information from graphics often hinders scientific evaluation. Chambers et al. (1983) and Cleveland (1995) offer specific ways to address these problems. The examples in Figure 2 do this using two of the most frequent graphical forms in psychology publications.

Figure 2 shows plots based on data from 80 graduate students in a Midwestern university psychology department, collected from 1969 through 1978. The variables are scores on the psychology advanced test of the Graduate Record Examination (GRE), the undergraduate grade point average (GPA), and whether a student completed a doctoral degree in the department (PhD). Figure 2A shows a format appearing frequently in psychology journal articles: two regression lines, one for each group of students. This graphic conveys nothing more than four numbers: the slopes and intercepts of the regression lines. Because the scales have no physical meaning, seeing the

slopes of lines (as opposed to reading the numbers) adds nothing to our understanding of the relationship.

Figure 2B shows a scatter plot of the same data with a locally weighted scatter plot smoother for each PhD group (Cleveland & Devlin, 1988). This robust curvilinear regression smoother (called LOESS) is available in modern statistics packages. Now we can see some curvature in the relationships. (When a model that includes a linear and quadratic term for GPA is computed, the apparent interaction involving the PhD and no PhD groups depicted in Figure 2A disappears.) The graphic in Figure 2B tells us many things. We note the unusual student with a GPA of less than 4.0 and a psychology GRE score of 800; we note the less surprising student with a similar GPA but a low GRE score (both of whom failed to earn doctoral degrees); we note the several students who had among the lowest GRE scores but earned doctorates, and so on. We might imagine these kinds of cases in Figure 2A (as we should in any data set containing error), but their location and distribution in Figure 2B tells us something about this specific data set.

Figure 3A shows another popular format for displaying data in psychology journals. It is based on the data set used for Figure 2. Authors frequently use this format to display the results of *t* tests or ANOVAs. For factorial ANOVAs, this format gives authors an opportunity to represent interactions by using a legend with separate symbols for each line. In more laboratory-oriented psychology journals (e.g., animal behavior, neuroscience), authors sometimes add error bars to the dots representing the means.

Figure 3B adds to the line graphic a dot plot representing the data and 95% confidence intervals on the means of the two groups (using the *t* distribution). The graphic reveals a left skewness of GRE scores in the PhD group. Although this skewness may not be severe enough to affect our statistical conclusions, it is nevertheless noteworthy. It may be due to ceiling effects (although note the 800 score in the no PhD group) or to some other factor. At the least, the reader has a right to be able to evaluate this kind of information.

There are other ways to include data or distributions in graphics, including box plots and stem-and-leaf plots (Tukey, 1977) and kernel density estimates (Scott, 1992; Silverman, 1986). Many of these procedures are found in modern statistical packages. It is time for authors to take advantage of them and for editors and reviewers to urge authors to do so.

Discussion

Interpretation

When you interpret effects, think of credibility, generalizability, and robustness. Are the effects credible, given the results of previous studies and theory? Do the features of the design and analysis (e.g., sample quality, similarity of the design to designs of previous studies, similarity of the effects to those in previous studies) suggest the results are generalizable? Are the design and analytic methods robust enough to support strong conclusions?

Novice researchers err either by overgeneralizing their results or, equally unfortunately, by overparticularizing. Explicitly compare the effects detected in your inquiry with the effect sizes reported in related previous studies. Do not be afraid to extend your interpretations to a general class or population if you have reasons to assume that your results apply. This general class may consist of populations you have studied at your site, other populations at other sites, or even more general populations. Providing these reasons in your discussion will help you stimulate future research for yourself and others.

Conclusions

Speculation may be appropriate, but use it sparingly and explicitly. Note the shortcomings of your study. Remember, however, that acknowledging limitations is for the purpose of qualifying results and avoiding pitfalls in future research. Confession should not have the goal of disarming criticism. Recommendations for future research should be thoughtful and grounded in present and previous findings. Gratuitous suggestions ("further research needs to be done . . .") waste space. Do not interpret a single study's results as having importance independent of the effects reported elsewhere in the relevant literature. The thinking presented in a single study may turn the movement of the literature, but the results in a single study are important primarily as one contribution to a mosaic of study effects.

Some had hoped that this task force would vote to recommend an outright ban on the use of significance tests in psychology journals. Although this might eliminate some abuses, the committee thought that there were enough counterexamples (e.g., Abelson, 1997) to justify forbearance. Furthermore, the committee believed that the problems raised in its charge went beyond the simple question of whether to ban significance tests.

The task force hopes instead that this report will induce editors, reviewers, and authors to recognize practices that institutionalize the thoughtless application of statistical methods. Distinguishing statistical significance from theoretical significance (Kirk, 1996) will help the entire research community publish more substantial results. Encouraging good design and logic will help improve the quality of conclusions. And promoting modern statistical graphics will improve the assessment of assumptions and the display of results.

More than 50 years ago, Hotelling, Bartky, Deming, Friedman, and Hoel (1948) wrote, "Unfortunately, too many people like to do their statistical work as they say their prayers—merely substitute in a formula found in a highly respected book written a long time ago" (p. 103). Good theories and intelligent interpretation advance a discipline more than rigid methodological orthodoxy. If editors keep in mind Fisher's (1935) words quoted in the *Analysis* section, then there is less danger of methodology substituting for thought. Statistical methods should guide and discipline our thinking but should not determine it.

REFERENCES

Abelson, R. P. (1995). *Statistics as principled argument*. Hillsdale, NJ: Erlbaum.
Abelson, R. P. (1997). On the surprising longevity of flogged horses: Why there is a case for the significance test. *Psychological Science*, 23, 12–15.
American Psychological Association. (1994). *Publication manual of the American Psychological Association* (4th ed.). Washington, DC: Author.
Bailar, J. C. , & Mosteller, F. (1988). Guidelines for statistical reporting in articles for medical journals: Amplifications and explanations. *Annals of Internal Medicine*, 108, 266–273.
Baker, B. L. (1969). Symptom treatment and symptom substitution in enuresis. *Journal of Abnormal Psychology*, 74, 42–49.
Benjamini, Y. , & Hochberg, Y. (1995). Controlling the false discovery rate: A practical and powerful approach to multiple testing. *Journal of the Royal Statistical Society*, 57 (Series B), 289–300.
Chambers, J. , Cleveland, W. , Kleiner, B. , & Tukey, P. (1983). *Graphical methods for data analysis*. Monterey, CA: Wadsworth.
Chartrand, J. M. (1997). *National sample survey*. Unpublished raw data.
Cleveland, W. S. (1995). *Visualizing data*. Summit, NJ: Hobart Press.
Cleveland, W. S., & Devlin, S. (1988). Locally weighted regression analysis by local fitting. *Journal of the American Statistical Association*, 83, 596–640.
Cohen, J. (1969). *Statistical power analysis for the behavioral sciences*. New York: Academic Press.
Cohen, J. (1988). *Statistical power analysis for the behavioral sciences* (2nd ed.). Hillsdale, NJ: Erlbaum.
Cohen, J. (1994). The earth is round (p. 05). *American Psychologist*, 49, 997–1003.
Cook, T. D., & Campbell, D. T. (1979). *Quasi-experimentation: Design and analysis issues for field settings*. Chicago: Rand McNally.

Cronbach, L. J. (1975). Beyond the two disciplines of psychology. *American Psychologist, 30,* 116–127.

Ehrenberg, A. S. C. (1975). *Data reduction: Analyzing and interpreting statistical data.* New York: Wiley.

Ehrenberg, A. S. C. (1981). The problem of numeracy. *American Statistician, 35,* 67–71.

Feldt, L. S. Brennan, R. L. (1989). Reliability. In R. L. Linn (Ed.), *Educational measurement* (3rd ed., pp. 105–146). Washington, DC: American Council on Education.

Fisher, R. A. (1935). *The design of experiments.* Edinburgh, Scotland: Oliver & Boyd.

Fleiss, J. L. (1994). Measures of effect size for categorical data. In H. Cooper & L. V. Hedges (Eds.), *The handbook of research synthesis* (pp. 245–260). New York: Sage.

Harlow, L. L. Mulaik, S. A. , & Steiger, J. H. (1997). *What if there were no significance tests?* Hillsdale, NJ: Erlbaum.

Holland, P. W. (1986). Statistics and causal inference. *Journal of the American Statistical Association, 81,* 945–960.

Holland, P. W., & Rubin, D. B. (1983). On Lord's paradox. In H. Wainer & S. Messick (Eds.), *Principles of modern psychological measurement* (pp. 3–25). Hillsdale, NJ: Erlbaum.

Hotelling, H., Bartky, W., Deming, W. E. , Friedman, M., & Hoel, P. (1948). The teaching of statistics. *Annals of Mathematical Statistics, 19,* 95–115.

Hurlburt, R. T., & Spiegel, D. K. (1976). Dependence of F ratios sharing a common denominator mean square. *American Statistician, 20,* 74–78.

Kahn, J. R., & Udry, J. R. (1986). Marital coital frequency: Unnoticed outliers and unspecified interactions lead to erroneous conclusions. *American Sociological Review, 51,* 734–737.

Keselman, H. J., Huberty, C. J., Lix, L. M., Olejnik, S. , Cribbie, R., Donahue, B., Kowalchuk, R. K., Lowman, L. L., Petoskey, M. D., Keselman, J. C., & Levin, J. R. (1998). Statistical practices of educational researchers: An analysis of their ANOVA, MANOVA, and ANCOVA analyses. *Review of Educational Research, 68,* 350–386.

Kirk, R. E. (1996). Practical significance: A concept whose time has come. *Educational and Psychological Measurement, 56,* 746–759.

Little, R. J. A., & Rubin, D. B. (1987). *Statistical analysis with missing data.* New York: Wiley.

McDonald, R. P. (1997). Haldane's lungs: A case study in path analysis. *Multivariate Behavioral Research, 32,* 1–38.

Messick, S. (1989). Validity. In R. L. Linn (Ed.), *Educational measurement* (3rd ed., pp. 13–103). Washington, DC: American Council on Education.

Rosenthal, R. (1966). *Experimenter effects in behavioral research.* New York: Appleton-Century-Crofts.

Rosenthal, R. (1994). Parametric measures of effect size. In H. Cooper & L. V. Hedges (Eds.), *The handbook of research synthesis* (pp. 231–244). New York: Sage.

Rosenthal, R. Rosnow, R. L. Rubin, D. B. (in press) *Contrasts and effect sizes in behavioral research: A correlational approach.* New York: Cambridge University Press.

Rosenthal, R., & Rubin, D. B. (1982). A simple general purpose display of magnitude of experimental effect. *Journal of Educational Psychology, 74,* 166–169.

Rosenthal, R., & Rubin, D. B. (1994). The counternull value of an effect size: A new statistic. *Psychological Science, 5,* 329–334.

Rubin, D. B. (1974). Estimating causal effects of treatments in randomized and nonrandomized studies. *Journal of Educational Psychology, 66,* 688–701.

Rubin, D. B. (1976). Inference and missing data. *Biometrika, 63,* 581–592.

Rubin, D. B. (1977). Assignment of treatment group on the basis of a covariate. *Journal of Educational Statistics, 2,* 1–26.

Rubin, D. B. (1978). Bayesian inference for causal effects: The role of randomization. *Annals of Statistics, 6,* 34–58.

Rubin, D. B. (1990a). Formal modes of statistical inference for causal effects. *Journal of Statistical Planning and Inference, 25,* 279–292.

Rubin, D. B. (1990b). Neyman (1923) and causal inference in experiments and observational studies. *Statistical Science, 5,* 472–480.

Scheines, R., Spirites, P. , Glymour, C., Meek, C., & Richardson, T. (1998). The TETRAD project: Constraint based aids to causal model specification. *Multivariate Behavioral Research, 33,* 65–117.

Schmidt, F. (1996). Statistical significance testing and cumulative knowledge in psychology: Implications for the training of researchers. *Psychological Methods, 1,* 115–129.

Scott, D. W. (1992). *Multivariate density estimation: Theory, practice, and visualization.* New York: Wiley.

Silverman, B. W. (1986). *Density estimation for statistics and data analysis.* New York: Chapman & Hall.

Snyder, P., & Lawson, S. (1993). Evaluating results using corrected and uncorrected effect size estimates. *Journal of Experimental Education, 61,* 334–349.

Thompson, B. (1996). AERA editorial policies regarding statistical significance testing: Three suggested reforms. *Educational Researcher, 25(2),* 26–30.

Thompson, B., & Snyder, P.A. (1998). Statistical significance and reliability analyses in recent JCD research articles. *Journal of Counseling and Development, 76,* 436–441.

Tukey, J. W. (1977). *Exploratory data analysis.* Reading, MA: Addison-Wesley.

Wainer, H. (in press). One cheer for null hypothesis significance testing. *Psychological Methods.*

Webb, E. J., Campbell, D. T., Schwartz, R. D., & Sechrest, L. (1966). *Unobtrusive measures: Nonreactive research in the social sciences.* Chicago: Rand McNally.

Unit 7

Key Points to Consider

❖ What are likely social consequences of policy decisions based on flawed research?

❖ What does the future hold for qualitative research in education?

❖ What arguments could be made in favor of applied research over basic research?

❖ How might qualitative and quantitative research be merged to make each approach more rigorous and useful?

 **Links**   **www.dushkin.com/online/**

These sites are annotated on pages 4 and 5.

Perhaps you have heard others express the idea, or even remarked yourself, that because research often yields conflicting findings there is little value in it. This is a common criticism of research that demands further examination. What it suggests, in effect, is that there is no point in conducting systematic study unless everyone can agree all of the time. Yet imposing this absolutism on research sets an unreasonable expectation. It is only natural that different studies of the same phenomenon conducted with different groups in different contexts are likely to yield some similarities and some differences. Contrary to naïve opinion, it is not a single, definitive study that "proves" anything. Rather, it is the weight of accumulated evidence gathered over time from which patterns emerge and new trends are spawned. The aim of research is to recommend rather than to dictate. Particularly in the social sciences, one worthy aim of research is to improve professional practice. If those of us in "the helping professions" (e.g., education, psychology, health care, sociology, and so forth) can improve their practice through research they can, in turn, do a better job of helping the population that they are expected to serve. Ideally, peoples' lives and situations would be improved. Simply stated, research aims have to do with the "so what?" question in research.

Unit 7 begins with Daniel Tanner's discussion of the social costs incurred when bad research is presented as an authoritative or definitive answer. The next two articles, by Reba Page and William Foote Whyte, consider where research might be headed next. Each author discusses a particular direction for research that appears to hold greater promise, based on what has already occurred in their fields. The final article, by Donn Weinholtz, Barbara Kacer, and Thomas Rocklin proposes the somewhat controversial idea that quantitative and qualitative research methods, thought by purists to be unmixable, might be blended into hybrids that counteract the weaknesses of the two types of methodology when used solely.

Research Aims: Improving Professional Practice

The Social Consequences Of Bad Research

In many cases it would seem that school practitioners can test research findings for practicability and generalizability more effectively than some of the editors of the leading educational research journals, Mr. Tanner contends.

By Daniel Tanner

THERE IS a sacred taboo in social research against addressing the problem of research bias. Now the word *taboo* comes from Tongan, the Polynesian language of the Tongans. As the anthropologists tell us, a taboo is the sacred and primitive tribal prohibition of an action or word—under pain of supernatural punishment. Hence I realize that I may be putting myself in mortal peril—if not from supernatural forces, then from the natural forces of professional tribal politics. However, if you'll pardon the pun, I may be saved by the "bell curve."

We are all too familiar with the relentless attacks on the public schools over the past half century by national commissions, by the mass media, by special-interest groups, and by individual school blamers. These attacks have come from within the profession as well as from outside it and from all parts of the political spectrum. Traditionally, the school blamers required no hard data to support their allegations and indictments, and politicians from the White House to the state house could blame the public schools

DANIEL TANNER *is a professor in the Graduate School of Education, Rutgers University, New Brunswick, N.J.*

for any and every short coming, even as they cut the allocations for elementary and secondary education.

Since the time of the so-called Coleman Report of 1966, educational researchers have been busy generating from their burgeoning data banks a deluge of increasingly elaborate empirical studies that examine the limitations of schooling rather than its potential for furthering social progress.[1] Gunnar Myrdal pointed out that the direction and findings of social research "normally come from the political interests that dominate the society in which we live."[2] Hence we find educational researchers at times moving as a flock in generating statistical data that portray the public schools as either utterly anemic[3] or beset by problems of such crippling proportions "that our entire public education system is nearing collapse."[4]

To many researchers and education policy makers the data would seem to indicate that the public schools are virtually brain dead. Myron Lieberman has gone a step further in the title of his book published by Harvard University Press: *Public Education: An Autopsy.*[5] With regard to the diagnoses that find the public schools moribund, as a long-time movie buff I cannot help but recall the scene from *Horse Feathers* in which Groucho Marx as Dr.

Hackenbush is taking someone's pulse and exclaims, "Either this man is dead or my watch has stopped."

Groucho was indeed using the right instrument to measure the patient's pulse, but merely using the right instrument is no guarantee of valid conclusions. To put the matter more soberly, as Myrdal did, the cultural and political setting will often tempt researchers "to aim opportunistically for conclusions that fit prejudices" and will shape "the approaches we choose in research,. . . the concepts, models, and theories we use, and the way in which we select and arrange our observations and present the results of our research."[6] The consequence, Myrdal argued, is systematic bias in our work—even in our manmade programming of computing machines.[7]

In recent years, as reflected by the journal *Educational Researcher,* a number of members of the American Educational Research Association have built their careers on the debate between qualitative research and quantitative research.[8] I had believed that John Dewey had dumped that issue into its final resting place back in 1929 when he wrote in *The Sources of a Science of Education* that all good research must be built on powerful qualitative ideas, that elaborate statistical measurements will have little sci-

From *Phi Delta Kappan,* January 1998, pp. 345-349. © 1998 by *Phi Delta Kappan.* Reprinted by permission.

entific value when the problems under investigation lack generalized significance, and, of course, that the same is true for nonstatistical research.[9]

Abandoning the Great Tradition

Regardless of the false dualism that divides social research into quantitative and qualitative camps, social researchers of either ilk appear to have abandoned what Myrdal called "the great tradition in social science"—namely, "for the social scientists to take a direct as well as indirect responsibility for popular education."[10]

Not only have social scientists largely abandoned their responsibility for popular education, but they have focused primarily on the limitations of public elementary and secondary education. One has only to look at the research generated over a period extending from Christopher Jencks' *Inequality* in 1972, which launched many careers on "no school effects" research, to the *Bell Curve* of 1994.[11] In effect, whether opportunistically or unwittingly, many of the most vocal and visible members of the social science research community have fallen in league with the political Right on issues of education policy.

With the findings of the Jencks study widely endorsed as valid by leading social science researchers, President Nixon's Commission on School Finance used Jencks' work to argue that schooling is inconsequential in the lives of other people's children—namely, the disadvantaged. Daniel Patrick Moynihan, then a professor of education and urban politics at the Kennedy School of Government at Harvard University and a consultant to the President, cited the report of the commission in holding that "with respect to school finance there is the strong possibility that we may be already spending too much."[12] Moynihan then concluded that "a final fact is that at a point, school expenditure does not seem to have any notable influence on school achievement," and "this discovery was one of the major events in large-scale social science."[13]

Can anyone imagine our professoriate in the social sciences generating research showing that a college education makes little difference in people's lives and that we may well be allocating too much public funding for higher education? On the contrary, the research findings on the effects of a college education on people's lives are invariably positive and judged to warrant increased expenditures.[14]

Seeming to anticipate the "no school effects" research, Gunnar Myrdal commented in 1968 that "there is truth in the biblical saying that, 'He that seeketh, findeth'; if a scientist seeks what isn't there, he will find it." He will find it, Myrdal continued, "as long as empirical data are scanty and he allows his logic to be twisted."[15] On the research problem of finding what isn't there, the humorist Robert Benchley once cautioned, "You can't prove that platypuses don't lay eggs by photographing platypuses *not* laying eggs." Hence, even though more than two-thirds of the variance in the research on school effects was unaccounted for, the researchers proceeded to treat this as a negative finding on school effects. In essence, the researchers prove the case by *not* finding something.

The lead article in the April 1994 issue of *Educational Researcher* bears the title "Does Money Matter?"[16] Just ask your spouse, neighbor, banker, dean, or university president—not to mention the Pentagon. I recall a TV interview some years ago in which a U.S. senator offered this candid comment: There are two things that are important in politics. The first is money, and I can't remember what the other one is." Incredibly, a quarter of a century after Jencks, we are still debating whether money matters in public elementary and secondary education. Somewhat belatedly the meta-analysis in the April 1994 issue of *Educational Researcher* found that, contrary to most of the earlier studies, the relationship between resource inputs and school outcomes is systematically positive—something that every teacher and parent has always known.[17] However, when the prevailing political policy is one of social and educational retrenchment, opportunity strikes for researchers to garner grants for themselves and to build their reputations by shattering the conventional wisdom.

According to Myrdal, our elaborate statistical techniques for generating and interpreting data often make our social research even more susceptible to bias. He argues that we need to put our value premises up front and put our research to the test of relevance and practical significance to our democratic social ideals.[18] As I noted above, many of those who posture as advocates of the disadvantaged have been quick to endorse the kind of research and public policy that begins with the limitations of schooling as opposed to the potentials.[19]

Returning to our good friend Groucho, Dr. Hackenbush may indeed have been using the right instrument and technique for taking the measurement, but his faulty premises guaranteed false findings. However, many researchers choose the instrument and set the conditions in an effort to prove their premises, or they set the stage for measuring that which is most easily measured. Albert Einstein put the matter quite clearly when he commented, "I have little patience with scientists who take a board of wood, look for the thinnest part, and drill a great number of holes where drilling is easy."[20]

Finding no connections is far easier than finding connections. The use of elaborate statistical techniques and hyper-abstract theoretical models to create the impression of scientific objectivity and to mask judgments and questionable premises is coupled with a cascade of unnecessarily technical and esoteric jargon that serves only to obscure issues, to mask the poverty of ideas underlying the research, and to isolate the communication within the cocoons of narrow academic specialties. In Myrdal's words, "While a great tradition in social science was to express reasoning as clearly and succinctly as possible, the tendency in recent decades has been for social scientists to close themselves off by means of unnecessarily elaborate and strange terminology, often to the point of impairing their ability to understand one another—perhaps occasionally even themselves."[21] This is no less the case with much so-called qualitative research.

The situation is such, Myrdal noted, that obscure technical language has become the instrument for spawning exercises in hyper-abstraction that spiral ever upward. One who is able to express ideas directly and with extraordinary clarity, such as John Kenneth Galbraith, observed Myrdal, is eyed with suspicion by his more pedestrian colleagues who refuse to recognize the contributions to knowledge that he has made.[22]

Politics of Standards

Recently, I was looking at an oversized, multicolored foldout from a publication issued in 1991 by the Council for Basic Education (CBE). It identified standards by grade level in each of the academic subjects. According to the CBE, the standards were gleaned from those developed by the national professional associations in the various academic disciplines and from state curricular frameworks, and, in the words of the CBE, they "represent the best wisdom currently available from the field."[23]

Now, get a load of this standard in science, cited by the CBE as formulated at the English Coalition Conference and issued by the National Council of Teachers of English and the Modern Language Association. It is to be attained by fourth-graders in the year 2000: fourth-grade students will "write and speak eloquently about observations and experiments." (I can only assume that the underlying wisdom of those who formulated this standard was that the fourth-graders of 1991 would still be in the fourth grade in the year 2000, struggling to meet this standard.) I ask you, how many academicians are able to "write and speak eloquently about observations and experiments"?

The current national standards movement can be traced to the failure of the nation's political leadership to meet the national goals that grew out of the Education Summit of governors, which was convened by President Bush in 1989. As a result of that summit, the Bush Administration produced its education strategy, called America 2000. The top goal was that, by the year 2000, "All children will start school ready to learn."[24] Back in 1989 the year 2000 seemed far off in the future—certainly beyond the governors' terms of office. So the current crop of governors and President Clinton shifted conveniently to rigorous and narrowly defined national standards for student testing. In effect, they sidestepped what was once the number-one national goal (which would have required massive social reconstruction on a scale comparable to the New Deal) and transferred the responsibility and accountability to "Mrs. Jones and her kindergartners."

On 8 September 1993 U.S. Secretary of Education Richard Riley held a press conference to release *Adult Literacy in America,* a study conducted by the Educational Testing Service (ETS) for the National Center for Education Statistics.[25] All three major network news programs that evening opened with an alarming story taken from Secretary Riley's press release declaring that most U.S. adults can't read. The following day, the front page of the *New York Times* carried a story headlined "Study Says Half of Adults in U.S. Can't Read or Handle Arithmetic."[26]

It doesn't take much intelligence to eye such sweeping pronouncements with suspicion. Yet the mass media immediately seized upon a report that made sensational copy. At the same time, the research methodology and findings in the report were accepted without challenge in academe. Here was yet another national report to use in cannonading our schools—a cannonade issued almost exactly a decade after *A Nation at Risk.*[27]

Even a cursory review of the premises and research methodology of the ETS national literacy study reveals gaping flaws that should have raised questions about the underlying motives of the research sponsors. First, the definition of literacy formulated for the study was utterly different from any that had been used previously by the U.S. Bureau of the Census or by any other national or international agency. For the ETS study, literacy was defined as "using printed and written information to function in society, to achieve one's goals, and to develop one's knowledge potential."[28] Aside from the ambiguity of the definition, it is doubtful that very many people in our society would claim that they have achieved their goals and have developed their knowledge potential, let alone voluntarily agree to submit to a lengthy written test to demonstrate that proficiency or to risk revealing their level of incompetence.

Adult Literacy in America claimed that it was based on a nationally representative sample of 13,000 adults (16 years of age or older) who submitted to a written test, coupled with interviews and tests conducted in 27,000 households in the U.S. In making a few simple calculations of my own, I find that the proportion of immigrants in the national sample far exceeded the proportional representation of immigrants in the national population. What's more, most of these immigrants had never attended U.S. schools. Also grossly overrepresented were disadvantaged minorities whose years of schooling, test scores, and economic conditions are below those of the national population. Furthermore, almost one in 10 males in the study were inmates of federal and state penitentiaries—hardly in a position "to function in society, to achieve one's goals, and to develop one's knowledge potential." The proportion of males incarcerated in federal and state prisons is actually less than 0.8%. Penitentiary inmates were overrepresented in this "scientific" sampling by almost 1,200%. The proportion of female inmates was also grossly overrepresented in the sample.

As expected, the test scores were positively and strongly correlated with years of schooling in the U.S. Of the 25% of residents in the 27,000 households who tested at the lowest level, almost one in five suffered from visual difficulties that impaired their reading of ordinary print materials under ordinary lighting conditions, let alone under the conditions of taking a timed test under the supervision of a stranger—the stranger being an ETS examiner in their home. In other words, they met the legal definition for being blind. More than one in four had physical, mental, or health difficulties that prevented them from participating in regular work, school attendance, housework, or other activities.

Furthermore, the report failed to indicate the percentages of people who declined to submit to the tests and to the questionnaires and interviews that required more than an hour of time under direct supervision. One might reasonably infer that busy people are less likely to make themselves available for such a test. Aside from the inherent biases in the research design, this factor may help account for the disproportionate representation of the incarcerated, the homebound, the debilitated, and the unemployed among subjects in the study.

It must also be acknowledged that one surely needs to know how to take a multiple-choice test to get through school or college, but one hardly encounters such tests in real life. Hence we must question whether such a test is a fair simulation of life conditions.

The validity of many of the test items must be regarded as suspect to say the least. In TV interviews, school critics made much of the finding that most adults in the study had difficulty deciphering a bus schedule. The schedule contained numerous distractors and conditional information in a hypothetical situation.[29] The school critics proceeded to declare that 80% of adults are unable to figure out which bus will get them home. To use Groucho's diagnosis, 80% of American adults are not finding their way home each day. Common sense should recoil at the way so-called authorities fashion their factoids in support of their biases—never submitting themselves to the test of the method of intelligence.

I am often amused when I should perhaps be appalled at seeing William Bennett or Gore Vidal, interviewed on TV as authors of national best-selling books, attacking the public schools for the allegedly endemic illiteracy of the adult American population. If people can't read, who is buying Bennett's *Book of Virtues* or Vidal's latest best seller? The fact is that, despite the concern that television and computer screens are distracting the population from old-fashioned books, the number of books sold annually per capita has not undergone a decline as predicted by many pundits, and Americans continue to spend more on books than on almost any other medium.[30]

We are all familiar with the impact of revisionism on historical and social science research, including education. It has become increasingly fashionable in some circles of the social sciences to build reputations and to convey the impression of scientific inquiry by generating hard data so as to overthrow conventional wisdom. Indeed, those researchers who have made use of elaborate mathematical and statistical techniques and computer-generated models of analysis have intimidated many of their colleagues, while others have taken the research seriously.

A notable example is the two-volume study by two noted economists, Robert Fogel of the University of Chicago and Stanley Engerman of the University of Rochester, published in 1974 under the title *Time on the Cross.* Fogel and Engerman set out to examine the economics of American slavery through advanced statistical techniques used by those who call themselves "econometric historians" and "cliometricians." Fogel and Engerman amassed data proving that "the slave diet was not only adequate, it actually exceeded modern recommended daily levels of the chief nutrients."[31] Among their other findings was that "the slave mortality rate in childbearing was lower than the maternal death rate experienced by southern white women."[32] Fogel and Engerman presented data to support the finding that "the average daily diet of slaves was quite substantial" and that "the energy value of their diet exceeded that of free men in 1879 by more than 10%.[33] Their reasoning was based on a comparison of the nutritive value of sweet potatoes, a staple of the slave diet, against that of white potatoes, a staple of the diet of the white population. Fogel and Engerman concluded further that "the material conditions of the lives of slaves compared favorably with those of free industrial workers" and that "over the course of his lifetime, the typical slave field hand received about 90% of the income he produced."[34]

Following the perverse premises of Fogel and Engerman and employing their analytical techniques, one can easily amass data to prove that a herd of milk cows on modern dairy farms enjoys a far better level of care and nutrition and a lower mortality rate in calf-bearing than does the general human population in child-bearing and that the cows receive, in the care given them, the equivalent of 90% of the income they produce. This allows the farmer a net profit of 10%." Of course, this defies all sense and sensibility, but it serves to illustrate how statistical data can be used to validate research premises that are dead wrong to begin with.

The Fogelman/Engerman study is another example of generating elaborate quantitative measures to support a perverse qualitative idea. One only has to read the eloquent indictment of slavery in Darwin's *Voyage of the Beagle* to realize that no amount of statistical data can convey the realities of slavery more scientifically than the impassioned words of Darwin.

Practicability and Generalizability

In an age of mounting specialism in research, it has been said that we are learning more and more about less and less. This has commonly been called the "knowledge explosion." Consequently, we have neglected the synthesis of knowledge that would allow us to generalize and use our knowledge to help solve practical problems of social significance. The nation—and indeed the world—suffers not from a knowledge explosion but from a problems explosion.

Professional schools, including schools of education, have a mandate to engage in research and to advance professional practice with the mission of improving society. This mission is not necessarily shared by all academic disciplines, and for this reason universities have schools of medicine, public health, social work, architecture, urban planning, engineering, agriculture, education, and so on. Unfortunately, much that is taken for social research serves no social purpose other than to embellish reputations in the citadels of academe and sometimes even to undermine the democratic public interest.

It is my contention that school practitioners and researchers should be able to evaluate the efficacy of educational research and to guide their own practice through a commitment to the best available evidence. In many cases it would seem that school practitioners can test research findings for practicability and generalizability more effectively than some of the editors of the leading educational research journals. A review of these journals reveals that many of the articles fail to meet the tests of practicability and generalizability.

For example, consider a not at all atypical lead article in the spring 1992 issue of the *American Educational Research Journal,* which addressed the problem of giving insufficient emphasis to higher-order thinking and problem solving in the classroom. Now this is clearly one of our most significant and pervasive curriculum problems. However, the author of the article, a Stanford professor and theorist in organizational behavior in education, proceeded to attack the problem from the vantage point of behavioral decision theory and the economics of organizations, rather than to treat it as a curriculum problem. As a consequence, the organizational theorist came up with a bizarre solution—a solution that nevertheless warranted its choice by the editors as the lead article. The organizational theorist proposed to have two types of teachers in the school: one type would specialize in teaching the basic skills to ensure that students at least develop these lower-order skills; the second type would specialize in higher-order thinking and problem solving. "We argue," she wrote, "that such a division would result not only in higher-quality education, but also in a more equitable delivery of services from classroom to classroom."[35]

Just imagine being a member of a school faculty divided evenly between those designated teachers of lower-order thinking and those annointed teachers of higher-order thinking and problem solving! Aside from the disastrous impact on faculty morale, there are the predictable perverse effects on the curriculum and learning—predictable because there is a vast body of curriculum research revealing conclusively that such a dualism between skills and thinking is counterproductive. From the time of the Winnetka Plan of the early 1920s, when such a division was actually instituted school-wide,[36] to contemporary work in areas such as "writing across the curriculum" failure is predictable when skills are severed from the ideas that govern thinking. Unfortunately, the organizational theorist formulated a solution without having reviewed the pertinent curriculum research literature.[37] Had she done so, she would have found a powerful and consistent pattern of evidence amassed over a period spanning three-quarters of a century that clearly invalidates her line of inquiry.[38] Actually, ordinary school experience and common sense should have been sufficient for the organizational theorist to realize that her line of inquiry was invalid from the beginning.

Unfortunately, in the social sciences and education, research reports in our journals rarely go back more than five years in reviewing the pertinent literature. J. Robert Oppenheimer commented, "The openness of this world derives its character from the irreversibility of learning; what is once learned is part of human life. We cannot close our minds to discovery."[39]

In science, once something has been discovered, it might later be disproved, but it does not need to be discovered anew. In education, we have a vast and rich knowledge base on which to build. If we do not build on that base, our research and school practices will shift unwittingly with whatever sociopolitical tide is dominant. The capacity to build on and draw from the knowledge base requires that our theory be tested continually for its power for generalizability and practicability in a wide range of situations. In social research, theory must have the generative power for revealing useful pathways to solutions of social significance.

Early in this century, John Dewey warned that educational *practices* must be the source of the ultimate problems to be investigated if we are to build a science of education.[40] We may draw from the behavioral sciences, but the behavioral sciences do not define the educational problems. The faculties of the professional schools draw on the basic sciences and behavioral sciences, but their mandate is mission-oriented, not discipline centered. Hence they must, in Dewey's words, "operate through their own ideas, plannings, observations, judgments."[41] To do otherwise in education "is to surrender the education cause."[42]

1. James S. Coleman et al., *Equality of Educational Opportunity* (Washington, D.C.: Office of Education, U.S. Department of Health, Education, and Welfare, 1966); and Christopher Jencks et al., *Inequality: A Reassessment of the Effect of Family and Schooling in America* (New York: Basic Books, 1972).
2. Gunnar Myrdal, *Objectivity in Social Research* (New York: Pantheon, 1969), p. 48.
3. Jencks et al., op. cit.
4. John I. Goodlad, *A Place Called School* (New York: McGraw-Hill, 1984), p. 1.
5. Myron Lieberman, *Public Education: An Autopsy* (Cambridge, Mass.: Harvard University Press, 1993).
6. Myrdal, p. 49.
7. Ibid., p. 44.
8. Larry V. Hedges, Richard D. Laine, and Rob Greenwald, "Does Money Matter? A Meta-Analysis of Studies of the Effects of Differential School Inputs on Student Outcomes," *Educational Researcher*, April 1994, pp. 5–14; and Eric A. Hanushek, "Money Might Matter Somewhere: A Response to Hedges, Laine, and Greenwald." *Educational Researcher*, May 1994, pp. 5–8.
9. John Dewey, *The Sources of a Science of Education* (New York: Liveright, 1929).
10. Myrdal, p. 41.
11. Jencks, op. cit.; and Richard J. Hernstein and Charles A. Murray, *The Bell Curve: Intelligence and Class Structure in American Life* (New York: Free Press, 1994).
12. Daniel P. Moynihan, "Equalizing Education: In whose Benefit?," *The Public Interest*, Fall 1972, p. 71.
13. Ibid., p. 73.
14. Alexander W. Astin, *What Matters Most in College* (San Francisco: Jossey-Bass, 1993); and Ernest T. Pascarella and Patrick T. Tereozini, *How College Affects Students* (San Francisco: Jossey-Bass, 1991).
15. Myrdal, p. 41.
16. Hedges et al., op. cit.
17. Ibid.
18. Myrdal, pp. 59, 63.
19. In addition to Moynihan and Jencks, I would also cite Samuel Bowles and Herbert H. Gintis, *Schooling in Capitalist America* (New York: Basic Books, 1976).
20. Albert Einstein, *Out of My Later Years* (New York: Philosophical Library, 1950), p. 63.
21. Myrdal, p. 42.
22. Gunnar Myrdal, "How Scientific Are the Social Sciences?," *Bulletin of the Atomic Scientists*, January 1973, pp. 31–37.
23. Council for Basic Education, "Standards: A Vision for Learning," *Perspective*, 1991. Table insert, n.p.
24. Ibid., p. 3.
25. Irwin S. Kirsch, Louis J. Jungeblut, and Andrew Kolstad, *Adult Literacy in America* (Washington, D.C.: U.S. Department of Education, 1993).
26. William Celis, "Study Says Half of Adults in U.S. Can't Read or Handle Arithmetic," *New York Times*, 9 September 1993, p. A-1.
27. National Commission on Excellence in Education, *A Nation at Risk: The Imperative for Educational Reform* (Washington, D.C.: U.S. Department of Education, 1983).
28. Kirsch, Jungeblut, and Kolstad, p. 2.
29. Ibid., p. 91.
30. *Book Industry Trends, 1996* (New York: Book Industry Study Group, 1996).
31. Robert W. Fogel and Stanley L. Engerman, *Time on the Cross: The Economics of Negro Slavery* (Boston: Little, Brown, 1974), p. 115.
32. Ibid., p. 123.
33. Ibid., p. 113.
34. Ibid., pp. 5–6.
35. Jane Hannaway, "Higher-Order Skills, Job Design, and Incentives: An Analysis and Proposal," *American Educational Research Journal*, Spring 1992, p. 20.
36. Carleton W. Washbume and Sidney P. Marland, Jr., *Winnetka: The History and Significance of an Educational Experiment* (Englewood Cliffs, N.J.: Prentice-Hall, 1963).
37. John L. Goodlad and Zhixin Su, "Organization of the Curriculum in Philip W. Jackson, ed., *Handbook of Research on Curriculum* (New York: Macmillan, 1992), pp. 327–44; and Wilford M. Aikin, *The Story of the Eight-Year Study* (New York: Harper, 1942).
38. Daniel Tanner and Laurel Tanner, *History of the School Curriculum* (New York: Macmillan, 1990).
39. J. Robert Oppenheimer, "Prospects in the Arts and Sciences," in *Man's Right to Knowledge* (New York: Columbia University Press, 1955), p. 113.
40. Dewey, p. 33.
41. Ibid., p. 76,
42. Ibid., p. 74.

Future Directions in Qualitative Research

REBA N. PAGE

University of California, Riverside

If "Question Authority" and "Question Everything" are apt watchwords for recent developments in qualitative research, the momentum they signal has not operated in isolation, but has evolved in tension with conserving tendencies that have sought to blunt or discredit critique. The charge of "political correctness," for example, has been a quick counter to postcolonial and feminist studies, just as "storytelling" and "anecdotal" have long been used to dismiss qualitative research in general.

Whether questioning authority or insisting on it, exchanges about research methodologies have sometimes been heated and, at other times, studiously indifferent. Both incarnations have prompted periodic calls for detente (see Agar, 1996; Bellack, 1978; Rist, 1977; Suter, 1998; see also Metz, [*Harvard Educational Review*, Spring 2000]).[1] Detente is not aimed at consensus, but, rather, seeks to configure a space for public deliberation where just criticisms can be accommodated and excess and unnecessary rupture avoided. Such a space is easily closed by ideological sniping, even in such seemingly abstract debates as those over research methodologies.

When early challenges to traditional research gained ground in the 1960s and 1970s, the envisioned truce was between the quantitative and qualitative methodologies. More recently, however, there have been calls for détente *within* the qualitative community. There is particular urgency now to get qualitative methodology's house in order so that it can sustain its place in the educational research community, especially with the revival of traditional methodology as an attractive corrective for the purportedly poor quality of educational research. The five essays in this symposium specify this urgency, grounding it close to home in schools, including schools of education. Collectively, the essays evoke questions about the core concerns of qualitative research, which are crucial to deciding how

to assess the proliferating varieties of qualitative methodology. They direct attention to the authority of disciplined (and multidisciplined) inquiry at a time when all kinds of knowledge, including practitioner-generated knowledge, are considered relevant to inquiry. And they note the difficulties in teaching qualitative research in schools of education, in part because of ambiguity about whether students are being trained to conduct scholarship or to develop a sociocultural sensibility, and in part because qualitative research is shifting and few scholars know themselves how to go about embodying in texts some of the new directions governing qualitative methodology, such as reflexivity or power. All these are debatable issues, and the five essays do not settle them. However, they do join the debate, and it is long overdue

Détente is particularly crucial for the reconstruction of academic disciplines in ways that make their knowledge and modes of inquiry applicable to contemporary concerns about schooling and education. Like détente, reconstruction requires conservation and critique, rather than a choice between breaking free of the bodies of knowledge or reining them in to secure an old order. To paraphrase one of the principal players in anthropology's current reordering, the dilemma is figuring out how to preserve that which one would also change (Marcus, 1998). The same tension is palpable in the essay written by Spindler and Hammond as they consider the strain between democratizing qualitative research, say with teacher research, and maintaining traditional anthropological standards.

In this sense, disciplines are stewardships. Those entrusted with the care of disciplines must act responsibly in conducting, supervising, maintaining, and transferring them. To act responsibly is a double move: it means being responsive to alternative perspectives on *their* terms, as well as offering a response in one's own terms so that the alternatives do not meet with silence (Page, 1997; Ricouer, 1976). Stewardship may sound ivory-towerish, but its concerns are as practical as they are intellectual. To be sure, it entails epistemological and methodological decisions

---

1 For a rhetorically interesting proposal for détente, see Gage (1989), who appears to propose a cease fire but, on close reading, gives all the advantage to the statistical forces.

about valued knowledge and how research should be done to advance it. However, it also involves a professional culture—which academic appointments to recommend, what criteria to use for graduate admissions (and thereby new recruits to a discipline), what programs to initiate, which texts to prescribe on a syllabus, and what standards to set for awarding grants, tenure, and dissertations.

Stewardship is no easy matter. Joseph Schwab (1969) described its core predicament thirty years ago when he argued that educators—more specifically, curriculum scholars—had taken flight from the practical, or moral, question of how a community determines the knowledge its schools should teach (including schools of education). He pointed out that choices about knowledge had to be made—there is always more to teach than there is time or capacity to learn—but the grounds for explaining choices were deeply uncertain. Paralleling Schwab, the five essays in this symposium suggest that educators continue to fly upward to "theory . . . metatheory . . . and metametatheory," often to the neglect of the substantive issues of education, or downward to "innocent" inquiry undisturbed by any preconceived construct or prior data as in the idiosyncratic stories produced by or about practitioners that are nonetheless put forward as research. In both cases, educators retreat from their vocation to the safety of spectatorship.

The predicament of justifying judgments is particularly salient in the qualitative research community, as agreement about canonical texts and orthodox practices thins. These five essays differ on whether *any* of the represented disciplines, including educational studies, is of value to the business of schooling. How is stewardship possible when there is little agreement about required readings or the criteria for acceptable research?[2] Yet in a transforming world, the future of qualitative methodology may lie less in whether it can be satisfactorily standardized or made more rigorously scientific and more in whether a professional community can reestablish stewardship amid the diffuse array of genres now laying claim to the label *qualitative research*. It will take acumen and experience to reconceptualize the methodology and allied disciplines. It will also take forthright, civil speech that will require commitment—and not a little courage.

The five essays in this Symposium exemplify the stewardship that makes an educational research community. All give eloquent, considered testimony to the contributions their disciplines have made to improved knowledge

and methods, and their usefulness for schooling and education. In addition, all testify to the challenges that have propelled new forms of qualitative research and growing self-consciousness and change in the contributing disciplines.

As the essays indicate, qualitative studies in psychology, anthropology, linguistics, sociology, and educational studies have clarified the individual and cultural differences that children and adults bring with them into classrooms and other educative settings; the often oblique manifestation of those differences, particularly in language; the difference the differences make, or that social institutions use the differences to make, for both cognitive and cultural mobility; and the deep-running ambiguity in school organizations that mediate modern society's pursuit of equally cherished but contradictory values of union and uniqueness. The authors credit qualitative methodology with providing important direction and means for inquiring into the unsuspected connections within and across the levels of individual, classroom, school, and society.

Reporting on the connections, which conventional categories may miss entirely, the essays also document the important new theories in education generated by qualitative research. In particular, they point to the relationships across seemingly incommensurate events such as local school lessons, wider historical contingencies, and more stable, institutionally embedded formations of race, social class, age, and so forth. At the same time, the insights of qualitative research have also reconfigured the disciplines themselves, reshaping *their* most fundamental concepts, procedures, and conclusions, and heightening awareness of the necessarily provisional character of their knowledge.

The essays also present sharp differences over the "exhausting" scope and depth of disciplinary knowledge, not to mention bewildering varieties of qualitative methodology and the difficulties inherent in how and whether research can be useful for educational practice. If the essays provide little in the way of consensus, they take on the issues of valuable knowledge and qualitative research, and they do it in responsive, responsible fashion. Their keen ideas, scrupulous positioning, and deliberative tone invite our participation as well.

Accordingly, I will mention some hopes I have for topics in these future debates, growing out of my reading of these five essays and my own experiences with qualitative research. I trust that other readers will make a list too. One topic in which I am keenly interested concerns affirming the possibility and value of qualitative studies focused on the substance of education. Conducting field research may seem a futile, irredeemably flawed endeavor, what with the crisis in representation, daunting asymmetries in research relations, and the distance of research from worldly events that cry out for action. While some studies have responded to the crises by creatively mixing reflexive and substantive data so that each informs the other (Kondo, 1990; Rogers, 1995; Tsing 1993), more have "fled" to theory, to disclaimers that qualitative studies are "only" descriptions or stories, or to the self-absorbed meth-

---

2 Tolerance for all possibilities of qualitative research is not a particularly desirable option because it may simply turn the matter of methodology over to the market. Although not discussed in recent reviews focused on programs in education (e.g., Lagemann & Shulman, 1999), California's public universities find themselves competing and not particularly successfully, with private institutions that, if more expensive, attract students with abbreviated seat-time requirements, credit for experience, instruction oriented to the "curbstone practicality" of familiar goals achieved by familiar means (Schwab, 1969, p.2), and dissertation requirements that can be met in a summer. As an ad in *The New Yorker* recently promised, "Doctoral Degree: Accredited, 1 to 2 years; 1 month residency."

odological accounts that lose sight of the subjects of study as they pursue researcher subjectivity.[3] Confronted by this disarray, graduate students are often reluctant even to claim research as a task in which they will engage.

However, I hope that "thick descriptions" of education will be encouraged, because they can illuminate the moral ambiguity characteristic of a world, including the research world, in which choices are more likely to be competing than clear-cut. Thick descriptions portray what Schwab called "the language of the practical" (1969) and what Magdalene Lampert,* calls the "strategic knowledge" that good teaching relies on. They present both description *and* analysis, convey the fine details as well as holistic features of particular cases, and let us see the value of local knowledge without accepting it at face value. On all counts, they allow us to move beyond simplistic notions of truth or anything-goes relativism to an affirmation of humanity, in both its promise and its tragedy. As humans, we persist in seeking to know others. Trying to comprehend the angle at which others come at the world, we are able to see them, but also ourselves in all our differences and similarities. We persist, even though we can never fully grasp another's perspective and even though we recognize that our desire to know can be a form of violence, not just an expression of interest. To interpret and reach toward other, and through other toward self, manifests our freedom, power, and connection in the world, even as interpretation also stands between us and the world, separating us from it, and affirming the tragic limits to our ability to know.

In thinking about the possibility and future of thick description, I also find intriguing George Marcus's proposal for "multi-sited" studies that "juxtapos[e] expert and governmental systems *and* . . . everyday lifeworlds, *both* within the same research frame of reference" (1998, p. 6).[4] The design is a theoretically interesting, structuralist departure in qualitative studies from the more widespread and often individualistic focus on reflexivity, voice, and identity. It provides for "studying up," but with the same degree of density that qualitative scholars have heretofore showered on people at the bottom or on the margins of societies. By giving qualitative attention to power, capitalism, or elites, qualitative studies would no longer be limited to merely providing illustrative cases of "the system," and their explanations could move beyond glossing or caricaturing "social structure" as some opaque, determining force. For example, critical ethnographies are often ironic contrasts between the researcher's critique of "the system" and the practitioner's adherence to it. However, studying the critic as much as the practitioner suggests that, notwithstanding the commonsensical assumption that critics stand outside "the system," no role is more "American"

than radical critique. Further, the relationship between critic and criticized is not contrastive but a joint social construction of mutual accusation; however counterintuitively, critique in such a relationship may contribute to maintaining rather than changing the status quo (see Page, 1994). Similarly, Nespor's (1997) study of Thurber Elementary School focuses less on classrooms than on the webs of social relations that tie the school to or sever it from cities, politics, businesses, neighborhoods, and popular culture. It shows us the school as an adjunct to a corporate economy, not the separate, strictly academic institution we more commonly assume it to be.

A second topic I hope will be debated concerns defining qualitative research and distinguishing it from other forms of meaning-making such as art, reflection, journalism, or meditation. Clarifying the genre, *research*, might help us think through who should do it and the preparation it requires. At the same time, it might also enhance our appreciation of the limits of research and the dangers inherent in reducing all meaning-making to research, including those posed by the university's own self-serving interests. For instance, calls for teacher research may be well-meaning efforts to honor teacher thinking and give it a deservedly central place in the corpus of knowledge about teaching. Such calls might also unintentionally minimize the caring, understanding, and respect that are fundamental to good teaching by overemphasizing knowledge of subject matter, styles of learning, or teaching strategies.

At the School of Education at the University of Wisconsin–Madison, which I attended after about a decade of teaching in U.S. high schools, I learned to think about research as systematic, self-conscious inquiry and about qualitative research as both a description and analysis of what particular people do and what they must know, often tacitly, that makes what they do understandable (Agar, 1996; Erickson, 1986; Hammersley & Atkinson, 1995; Spindler, 1982). I also learned that research could—and should—be made to speak not only to theory and methodology, but also to practice and policy. In short, research was itself praxis.

This definition suggests the precarious and unsettling balancing act qualitative research presents, why it is so difficult to teach—almost as difficult as teaching teaching—and the potential of interdisciplinary or multi-disciplinary programs of preparation. On the one hand, conducting a self-conscious study of any instance of education requires having information about what is already known about educative processes. One cannot recognize what is unusual and what is routine in a classroom observation, particularly in one's own culture, unless one knows first what others have seen in other classrooms. Similarly, conducting systematic inquiry requires an explicitly formulated theory. One has to know the theories that are available if one is to be able to make an informed choice from the variety that is available.

---

3 Criticism of Geertz (1973), who raised the concept "thick description" to prominence, resides in Geertz's apparent refusal to take his own critique of the limits of representation seriously enough and, instead, to continue to write as though he has understood something of others.
4 Agar (1996) makes a comparable recommendation.

On the other hand, disciplinary training can also function as a set of blinders as much as a focusing lens. It directs attention to particular processes and away from others and, held to too tightly, it can prevent participant-observers from learning anything in fieldwork. In this regard, drawing on several rather than a single discipline may be particularly valuable. Alternate lenses may expose variegated aspects of a case and provide for the development of "thicker," more complexly layered explications (see, for example, Metz, 1986; Page, Samson, & Crockett; 1998, Spindler & Spindler, 1982).

If disciplines are valuable, borrowing from any one of them, much less several, is daunting. In my graduate classes at Wisconsin, Professor Michael Apple warned that borrowing from areas outside one's expertise takes knowledge out of the self-correcting context of a disciplinary community. Done glibly or superficially, it can result in misinterpretations and the unwitting reproduction of misinterpretations. The only option, he said, was serious, sustained reading in a specific discipline, coupled with continuing discussion with fellow students in education and from other academic departments who were doing the same.

Furthermore, my own experience as a professor of education is that students are intrigued by interdisciplinary studies and experimental modes of representation. However, they often flounder if they take up interdisciplinary studies, such as cultural studies, all at once. They seem to do better when they first become well established in a single discipline and later add training in others. Of course, the danger is that the first discipline takes so much time and energy that students never get to a second. Another danger is that students will become so taken with studies in critical theory, popular culture, or the disciplines that they will "flee" educational matters altogether. Students also find creative models of qualitative research liberating. They want to write vivid, moving stories that someone will actually read. However, they are less aware that story-like models may not be considered legitimate by people who make decisions about hiring and tenure. One tactic I use to move between conventional and creative materials is to ground courses in traditional constructs, methods, and empirical studies, but to couple them with practices that provide for reading them across the grain (Page, 1997).

A final point for public deliberation is how debate can occur, given the size and diverse interests and expertise of participants in the educational research community. Lampert suggests that new technologies may be crucial. Hypertext, for example, represents the complexities of teaching in a more compelling and readily accessible form than written or spoken texts, and the representations can be disseminated electronically to distant audiences. Metz and Heath suggest that we may need experts who are especially knowledgeable about and adept at bridging research paradigms and bridging research and practice. Other scholars have described additional ways of thinking about the nature of educational community, including arrangements that are collaborative but that distribute tasks differentially, according to the diverse roles and interests of participants (Boostrum, Jackson, & Hansen, 1993; Greeno et al., 1999).

George Spindler, with his late wife Louise Spindler (1982), suggested an older and more homely technology: teaching. They advise educators not to underestimate the possibilities for discourse and dissemination in their classrooms. As the Spindlers put it:

> In some ways the classroom or seminar is the most salubrious setting for the transmission and diffusion of ethnographic case study material and the lessons to be learned from it. The classroom is more flexible and less permanent than the printed page. One can be wrong, find out, and correct oneself. Nuances can be better communicated, and there is less chance of damage to the object of study. (p. 27)

Put another way, we might consider that if we treat our students well, many of whom are or will go on to be teachers themselves, they will remember and treat their students well. Although this is not grand "scaling up," modest expectations may be more in keeping with the nature of scholarly work and its relationship to the complexities of practice. Certainly the Spindlers have used their method to shape the thinking and practice of thousands of students.

In whatever forms—including the form offered by this Symposium—public deliberation carries no promise of consensus about what qualitative research is, who should do it, whether it is of value, or other epistemological and professional questions. Yet such deliberation is important because community is constituted in communication (Dewey, 1966). In deliberation with each other, whether face-to-face or through texts, we make public not only our *knowledge* that there are differences between us, but also our *respect* for those differences (Greene, 1985; Heath, 1982; Maclean, 1992; Miller, 1998). Deliberation is a pledge—an act of obligation—in which we demonstrate a common world whose most fundamental characteristic is humane respect for diversity.

*See *Harvard Educational Review,* Spring 2000.

References

Agar, M. (1996). *The professional stranger: An informal introduction to ethnography* (2nd ed.). San Diego: Academic Press.

Bellack, A. (1978). *Competing ideologies in research on teaching* (Uppsala Reports on Education No. 1). Uppsala, Sweden: Uppsala University, Department of Education.

Boostrum. R., Jackson, P., & Hansen, D. (1993). Coming together and staying apart: How a group of teachers and researchers sought to bridge the "research/practice gap." *Teachers College Record, 95,* 35–44.

Dewey, J. (1966). *Democracy and education.* New York: Free Press. (Original work published 1916)

Erickson, F. (1986). Qualitative methods in research on teaching. In M. Wittrock (Ed.), *Handbook of research on teaching* (3rd ed., pp. 119–161). New York: Macmillan.

Gage, N. (1989). The paradigm wars and their aftermath: A "historical" sketch of research and teaching since 1989. *Educational Researcher, 18,* 4–10.

Geertz, C. (1973). *The interpretation of culture: Selected essays.* New York: Basic Books.

Greene, M. (1985, Fall). Public education and the public space. *Kettering Review,* 55–60.

Greeno, J., McDermott, R., Cole, K., Engle, R., Goldman, S., Knudsen, J., Lauman, B., & Linde, C. (1999). Research, reform, and aims in education: Modes of action in search of each other. In E. Lagemann & L. Shulman (Eds.), *Issues in educational research* (pp. 299–335). San Francisco: Jossey-Bass.

Hammersley, M., & Atkinson, P. (1995). *Ethnography: Principles in practice* (2nd ed.). London: Routledge.

Heath, S. (1982). Questioning at home and at school: A comparative study. In G. Spindler (Ed.), *Doing the ethnography of schooling: Educational anthropology in action* (pp. 102–131). New York: Holt, Rinehart & Winston.

Kondo, D. (1990). *Crafting selves: Power, gender, and discourses of identity in a Japanese workplace.* Chicago: University of Chicago Press.

Lagemann, E., & Shulman, L. (1999). *Issues in education research: Problems and possibilities.* San Francisco: Jossey-Bass.

Maclean, N. (1982). *Young men and fire.* Chicago: University of Chicago Press.

Marcus, G. (1998). *Ethnography through thick and thin.* Princeton, NJ: Princeton University.

Metz, M. (1986). *Different by design: The context and character of three magnet schools.* London: Routledge.

Miller, J. H. (1998). Literary and cultural studies in the transnational university. In J. C. Rowe (Ed.), *"Culture," and the problems of the disciplines* (pp. 45–68). New York: Columbia University Press.

Nespor, J. (1997). *Tangled up in school: Politics, space, bodies, and signs in the educational process.* Mahwah, NJ: Lawrence Erlbaum.

Page, R. (1994). Do-good ethnography. *Curriculum Inquiry, 24,* 479–502.

Page, R. (1997). Teaching about validity. *International Journal of Qualitative Studies in Education, 10,* 145–155.

Page, R., Samson, Y. & Crockett, M. (1988). Reporting ethnography to informants, *Harvard Educational Review, 68,* 299–333.

Ricouer, P. (1976). *Interpretation theory: Discourse and the surplus of meaning.* Fort Worth: Texas Christian University Press.

Rist, R. (1977). On the relations among educational research paradigms: From disdain to détente. *Anthropology and Education Quarterly, 8,* 42–49.

Rogers, A. (1995). *A shining affliction.. A study of harm and healing in psychotherapy.* New York: Viking.

Schwab, J. (1969). The practical: A language for curriculum. *School Review, 78,* 1–23.

Spindler, G. (1982). *Doing the ethnography of schooling: Educational anthropology in action.* New York: Holt, Rinehart & Winston.

Spindler, C., & Spindler, L. (1982). Roger Harker and Schönhausen: From familiar to strange and back again. In G. Spindler (Ed.), *Doing the ethnography of schooling: Educational anthropology in action* (pp. 20–46). New York: Holt, Rinehart & Winston.

Suter. L. (1998, April). Report of a workshop on issues in mathematics and science education research methods. In L. Suter (chair), *Research methods in mathematics and science education research: Report of a workshop.* Symposium conducted at the meeting of the American Educational Research Association, Montreal.

Tsing, A. (1993). *In the realm of the Diamond Queen: Marginality in an out-of-the-way place.* Princeton, NJ: Princeton University Press.

RETHINKING SOCIOLOGY: APPLIED AND BASIC RESEARCH

WILLIAM FOOTE WHYTE

In this article, Whyte makes eight criticisms of conventional sociology. He then suggests ways of improving sociology through an emphasis on applied research and active field work.

To strengthen the scientific value of sociology, first we need to concentrate on social structures and social systems: organizations and organizational relations and inter-organizational relations. I argue that this is the best way to focus on elements that can yield scientific uniformities.

This means focusing on groups from families and kinship systems to organizations, from informal groups to formally organized associations, from private businesses to governmental organizations, and including the large variety of nongovernmental organizations (NGOs) from colleges and universities to social service agencies and organizations designed to organize public opinion for or against some cause.

Individuals play out their roles within such organizational contexts, shaped by them but not entirely controlled by them. To explain individual behavior, this is where we begin.

Second, we need to combat the assumed separation between basic and applied research, and the status distinctions, that go with that separation, with the basic researchers viewed as the real social scientists whereas the applied researchers are seen as little more than technicians. As Paul F. Lazarsfeld et al. (1967; 1975) maintained all his work-life, research can be basic as well as applied—basic in contributing to general knowledge, applied in terms of practical applications.

This has not been the predominant view of what are often called mainstream sociologists. They are only concerned with what they call basic knowledge.

This is seen in two reviews of sociological knowledge a generation apart: by Robert B. L. Farms (1964) and by Neil Smelser (1988). In neither of these works was a single chapter devoted to applied sociology. The authors seemed to assume that anything found in an applied project did not constitute real knowledge.

As Kurt Lewin often said (but never wrote down), "There is nothing as practical as a good theory." The corollary of that statement is that we can never know if a theory is good until it is tested out in practice.

Third, we need to challenge the common sociological fixation on the statistical testing of hypotheses. It is often assumed that if a sociologist has not submitted one or more hypotheses to statistical testing, she or he has not done real research. Many important sociological questions do not yield to the neatness of statistical testing.

In the 1980s and 1990s, a group of Cornellians was studying social and economic processes involved in the transformation of the Xerox Corporation from a business that had invented the photocopying process, and yet was losing out to Japanese and other competitors (when its patent protection ran out), into a business that had reshaped itself and was beginning to regain its lost shares of the world market. This involved analysis of a series of changes taking place over an eleven-year period. Can you imagine an hypothesis or set of hypotheses that would cast light on the sequence of those changes?

Even when it makes sense to test a hypothesis, the result is a finding that the items measured represent a small fraction of the possible variation. They give few clues as to which actions are likely to lead to which results.

From *American Sociologist,* Spring 1998, pp. 16-20. © 1998 by Transaction Publishers, Inc. All rights reserved. Reprinted by permission.

What alternatives for hypothesis testing can we propose? As I have pointed out (1997), we need first to establish a legitimate field of comparison instead of assuming that we can compare Xerox with all large organizations. We assumed that: the Xerox experience would most likely apply to organizations that were not only large but also were heavily involved in manufacturing and marketing in widespread international markets. As we compare the Xerox experience with comparison firms, we should arrive at certain uniformities of behavior and organization. That is a more complex process than significance testing but one that is more likely to yield practical results.

Following that strategy enhances a manager's chances of leading an effective change process, and the organizational researcher can draw on all ever-expanding academic literature on major organizational changes.

Fourth, survey researchers have concentrated primarily on the measurement of attitudes, values, and perceptions. If we want to predict behavior, those subjective states give us unreliable clues. To be sure, the survey researcher can study behavior indirectly through questioning people about certain aspects of past behavior, but the reliability of such reports can be questioned when the respondent is asked about behaviors one is expected to do—such as church attendance or attendance at union meetings.

Studying behaviors requires field work, a much more labor-intensive activity. Generally the principal researcher must do some of the fieldwork him- or herself, not delegating all of it to students or hired assistants. To be able to predict or to influence behavior, researchers need to develop a baseline on past and present patterns of behavior.

Fifth, mainstream sociologists have focused primary attention on social relations. They have neglected the important theoretical contribution of Eric Trist (1981) with his formulation of "socio-technical systems." Trist points out that any work organization is not only a social system but also a technical system that structures the work that needs to be done.

As I have noted, mainstream sociologists are concerned only with what they call basic research. Applied sociologists studying work organizations necessarily study the linking of social and work relations.

Sixth, there has been a decline in field work. This is related to the dominant sociological focus on survey research. In a leading sociological department in the 1980s, I found that the predominant way of doing research for the doctoral thesis simply involved taking a questionnaire previously used in the department or one available elsewhere. The student then figured out one or more hypotheses that had not been tested in that research, ran these new correlations and reported the results.

When I reported this at a meeting of the Southern Sociological Society, a professor from Penn State told me what had recently happened in his department, They had invited nine candidates for an assistant professorship to present a report on their doctoral theses. All but one simply reported the results of a survey, without having done any field work. When professors asked the candidates what behavior might explain what they had found, they were at a loss to answer. The eight candidates seemed to assume that if they had the statistical data, that should be enough to satisfy any sociologist.

Let me make it clear that I am not arguing against the use of survey research. I have used surveys in various projects but always in conjunction with field research (Whyte and Alberti 1976). I have found that that combination yields vital new information on what has been going on in the field.

Seventh, sociologists who have been lured by the gospels of deconstructionism and post-modernism should abandon what I believe is a passing fad and return to the challenge of advancing sociology as a social science (Whyte 1997).

Various Ways of Doing Applied Research

Applied social research comes in various forms. We need to distinguish one form from others to make it clear what we are talking about.

Perhaps the most common form is what I call the professional expert model. The sociologist is called upon by a client to study a research or action program and report to the client the findings of that study. She or he may then be asked to make recommendations for action. Beyond that point the sociologist has no more responsibilities. This form requires the sociologist to deviate very little from the traditional academic role.

If the sociologist wants to get directly involved with the organizations studied, we can define three distinctly different roles to play:

1. Action research. Here the sociologist assumes primary responsibility for choosing the action objectives and for guiding the actions designed to bring them about.

2. Participatory research. Here the sociologist participates fully with the members of the organization studied but the project has no action objectives. It is designed simply to yield further information and ideas.

3. Participatory action research (PAR). Here the sociologist participates fully with one or more members of the organization studied through the various stages of the research, from design to data gathering, from analysis to the generation of new actions.

It is important to recognize the distinctions among the above types. There call be action research without participation—in fact, at one time this was the most common type. Here the researcher seeks to direct and control the actions. In past studies the researcher participated with the people studied and yet neither party was seeking anything more than the generation of information and ideas.

In recent years, with several collaborators, I have been involved in PAR projects in the Xerox Corporation (Whyte 1989), the Mondragon cooperative complex (Greenwood, Gonzales et al. 1991), and the University of Pennsylvania (Greenwood, Whyte and Harkavy 1993). Einar Thorsrud (1977) has also written about earlier projects that met all the requirements of PAR, but were given different titles by their principal authors.

Those of us who have been using PAR have found this a powerful method both for gaining new knowledge and for getting practical results. By teaming up with members of the organization studied, we can provide a semi-experiment in the field that tests us to find if we have really arrived at practical answers as well as confirmed knowledge.

References

Faris, Robert B. L. 1964. Handbook of Modern Sociology. Chicago: Rand McNally.

Greenwood, D., Gonzalez, J., et al. 1992. Industrial Democracy as Process: Social Research for Action in the Fagor Cooperative Group of Mondragon. Assen Maastrict: Van Gorcum.

_____, W. Whyte and Ira Harkavy. 1993, "Participatory Action Research as a Process and as a Goal," *Human Relations* 46(2):175–92.

Lazarsfeld, Paul F., W. Sewell, and H. Wilensky (Eds.). 1967. The Uses of Sociology. New York: Basic Books.

_____, Pasanella, A. and J. Reitz, 1975. An Introduction to Applied Sociology. New York: Elsevier.

Smelser, Neil. 1988. Handbook of Sociology. Newbury Park, CA: Sage Publications.

Trist, Eric. 1981. The Evolution of Socio-Technical Systems: A Conceptual Framework and an Action Research Program. Toronto: Ontario Ministry of Labor.

Thorsrud, Binar. 1977. "Democracy at Work: Norwegian Experience with Non-Bureaucratic Forms of Organization," *Applied Behavioral Science* 13(3): 410–21.

Whyte, William Foote, 1989, "Advancing Sociological Knowledge through Participatory Action Research." *Sociological Forum* 4:367–85.

_____, 1997. Creative Solutions to Field Problems Reflections on a Career. Walnut Creek, CA: Altamira Press

Whyte, William Foote and Giorgio Alberti. 1976. Power, Politics, and Progress: Social Change in Rural Peru, New York: Elsevier.

William Foote Whyte is professor emeritus in Cornell's School of Industrial and Labor Relations and is Research Director of Programs for Employment (PEWS) in the ILR extension division. He is the author or co-author of twenty books, including *Street Corner Society*. Address for correspondence: William Foote Whyte, 223 Savage Farm Drive, Ithaca, NY 14850-6501.

PEARLS, PITH, AND PROVOCATION

Salvaging Quantitative Research With Qualitative Data

Donn Weinholtz
Barbara Kacer
Thomas Rocklin

Through presentation of two case studies, this article illustrates just how ambiguous and misleading results from quantitative studies can be if not supplemented by qualitative data. The focus is on the salvaging power of qualitative methods and their ability to ensure some return on an investment that might otherwise be partially or completely lost.

It is no longer provocative to merely announce that quantitative and qualitative research methods can be fruitfully combined. The point has already been made repeatedly (e.g., Fielding & Fielding, 1986; Miles & Huberman, 1984; Reichardt & Cook, 1979). Furthermore, even those expressing strong misgivings about the "capture of qualitative inquiry by the quantitative approach," due to the accompanying blurring of important underlying objectivist and realist assumptions, acknowledge that "at the level of applying specific individual procedures...the two approaches can be mixed" (Smith & Heshius, 1986, p. 4). Consequently, we will not argue here over whether quantitative and qualitative approaches can be combined. Rather, via presentation of two case studies we will illustrate just how ambiguous and misleading results from quantitative studies can be if not supplemented by qualitative data. In doing so, we will address an issue generally ignored in the literature and also show how use of supplemental qualitative methods by quantitative researchers can serve as a prudent hedge against obtaining inconsequential or erroneous results.

The first case that we will discuss illustrates how qualitative data can permit insightful interpretation of studies that yield no significant quantitative findings. The second will demonstrate how qualitative data can permit detection of errors in quantitative data analysis procedures by providing important reference points for numeric values. In both cases, even though substantial care was taken by the researchers in their quantitative designs, the qualitative data played an important role in rendering the studies useful. Thus we will focus on the "salvaging power" of qualitative methods in reference to their ability to ensure some return on an investment that might otherwise be partially or completely lost.

A STUDY OF SMALL GROUP INSTRUCTION OF COMPUTER APPLICATIONS

The first case, previously reported by Kacer, Weinholtz, and Rocklin (1991), investigated the impact of small group instruction on attitude and achievement of students learning computer applications (e.g., word processing, spreadsheets, and databases). Forty-nine teacher education students (44 females, 5 males) were randomly assigned to either an individual (n = 15) or a group (n = 17 dyads) condition. Using the Appleworks program to learn the three designated computer applications skills, subjects met in their individual or group conditions for 3 consecutive weeks to complete an instructional assignment for each of the three applications. (On these assignments, subjects within the dyadic condition each received the same score for their performance.) Also, subjects from both conditions were individually administered a comprehensive postinstructional test, involving creating new files and manipulating existing files. Finally, before and after instruction, all subjects completed a questionnaire measuring attitude toward instruction.

In addition to the numerically scored and analyzed assignments, tests, and questionnaires, the researchers collected two types of qualitative data. First, subjects in both the individual and group conditions were audiotaped while working at their computers on their instructional assignments. Second, at the conclusion of the study, subjects from each condition (4 individuals plus 9 members from dyads) were randomly selected for debriefing interviews. Following completion of the study's quantitative data analysis, these qualitative data were analyzed via the review and categorical coding of transcribed audiotapes and interview notes, as prescribed by Lofland (1971).

To briefly summarize the results of the quantitative analysis, neither multivariate nor univariate analysis of variance procedures revealed significant differences between individuals and groups on either the assignment, test, or attitude measures. The researchers found the results encouraging, in that dyadic computer use made more efficient use of equipment without incurring any penalty in learning. But they were also disappointed. Based on personal experience and an extensive review of the small group instruction literature, it had been assumed that distinctive differences between individuals and dyads would exist, but the carefully developed quantitative comparison provided no indication of any difference, nor any clue as to where differences, if they existed, might be found.

Faced with this situation, the traditional quantitative researcher is forced to review the research effort in an attempt to either explain the present findings or design future research. The researcher asks, "Did we have adequate statistical power?" "Were our measures adequately reliable and valid?" "Was our treatment powerful enough?" "Was the treatment implemented as planned?" "Did subjects perceive stimuli (or understand questions, or react to manipulations) as we expected?" Some of these questions can be answered rather directly (e.g., statistical power, reliability of measures). But these are the very questions that can and should be answered before the research is conducted. Other questions (e.g., treatment integrity, subjects' reactions) cannot be answered a priori. Neither can they necessarily be answered from any of the data collected in the quantitative research. Worst of all, the specific form of some of these questions cannot be anticipated before the data are collected.

Qualitative data can play a particularly useful salvaging role both in understanding the findings and in suggesting future research. In the small group instruction/computer applications study, this certainly proved to be the case. Analysis of 11 randomly selected, transcribed audiotapes revealed that students working in the individual condition asked three times the number of questions of available teaching assistants as did students working in dyads. This finding indicated that rather than establishing a pure comparison between individual and group performance and attitudes, the study compared group performance with that of a condition that was something akin to a tutor-tutee relationship. Furthermore, conversations within dyads consistently indicated delayed use of the keyboard and the initiation of planning activities, whereas students in the individual condition regularly turned directly to use of the keyboard and asked questions of teaching assistants that indicated little in the way of planning activities. Finally, dyads asked a greater percentage of conceptual-level questions (45% to 33%) than did individuals, and the questions raised by dyads consistently indicated conceptual understanding, whereas those from individuals revealed bewilderment.

Analysis of the interview data also revealed differences between the two conditions. Those from the individual condition all indicated that the classroom experience had been enjoyable and that instruction had been helpful. Beyond these points, no clear opinion patterns emerged. However, interviews with dyad members offered additional information. For example, learning from one's partner, relatively independent of the instructor, was consistently reported. Also, feedback from one's partner was valued, as was the knowledge that one's partner was putting forth a conscientious effort. As one student put it, "1 would rather do my own work and make sure it's done correctly than be with somebody else who doesn't do it and gets the same grade that I do."

In combination, the audiotape data and interview data did not change the "no-difference" quantitative findings, but they did make the numeric results more understandable and interesting. They made it clear that the study's individual condition had unexpectedly metamorphosed into a modified group condition. Also, they provided evidence that the study's outcome measures were insensitive to an apparent higher level learning outcome within the dyad condition. Finally, they revealed a condition (lack of perceived mutual effort) that might undermine group performance.

These qualitative findings helped to establish connections with previous research, such as Webb's (1984) finding that individuals and small groups working on computer tasks (although showing no achievement differences) adopted different learning strategies. Even more important, they suggested enticing directions for future research. For example, the individual condition might be more carefully controlled and additional higher order learning measures might be incorporated. Also, interactions and attributions of lower performance dyads might be analyzed to further assess the impact of perceived mutual effort on group performance. From such analyses, recommendations for enhancing mutual effort might be developed and tested.

All of these possibilities were truly exciting. They provided insight and momentum to a research initiative that otherwise would have stalled due to lack of plausible explanations for the outcomes of the original study. Using a term made popular by Parlette and Hamilton (1972), the qualitative findings "illuminated" the quantitative results, thereby decreasing the need for the researchers to offer shot-in-the-dark interpretations about what occurred during the study

A STUDY OF TEACHING BY UNIVERSITY HOSPITAL ATTENDING PHYSICIANS

The second case actually involved two studies, one correlational the other experimental, linked together in a single effort to modify and improve the teaching of university hospital attending physicians (clinical faculty) in the small group teaching and working setting known as attending rounds. Attending rounds occupy approximately 2 hours per day and involve several medical students, first-year resident physicians, a senior resident physician, and the presiding attending physician in a rich, experiential teaching and learning activity.

Briefly, the correlational study (Weinholtz, Everett, Albanese, & Shymansky, 1986) involved collection of behavioral data on the attending round teaching of 41 attending physicians.

Each physician was observed for 8 to 10 hours (1 week's attending rounds), and teaching behaviors were recorded by trained observers carrying portable computers programmed to accept data from the Attending Round Observation System (Weinholtz, Albanese, Zeitler, Everett, & Shymansky, 1986), a behavioral recording scheme specifically designed for use in the setting under study. Following each observation period, the medical students and residents on each attending physician's team were asked to rate specific aspects of the attending physician's teaching as well as his or her overall teaching performance. Students also completed two open-ended items regarding the attending physician's teaching, and observers scored brief qualitative diaries regarding each day's activities. Correlations were calculated between percentages of time that attending physicians allocated to particular teaching activities and to the learners' ratings of teaching effectiveness.

In addition to yielding correlational findings indicative of teaching behaviors that learners perceived to be effective, this study provided baseline teaching behavior data that were used as the premeasures in the follow-up experimental study designed to assess whether one-shot instructional consultations could yield changes in attending physician teaching behaviors and ratings by learners of teaching effectiveness (Weinholtz, Albanese, Zeitler, & Everett, 1989). Fourteen of the 28 physicians who were able to continue into the second phase were randomly assigned to a treatment condition and 14 were assigned to a control group. Those in the treatment group received a consultation 1 to 3 weeks prior to a second round of observations and ratings. The consultations provided the attending physicians with feedback on their prior behavioral data, ratings data, and on the qualitative comments from learners and observers. This feedback was used to negotiate a set of target areas in which the attending physicians might experiment with new teaching approaches.

The 14 attending physicians assigned to the control group also received consultations, but not until after the second round of observation and ratings. In addition to the behavioral and ratings data collected as outcome measures, all attending physicians participating in the study completed a brief evaluation form focusing on the observation and consultation process.

The correlational study identified 18 teaching behaviors, occurring across various attending round contexts and settings, that were pertinent for use in the consultations. The experimental study revealed that the consultations did provoke behavioral change, but that increase in learner ratings of teaching was not significantly different from a similar increase in the control group ratings. Also, the attending physicians' evaluations of the observation and consultation process were highly positive. In combination, these two quantitative studies were quite successful in making a contribution to a relatively uncharted area of educational research. They were published and are now frequently cited in the clinical, medical education literature. So, what is the issue here?

The issue is that, if not for the collection of a modest amount of qualitative data (the learner responses to two open-ended questions on the teacher rating form and the brief diaries maintained by the observers), the study would have foundered due to an undetected and potentially catastrophic data analysis error. To make a long and painful story relatively short, the initial correlational analysis revealed some fairly straightforward and also some relatively "counterintuitive" findings. Based on these findings, consultations for the experimental phase were to be devised. However, while designing the consultations the learner comments and observer diaries (which were added to the study almost as an afterthought) had to be consulted. While developing the first consultation, a striking problem became apparent. The physician's behavioral profile was grossly inconsistent with the qualitative comments and accounts. A quick check revealed that this was also the case for the data on several other physicians. Somewhere, something had gone wrong, but it was not clear where.

Eventually, the source of the error was found. Approximately halfway through the correlational study, a mistake had been made in the assignment of identification numbers to the attending physicians. Down the line, there was a resulting mismatch of behavioral and ratings data through half of the two data sets. This resulted in one physician's behavioral data being correlated with another's ratings data. (No wonder there were counterintuitive findings!) The entire correlational analysis had to be repeated.

Fortunately for all involved, the data for the attending physician scheduled for the first consultation just happened to have come from the second half of the data sets where the error existed. This was a stroke of luck, but even with that luck the discovery, made in the waning hours before the first consultation was supposed to have been delivered, would never have occurred without the collection of the small amount of qualitative data that was designed into the studies. Without that data, consultations would have been offered and recommendations made based on an error-filled analysis. Half of the physicians would have been offered supposedly "hard," "numeric" observational profiles of their (actually others') teaching behaviors. We can only guess how they would have reacted. Some might have scratched their heads and said, "Gee, I didn't realize that I did that," but some (quite rightfully) would probably have announced that their profiles were preposterous because they never engaged in some of the behaviors presented to them.

Obviously, the error described here could have been detected by more carefully grooming the data. However, many precautions had been taken. The researchers involved thought they had monitored the data as carefully as possible. It was one research assistant's half-time job just to tend to the data sets, and that individual's efforts were double-checked by one of the researchers. What happened (as can happen so often) was one minor human error that occurred while navigating in a sea of numbers, an error not detected by either of two individuals. In this downwardly spiraling scenario, a relatively small amount of qualitative data (without prior intent on the part of the researchers) served as a failsafe mechanism preventing a horrible waste of invested time and energy. Although the experimental study timetable was thrown off schedule by having to redo the correlational analysis, both studies were salvaged because the qualitative data cast the numbers in verbal description that made the error much more readily detectable. We can only wonder how many other studies have suffered irreparable damage from not having a qualitative safety net in place. There is no way to gauge the extent of this sort of problem because researchers do not often report such embarrassments. However, even if the problem is infrequent, the cost is too great to those involved not to take precautions against such consequences.

FURTHER LESSONS

Beyond the points already made, what lessons can be derived front these two cases? First, the collection of qualitative data was neither a particularly obtrusive nor labor-intensive effort. The audiotapes in the small group/computer study were the only data recorded simultaneously with quantitative data collection, and there is no evidence that the tape recorder altered individual or group responses to the assignments. The debriefing interviews at the end of this study were the single most time-consuming effort, but the use of a random sample of subjects for interviewing made the task manageable (while admittedly sacrificing some data).

Second, analysis of the data required additional time and effort, especially in the small group/computer study. However, the insights gained in both studies clearly warranted the additional investment, which was quite small compared to the overall effort required for mounting and executing their quantitative components.

Third, both studies had a small group focus, and qualitative research methods are particularly suited for highlighting group processes not easily captured by quantitative measures. Other researchers conducting quantitative studies involving small group conditions would seem particularly well advised to incorporate supplemental qualitative methods. Nevertheless, even those not investigating small group phenomena could benefit substantially from doing so, particularly by making efforts to ensure that their experimental treatments have had their expected impact. For such purposes, debriefing interviews can be particularly effective.

To illustrate, a doctoral student on whose dissertation committee one of us was once asked to sit completed an elegant multivariate analysis of variance in a study comparing group performances on speeded achievement tests (Conboy, 1986). The critical variable in the study was the imposition of awareness levels of target goals for the different groups. It was assumed that creation of high awareness levels (particularly of initial failure) would enhance motivation (and consequently performance). However, the extraordinarily careful analysis revealed little other than an obscure interaction. On the other hand, a "manipulation check" via a short debriefing interview conducted by the researcher (again almost as an afterthought) revealed that "fewer than 20% of the subjects could identify their assigned goals on difficult problems, and only 35% could do so on easy problems." This poststudy assess-

ment provided ample evidence that the expected treatment never really took hold, a useful finding that might have yielded even more valuable information if more in-depth, probing interviews of subjects had been conducted following completion of the quantitative data collection. How many times is the impact of a treatment rejected when the treatment has not really been established? We simply do not know, but it is plausible that in most experimental studies debriefing interviews in combination with unobtrusive observations could determine if a "take" occurs.

Conducting research of any kind is a high-stakes endeavor. It is not just one's intellectual acumen that is tested; one's career and academic credibility are held in the brink. It simply does not make sense to conduct "black box" studies that yield bewildering results. For quantitative researchers, the judicious use of qualitative methods offers an efficient and powerful tool for self-correcting studies gone astray Much good work can be salvaged through forethought of design.

REFERENCES

Conboy, J. E. (1986). *Goal awareness and self-efficacy as determinants of the constructive effects of failure.* Unpublished doctoral dissertation, University of Iowa, Iowa City.

Fielding, N. G., & Fielding, J. L. (1986). *Linking data.* Beverly Hills, CA: Sage.

Kacer, B., Weinholtz, D., & Rocklin, T. (1991). The impact of small group instruction upon attitude and achievement of students' learning computer applications. *Computers in the Schools, 8,* 357–360.

Lofland, J. (1971). *Analyzing social settings.* Belmont, CA: Wadsworth.

Miles, M., & Huberman, M. (1984). *Qualitative data analysis.* Beverly Hills, CA: Sage.

Parlette, M., & Hamilton, D. (1972). *Evaluation as illumination: A new approach to the study of innovative programmes.* Occasional Paper 9, Center for Research in the Educational Sciences, University of Edinburgh.

Reichardt, C., & Cook, T. (1979). Beyond qualitative versus quantitative methods. In T. Cook & C. Reichardt (Eds.), *Qualitative and quantitative wetlands in evaluation research* (pp. 7–32). Beverly Hills, CA: Sage.

Smith, J. K., & Heshius, L. (1986). Closing down the conversation: The end of the quantitative-qualitative debate among educational inquirers. *Educational Researcher,* 15(1), 4–12.

Webb, N. M. (1984). Microcomputer learning in small groups: Cognitive requirements and group processes. *Journal of Educational Psychology, 76,* 1076-1088.

Weinholtz, D., Albanese, M., Zeitler, R., & Everett, G. (1989). Effects of individualized observation with feedback on attending physician clinical teaching. *Teaching and Learning in Medicine, 1*(3), 128-134.

Weinholtz, D., Everett, G., Albanese, M., & Shymansky, J. (1986). The attending round observation system: A procedure for describing teaching during attending rounds. *Evaluation & the Health Professions, 9,* 75-89.

Weinholtz, D., Albanese, M., Zeitler, R., Everett, G., & Shymansky, J. (1986). Effective attending physician teaching: The correlation of observed instructional activities and learner ratings of teaching effectiveness. In *Proceedings of the Twenty-fifth Annual Research in Medical Education Conference* (pp. 273-278). Washington, DC: Association of American Medical Colleges.

Donn Weinholtz, Ph.D., is the dean of the College of Education, Nursing and Health Professions at the University of Hartford.
Barbara Kacer, Ph.D., is an associate professor of education at Western Kentucky University.
Thomas Rocklin, Ph.D., is a professor of education at the University of Iowa.

quantitative attitudes questionnaire (QAQ), 134–137; development of, 135
quantitative research approaches, 40–42
quantitative-qualitative dichotomy of Halfpenny, 33
quasi-experimental research approach, 40–41
Question-Answer Relationships (QAR), 172
Quetelet, Adolphe, 13

AE Article Review Form

We encourage you to photocopy and use this page as a tool to assess how the articles in **Annual Editions** expand on the information in your textbook. By reflecting on the articles you will gain enhanced text information. You can also access this useful form on a product's book support Web site at **http://www.dushkin.com/ online/.**

NAME: _____ DATE: _____

_____

TITLE AND NUMBER OF ARTICLE:

_____

BRIEFLY STATE THE MAIN IDEA OF THIS ARTICLE:

_____

LIST THREE IMPORTANT FACTS THAT THE AUTHOR USES TO SUPPORT THE MAIN IDEA:

_____

WHAT INFORMATION OR IDEAS DISCUSSED IN THIS ARTICLE ARE ALSO DISCUSSED IN YOUR TEXTBOOK OR OTHER READINGS THAT YOU HAVE DONE? LIST THE TEXTBOOK CHAPTERS AND PAGE NUMBERS:

_____

LIST ANY EXAMPLES OF BIAS OR FAULTY REASONING THAT YOU FOUND IN THE ARTICLE:

_____

LIST ANY NEW TERMS/CONCEPTS THAT WERE DISCUSSED IN THE ARTICLE, AND WRITE A SHORT DEFINITION:

ANNUAL EDITIONS revisions depend on two major opinion sources: one is our Advisory Board, listed in the front of this volume, which works with us in scanning the thousands of articles published in the public press each year; the other is you—the person actually using the book. Please help us and the users of the next edition by completing the prepaid article rating form on this page and returning it to us. Thank you for your help!

ANNUAL EDITIONS: Research Methods 01/02

ARTICLE RATING FORM

Here is an opportunity for you to have direct input into the next revision of this volume. We would like you to rate each of the 32 articles listed below, using the following scale:

1. Excellent: should definitely be retained
2. Above average: should probably be retained
3. Below average: should probably be deleted
4. Poor: should definitely be deleted

Your ratings will play a vital part in the next revision. So please mail this prepaid form to us just as soon as you complete it. Thanks for your help!

RATING	ARTICLE
	1. Back from Chaos
	2. The Connection between Research and Practice
	3. Evolution of Qualitative Research Methodology: Looking beyond Defense to Possibilities
	4. Quantitative Research Approaches
	5. What Is (and Isn't) Research?
	6. Human Subjects and Informed Consent: The Legacy of the Tuskegee Syphilis Study
	7. Types of Errors in Synthesizing Research in Education
	8. Ethics, Institutional Review Boards, and the Changing Face of Educational Research
	9. Standards of Evidence in Historical Research
	10. Research Students' Early Experiences of the Dissertation Literature Review
	11. The Best Kept Secret in Counseling: Single-Case (N=1) Experimental Design
	12. Issues in Teaching Participatory Action Research
	13. Practical Issues for Teachers Conducting Classroom Research
	14. Videotaped Behavioral Observations: Enhancing Validity and Reliability
	15. The Future of Focus Groups
	16. Self-Assessment at Work: Outcomes of Adult Learners' Reflections on Practice
	17. Using Electronic Mail to Conduct Research

RATING	ARTICLE
	18. Daily Data Collection: A Comparison of Three Methods
	19. Quantitative Attitudes Questionnaire: Instrument Development and Validation
	20. Misconceptions about Sample Size, Statistical Significance, and Treatment Effect
	21. On Writing Qualitative Research
	22. A Primer in Survey Research
	23. The New Frontier in Qualitative Research Methodology
	24. Action Research: Empowering Teachers to Work with At-Risk Students
	25. The Need for Better Ethical Guidelines for Conducting and Reporting Research
	26. Education Should Consider Alternative Formats for the Dissertation
	27. Chance and Nonsense: A Conversation about Interpreting Tests of Statistical Significance, Parts I and II
	28. Statistical Methods in Psychology Journals: Guidelines and Explanations
	29. The Social Consequences of Bad Research
	30. Future Directions in Qualitative Research
	31. Rethinking Sociology: Applied and Basic Research
	32. Salvaging Quantitative Research with Qualitative Data

We Want Your Advice

(Continued on next page)

ANNUAL EDITIONS: RESEARCH METHODS 01/02

NO POSTAGE
NECESSARY
IF MAILED
IN THE
UNITED STATES

BUSINESS REPLY MAIL
FIRST-CLASS MAIL PERMIT NO. 84 GUILFORD CT

POSTAGE WILL BE PAID BY ADDRESSEE

McGraw-Hill/Dushkin
530 Old Whitfield Street
Guilford, CT 06437-9989

ABOUT YOU

Name _____ Date _____

Are you a teacher? ☐ A student? ☐
Your school's name
_____

Department
_____

Address _____ City _____ State ____ Zip ____

School telephone # _____

YOUR COMMENTS ARE IMPORTANT TO US !

Please fill in the following information:
For which course did you use this book?
_____

Did you use a text with this *ANNUAL EDITION*? ☐ yes ☐ no
What was the title of the text?
_____

What are your general reactions to the *Annual Editions* concept?
_____

Have you read any particular articles recently that you think should be included in the next edition?
_____

Are there any articles you feel should be replaced in the next edition? Why?
_____

Are there any World Wide Web sites you feel should be included in the next edition? Please annotate.
_____

May we contact you for editorial input? ☐ yes ☐ no
May we quote your comments? ☐ yes ☐ no